UFOs
The Public Deceived

Philip J. Klass

Prometheus Books

59 John Glenn Drive
Amherst, NewYork 14228-2197

Published 1983 by Prometheus Books

Library of Congress Card Catalog No.: 83–60202
ISBN 0–87975–322–6

Printed in the United States of America on acid-free paper

To my good wife, Nadya, with
appreciation for her understanding
tolerance of her only competitor
for my time and attention—but a
very demanding one.

Contents

Introduction

"C.I.A. Papers Detail U.F.O. Surveillance" was the headline on the feature story. The article did not appear in one of the sensationalist tabloids but in the respected *New York Times*, on January 14, 1979. The article stated:

> Phoenix, Jan. 13—Documents obtained in a lawsuit against the Central Intelligence Agency show that the agency is secretly involved in the surveillance of unidentified flying objects and has been since 1949, an Arizona-based U.F.O. group said yesterday.
>
> The C.I.A. has repeatedly said that it investigated and closed its books on U.F.O.'s during 1952, according to Ground Saucer Watch, a nation-wide research organization of about 500 scientists, engineers and others who seek to scientifically prove or disprove the existence of U.F.O.'s, but 1,000 pages of documents, obtained under a freedom of information suit, show "the Government has been lying to us all these years," it said.
>
> "After reviewing the documents, Ground Saucer Watch believes that U.F.O.'s exist, they are real, the U.S. Government has been totally untruthful and the cover-up is massive," William Spaulding, head of the group said.... Among the documents are several detailed reports of Air Force attempts to either intercept or destroy U.F.O.'s....
>
> Mr. Spaulding says the documents show that there are links and patterns in the sightings. From the evidence, he says, he believes U.F.O.'s are here on surveillance missions. "We find a concentration of sightings around our military installations, research and development areas," he said....
>
> Mr. Spaulding said he has sworn statements from retired Air Force colonels that at least two U.F.O.'s have crashed and been recovered by the Air Force. One crash, he said, was in Mexico in 1948 and the other was near Kingman, Ariz., in 1953. He said the retired officers claimed they got a glimpse of dead aliens who were in both cases about four feet tall with silverish complexions and wearing silver outfits that "seemed fused to the body from the heat."

1

Mr. Spaulding said his group is waiting now for a Federal judge to rule on the last phase of its C.I.A. suit, which seeks access to 57 items that would provide "hard evidence" of U.F.O.'s or "retrievals of the third kind." That evidence includes motion pictures, gun camera film and residue from landings, he said . . . .

Five days later the *Washington Post* carried a front-page feature article, authored by Ward Sinclair and Art Harris, under the headline: "WHAT WERE THOSE MYSTERIOUS CRAFT?" The article was syndicated and later published by many other major newspapers, some of which used more ominous headlines. For example the *Denver Post* called its account: "SIGHTINGS NEAR BASES: U.S. REPORTS VISITS OF UFOs." The *New York Post* headlined its version: "UFOs SIGHTED AT MISSILE SITES: SECRET DEFENSE REPORTS BARED." The *Washington Post* article reported:

During two weeks in 1975, a string of the nation's supersensitive nuclear missile launch sites and bomber bases were visited by unidentified low-flying and elusive objects, according to Defense Department reports.

The sightings, made visually and on radar by air and ground crews and sabotage-alert forces, occurred at installations in Montana, Michigan and Maine, and led to extensive but unsuccessful Air Force attempts to track and detain the objects.

Air Force and Defense Department records variously describe the objects as helicopters, aircraft, unknown entities and brightly lighted, fast-moving vehicles that hovered over nuclear weapons storage areas and evaded all pursuit efforts.

In several instances, after base security had been penetrated, the Air Force sent fighter planes and airborne command planes aloft to carry on the unsuccessful pursuit. The records do not indicate if the fighters fired on the intruders . . . .

Yet another Air Force intelligence report indicated extensive interest in a 1976 incident over Iran, when two Iranian Air Force F-4 Phantom fighter planes were scrambled to encounter a brightly lighted object in the skies near Tehran . . . .

In the wake of the *Washington Post* article, the Associated Press sent out a story that began: "Strange flying visitors to several defense installations in recent years are reported in nearly 1,000 pages of documents released by the Central Intelligence Agency." United Press International distributed a similar account to its subscribers.

In November 1975, shortly after the unexplained incidents at vital SAC bases, the wire services carried a report that a young man named Travis Walton, of Snowflake, Arizona, seemingly had been abducted by a UFO and that the incident had been witnessed by six other members of a lumber-trimming crew. Several days later, with Walton still missing, the wire services reported that the six crew members had taken a polygraph test, which five had passed, while the sixth was inconclusive. Shortly afterward, young Walton reappeared and told of having been held hostage aboard a UFO. Later the wires reported that young Walton had taken and passed a lie-detector test. This incident would ultimately be endorsed as the most significant UFO event of 1975 by a panel of experienced "UFOlogists," many of them with impressive academic degrees.

The October 14, 1979, edition of the *New York Times Magazine* carried a major feature story on UFOs, headlined: "U.F.O. FILES: THE UNTOLD STORY." The subhead read: "Though officials have long denied that they take 'flying saucers' seriously, declassified documents now reveal extensive Government concern over the phenomenon."

Less than two months earlier, in northwestern Minnesota, a deputy sheriff, Val Johnson, radioed a report that while driving in a rural area in the early morning hours, he had encountered a large glowing UFO that had "attacked" his patrol car. When another law-enforcement officer arrived at the scene, he found the windshield of Johnson's car was badly cracked, one headlight was broken, there was a dent atop the hood, and two radio antennas on the roof were bent back at sharp angles.

It is hardly surprising that a Gallup Poll conducted in mid-1978 indicated that 57 percent of the adult American population believes that UFOs "are real," an increase of 24 percent over the figure obtained in a similar survey in 1966. Gallup reported that for adults with a college education, the "belief" figure was an even higher 66 percent. When *Industrial Research/Development* magazine surveyed its readers in 1979, it found that 61 percent of the respondents believe that UFOs "probably" or "definitely" exist.

Are extraterrestrial craft penetrating the airspace over some of this nation's vital military facilities? Are UFOs abducting innocent persons with increasing frequency—at least two hundred victims by the latest count? And do they sometimes make physical attacks? Is the U.S. government involved in a massive coverup that dwarfs the Watergate scandal both in longevity and importance?

Or has the public been deceived by those eager to promote belief in UFOs, abetted by seemingly responsible news media that have shirked their responsibility to investigate thoroughly before publicizing extraordinary claims?

For much too long, the public has been misled by half-truths, by coverup, and by outright falsehoods. Paraphrasing the late Adlai Stevenson, it is time to talk sense to the public about unidentified flying objects.

1

A Government Coverup?

Since mid-1947, when UFOs first burst upon the public's consciousness, there have been charges that the U.S. government was withholding significant information. One of the first to level this charge was Donald Keyhoe, a retired Marine Corps officer turned freelance writer, who first popularized UFOs and claimed they were extraterrestrial spacecraft.

The birth of the so-called UFO era coincided with that of the Cold War, when the Soviet Union acquired nuclear weapons and a large fleet of long-range bombers that exposed the U.S. to the risk of nuclear attack. For this reason, the location and coverage of U.S. air-defense radars was considered top-secret information because of its potential value to an enemy contemplating a surprise attack. Thus, if a military radar operator reported seeing mysteriously acting "blips" on his scope, his report would be classified "secret" lest it reveal the location and coverage of the radar.

World War II had seen the development of the atomic bomb and the long-range German V-2 ballistic missile, whose technology would open the way to space travel. Many previous science-fiction ideas were fast becoming "science-fact." Thus it is not surprising that even within the U.S. Air Force there were a few who leaped to the conclusion that some UFOs might be explained as extraterrestrial craft reconnoitering earth, possibly with hostile intent. Others were concerned that they might be Soviet craft developed from advanced-design concepts obtained from captured German scientists. Thus there was understandable justification for some military secrecy in the early years of the UFO era, and hence for Keyhoe's early charges of government coverup.

But by the early 1950s, the prevailing view within the USAF was that UFO reports did not involve extraterrestrial craft, and probably not Soviet craft either, and so there was a general easing of prior secrecy. In late 1969, when the USAF announced it was closing down its Project Blue Book UFO investigations office at Wright-Patterson Air Force Base, in Dayton, Ohio, all of its UFO files were transferred to the Air Force Archives at the Air University, Maxwell Air Force Base, Alabama. There the files were open to UFO researchers, but because the archives building also contained classified files on other subjects, researchers wanting to visit the UFO archives first had to make arrangements through the Pentagon. Thus an aura of secrecy persisted. Then, in the spring of 1976, arrangements were made to turn over all of the Project Blue Book files to the National Archives in Washington, D.C. Microfilm copies of the roughly 80,000 pages of material, including photos, now were open to anyone without restriction and a microfilm copy of the complete collection could be purchased by those with sufficient interest and funds.

But when the files became available to the public in July 1976 another cry of censorship was heard from some UFOlogists. They reported that many of the names of persons who had submitted the UFO reports, or been involved in the incidents, had been blacked out. This was true—but not because of any USAF desire to withhold information about UFOs. In 1974 the U.S. Congress had passed the Privacy Act, and it was this that required the USAF to delete some, but not all, names. If a UFO report had been submitted by a civilian not employed by the government, that person's name had to be blacked out. If the report came from military personnel or a government employee, the name also had to be deleted *if* the UFO sighting had occurred during personal time. But if the incident occurred when the person was at work, that is, on "company time," then the name could remain intact.

UFOlogists pored over the Project Blue Book files, and some ordered the complete microfilm duplicate for more detailed study. But none could find any evidence to support the frequent, earlier charges of a "UFO cover-up."

Even before Project Blue Book files became available in the National Archives, there were some within the UFO movement who charged that Project Blue Book was merely a "public relations cover" and that the government's center of UFO investigations was really in the then supersecret Central Intelligence Agency. This idea gained some credence when the September 3, 1966, issue of *Saturday Review* magazine revealed that the CIA had been responsible for secretly convening a panel of leading scientists January 14–17, 1953, to evaluate the UFO question. The group had been headed by Dr. H. P. Robertson of the California Institute of Technology.

The existence of the Robertson Panel study earlier became known to UFOlogists, but the 1966 article by the *Saturday Review*'s science editor, John Lear, was the first documented disclosure that the CIA had been sufficiently interested in UFOs to sponsor a meeting. That such a panel had been convened was first disclosed by Edward J. Ruppelt, a former USAF captain who had headed Project Blue Book at the time of the meeting. The disclosure, in Ruppelt's book *The Report on Unidentified Flying Objects* (Doubleday and Co.), published in 1956, sparked a rash of inquiries. Finally, on April 9, 1958, the USAF released the following:

REPORT OF THE SCIENTIFIC PANEL ON UNIDENTIFIED FLYING OBJECTS

17 January 1953

1. The undersigned Panel of Scientific Consultants has met at the request of the Government to evaluate any possible threat to national security posed by Unidentified Flying Objects ("Flying Saucers"), and to make recommendation [sic]. The Panel has received the evidence as presented by cognizant Governmental agencies, primarily the United States Air Force, and has reviewed a selection of the best documented incidents.

2. As a result of its considerations, the Panel concludes: That the evidence presented on Unidentified Flying Objects shows no indication that these phenomena constitute a direct physical threat to the national security.

We firmly believe that there is no residuum of cases which indicates phenomena which are attributable to foreign artifacts capable of hostile acts, and that there is no evidence that the phenomena indicate a need for the revision of current scientific concepts.

3. In the light of this conclusion, the Panel recommends: That the national security agencies take immediate steps to strip the Unidentified Flying Objects of the special status they have been given and the aura of mystery they have unfortunately acquired.

We suggest that this aim may be achieved by an integrated program designed to reassure the public of the total lack of evidence of inimical forces behind the phenomena. [The document was signed by:]

> H. P. Robertson, Chairman; California Institute of Technology
> Luis W. Alvarez; University of California
> Lloyd V. Berkner; Associated Universities, Inc.
> S. A. Goudsmit; Brookhaven National Laboratories
> Thornton Page; John [sic] Hopkins University

Lear's article not only was the first to reveal CIA involvement, but it also disclosed that the "Panel Report" released by the USAF in 1958 was only a brief summary of a much more detailed report on the meeting written by Fred Durant III, then a consultant to the CIA, who participated in the meeting. Lear's article disclosed that he had obtained a "sanitized" (that is, censored) version of the Durant Report through Major Hector Quintanilla, Jr., who then headed Project Blue Book. Further, that Quintanilla had asked the CIA to authorize release of the full Durant Report, but it was willing to make public only the sanitized version.

While Lear's article indicated that he was skeptical over the claims of extraterrestrial visitors made by UFOlogists after he had reviewed the Blue

Book files in Dayton, he also was clearly disturbed over the CIA's censoring of the Durant Report. Lear wrote:

> CIA's insistence on editing [the Durant Report] in the face of an Air Force request for unequivocal declassification of a thirteen-year old document is unfortunate. The very exercise of censorship suggests that vital information of long-range significance may be withheld for strategic reasons. That the CIA, not the Air Force, is the censor is susceptible to interpretation as a sign that whatever data is missing has clandestine implications — precisely the claim that UFO fans have been making for years.

The extent of the CIA's interest and involvement in UFOs might have remained a matter of legitimate conjecture, and a cause celebre for the UFO movement, were it not that in early 1975 the U.S. Congress passed a Freedom of Information Act (FOIA). This new law enabled citizens to obtain information from any government agency, including even the CIA, unless that agency could demonstrate beyond all doubt that its release would be gravely injurious to the national security. Under FOIA, citizens can bring legal action in the U.S. Courts, if other procedures fail, to force any government agency to substantiate its claim that the release of any information would seriously jeopardize national security.

William Spaulding, of Phoenix, Arizona, who directs a small UFO organization called Ground Saucer Watch (GSW), had long been a proponent of the idea that the CIA not only was withholding significant information on UFOs but was really the secret center of the U.S. government's ongoing investigation in the field. Two other strong proponents of this hypothesis were Mr. and Mrs. L. J. Lorenzen, of Tucson, Arizona, who direct one of the nation's oldest and largest UFO organizations, known as Aerial Phenomena Research Organization (APRO).

GSW's Spaulding was one of the nation's first UFOlogists to take advantage of the Freedom of Information Act. On June 7, 1975, he wrote to the CIA asking for a complete copy of the Durant Report on the Robertson Panel meeting. On June 16, the CIA's FOIA Coordinator, Robert S. Young, replied saying that the 24-page report and two of its original appendices (Tab A and Tab C) had been declassified and that an effort was being made to declassify Tab B, which involved material from "another agency." On June 30, the CIA spokesman wrote Spaulding to say that the complete report had been declassified and a copy was enclosed.

If Spaulding expected to find "the smoking gun" that would confirm his claims of a CIA coverup of significant UFO secrets, he must certainly have been disappointed as he read the complete Durant Report. Most of it had been made public in early 1969 with publication of the final report on a government-funded UFO study conducted by the University of Colorado under the direction of Dr. Edward U. Condon. His *Scientific Study of Unidentified Flying Objects* (Bantam Books) contained the full Durant

Report except that the names of the panel members expressing specific viewpoints had been deleted, and Tab C, listing military and CIA officials who had briefed the panel scientists, also was omitted.

There was one other small deletion in the version published in 1969: the name of the organization that had conducted a computer analysis of UFO reports in the early 1950s, under USAF sponsorship. This was the Battelle Memorial Institute, which had been reluctant to admit its involvement in the UFO controversy. But Battelle's identity had long been known to UFOlogists. This was the "other agency" whose approval finally had been obtained in June 1975, enabling the CIA to release to Spaulding the complete, unexpurgated version of the Durant Report on the Robertson Panel meeting held in early 1953, nearly a quarter of a century earlier.

But Spaulding's suspicions of a UFO coverup by the CIA continued, and in 1976 they were fanned by a new GSW member, W. Todd Zechel, of Prairie du Sac, Wisconsin. Zechel claimed he had first-hand knowledge of a massive UFO coverup as a result of having been employed for ten years by two civilian intelligence agencies, one of which Zechel said was the National Security Agency. (NSA is responsible for intercepting and decoding foreign communications and for devising means to improve the security of U.S. communications.) By the spring of 1977, Spaulding had named Zechel to the newly created post of director of research for GSW.

In GSW's quarterly newsletter to its membership, Zechel was described as follows:

> . . . one of our country's leading authorities on the suppression of UFO evidence by the intelligence community. His background in working with the National Security Agency (NSA) in an overt role, and for another agency in a covert role, enables him to speak with authority on intelligence operations. He left intelligence work in 1974 after ten years of distinguished service, deciding to bring to the attention of the American public the details of a long-standing conspiracy . . . to suppress the facts about UFOs.

This prompted Spaulding later to write: "In reality, Air Force Project Blue Book was no more than a PR front, primarily covering for the secret research being conducted by the CIA . . . "

Spurred by Zechel's claims of what he said he had learned during his many years in the "intelligence community," Ground Saucer Watch filed a suit under FOIA on September 12, 1977, against the CIA in the U.S. District Court, Eastern District of New York. Attorney for GSW was Peter A. Gersten, member of the firm of Rothblatt, Rothblatt, Seijas and Peskin, Bronx, New York. As Gersten later explained to me, he had had an interest in UFOs since his youth and had read of the alleged coverup in numerous UFO books. When the Freedom of Information Act was passed, Gersten told me, he had written to several major UFO organizations to volunteer his services for an FOIA action. GSW was the only UFO group to respond, Gersten said.

Under the terms of the original filing, GSW sought "a true copy of the original Robertson Panel Report" and "a true copy of Tabs A, B, and C" of that report, indicating a continuing suspicion that the copies earlier supplied to Spaulding were spurious or incomplete and that the CIA was violating the law of the land. GSW made several other specific requests and concluded by asking that the CIA supply "all records relating to UFOs." During subsequent months, Gersten submitted an interogatory discovery motion containing more than six hundred specific UFO incident requests, and he agreed to transfer the litigation to the U.S. District Court in Washington.

On August 17, 1978, the Assistant U.S. Attorney for the District of Columbia, William H. Briggs, the legal representative of the CIA, telephoned Gersten to propose that GSW amend its complaint to ask the CIA to conduct "a reasonable search" of its files for all UFO-related materials. Gersten and GSW were greatly surprised by the CIA's proposal. As Gersten later told me: "Why they agreed to search their complete files when they didn't have to, I don't know the answer. But they did." In other words, if the CIA was anxious to hide its UFO activities, why had the agency offered to supply more information than GSW had specificially asked for? GSW agreed to the proposal and U.S. District Court Judge John Pratt then issued an official order requiring the CIA to make "a reasonable search" within ninety days and to release all UFO-related materials, except for any that could rightfully be withheld because of national security considerations.

On December 20, 1978, a one-page press release announcing "CIA RELEASES UFO DOCUMENTS" was distributed to the news media in Washington, D.C. It had been prepared by an organization called Citizens Against UFO Secrecy (CAUS) that had been formed a few months earlier by W. Todd Zechel. The CAUS press release said that the CIA had released approximately 900 pages of UFO-related material on December 15, as required by the U.S. District Court order, and that the materials "are currently being studied by officials of Citizens Against UFO Secrecy."After briefly acknowledging the role played by GSW in obtaining the CIA material, the CAUS press release said the "documents are dated from the 1950s, 1960s and 1970s, demonstrating continuous interest on the part of the agency despite frequent public denials. The significance of the information contained in the documents will not be known until after they have been fully analyzed."

Although CAUS had five days to study the CIA material, clearly it was not able to find any evidence of a significant coverup. But the press release noted that there were "nearly 200 additional documents" (a document being one or more pages of material) in the CIA files that had not yet been released because the material had originated with other agencies, such as the Defense Department. These documents were being referred to the other agencies to determine if they could be made public. (The bulk of this material was soon released.) Additionally, CAUS noted, there were fifty-seven more documents which the CIA said could not be released on national security grounds.

Several months earlier, after learning of the GSW suit, I had written to the CIA's Information and Privacy coordinator, requesting copies of all UFO-related material released under FOIA. On October 4, I received 118 pages of material which the CIA earlier had released to CAUS. On December 26, nine days after the 900 pages of additional UFO-related material were released, but before I had received my copy from the CIA, I telephoned Spaulding to ask for his appraisal of the new batch of data. (Spaulding and I had developed a close working relationship when we jointly investigated the alleged UFO abduction of Travis Walton, an award-winning UFO case to be discussed in Chapters 18–23.)

Spaulding told me on December 26 that he had not yet received the CIA material. But he said that he had talked with attorney Peter Gersten, who had studied the newly released material, and that Gersten had not found any startling disclosures. On January 12, I left for a two-week ski vacation. A new guest at my ski lodge arrived with a copy of the January 14 *New York Times,* containing a major article headlined: "C.I.A. PAPERS DETAIL UFO SURVEILLANCE," with a subhead reading: "Agency's Secret Studies Convince Arizona Research Group That Flying Saucers 'Are Real.'"

As I read the article in the *Times* (highlights of which were quoted in the Introduction to this book), I was amazed to read Spaulding's claim that the newly released CIA material showed that "the U.S. Government has been totally untruthful and the cover-up is massive," and of his claim of evidence to indicate that the U.S. government had recovered two flying saucers and their occupants. Had such an article appeared in one of the sensationalist tabloids, it could be dismissed as nonsense. But presumably the *New York Times* would not have carried such a story unless its reporter had personally studied the CIA documents.

The thrust of the article did not square with Spaulding's statement to me less than three weeks earlier. Nor did it square with my twenty-seven years experience (by 1978) as the senior avionics editor for *Aviation Week and Space Technology* magazine (which sometimes is called "Aviation Leak" because it so often publishes sensitive material that the Defense Department, the CIA, State Department, and White House would prefer to keep under wraps). *Aviation Week* editors, and especially Robert B. Hotz, its editor-in-chief for more than a quarter century, had long had many well-placed sources. Yet never in my long years with the magazine had we ever heard the slightest hint that the USAF, the CIA, or any other government agency knew anything more about UFOs than had been made public since the early 1950s.

Upon returning to Washington in late January, I found the CIA-released documents waiting for me, some 879 pages. For the next several weeks I eagerly studied the massive stack of material, searching for the evidence that had prompted Spaulding to say, and the *New York Times* to report, that "the U.S. Government has been totally untruthful and the cover-up is massive." The CIA documents revealed quite the opposite.

2

The CIA Becomes Interested

The 879 pages of CIA material released in mid-December included fifty-four pages containing an English translation of a Soviet bibliography listing articles on parapsychology. Perhaps it was included because a tiny handful of UFOlogists claim that UFOs may really be "psychic phenomena" rather than extraterrestrial craft. Another sixty sheets contained brief UFO sighting reports that had been clipped from foreign newspapers and submitted to the CIA by U.S. embassies abroad. Most of the items were more than twenty years old. UFO groups such as APRO, with extensive membership overseas, had far larger and more impressive collections of such foreign-sighting reports.

More than one hundred of the pages were letters from dedicated UFOlogists seeking UFO-related material and the CIA's replies, all of which long had been in the public domain. Much of this correspondence came from one persistent UFOlogist and dealt with his theory that UFOs were the product of the CIA and were being employed to test psychological-warfare concepts, using the American public as a guinea pig. Still other sheets were copies of letters sent to the CIA by congressmen on behalf of their constituents, some of whom submitted UFO-sighting reports.

Among the formerly classified sheets were roughly two dozen first-hand UFO-sighting reports from the USSR and Communist Bloc countries, sufficiently censored so that it is impossible to tell whether the source was a U.S. citizen assigned to the USSR or a Soviet citizen. One of these was submitted by an American scientist who reported being asked by a Russian scientist "if the U.S. forecast [weather service] center was ever bothered with UFO sightings. He [Soviet scientist] explained that at one time the [censored] and [censored] in particular, had been plagued with calls and questions about UFO sightings. He said that some of their scientific balloon flights had prompted some of them [UFO reports]." Clearly, high-altitude scientific balloons and weather balloons generated UFO reports in the USSR, just as they do in the U.S.

The stack of CIA-released material contained a considerable number of duplicate sheets, including multiple copies of the Robertston Panel report as well as internal memoranda. If a CIA official wrote a memo on UFOs and sent copies to "X" and to "Y" while keeping a copy for his own files, when the agency made this FOIA sweep of its files and if there were two or three copies of the memo, then it duplicated and released every copy lest it be accused of withholding any information. Sometimes the recipient had penned an annotation on his copy that was not on the original.

Out of the 879 pages of material released in December, plus another 118 pages released earlier to Zechel—a total of nearly a thousand sheets—there were fewer than 350 pages that had once been classified and which could be said to provide any useful insight into the CIA's interest in UFOs and its efforts to probe the mystery. *Thus, over the 30-year period from 1949 to 1979, CIA officials and employees had written an average of only one page of classified UFO-related material per month.* If the CIA or government had evidence that UFOs were extraterrestrial craft one might expect that there would be a hundred or a thousand times as many memoranda on the subject. The great bulk of the CIA memoranda had been written over a one-year period, from mid-1952 to mid-1953, and there was very little of significance written in the subsequent twenty-five years.

The early memoranda, usually stamped "Secret," reveal why the CIA was interested in the UFO mystery, what steps were taken in the late-1952 period to resolve the issue, and when the agency's formal interest ended. Most important, they reveal why the CIA sought, without success, to keep secret its early interest in the subject.

The earliest document in the recently declassified CIA files is an internal memorandum, dated March 15, 1949, from a Dr. Stone, in the Office of Scientific Intelligence, to a Dr. Machle, also of OSI, that begins: "A rapid perusal of your documents [on UFOs] leaves one confused and inclined to supineness." The memo goes on to discuss a variety of different possible explanations for UFO sightings, including "extraterrestrial space ships."

The memo concludes:

> Studies on the various possibilities have been made by Dr. Langmuir of GE [world-renowned scientist in the General Electric research laboratory], Dr. Valley of MIT [Massachusetts Institute of Technology expert on air defense], Dr. Lipp of Project Rand [an Air Force "Think Tank"], Dr. Hynek of Ohio State [University] and [USAF] Aero Medical Lab. That the objects are from outer space or are an advanced aircraft of a foreign power is a possibility, but the above group have concluded that it is highly improbable. In discussions of this subject with Mr. Deyarmond at Wright Patterson Air Force Base, he seemed to think, and I agree, that the "flying discs" will turn out to be another

"sea serpent." However, since there is even a remote possibility that they may be interplanetary or foreign aircraft, it is necessary to investigate each sighting.

The next entry in the CIA files is dated more than three years later, July 29, 1952, and is an internal memorandum from Ralph L. Clark, acting assistant director for scientific intelligence to the deputy director for intelligence. Clark wrote: "In the past several weeks a number of radar and visual sightings of unidentified aerial objects have been reported. Although this office has maintained a continuous review of such reported sightings during the past three years, a special study group has been formed to review this subject to date. O/CI [Office of Current Intelligence] will participate in this study with O/SI [Office of Scientific Intelligence] and a report should be ready about 15 August."

The radar and visual UFO sightings to which Clark referred occurred in the Washington, D.C., area during the early hours of July 20, 1952, when mysterious "blips" showed up on the radarscopes at Washington National Airport, and a week later during the night of July 27, suggesting that the nation's capital was under UFO surveillance, perhaps as a precursor to an attack. During the second incident, the USAF showed sufficient concern to dispatch F-94 interceptor aircraft from the New Castle County AF Base, Delaware. The second incident generated alarming headlines in newspapers across the nation, such as: "FIERY OBJECTS OUTRUN JETS OVER CAPITAL— INVESTIGATION VEILED IN SECRECY FOLLOWING VAIN CHASE."

The Pentagon hurriedly called a press conference on July 28, at which Major General John Samford, the USAF's chief of intelligence, sought to reassure the public. Washington's *Times Herald* phrased it: "A.F. OFFICIALS SEEK TO QUELL PUBLIC ALARM." Samford said that analysis of the two incidents revealed "no pattern of anything remotely consistent with any menace to the United States," and suggested that the mysteriously behaving radar blips might be the result of "temperature inversions." (A subsequent investigation by the Civil Aeronautics Administration confirmed that such spurious radar blips were quite common on its radars and were caused by temperature inversions as detailed in a technical report published in May 1953.)

However, the *Times Herald,* like many other newspapers, was not impressed. It reported that "the fact that the objects appeared on radar proved that the objects represented some type of solid or semi-solid." It added that the fact that the radar blips "alternately disappeared and reappeared" eliminated any possibility that they might have been caused by conventional aircraft. The newspaper quoted one of the interceptor pilots as saying he had visually sighted "several bright lights" but was unable to "close" on them even at a speed of 600 mph.

Understandably, the incidents generated concern in the White House, and a CIA document dated August 14, 1952, indicates that the USAF received "an official query from the White House." It would be surprising if the White House had not also made an inquiry to the director of Central Intelligence, Walter B. Smith, who in turn had sought a situation report from appropriate lower-echelon officials in the CIA, although there is no evidence for this in the released documents.

In a memo dated August 1, 1952, from Edward Tauss, then the acting chief of the Weapons and Equipment Division, to his superior, the deputy assistant director for scientific intelligence, Tauss stated that less than one hundred of the more than one thousand UFO reports submitted to the USAF remain "unexplainable" and added that "it is probable that if complete information were available for presently 'unexplainable' reports, they, too," could be explainable in prosaic terms. But Tauss added: "so long as a series of reports remains 'unexplainable' (interplanetary aspects and alien origin not being thoroughly excluded from consideration) caution requires that intelligence continue coverage of the subject."

Tauss recommended that the CIA continue to monitor the situation, in cooperation with the USAF. He added: "It is strongly urged, however, that no indication of CIA interest or concern reach the press or public, in view of their probable alarmist tendencies to accept such interest as 'confirmatory' of the soundness of 'unpublished facts' in the hands of the U.S. Government." In other words, any public disclosure of CIA interest in UFOs might seem to confirm claims by UFO promoter and writer Keyhoe and others that the U.S. government had good reason to suspect that some UFOs might be extraterrestrial spacecraft. Tauss concluded by saying that arrangements had been made with the USAF's Air Technical Intelligence Center (ATIC), at Wright-Patterson AF Base, "for a thorough and comprehensive briefing related to this subject" on August 8 and that his office would then prepare a detailed report on the subject.

Another previously classified CIA memorandum containing "Minutes of Branch Chief's Meeting of 11 August 1952" indicates that responsibility for the UFO investigation had been assigned to the Physics and Electronics Division of the Office of Scientific Intelligence and that A. Ray Gordon had been named project officer. Following the August 8 briefing by the USAF in Dayton, three different papers were prepared by those who attended, to brief top CIA officials on the currently available knowledge of the UFO problem. The date of the top-level briefing is not indicated but the three papers were dated August 14, August 15, and August 19, 1952. Presumably all were presented at the same time. I shall now present in detail relevant sections of these documents.

The August 14 document tells of the Office of Scientific Intelligence's decision:

> . . . [to] make an evaluation of the Air Force study, its methodology and coverage, the relation of its conclusions to various theories which have been

propounded and to try to reach some conclusions as to the intelligence implications of the problem—if any. In view of the wide interest within the Agency, this briefing has been arranged so that we could report on the survey. It must be mentioned that outside knowledge of Agency interest in Flying Saucers carries the risk of making the problem even more serious in the public mind than it already is, which we and the Air Force agree must be avoided.

In order to supply both breadth and depth to the survey we have reviewed our own intelligence, going back to the Swedish sightings of 1946; reviewed a large number of individual official reports, recent press and magazine coverage and the main popular books. Indexes of the Soviet press were scanned [for mention of any Russian UFO sightings]. We interviewed a representative of the Air Force Special Study Group. Following this, we spent a day at Wright Field in a thorough discussion with the officers conducting the ATIC study, and finally we took the problem to a selected group of our own consultants, all leaders in their scientific fields.

The first briefing paper, after discussing the history of the UFO mystery, then shifted to a discussion of the "four major theories" advanced to explain UFO reports:

First, that it is a U.S. secret weapon development. This has been denied officially at the highest level of government and to make doubly certain we queried Dr. Whitman, Chairman of the Research and Development Board. On a Top Secret basis, he, too denies it. However, in the light of the Manhattan District [atomic bomb] early super security, two factors might be mentioned which tend to confirm the denials—first, the official action of alerting all Air Force commands to intercept [UFOs], and second, the unbelievable risk aspect of such flights in established airlanes.

The second theory is that these are a Russian development. Though we know that the Russians have done work on elliptical and delta wing principles, we have absolutely no intelligence of such a technological advance as would be indicated here in either design or energy source. Further, there seems to be no logical reason for the security risk which would be involved [in flying craft over the U.S.] and there has been no indication of a reconnaissance pattern [i.e. over strategic targets]. However, it should be mentioned that there is a totally unsupported thesis that this may be a Russian high altitude development of the World War II Jap balloon effort using preset flares and the resulting US press reports to check flight tracks. [Not mentioned was the fact that the USAF/CIA were then using such high-altitude Skyhook balloons, developed by the Navy, for top-secret photo-reconnaissance missions over the USSR.]

The third theory is the man from Mars—space ships—interplanetary travellers. Even though we might admit that intelligent life may exist elsewhere and that space travel is possible, *there is no shred of evidence to support this theory at present . . . .* [Emphasis added.]

It should be emphasized and remembered that the foregoing was part of a *"secret" briefing* for *top* CIA officials, based on the results of the agency's own investigation and its briefing by USAF intelligence officials, which in turn had been spurred by White House interest and concern. *It is inconceivable that some unnamed party in the U.S. government had captured a crashed flying saucer in 1948,* as Spaulding publicly claimed, *but that all information on the incident had been kept secret from the CIA, the USAF and from the White House,* while full details of the incident would be known to two relatively low-level officers, who supplied sworn statements to Spaulding.

> The fourth major theory [the CIA briefing paper stated] is that now held by the Air Force, that the sightings, given adequate data, can be explained either on the basis of misinterpretation of known objects, or of as yet little understood natural phenomena.

The second briefing paper, dated 15 August 1952, began:

> In the next few minutes, I intend to touch briefly upon the official [USAF] explanations of the great majority of sightings of unidentified flying objects (or UFO's) and mention possible phenomena which may account for some of the open [unexplained] cases. Before we elaborate upon the current explanations I would like you to keep in mind certain facts which are generally common to all reports. First, is the earnestness of those making reports. These people are certain that they have seen *something*. Secondly, objects sighted almost always are reported to be against the sky thereby providing no point of reference. Thirdly, without a reference point, a valid estimation of size, speed, distance of relative motion [sic] is virtually impossible. *Finally, no debris or material evidence has ever been recovered following an unexplained sighting.*
>
> In each case of reported sightings exists the personal element. This is the combined effect of psychological and physiological factors which individually or together may have outstanding importance in the accuracy of a person's report. *These factors generally cannot be determined adequately.* The psychological factors are: Mental conditioning by newspaper stories of earlier reported sightings; Individual emotional response with respect to the unknown; Desire for publicity resulting in 'embroidering' of facts or complete fabrication; Emotion of chase of interceptor pilots. [Emphasis added above.]

The briefer then discussed some UFO incidents, including one involving Captain Ruppelt, then head of Project Blue Book, which:

> . . . points up interesting psychological factors. The time was near dusk. Ruppelt was called out to witness a sighting of three red lights in the sky. Even through [using] binoculars, he could not determine their nature. An F-94 interceptor climbed to 43,000 feet. At this altitude the pilot could see clearly that the objects were a cluster of three Skyhook balloons still well above him, sailing an even course across the sky. By this time, telephone reports had started to come in. The objects were described as violently maneuvering "saucers" of various shapes and colors. Even "looping" maneuvers were reported. The medical staff at Wright Field, including the senior psychologist, witnessed the sighting. *The*

next day this staff turned in a report stating that, despite the official statement that these objects were balloons, they felt that this was in error and that the sighting must have been of some other unknown origin. [Emphasis added.]

. . . in the daytime, aircraft, particularly those that are unpainted, can give extremely brilliant reflections of sunlight. An interesting case under known conditions is one which occurred last year in Maryland. A group of aircraft design engineers went into the country to witness tests of their own jet airplane. The three test aircraft, with unpainted wings and red fuselages, passed directly overhead. All engineers agreed that if they had not *known* what the objects were, and since they could not observe the silver wings against the sky, they would have reported the red fuselages as flaming trails and they would have imagined objects emitting them.

[The briefing paper described] a pulsating bright yellow light [was] reported moving through the sky near Pittsburgh, Pennsylvania. For months this report was relegated to the "unexplained" file. A few weeks ago in Washington, a man who was familiar with this report saw an anti-collision light installation on a Capital Airlines airplane. This new safety device, a light mounted on the nose of the airplane, oscillates back and forth laterally similar to those installed on some ambulances and police cars. A check with Capital Airlines revealed that an airplane fitted with such a light had "checked in" while flying near Pittsburgh at the exact time and place of the reporting [sic] [UFO] sighting.

After discussing other trigger-mechanisms for UFO reports, including bright celestial bodies such as Venus and meteor/fireballs, the briefing paper noted that temperature-inversions and air-turbulence can create "optical as well as radar aberrations," that is, an unidentified object. "In one case of a ground radar sighting in Maryland the pilot of an interceptor aircraft with his AI [airborne intercept] gear [radar] 'locked on' a 'blip,' found himself on a steeply sloping downwards course at low altitude. This occurred three times indicating that the target was on the ground and that the course of the [aircraft] radar beam had been distorted."

The briefer cited another radar-UFO incident that had occurred at Frenchmen's Flat, Nevada: "Blips in formation were picked up on the radar scope. They were reported to be traveling at terrific speed at 30,000 feet. It happened that the reporting station had a searchlight and it was turned on in the direction of the radar sighting. It was immediately discovered that the objects were Canadian geese flying at 300 feet altitude."

The briefing paper said that the USAF had been able to explain roughly 80 per cent of the UFO reports it received and believed that another 10 per cent could be explained if more information, or more accurate information, were available.

This still leaves ATIC with a possible 10% of sightings for which there is no available explanation. Considering that the remaining cases might have been caused by little understood natural phenomena, the OSI Panel conferred at length with three of our consultants in Boston. These men are outstanding in the fields of geophysics, electronics and chemistry. They emphasized to us that there are so many scientific frontiers which have as yet been little explored or charted. In those areas occur phenomena which may account for things actually seen. They listed three categories: atmospherics, ionization and extraterrestrial phenomena [that is, cosmic rays].

The briefing paper noted that optical and radar effects caused by temperature inversions were *not* well understood, nor was there a complete understanding of possible effects of the ionosphere. Also cited was ball lightning, "a luminous [plasma] phenomena which has been reported for centuries" which is not understood. "This list could be extended at length. Suffice to say, our ignorance of the nature and controlling factors of all of the above is immense. Effects of interaction between these natural phenomena and radioactive material in the air [from nuclear weapons tests] can only be conjectured. The appearance of unusual optical or radar sightings caused by these phenomena is possible."

The briefer concluded by pointing out some of the seemingly mysterious characteristics reported in some UFO sightings and added: "Here we run out of even 'blue yonder' explanations that might be tenable, and we still are left with numbers of incredible reports from credible observers." (This phrase would later become the cornerstone of UFO-proponents' argumentation.)

The final briefing paper, dated August 19, mentioned that a search for UFO reports in the Soviet press had turned up "not one report or comment . . . . This could only result from an official policy decision and of course raises the question of *why* and whether or not these sightings could be used from a psychological warfare point of view either offensively or defensively. Air Force is aware of this and had investigated a number of the civilian [UFO] groups . . . ." The briefer cited one UFO group which he said "has substantial funds, strongly influences the editorial policy of a number of newspapers and has leaders whose connections may be questionable." It should be recalled that in 1952 there was serious public concern over possible Communist infiltration and subversion.

> Air Force is watching this organization because of its power to touch off mass hysteria and panic. Perhaps we, from an intelligence point of view, should watch for any indication of Russian efforts to capitalize upon this present American credulity.
>
> Of even greater moment is the second danger. Our air warning system will undoubtedly always depend upon a combination of radar scanning and visual observation. We give Russia the capability of delivering an air attack against us . . . . At the moment of attack, how will we, on an instant basis, distinguish hardware [enemy bombers] from phantom [UFO]? . . . until far greater knowledge is achieved of the causes back of the [UFO] sightings . . . we will run increasing risk of false alerts and the even greater danger of tabbing [identifying] the real as false. This is primarily an operational research problem but

as long as it exists it will have intelligence implications because of its bearing on air vulnerability [to enemy bomber attack].

Our purpose in this survey has been to examine what *is* being done and make some assessment of its validity. The Air Force study is valid. On a case by case basis, the great bulk of the sightings have been and will continue to be explained—but the limited case-approach will never solve this second real problem—positive identification . . . we proposed to discuss the research problem with the Research and Development Board and to pass on to the Air Force an offer from M.I.T. to assist in a study of some of the fundamentals. We suggest that the psychological possibilities both for and against us should be investigated.

Thus these formerly "secret" CIA documents reveal that there was serious, and justifiable, concern about the "UFO problem" within the agency and within the USAF—but *not* because there was any evidence that any UFOs were either extraterrestrial or Soviet craft. Rather, because the USSR, with its growing fleet of long-range bombers and its newly acquired atomic bombs, could conceivably exploit UFO-mania within the U.S. to stage a surprise attack. The first eyewitness reports of approaching enemy bombers could too easily be dismissed as prosaic UFO reports, until the first atomic weapons began to explode. Thus, in the summer and fall of 1952, there was good reason for the CIA to invoke secrecy to cloak its interest in the UFO problem, and the real reasons for that interest. To publicly disclose this interest, and the reason for agency concern, would simply have alerted the USSR to the *possibility* that it *could* plan to exploit UFOs to mask a surprise nuclear attack.

3

Famous Robertson Panel Report

American television viewers received a UFOlogist's version of the contents of the CIA papers on UFOs when GSW's Spaulding appeared on the National Broadcasting Company's popular "Tomorrow" show, hosted by Tom Snyder, on February 2, 1979. When Snyder invited Spaulding to read from some of the previously secret CIA documents he had brought along, Spaulding responded with the following comment:

> In a document to the Director of the Central Intelligence Agency, under conclusions, called [dealing with] flying saucers, they [UFOs] pose two elements of danger which have national security implications. The first involves mass psychological considerations and a second concerns the vulnerability of the United States to air attack. And I'm paraphrasing exactly [sic] here. And another document from Chadwell, who was the director of the OSI [Office of Scientific Intelligence] in the CIA: "I consider this problem to be of such importance that it should be brought to the attention of the National Security Council in order that a community-wide coordinated effort towards its solution may be initiated."

Tom Snyder responded to Spaulding: "So there's plenty of documentation there that they know."

Spaulding replied: "There are many, many other pages that we just wouldn't have time to read."

Television viewers could readily conclude from this tiny amount they had heard, that the memo, written by H. Marshall Chadwell more than a quarter-century earlier (September 24, 1952), was expressing concern that UFOs were, or might be, extraterrestrial craft that posed a potential threat to the United States.

In actual fact, the Chadwell memo, when read in its entirety, reveals quite the opposite.

The memo highlights the results of the CIA's several months of study of the UFO problem and the conclusions reached by its Office of Scientific Intelligence. Chadwell wrote: "It was found that the only unit of Government currently studying the problem is the Directorate of Intelligence, USAF, which has charged the Air Technical Intelligence Center [ATIC] with responsibility for investigating the reports of sightings. At ATIC there is a group of three officers and two secretaries . . . [which] conducts investigations of the [UFO] reports, consulting as required with other Air Force and civilian technical personnel . . ."

Considering that the USAF is charged with defending the nation against air attack, whether from terrestrial or extraterrestrial craft, if the USAF had captured a flying saucer in 1948 as Spaulding and others claim, it was being derelict to its duty by assigning only three officers, the highest ranking of whom was a captain, to the UFO investigations effort.

The Chadwell memo noted that the USAF effort to investigate UFO reports on a case-by-case basis

> . . . does not solve the more fundamental aspects of the problem . . . to determine definitely the nature of the various phenomena which are causing these [seemingly unexplainable] sightings, and to discover means by which these causes, and their visual or electronic effects, may be identified immediately. The CIA consultants stated that these solutions would probably be found on the margins or just beyond the frontiers of our present knowledge in the fields of atmospheric, ionosopheric and extraterrestrial [i.e. such as cosmic rays] phenomena, with the added possibility that the present dispersal of nuclear waste products might also be a factor. [Chadwell said the consultants had recommended a study to look into these more basic issues and recommend appropriate research.]
>
> The flying saucer situation contains two elements of danger which, in a situation of international tension, have national security implications. These are: Psychological — With world-wide sightings reported, it was found that, up to the time of the investigation, there had been in the Soviet press no report or comment, even satirical, on flying saucers . . . . With a State-controlled press, this could result only from an official policy decision. The question, therefore, arises as to whether or not these sightings: (1) could be controlled, (2) could be predicted, and (3) could be used from a psychological warfare point of view, either offensively or defensively. The public concern with the phenomena . . . indicates that *a fair proportion of our population is mentally conditioned to the acceptance of the incredible. In this fact lies the potential for the touching-off of mass hysteria and panic.* [Emphasis added.]

The second element of danger, Chadwell said, was

> *Air Vulnerability* — The United States Air Warning System will undoubtedly always depend upon a combination of radar screening and visual observation. The U.S.S.R. is credited with the present capability of delivering an air attack

against the United States, yet at any given moment now, there may be current a dozen *official* unidentified sightings plus many unofficial ones. At any moment of attack, we are now in a position where we cannot, on an instant basis, distinguish hardware from phantom, and as tension mounts we will run the increasing risk of false alerts and the even greater danger of falsely identifying the real as phantom . . . .

[The Chadwell memo further acknowledged that] both of these problems are primarily operational in nature [and thus of concern to the USAF] but each contains readily apparent intelligence factors [of concern to the CIA]. From an operational point of view, three actions are required:

(a) Immediate steps should be taken to improve identification of both visual and electronic phantom so that, in the event of an attack, instant and positive identification of enemy planes or missiles can be made.

(b) A study should be instituted to determine what, if any, utilization could be made of these phenomena by United States psychological warfare planners and what, if any, defenses should be planned in anticipation of Soviet attempts to utilize them.

(c) In order to minimize risk of panic, a national policy should be established as to what should be told the public regarding the phenomena . . . .

Other intelligence problems which require determination are:

(a) The present level of Soviet knowledge regarding these phenomena.

(b) Possible Soviet intentions and capabilities to utilize these phenomena to the detriment of the United States security interests.

(c) The reasons for silence in the Soviet press regarding flying saucers . . . .

[The memo then recommended] additional research, differing in character and emphasis from that presently being performed by the Air Force, will be required to meet the specific needs of both operations and intelligence. Intelligence responsibilities in this field as regards both collection and analysis can be discharged with maximum effectiveness only after much more is known regarding the exact nature of these phenomena.

Only then did the concluding statement—from September 24, 1952, one should remember—that Spaulding had quoted on NBC-TV appear: "I consider this problem to be of such importance that it should be brought to the attention of the National Security Council in order that a community-wide coordinated effort towards its solution may be initiated."

In the fall of 1952, with the Cold War getting hotter and the United States becoming increasingly vulnerable to a surprise nuclear attack from the growing Soviet fleet of strategic bombers, Chadwell's concerns over the implications of the UFO phenomena were quite justified. *But these concerns were quite different from those conveyed by Spaulding to millions of NBC-TV viewers in 1979.*

The declassified CIA files show that on October 2, 1952, Chadwell sent a similar memo to the director of Central Intelligence in which the problem, facts, conclusions and recommendations were stated more succinctly, with a more detailed discussion contained in an appendix (Tab A). Included was a draft memorandum that had been prepared for signature by the CIA director, intended for possible submission to the National Security Council, to inform NSC "of the implications of the 'flying saucer' problem and request that [CIA] research be initiated." Also enclosed was a draft memorandum for the director of the Psychological Strategy Board, suggesting "that CIA, with the cooperation of PSB and other interested departments and agencies, develop and recommend for adoption by the NSC a policy of public information which will minimize concern and possible panic resulting from the numerous sightings of unidentified flying objects."

A dissenting view is found in a memorandum to the CIA's deputy director for intelligence, dated October 13, 1952, written by James Q. Reber, CIA's assistant director for intelligence coordination. Reber acknowledged: "Determination of the scientific capabilities of the USSR to create and control Flying Saucers as a weapon against the United States is a primary concern of the CIA/OSI." But he added: "Its review of existing information does not lead to the conclusion that the saucers are USSR created or controlled." Reber seemingly opposed the idea that the CIA should initiate a fundamental research effort into natural phenomena that might be responsible for unexplained UFO reports. "The institution of fundamental scientific research is the primary responsibility of the Defense Department," Reber's memo said, and he continued: "It is far too early in view of the present state of our knowledge regarding Flying Saucers for psychological warfare planners to start planning how the United States might use U.S. Flying Saucers against the enemy. When intelligence has submitted the National Estimate on Flying Saucers there will be time and basis for a public policy to reduce or restrain mass hysteria."

Another memo, dated October 14, 1952, signed by Ralph L. Clark, then acting assistant director for scientific intelligence, indicated that a meeting of appropriate CIA officials would be held on October 20 or 21, to try to resolve these differences so an "agreed program can then be forwarded to the DCI and possibly the Secretary of Defense and the balance of the National Security Council as an established program . . . ." The memo indicated that in addition to CIA officials the meeting would be attended by Major General John A. Samford, USAF director of intelligence, and Dr. Walter G. Whitman, chairman of the Defense Department's Research and Development Board. The reason Whitman was included is evident in a memorandum to the director of Central Intelligence written by Chadwell on December 2, 1952. Whitman was to "investigate the possibility of undertaking research and development studies through Air Force agencies. On approximately 6 November, we were advised by Chairman, R&DB [Whitman] that inquiries in the Air Staff did not disclose 'undue concern' over this matter [unexplained UFO reports], but that it had been referred to the Air Defense Command for consideration."

But Chadwell was less sanguine than the USAF, as a result of another briefing of CIA representatives by the USAF on November 25. Chadwell's memo stated:

> At this time, the reports of incidents convince us that there is something going on that must have immediate attention. The details of some of these [UFO] incidents have been discussed by AD/SI [assistant director of scientific intelligence] with DDCI [deputy director of Central Intelligence]. Sightings of unexplained objects at great altitudes and travelling at high speeds in the vicinity of major U.S. defense installations are of such nature that they are not attributable to natural phenomena or known types of aerial vehicles. . . . [Chadwell said his office] is proceeding to the establishment of a consulting group of sufficient competence and stature to review this matter and convince the responsible authorities in the community that immediate research and development on this subject must be undertaken.

The consulting group to which Chadwell referred would emerge as the now-famous Robertson Panel.

The UFO problem was one of several discussed by the Intelligence Advisory Committee (IAC), when it met on December 4, according to the minutes of the meeting. Members of the IAC included the directors of intelligence for the USAF, Army, Navy, Atomic Energy Commission, State Department, Joint Chiefs of Staff, and an assistant to the director of the Federal Bureau of Investigation. Also, there were an additional fifteen specialists from the CIA, Defense and State Departments.

If the United States had really captured a flying saucer and its extraterrestrial occupants more than four years earlier, this fact would have been known to one or more members of this highest-level group of intelligence specialists. Yet the once "secret" minutes show that the group concluded that the CIA should "enlist the services of selected scientists to review and appraise the available [UFO] evidence in the light of pertinent scientific theories."

A memo by Chadwell to the CIA director on December 10 indicated that in response to this recommendation, he had contacted Dr. H. P. Robertson, of the California Institute of Technology, a physicist, who formerly had been director of research for the Defense Department's Weapon System Evaluation Group, "toward establishing a panel of top scientists and engineers in the fields of astrophysics, nuclear energy, electronics, etc., to review this situation . . . . It is hoped to organize the panel and undertake substantive scientific review of this subject within the next two to three weeks." Another Chadwell memo, dated January 9, 1953, indicates that it had been decided to expand the panel of experts from three to five. It would include, in addition to Robertson, Dr. Samuel Goudsmit, Brookhaven National Laboratories, a nuclear physicist; Dr. Lloyd V. Berkner, Associated Universities, a specialist in geophysics; Dr. Luis Alvarez, University of California, a recognized expert on radar and electronics; and Dr. Thornton W. Page, Johns Hopkins University, an astronomer and astrophysicist.

The distinguished group of scientists convened on January 14, without Berkner, who was not able to join the group until January 16. The USAF presented seventy-five of the "best documented" UFO case histories of reports submitted in 1951–52. The scientists viewed color home-movies of two UFOs that had been taken at Great Falls, Montana, on August 15, 1950, and others that had been taken near Tremonton, Utah, on July 2, 1952. The panel concluded that the two bright images photographed at Great Falls were caused by bright sunlight reflecting off the vertical tail-surfaces of two F-94 interceptors which were known to have landed at the local airbase a short time later.* And the scientists concluded that the multiple bright images on the Tremonton film were caused by sunlight reflecting off the underside of seagulls known to populate the region.

After considering the best evidence available on the UFO mystery, the following report, classified "Secret" at the time, was prepared and signed by the five scientists.

> 1. Pursuant to the request of the Assistant Director for Scientific Intelligence, the undersigned Panel of Scientific Consultants has met to evaluate any possible threat to national security posed by Unidentified Flying Objects ("Flying Saucers"), and to make recommendations thereon. The Panel has received the evidence as presented by cognizant intelligence agencies, primarily the Air Technical Intelligence Center [USAF], and has reviewed a selection of the best documented incidents.
> 2. As a result of its considerations, the Panel *concludes:*
>> (a) That the evidence presented on Unidentified Flying Objects shows no indication that these phenomena constitute a direct physical threat to national security.
> We firmly believe that there is no residuum of cases which indicates phenomena which are attributable to foreign artifacts capable of hostile acts, and that there is no evidence that the phenomena indicate a need for the revision of current scientific concepts.
> 3. The Panel further *concludes:*
>> (a) That the continued emphasis on the reporting of these phenomena does, in these parlous times, result in a threat to the orderly functioning of the protective organs of the body politic.
> We cite as examples the clogging of channels of communication by irrelevant reports, the danger of being led by continued false alarms to ignore real indications of hostile action, and *the cultivation of a morbid national psychology in which skillful hostile propaganda could induce hysterical behavior and harmful distrust of duly constituted authority.* [Emphasis added.]
> 4. In order most effectively to strengthen the national facilities for the timely recognition and the appropriate handling of true indications of hostile action, and to minimize the concomitant dangers alluded to above, the Panel *recommends:*

---

*For a detailed account of the Great Falls film, see my *UFOs Explained* (Random House, 1974), Chapter 16.

(a) That the national security agencies take immediate steps to strip the Unidentified Flying Objects of the special status they have been given and the aura of mystery they have unfortunately acquired;

(b) That the national security agencies institute policies on intelligence, training, and public education designed to prepare the material defenses and the morale of the country to recognize most promptly and to react most effectively to true indications of hostile intent or action.

We suggest that these aims may be achieved by an integrated program designed to reassure the public of the total lack of evidence of inimical forces behind the phenomena, to train personnel to recognize and reject false indications quickly and effectively, and to strengthen regular channels for the evaluation of and prompt reaction to true indications of hostile measures.

It is interesting to contrast these original Robertson Panel conclusions with the modified version first released in 1958 after the existence of the Panel originally became known to the public through the Ruppelt book. The "sanitized" version deleted reference to the fact that the Panel had been convened at the request of the CIA. More importantly, the sanitized version deleted the strongly expressed concern that the UFO phenomenon could be exploited by potential enemies contemplating a nuclear attack to clog communication channels and disrupt U.S. air defenses, as well as to "induce hysterical behavior and harmful distrust of duly constituted authority."

This censorship of Panel-member concerns, originally written with the idea that such would be seen only by top intelligence and military officials, made good sense in the 1950s, when the growing Soviet arsenal of atomic weapons and long-range bombers appeared to threaten the nation's survival. If the USSR had so far ignored "flying saucers" as a foible of the "capitalistic world," there was good reason not to call attention to the fact that the Soviet Union could exploit UFOs for military purposes. For example, a few suitably placed Soviet "trawlers" could release hundreds of weather balloons, modified to carry battery-operated flashing lights, just prior to a strategic bombing attack and thereby saturate and confuse USAF air defense.

Because of these constraints imposed by very real national security considerations, the sanitized version of the Robertson Panel conclusions released in 1958 could not specify the true nature of the concerns. And this sanitized report, when it became public, provided ammunition for UFO-proponents to claim that the U.S. government intentionally was debunking flying saucers because it feared panic if the public learned that the earth was being visited by extraterrestrial craft. This ironic twist of events would defeat the important recommendation of the Robertson Panel that UFOs be stripped of "the aura of mystery they have unfortunately acquired."

4

What the CIA Papers Reveal

During the fall of 1952, the CIA's Office of Scientific Intelligence had pushed for a major scientific investigation into natural phenomena to account for the UFO reports that the USAF had difficulty in explaining, and to look into possible psychological-warfare implications of UFOs. The now declassified CIA files reveal that draft letters were prepared for the director of Central Intelligence to submit to the National Security Council, proposing that such an effort be authorized by a National Security Council Intelligence Directive (NSCID).

But these plans were completely abandoned in the wake of the Robertson Panel findings. On February 18, the CIA's James Q. Reber, in transmitting a copy of the two-page Robertson Panel conclusions to the Intelligence Advisory Committee, wrote: "The results of the panel's studies have moved CIA to conclude that no National Security Council Intelligence Directive on this subject is warranted."

Two days earlier, Fred C. Durant III, who had served as recording-secretary for the Robertson Panel, completed a comprehensive 24-page report detailing the deliberations of the panel. Durant, then employed by the Arthur D. Little Company, a consulting-engineering company, was serving as a consultant to the CIA because of his extensive background in rocketry and space technology. Durant was one of the early "space-enthusiasts," at a time when the idea of space travel was viewed by some as science-fiction. In 1952–53, he was both president of the American Rocket Society and head of the International Astronautical Federation. If the USAF files on UFOs contained any indication that the earth was being visited by extraterrestrial craft, such evidence would certainly have been welcomed by a space-enthusiast like Durant, for it could provide the incentive for a major U.S. space program—as the USSR's Sputnik would do five

31

years later. This provides valuable perspective for the contents of the
Durant report on the Robertson Panel deliberations.

Durant wrote:

> The Panel Members were impressed (as have been others, including O/SI
> personnel) in the lack of sound data in the great majority of case histories;
> also, in the lack of speedy [USAF] follow-up due primarily to the modest size
> and limited facilities of the ATIC section concerned . . . . [After citing a
> number of the more significant UFO cases considered by the Robertson Panel,
> he continued]: the Panel concluded that reasonable explanations could be sug-
> gested for most sightings and "by deduction and scientific method it could be
> induced (given additional data) that other cases might be explained in a similar
> manner." . . . Furthermore, it was considered that, normally, it would be a
> great waste of effort to try to solve most of the sightings, unless such action
> would benefit a training and educational program . . . . It appeared obvious
> that there was no single explanation for a majority of the things seen.

Another agency representative who had attended the Robertson Panel
meeting in Dayton was Lieutenant Colonel Frederick C. E. Ober (USAF), a
member of the Physics & Electronics Division of the Office of Scientific Intelligence. On January 27, only ten days after the panel meeting, Ober wrote
a memo to his division chief that reveals a decided lack of interest in further
UFO studies. The memo says:

> Weapons Division has a considerable file [of UFO-related material] which
> according to [D. B.] Stevenson, they would like to dispose of because of the
> findings of the Advisory Group [Robertson Panel] that "flying saucers" pose
> no present threat to the United States security. Mr. Durant feels that the
> material in the Weapons Division file should be maintained in one of the
> substantive Divisions of OSI and has suggested that P & E [Physics and Elec-
> tronics] Division take them over and maintain them. Mr. Stevenson of
> Weapons Division currently has the material and estimates that several hours
> per week will be required to keep it current. He indicates that he is suggesting
> to Mr. [Edward] Tauss, Chief of Weapons Division, that P & E Division get
> the files . . . I personally don't see why P & E Division has any greater interest
> in this material than Weapons Division.

In other words, since it now was apparent that UFOs would not be the
object of a CIA research effort, Ober was objecting to his group being sad-
dled with taking over and maintaining agency files on the subject, particularly since this might involve "several hours per week" of clerical effort.
This is especially revealing in view of a government bureaucracy's well-
known proclivity for *seeking jurisdiction* over important programs that are
likely to result in expanding staff and budget!

Other memoranda in the declassified CIA files reveal that other agency
officials were equally anxious to get rid of their UFO-related materials in

the wake of the Robertson Panel report. For example, a memo from Durant to his superior, Philip G. Strong, dated March 31, 1953, begins: "Jack Heckert telephoned yesterday and told me that O/CI [Office of Current Intelligence] is no longer following reports of U.F.O.'s. Jack has the O/CI file of U.F.O. dispatches and wanted suggestions as to where to send it . . . . It would seem wise for O/SI to keep a watch on U.F.O. reports in view of possibly greater activity this summer." Durant then suggested that Strong "Designate Chief, Applied Science Division, as coordinator of reports on U.F.O.'s with the suggestion that Mr. David E. Stevenson be named 'action man.' . . . Request O/CI turn files now in custody of John Heckert over to Stevenson for perusal. *I believe very little material would be worth saving except as samples of indicative or unusual reports. The rest I recommend be destroyed."* [Emphasis added.] A memo from Chadwell, dated May 27, 1953, to the chief of the Physics and Electronics Division, disclosed his decision: "Responsibility for maintaining current knowledge of reports of sightings of unidentified flying objects is hereby assigned to your division . . ."

The head of the P & E Division, Todos M. Odarenko, responded with a memo dated July 3, 1953, noting that the May 27 memo "did not stipulate the priority of this project versus the normal responsibilities of this Division, nor indicated [sic] the depth or scope of required knowledge . . ." Odarenko's memo noted that his own review indicated that "a close follow-up of the project including a careful analysis of all incoming information and the corresponding liaison with sources would require *continuous efforts of two analysts, a file clerk* and a considerable typing load." [Emphasis added.] This would hardly seem to be an excessive expenditure of effort if the CIA really knew that UFOs were extraterrestrial craft reconoitering earth, or suspected that they might be Russian craft engaged in similar missions.

The memo continued:

> In view of the findings of the Board [Robertson Panel] that a close inspection of the available material does not postulate a serious, direct threat to national security, and that no information has been obtained since the Board's conclusion to necessitate their modifications, it was concluded that:
> (a) the project will be considered as inactive
> (b) the incoming material will be reviewed periodically to segregate references to recognizable and explainable phenomena from those which come under the definition of "unidentified flying objects"
> (c) all material on unidentified objects will be deposited in the files for future reference unless it raises an immediately recognizable problem of concern to national security.
> With the above premise . . . it is planned to handle the project with a part-time use of an [one] analyst and a file clerk. To provide filing facilities, one additional filing cabinet will be requested.

There is an interesting memo in the now-declassified files, dated December 8, 1953, dealing with a newly published book titled *Flying Saucers from Outer Space* by Donald Keyhoe, one of the earliest writers to popularize the subject. The memo from Philip Strong to his superior, the CIA's assistant director for scientific intelligence, said the book had been "reviewed by one of our consultants with particular reference to possible security violations concerning CIA's part in the flying saucer investigation." The consultant's comments included the following:

> The book itself is highly readable, but the content is highly distorted and filled with so many half-truths and inferences I feel certain that the author is knowingly committing a perpetration [sic]. The author . . . implies that the Air Force is deliberately concealing positive conclusions from the public . . . Keyhoe states . . . that a friend of his, with high level "contacts," told him about February 17, 1953, that CIA "people" advised the Air Force to put out a report debunking the saucers, tell the public the project was ended and then carry it on underground, Top Secret . . . CIA is supposed to have made these recommendations following a "secret high level briefing." There is no apparent knowledge of the CIA panel meetings, *although the [Robertson] Panel's recommendations might have been interpreted by a fanatical saucer "believer" as "debunking." However, there was certainly no recommendation that suggested hiding any information from the public.* [Emphasis added.]

On December 17, 1953, the chief of the Physics and Electronics Division, sent a three-page memo, classified "Secret," to the CIA's assistant director for scientific intelligence, in response to a request, providing a report on the "Current Status of Unidentified Flying Objects (UFOB) [sic] Project." Odarenko's memo said that insofar as the CIA was concerned, "the project has been confined to maintaining awareness of the activities of other agencies (notably the USAF) in the unidentified flying objects business and to maintenance of files." It continued: "The Air Force continues to maintain, but with apparently decreasing emphasis, its interest in UFOB's. . . . The Navy, in spite of press reports to the contrary, is presently devoting only part of one ONI [Office of Naval Intelligence] analyst's time to maintaining cognizance of UFOB's . . . The Army has evidenced little or no interest in UFOB's . . ." If a *second* crashed "saucer" had been recovered earlier in the year from near Kingman, Arizona, as GSW's Spaulding later indicated to the *New York Times,* either the CIA had not been informed of the incident or Odarenko thought it too inconsequential to mention to his superior!

The CIA was quick to recognize the potential implications of a new Canadian program to construct a small experimental aircraft shaped like the traditional flying saucer. Developed by the Canadian affiliate of Britain's A. V. Roe, Ltd., with some financial support from the USAF, the concept never went beyond a small-scale model that simply hovered a few feet off the ground, powered by a conventional jet engine. But it was an air-craft concept that deserved to be monitored, the CIA concluded. In a "secret" memorandum for the record, dated June 14, 1954, it was agreed that the assistant director for scientific intelligence would be responsible for "all intelligence measures required to identify, to assess and to report the use by any foreign power or nation of non-conventional types of air vehicles, such as or similar to the 'saucer-like' planes presently under development by the Anglo/British/Canadian efforts."

The same memo reaffirmed that the Physics and Electronics Division would "continue to be responsible for the OSI [Office of Scientific Intelligence] project on 'unidentified' flying objects, will maintain the OSI central file on such objects and will make available to ASD/SI the material of this file *which might bear directly or indirectly upon man-made non-conventional air vehicles capable of 'weapon' applications . . .*" [Emphasis added.] This explains why the CIA would continue to monitor "UFO" reports from overseas, especially from Communist Bloc countries.

The next memo of import, dated August 8, 1955, from the chief of the Physics and Electronics Division, sent to the acting assistant director for scientific intelligence, *recommends that his division be relieved of its duty of monitoring UFOs.* Odarenko noted that during the two years that his group had been assigned to monitor UFO matters, "no intelligence of concern to national security has been developed from the project." He pointed out that the coming year's assignments in other areas "requires that all non-essential activities be terminated," and that his division had been spending "between 10 and 25 analyst hours per month" in reviewing UFO matters and "about half that much clerical time."

"In view of the fact that no positive intelligence of significance has been produced under the subject [UFO] project, *it is recommended that the project be terminated and the files thereof be placed in dead storage.*" [Emphasis added.] The released CIA files do not contain a written response to this recommendation.

However, a memorandum for the record, dated February 9, 1956, sign-ed by W. E. Lexow, chief of the Applied Science Division, refers to a memorandum dated January 9, 1956, which assigned responsibility for "non-conventional types of air vehicles" to his division. Lexow's memo states:

> Files will be maintained in ASD on incoming raw reports where, *in our judgement,* the subject matter may provide information bearing on *foreign* weapons' system research or development. . . . [Further, reports] which could conceivably provide information on foreign fundamental science develop-ments will be forwarded to the Fundamental Science Area . . . Reports which fit under none of the above will be destroyed. . . . A chronological file of all OSI correspondence and action taken in connection with the United States U.F.O. program will be maintained in ASD. A file of finished intelligence

reports published by members of the United States intelligence community on U.F.O. will be maintained in ASD . . . It has been recommended *that the raw intelligence and the obsolete finished reports on U.F.O. now filed in Electronics Division be destroyed.* [Emphasis added.]

Any hope of terminating the agency's meager UFO-report monitoring activities was frustrated by a memo dated March 26, 1956, from the CIA's new deputy director for intelligence, Robert Amory, Jr., who seemingly was unaware of what had transpired in 1952–53. In a brief memo to Herbert Scoville, Jr., then assistant director for scientific intelligence, Amory said he recently had chanced to see an article in a popular French magazine about a curious UFO incident in France. He asked: "Are we keeping in touch with the Air Force center on these things? Does it [USAF] concern itself with foreign 'sightings' such as the above?" The CIA official concluded: "I am also informed that in the coming year Mars will reach its closest point to the Earth in a long period. Outlandish as it may seem, I do feel that OSI has the responsibility to keep its finger on this general subject if for no other purpose than to arm the front office with the refutation of the more spectacular reports."

Scoville replied that the French magazine article did not provide enough information to identify the UFO and "gives the impression that the sighting has been considerably exaggerated in order to produce a more sensational story." He went on to say that if a thorough investigation were made "most likely an identification could be made . . . We do maintain close liaison with the Air Force . . . on reports of unidentified flying objects . . ." Scoville confirmed that Mars would be very close on September 7, 1956, providing astronomers with "a rare opportunity to study Mars . . . However, as you suggest, this unusual event may precipitate a large number of reports on 'flying objects' and 'little green men' from Mars. This Office will follow the general subject closely, and keep you informed on the more spectacular published reports."

The next internal memo of import, dated September 21, 1957, written by Scoville to the acting director of Central Intelligence, describes a curious incident that had occurred on September 20, in which a UFO reportedly was tracked by Air Defense Command radars

. . . on a relatively straight course from the eastern tip of Long Island to the vicinity of Buffalo. The object was reportedly moving westward at an altitude of 50,000 feet and speed of 2,000 kts. "Jamming" [interference] was reported by several radars in this vicinity and westward as far as Chicago.

In a subsequent briefing for representatives of the IAC [Intelligence Advisory Committee], the US Air Force reported that the original reports had been degraded somewhat by information that: (a) there was a 11 minute break [discontinuity] in the [radar] track; (b) weather conditions in the area were of the type which have in the past produced false radar pips and electronic interference; (c) B-47s of SAC [Strategic Air Command] were in the area near Chicago on an ECM [Electronic Countermeasures/Jamming] training flight. The ADC has not completed its investigation of this incident, but in any event it now seems clear that the phenomena reported west of Buffalo were not related to the UFO . . . . [Scoville's memo went on to consider the possibility that the object might have been a Soviet reconnaissance flight but he concluded that this seemed most unlikely.] Considering the facts that the ADC investigation is incomplete, and that weather phenomena are increasingly likely explanations of the original report, we recommend that no IAC meeting be called on this subject at this time.

The CIA files contain a brief memo from Philip G. Strong to the assistant director for scientific intelligence, dated October 26, 1957, saying that Dr. Robertson had called to inform him that the Air Force had requested permission to declassify the two-page report by the Robertson Panel. Strong said he told Robertson that he would take up the matter with the USAF. In subsequent weeks, Strong contacted the five panel members to see if any objected to making the two-page report public. One letter from Berkner indicated that he had no objection to declassifying the report but *strongly opposed any mention of the CIA's role in convening the panel.* After considerable discussion with panel members, it was agreed that a "sanitized" version would be prepared that deleted any mention of the intelligence agency's role. Also paragraphs would be deleted and revised to avoid calling the attention of Soviet strategists to the idea that they might be able to exploit UFOs to mask a surprise bombing attack by saturating early-warning channels. This sanitized version was sent to the USAF by Strong on December 20, 1957.

But on the night of March 8, 1958, the cat escaped from the bag—as far as the CIA's involvement went—when UFO-writer and promoter Donald Keyhoe was interviewed on the Columbia Broadcasting network by Mike Wallace. This served to unleash a barrage of letters during the coming months from a Dr. Leon Davidson to the director of Central Intelligence, Allen Dulles, to the Air Force, and to members of the Robertson Panel, seeking confirmation of the CIA's involvement and the release of the Panel's full report. Davidson's letters, agency memoranda triggered by his letters, and replies to Davidson make up the bulk of the material in the CIA-released files for the year 1958. In fact, letters from and to Davidson, between the CIA and members of the Robertson Panel, make up *more than five percent* of all of the CIA-released files.

In a letter to panel member Berkner, dated April 11, 1958, Dr. Davidson, a chemical engineer who had worked in the nuclear-weapons program, stated:

> It is my belief, unchanged since I first started to study this subject at Los Alamos in 1950, that activities of the U.S. Government are responsible for the

flying saucer sightings of the last decade. I now believe that the agency which bears most of the responsibility for causing and abetting the reports is the Central Intelligence Agency, while the technical and (shall we say) logistical support comes from the Navy. The Air Force has been relegated to the position of scapegoat, and its "investigations" are diversionary tactics necessary to the psychological warfare strategy.

On July 3, 1958, Davidson wrote another letter to CIA Director Dulles and posed the following question, asking for an "unequivocal catagorical" response:

> Has the CIA, alone or in cooperation with other Agencies, at any time since January 1951, and particularly in the early summer of 1952, been engaged in advising, inspiring, producing, promulgating, disseminating, causing, or encouraging the birth and/or spread of stories relating to the appearance of flying saucers (or UFO's) in the sky, or on radar screens, or on land, some of which have associated with them, or may have associated with them, passengers or crew members who seem to encourage observers to believe that they come from other planets than Earth? . . . I would normally be hesitant about sending such a fool-hardy question to a person in your position, but I believe that I have ample circumstantial evidence to justify at least posing the question to you. The fact that your agency has a legitimate interest in carrying out "psychological warfare" (but against whom??), and there is no public, and scarcely any private, accounting for the hundreds of millions of dollars which the CIA has spent, seem sufficient to allow at least the possibility that the CIA would be involved in such activities.

In a letter to another Robertson Panel member, Dr. Thorton Page, Davidson wrote on July 6, indicating the genesis of his suspicions:

> From correspondence I have had . . . I gather that "psychological warfare" applications of flying saucer phenomena was of interest to the CIA . . . . [In this, of course, Davidson was correct, but CIA interest was in how the USSR might make use of UFOs against the United States, or vice versa, not against the American public. He concluded:] I do not believe that a "1984" type of thought control should be allowed to develop in America. As I see it, if the CIA or the OCB, or whoever is calling the tune, can keep on getting away with this "saucer" activity, then the people will eventually be unable to believe their own eyes and ears. The manipulated world of which Orwell wrote will be upon us . . . .

During the next few years there were no significant developments on the UFO front, so far as the CIA files reveal, until a rash of UFO sightings that occurred in 1964 prompted the director of Central Intelligence to request an "Evaluation of UFOs" from the then assistant director for scientific intelligence, Donald F. Chamberlain. John McCone, who headed the CIA in 1964, had assumed that post in November 1961, some years after the agency's initial, and brief, UFO investigation.

Chamberlain responded with a memo on January 26, 1965, which acknowledged that

> . . . there has been a recent spate of reports of UFOs (unidentified flying objects) in news media. Widely publicized UFO reports during the past 18 months include: the July [date indistinct] Sunnyvale, California, incident in which the UFO was later identified as an aircraft; two UFOs reportedly associated with the Gemini [spacecraft] launching in April, which probably were due to fragments causing radar reflection; and the Patuxent, Maryland, incident in December 1964, in which two objects were apparently tracked by radar, but later analysis attributed the sightings to malfunctioning radar circuitry. Evaluation of these and other reported phenomena reveals no evidence that UFOs are of foreign origin or are a threat to the security of the United States.
>
> The Office of Scientific Intelligence monitors reports of UFO's, including the official Air Force investigation reports, and concurs with the Air Force conclusions, which are unclassified and available to scientific investigators.

Chamberlain's memo noted that of the many hundreds of UFO reports received during 1964, the USAF had classified only three percent of them as "unidentified." *The contents of this memo clearly indicates that there had been no change of viewpoint either within the USAF or the CIA on the UFO question during the twelve-year interval since the Robertson Panel report.*

The CIA files disclose that on July 19, 1966, a Mrs. Sara B. Hunt, from the Secretary of the Air Force's Office of Information, visited the CIA's D. B. Stevenson to ask that the CIA declassify the entire 24-page (plus appendices) Durant Report of 1953, which detailed the deliberations and conclusions of the Robertson Panel. This prompted a memo by Stevenson to his superior, dated July 20, saying that the USAF request "was triggered by the May 12 *CBS Reports* program," in which references to CIA involvement in the convening of the panel had been made, which in turn had sparked press queries. The Stevenson memo noted: "Mrs. Hunt said that the Air Force is now trying to declassify all U.S. Government work on UFO's." (Yet more than a decade later there still are persons who accuse the USAF of seeking a continuing "cover-up" on UFOs.)

Stevenson's memo expressed reservations over whether the full Durant Report could be released. In another Stevenson memo dated August 12, he indicated that the USAF was getting impatient to obtain release of the Durant Report as evidenced by a telephone call from Mrs. Hunt. Stevenson said he had told her that a sanitized version of the Durant Report, that omitted certain material, was then being retyped. The memo noted that Mrs. Hunt said the USAF was anxious to make the Durant Report available to John Lear for an article he was writing for *Saturday Review* (which would be published in the September 3 issue).

What Stevenson, and possibly Mrs. Hunt, did not know was that a copy of the original, unexpurgated Durant Report recently had been shown to a man who would soon emerge as an aggressive spokesman for the UFO movement. The man was Dr. James E. McDonald, an atmospheric physicist from the University of Arizona. When McDonald had visited the Project Blue Book offices on June 6 to peruse its UFO files, he had seen a copy of the Durant Report that had been declassified erroneously and he had been allowed to take notes on the report. Someone had stamped the report "Downgraded at 3-year intervals; declassified after 12 years," which is a standard Defense Department procedure for most of its documents, and the Durant Report now was thirteen years old. But because the CIA had originated the report, it was the only agency that had the authority to declassify it.

McDonald returned to Dayton on June 30 and asked for permission to make a photocopy of the complete Durant Report; at that time he was told that the USAF would need CIA permission. By this date the USAF seemingly had recognized that it had "goofed" in letting McDonald see the report on June 6 and take notes on its contents. When McDonald returned to Dayton again on July 20, he was told that the CIA had decided to reclassify the Durant Report. This was the day after Mrs. Hunt had first visited Stevenson and learned of his reluctance to make the full report public.

The CIA files show that on August 15, 1966, the agency's deputy director of scientific intelligence, Karl H. Weber, wrote to the USAF Office of Information in the Pentagon to say that the full Durant Report "cannot be downgraded," that is, declassified. Weber said that a sanitized version had been prepared for release that omitted the names of personnel and participating organizations. Weber noted that the panel members themselves wanted to avoid release of the fact that the CIA sponsored the original meeting. "We are most anxious that further publicity not be given to the information that the panel was sponsored by the Central Intelligence Agency," Weber's memo said. "Further, we cannot authorize the listing of personnel participating in the discussions . . ." This referred to persons who had briefed panel members, some of whom were employed by the CIA.

In retrospect, the CIA's decision to release a "slightly censored" version of the Durant Report was ill-considered. It would generate suspicions that possibly significant material had been deleted; even the *Saturday Review*'s Lear, who was sympathetic to the USAF/CIA view on UFOs was puzzled. (Today it is obvious that the deletions were inconsequential.) But this would serve to focus more, not less, public attention on the fact that the Robertson Panel had been convened under CIA auspices.

On August 31, 1966, the USAF asked the University of Colorado to undertake an independent investigation into the UFO question. The action was the result of oft-repeated charges that the USAF either had not done a sufficiently rigorous investigation or that it was guilty of covering-up what it had discovered. As a result of the rise in UFO reports in the mid-1960s, brief hearings on the subject had been held on April 5, 1966, by the House

Armed Services Committee, and the Air Force Scientific Advisory Board had recommended an independent study by a respected university or group of universities. The University of Colorado agreed to conduct the new UFO investigation, and in October it named Dr. Edward U. Condon to head the effort. Condon, a highly respected physicist at Colorado, earlier had headed the National Bureau of Standards.

The CIA files contain a memo from Arthur C. Lundahl, then director of the CIA's National Photographic Interpretation Center (NPIC), in Washington, telling of a request from the USAF that the center assist the Condon team in evaluating "alleged UFO photos." Lundahl's memo of February 7, 1967, to the CIA deputy director for intelligence, requested permission for five members of the University of Colorado team to visit the center to learn about its facilities and techniques for analyzing reconnaissance photos. Another Lundahl memo, dated Februray 23, reports on the highlights of a February 20 visit by Dr. Condon and four other project scientists. Still another memorandum-for-the-record, dated May 8, 1967, indicates that an NPIC analyst had briefed Condon and several associates on May 5 on the results of NPIC's analysis of a UFO photo taken by a barber in Zanesville, Ohio. (The photo was shown to be a hoax.)

In early 1969, a lengthy report on the University of Colorado's UFO investigation was published. Although the Colorado team, like the USAF, had encountered cases that it could not explain, Dr. Condon endorsed the USAF's conclusions that "the whole class of UFO reports so far considered does not pose a defense problem," that is, that there was no evidence of extraterrestrial craft. Condon concluded that "nothing has come from the study of UFOs in the past 21 years that has added to scientific knowledge . . . further extensive study of UFOs probably cannot be justified in the expectation that science will be advanced thereby."

The University of Colorado study and conclusions were reviewed by a special panel convened by the highly respected National Academy of Sciences. This panel endorsed Condon's conclusions by stating that "no high priority in UFO investigations is warranted by data of the past two decades." The panel added: "On the basis of present knowledge, the least likely explanation of UFOs is the hypothesis of extraterrestrial visitations by intelligent beings." On that basis, the Air Force announced on December 17, 1969, that it was terminating its Project Blue Book and would no longer investigate UFOs. The announcement said that all of the Project Blue Book files and records would be "retired" to the USAF Archives at Maxwell Air Force Base, Alabama.

The Condon Report and the USAF decision to close down Project Blue Book left the UFO movement in a state of shock and disarray. If the government "knew" that UFOs were extraterrestrial craft, how could it get out of the UFO field? This suggested to some that Project Blue Book had been only a "public relations front" and that the government's UFO investigating activities really were centered in another agency—the CIA. After all, it had been the CIA that had convened the Robertson Panel in 1953, and which had been so anxious to keep CIA-sponsorship secret. Clearly, went the UFOlogists' reasoning, the CIA was the real UFO-investigating agency and its efforts could now continue in secrecy while the public had been fooled into thinking the government no longer was interested in the subject. (Who then could have predicted that Congress would later pass a Freedom of Information Act that would oblige the CIA to disgorge its UFO files?)

An internal CIA memo dated July 29, 1970, from the deputy director for scientific intelligence to the deputy director for science and technology, comments on a letter written by a person named Vartorella, not otherwise identified. The memo begins:

> The central theme of this letter is "that the CIA has used—or is using—the Condon Report as a whitewash designed to cover a CIA-initiated program begun prior to January 1953." This allegation is not new and, of course, is ridiculous. Confirmed UFO believers are constantly searching for ways to discount the conclusions of every responsible group that ever considered the UFO problem—whether they be Swedes, British, the U.S. Air Force, the CIA, or the Condon Committee. A review of the files on the last two decades shows the following. The only formal CIA involvement in a UFO investigation was in the one conducted by the Robertson Panel in 1953 . . . *This was the high point in CIA involvement in the UFO matter.* [Emphasis added.] We had no organized effort on the subject. One or two analysts maintained some kind of watch on reports under Phil Strong's general guidance . . . .

The next internal CIA correspondence on the subject in the released files, dated April 4, 1976, consists of a series of telegraphic messages in which the names have been deleted, because of Privacy Act considerations and the fact that current CIA employee-positions generally are not made public. Apparently some American scientist submitted a "UFO study" to the CIA to ask whether it should be classified for national-security reasons. Possibly it dealt with a question that has occupied UFO believers: If UFOs are extraterrestrial craft, what novel type of propulsion is used to achieve the remarkable performance characteristics that sometimes are reported? (This is comparable to speculating that if a thousand angels really can dance on the head of a pin, what kind of shoes do they wear to keep from falling off.)

A telegraphic message dated April 26, 1976, says:

> Per the request in Reference (B), we attempted to obtain analytical guidance on the UFO [censored] subject. We contacted the A/DDS & T [Acting Deputy Director for Science and Technology] (Dr. [censored]) to see if he knew of any official UFO program and also to attempt to answer some of the

questions posed by [censored]. Dr. [censored] exhibited interest in [censored] which was handcarried to his office. After a short examination of its contents Dr. [censored] advised us that he would personally look into the matter . . . *It does not seem that the Government has any formal program in progress for the identification/solution of the UFO phenomena . . . . At the present time, there are offices and personnel within the agency who are monitoring the UFO phenomena, but again, this is not currently on an official basis.* Dr. [censored] feels that the best approach would be to keep in touch with and in fact develop reporting channels in this area to keep the Agency/community informed of any new developments. In particular, any information which might indicate a threat potential would be of interest, as would specific indications of foreign developments or applications of UFO related research . . . .

We wish to stress again, that there does not now appear to be any special program on UFOs within the intelligence community and this should be relayed to [censored]. [Emphasis added.]

Another memo, also censored, dated May 27, 1976, suggests that the CIA had received additional material from the person who had earlier submitted the "UFO Study," and this was being sent to Dr. [censored] within the CIA. The memo says:

Our source felt that [censored] work might be of interest to the US Government and that it should be evaluated by the Agency. The source also felt that it could be analyzed outside the context of its UFO connection if necessary to remove it from a controversial subject. As before we are faced with the problem of having UFO related data which is deemed potentially important for the US by our S & T [Science and Technology] sources evaluated. As you are aware, *at this time there is no channel or working group to which we can turn for this type of analysis and dissemination.* Thus, if it is acceptable to you we will continue to periodically advise you or your designee of any new or potentially important developments which might arise from current independent scientific research on the UFO phenomena. [Emphasis added.]

Clearly, as of May 27, 1976, there still was no group within the CIA that was actively interested in, or investigating UFOs, on an official basis.

A final entry in the CIA files, dated July 14, 1976, addressed to a Mr. [censored] begins:

At a recent meeting to evaluate some material from [censored], you mentioned a personal interest in the UFO phenomena. As you may recall, I mentioned my own interest in the subject as well as the fact that DCD had been receiving UFO related material from many of our S & T sources who are presently conducting related research. These scientists include some who have been associated with the Agency for years and whose credentials remove them from the "nut" variety. The attached material came to my attention through these sources and it appears to have some legitimate FI [foreign intelligence] or community interest potential . . . In view of the expertise associated with your

office, as well as your own interest in the subject, I felt you might like to see
the material. (If you need additional information or if you feel there is some
potential, I would be glad to discuss this with you. If not, please feel free to
destroy the material.)

If the recipient showed any official, or personal, interest, this is not
shown by further memoranda on the subject. That these two employees of
the CIA should have a personal interest in UFOs is not surprising, for the
subject had widespread appeal. But this final once-classified series of
memoranda clearly indicates that as of mid-1976, there was no active UFO-
investigatory effort under way within the CIA.

Yet it was these CIA documents, briefly summarized on the preceding
pages, that resulted in a front-page story in the respected *Baltimore Sun:*
"FILES INDICATE U.S. IS NOT TELLING ALL IT KNOWS ABOUT UFO's," and an
article in the *New York Times* headlined: "C.I.A. PAPERS DETAIL U.F.O.
SURVEILLANCE." *US* magazine published an article March 6, 1979, that
began: "Do you believe in U.F.O.'s? Well, the C.I.A. does. At least, it's
been tracking and photographing them for the past 30 years – and William
Spaulding, head of Ground Saucer Watch . . . has 950 pages of C.I.A.
documents as proof."

Following my initial study of the CIA files, on February 5, 1979, I called
Peter Gersten, Spaulding's attorney, who had been the first to receive the
documents and who could be expected to have studied them carefully.
When I asked Gersten if his study had revealed any evidence of a government coverup, he replied: "As far as the conspiracy is concerned, there is no
indication at all that there is a conspiracy. And as far as a coverup – coverup meaning that they are not volunteering documents – I would think that
the documents they have released seriously damages the theory of a
coverup."

Gersten said he still believed there was some physical basis for all the
UFO reports, but was inclined to suspect that UFOs were some secret
American or Russian craft. "I have come to the conclusion, separate and
aside from all this ETH [extraterrestrial hypothesis] baloney and so forth,
that there was a technology back in the late forties and early fifties [that had
been] developed – what was being seen later on, for one reason or another.
All of this is being interpreted as from other planets. But there is no
evidence of that."

In the late 1940s and early 1950s, it was understandable that some persons suspected that UFOs might be a secret U.S. or Soviet development. But
if UFOs were a U.S. development, saucer-shaped craft would long ago have
begun to enter the U.S. Air Force inventory and the UFO mystery would
then have been resolved. Yet both the U.S. and USSR continued to spend
billions of dollars to design and build "old-fashioned" conventional military
aircraft in the intervening decades.

Thus Gersten, unable to find any evidence in early 1979 of a government coverup in the many hundreds of pages of released CIA papers, felt obliged to turn to the "secret terrestrial weapon" hypothesis that many years earlier had been abandoned by more knowledgeable, experienced UFOlogists.

5

The Withheld Evidence

The CIA did not release all of its UFO-related papers in late 1978. It refused to declassify some fifty-seven pages on the grounds that they might compromise U.S. security. The agency did not elaborate, but at least one possibility comes to mind. It will be recalled that in 1952, CIA officials noted with interest that there was no mention or discussion of UFO sightings in the tightly controlled Soviet news media. This had prompted suspicions that UFOs might be a Russian psychological-warfare device. It is therefore reasonable to suppose that U.S. secret agents within the USSR were asked to probe their military and intelligence contacts to obtain Soviet views on UFOs and to ascertain whether UFOs might be a Soviet development. Thus it seems reasonable to assume that at least some of the unreleased material deals with the responses, activities and names of secret agents within the USSR.*

When Gersten and I talked on February 5, 1979, he told me that his study of the many hundreds of pages of CIA-released material failed to show any conspiracy or coverup, and he expressed no concern over the fifty-seven pages that were withheld. But the idea that the U.S. government is involved in a massive coverup of *significant* UFO information has been the cornerstone of belief of UFO proponents for more than three decades — much too long to be easily abandoned.

Within a year Gersten decided to take legal action to try to force the CIA to release the remaining fifty-seven pages, but his request was rejected by the U.S. District Court, in Washington, D.C., on May 30, 1980. Meanwhile,

---

*Another possible explanation for not releasing some CIA reports is that they may have come from intelligence agencies in allied countries. It is a long-standing CIA policy never to disclose such sources.

Freedom of Information Act requests for UFO-related material directed to the National Security Agency (NSA) and the Defense Intelligence Agency had brought the release of several hundred pages of UFO reports, most of them dating back many years, many from overseas sources. But NSA, like CIA, had withheld some material on security grounds. Because NSA's principal function involves the interception and decoding of foreign-government encrypted communications, it is possible that the release of some papers could reveal that NSA has been able to decode messages that the USSR, for example, previously believed to be secure. Unreleased documents may involve Kremlin communications to its embassy in Washington seeking information on USAF investigations into UFO incidents involving military aircraft, for example.

On June 25, 1980, Gersten issued a press release announcing that he had filed suit against NSA and the Defense Intelligence Agency, as well as the Federal Aviation Administration, to try to force the release of all withheld documents and that he was appealing the court decision on the CIA's withheld pages. On September 5, 1980, Gersten appeared at a press conference in Washington, sponsored by the Fund for UFO Research, at which an appeal was made to the government to release all UFO-related material. Following the press conference, I talked with Gersten and asked him if he had found any new evidence to support a government coverup charge. Gersten replied: "There is no evidence that I can see that the government is intentionally withholding anything, or misleading anybody. I think it's just . . . bureaucratic bungling . . ."

Within a year, based on the same evidence, Gersten would make contradictory claims. The occasion was a conference sponsored by the Mutual UFO Network (MUFON), held July 25–26, 1981, in Cambridge, Massachusetts. In a paper given there and later published by MUFON, Gersten spoke of evidence obtained from

> . . . 3,000 pages of previously classified documents on UFOs released during the past four years by the Departments of State, Army, Navy and Air Force, and by the Federal Bureau of Investigation, the Central Intelligence Agency, the National Security Agency and the Defense Intelligence Agency.
>
> Certain official government documents on the subject of UFOs give evidence that (1) some UFOs are unconventional aerial objects; that (2) these unconventional aerial objects perform in ways that are beyond the range of present day technological development; and (3) that these unconventional aerial objects with high performance characteristics have posed a threat to the national security of the United States and may have human survival implications as well.
>
> If the evidence contained in these documents were to be presented in court, it would provide overwhelming proof that UFOs do exist and that some UFOs are unconventional aerial objects. . . . [He charged that] there is evidence that our government has continually misinformed the public concerning the true

significance of the "UFO problem" . . . The evidence is clear and convincing that the federal government has systematically misinformed the American people about the real threat to our national security posed by such UFO encounters.

If Gersten is correct, it means that eight presidents, ranging from Harry S. Truman to Ronald Reagan, and an even greater number of directors of the CIA, secretaries of defense, and hundreds of high-level military officers have either been too dumb to recognize what is so obvious to Peter Gersten, or have been derelict in discharging their sworn obligations.

Since Gersten claims "proof" is found in the 3,000 pages in his possession, one might expect that he would end the litigation to try to force the CIA to release the remaining fifty-seven pages and also for some 135 pages of material which NSA is unwilling to release. But in fact Gersten continued his litigation against the NSA, taking it as high as the U.S. Supreme Court, which declined to review a lower court's action in rejecting Gersten's petition.

Gersten explained his rationale for continued litigation in his MUFON paper: "These government documents have given us the opportunity to see what the government should be aware of—what the government should know about UFOs. But it is difficult to say exactly what the government *does* know about UFOs because I do not have in my possession all the government UFO documents."

These withheld 192 pages of material will remain a cause célèbre for the UFO movement. UFO proponents will claim that if the government could be forced to release these pages they would provide the long-sought "smoking gun" and reveal that the U.S. government has for at least thirty years known that UFOs are extraterrestrial craft. Perhaps there would be confirmation that one or more such craft have been recovered.

The extraordinarily small number of pages being withheld contradicts this desperate hope. If the U.S. government obtained positive evidence that even one UFO was an extraterrestrial craft thirty years ago, that would represent one of the most extraordinary events in the history of the world and would impact heavily on many branches of government, including the White House, the Defense Department, the CIA, and the State Department. It is inconceivable that these large bureaucracies collectively would generate a total of only 192 pages of super-secret memoranda over a period of three decades, *or an average of only six sheets per year from all interested agencies.* Or that they would continue to write many more classified internal memoranda claiming ignorance of what was behind the UFO phenomenon and recommending investigations to resolve the issue.

If and when the U.S. government learns that the earth has been visited by an extraterrestrial craft, I am certain that more than 192 pages of memoranda on the subject will be generated by interested government agencies within a few days; that many thousands will be written within a year;

and that it will be impossible to keep the startling fact from the public.

But these 192 pages of unreleased material will continue to be cited by UFO proponents as "hard evidence" that the U.S. government, after more than a third of a century, continues to try to cover up the biggest non-secret of all time.

6

An Airline Pilot's UFO

Had you been one of the many thousands of persons who listened to the popular evening talk show broadcast over San Francisco's powerful KGO radio station on March 31, 1975, you could easily have been convinced that there are strange-looking craft in our skies. You would have heard a senior United Airlines captain report that not only he had seen a disk-shaped UFO in broad daylight but also that he had managed to photograph it in color. In the public's mind, airline pilots are viewed as persons whose integrity and veracity is beyond question.

I was one of two guests on the "Art Finley Show" that evening, with Paul Cerny, then chairman of MUFON's Bay Area chapter and now its western regional director. After Cerny and I had crossed verbal swords on UFOs (I in my traditional skeptic's role), we then responded to questions and comments telephoned in by listeners throughout the Pacific Coast and Rocky Mountain states. One caller said he was a senior captain with a major airline, which he declined to identify except to say that "we fly the friendly skies," that is, United Airlines.

The airline captain, who declined to give his name on the air, said the incident had occurred around 4:00 P.M., in September 1958, when he was then flying as co-pilot on a DC-6 airliner enroute from Seattle to Los Angeles, cruising at an altitude of about 14,000 feet. He said he had spotted a disk-shaped object to the west as it approached his aircraft, which it subsequently overtook and passed. The pilot said he had recently purchased a new camera which he had with him in the cockpit, loaded with film. He said he quickly grabbed the camera and photographed the UFO through the green sunshield positioned over the right-hand window. The pilot said he had sent a copy of the resulting color transparency "to Major Keyhoe's organization," that is, National Investigations Committee on Aerial Phenomena (NICAP), which at that time was the nation's largest UFO organization. The pilot said the photo had been analyzed "but [they] could find no spectral lines."

At this point our discussion was interrupted for the hourly news report. Cerny and I asked the pilot to remain on the telephone line so we could talk to him privately (off-the-air) and he agreed to do so. During the subsequent private conversation, the pilot gave us his name: Joseph H. Mathes. I asked him if he had the original color transparency of the UFO, and he assured me that he did. I expressed an interest in obtaining a copy, along with the report he said he had written shortly after the incident, and I offered to send him a copy of my book, *UFOs Explained,* if he would send me a copy of his UFO photo and report. Mathes agreed to do so. Cerny also talked with him and requested a copy of the report and photo for use by MUFON.

Within a few days, after returning to Washington, I promptly mailed a copy of my book to Captain Mathes. After a month had elapsed without a response, I wrote to him on May 11, asking if he had received my book and when I might expect to receive a copy of his UFO photo and report. Mathes replied on May 18 and thanked me "for the gift." He explained that because of his busy schedule he had not found time to read my book until quite recently. He complimented me on some aspects of the book but challenged others in a manner that indicated he was a "UFO believer," which is his (or anyone's) inalienable right.

But Mathes did not enclose the long-awaited UFO photo or report. Instead, there was a brief postscript which said: "As formerly advised, please contact NICAP for information on 1958 report & slide." There had been no "formerly advised" from Mathes. I replied on May 27, responding to some of his challenges on UFO cases, and concluding: "I feel you have not kept your part of the bargain. I agreed to send you an autographed book without charge and you were to at least try to find your original report and slide . . . . Surely for so important an incident and photo . . . you must have put them away in a valuable, safe location . . . . At least try to find them for me."

Mathes replied on May 31, devoting nearly four typewritten pages to a further challenge of my views on UFOs. Only at the bottom of the last page did he mention the UFO photo and report, saying that he had "not put [his] report and UFO slide away in a safe place, unfortunately." He claimed he was unable to locate them and added that the incident now was quite "old and not all that important." Mathes concluded his letter: "Have a happy and enjoyable summer season. Life has many beautiful things to offer besides investigating *a group of shy, well-meaning visitors to our beloved planet.*" [Emphasis added.]

On July 1, 1975, I wrote to the head of NICAP, Jack Acuff, with whom I had cordial relations. I recounted the Mathes incident and asked if Acuff would search NICAP files for a copy of the pilot's report and photo, as well as the spectral analysis that Mathes said that NICAP had made. Acuff responded on July 3 saying he had checked the files but could find neither the Mathes report nor his photo. I then recalled that in 1964, several years after the date of the Mathes incident, NICAP had prepared and published a 184-page report, entitled *The UFO Evidence,* which contained the most impressive UFO reports and photos it had, for distribution to members of Congress and the news media. I turned to this, to the section devoted to UFO reports from airline and military pilots. *But there was no mention of any report from Mathes.* Then I turned to another section that listed the sixty-four most impressive UFO photos submitted to NICAP between 1946 and 1962. *There was no mention of a color photo from Mathes.*

On July 7, I wrote to Captain Mathes, informing him that NICAP had no record of ever having received either his UFO report or photo, and I noted that neither was mentioned in NICAP's 184-page report. My letter concluded by offering him an "out." Was it possible, I asked, that he had not sent his photo and report to Major Keyhoe/NICAP, as he first said, but to another UFO organization? My letter was returned, unopened, marked: "Refused by Addressee. Return to Sender."

I began to wonder if Mathes was a senior captain with United Airlines, or whether this claim, like his UFO photo, was also bogus. On August 3, I wrote to a friend who is employed at the United Airlines flight-training center in Denver to ask if he could check company records to determine if Mathes was a captain with United. Two weeks later this friend replied that it had not been necessary to check the records because he had met Mathes in late 1973, when he came to Denver for his semiannual pilot-proficiency check. My friend, who had a long-standing interest in UFOs, said that Mathes had told him that he and a team of electronic and computer experts in California were working to "crack the code" that would enable them to communicate with the extraterrestrial visitors who pilot UFOs!

Another curious incident, involving MUFON's Paul Cerny, had occurred during the same talk-show on station KGO. At one point in our discussion, Cerny suggested that the real reason I was a UFO skeptic and debunker was that I was being paid by the Central Intelligence Agency, the USAF, or some other government agency. I reminded Cerny that he had made a similar allegation in the late 1960s when we had appeared together on a Bay Area television program. At that time, I reminded him, I had offered to pay him $10,000 if he could substantiate his charge. When he again raised the issue on the KGO program, I said that because there had been inflation since my earlier offer was made, I would now raise the figure to $25,000. I said I would pay him this amount if he could prove I had ever received any money from any government agency at any time, except for a small Social Security payment on the death of my mother and an even smaller refund one year for overpayment of my federal income tax.

To help Cerny obtain the evidence he needed to collect the $25,000, I offered to send him a photocopy of my federal tax returns, beginning in 1966 when I first entered the UFO field, if he would let me examine his federal tax returns for the same period. I pointed out that if he found evidence of government payments in my tax returns, he could collect the $25,000. If he found no such evidence but could prove his charge by other means, then he could not only collect the $25,000 but also could have me sent to prison for tax evasion. *Cerny agreed to send me his federal tax returns as soon as he received mine.* When I returned to Washington, I mailed Cerny a photocopy of my 1966 tax return on May 10, 1975. In my accompanying letter I said that when I received his tax return for 1966, I would then send him mine for 1967 and we would follow this procedure until each had sent the other all of his tax returns. But my letter, with its 1966 tax return, was returned, unopened, marked: "Refused. Please Return to Sender," and signed "P. Cerny."

I heard no more from either Captain Mathes or Cerny. But in mid-February of 1982, I was told that Cerny and Mathes had concocted the story of the pilot's UFO sighting and photo in advance of the KGO program to confront me with a seemingly irrefutable UFO report from a senior airline captain and a daylight photo to support his story. I learned this from John Merrell, of Beaverton, Oregon, a young UFOlogist, whose experience in investigating cases first-hand had converted him into a skeptic. Merrell told me he had corresponded with Mathes and talked with Cerny in the spring of 1975 and that a letter from Mathes revealed that he and Cerny were friends at the time of the KGO broadcast, although each had pretended on the phone that they were complete strangers.

Merrell sent me a copy of the letter from Mathes, dated May 11, 1975, barely six weeks after the KGO broadcast. In the letter Mathes recommended that Merrell "contact one Paul Cerny, a personal friend of mine . . ." In the same letter, Mathes informed Merrell that if he was "deeply serious about learning the real purpose and validity of UFOs, and their reason for visiting this planet, I would be happy to forward to you a copy of *The Amnesia Factor* . . . I wrote the book in conjunction with Lenora Huett, my co-worker." Merrell obtained a copy of the book and later sent it to me.

The back cover of *The Amnesia Factor* summarizes its contents as follows: "Two Extra-terrestrial Guides Speak Through the Unexpected Voice of a Gentle and Gifted 'Channel.' Through a series of taped interviews in which two beings in different times and dimensions speak through Lenora Huett, J. H. Mathes writes compellingly of what they said about him, about mankind, space, other worlds, and God." In the introduction to the 169-page book, the reader is told that Mathes "maintained a firm, skeptical stance throughout three decades concerning ESP phenomena. But one sunny afternoon in 1971, he was introduced to Lenora . . . . Within ten short minutes with Lenora, his limited opinions had to be radically revised. He quickly determined that her telepathic ability was genuine by asking complex questions clearly beyond her field of knowledge."

During this initial session, Mathes wrote, "we soon discovered that Lenora knew nothing about UFOs, nor did she have any real interest in such things. Paul [whose last name is not given but who sounds like Paul Cerny] then began projecting [UFO] slides onto the screen. As a test, he asked Lenora if the UFO in the picture was real or fake. Gradually overcoming her shyness, Lenora faintly murmured, 'That one feels like a fake.' Then another UFO flashed onto the screen and she hesitated, looking far away. Suddenly she stated, 'That's the real thing.' Then another lighted the screen. Leaning forward, she stated, 'That, too is a real object. I can sense that there was life aboard that craft.' We stared at Lenora. Somehow, I could tell that she had been accurate," Mathes wrote in the book.

But the most impressive part of Mrs. Huett's performance was yet to come. "Paul lapsed into his lecture format by stating the circumstances surrounding each sighting. 'This photograph was taken by a scientist . . . We'd like to find out if UFOs are able to penetrate into dimensions other than ours.' Lenora leaned back, closed her eyes very briefly, then surprised us all by rattling forth the following strange message: THEY COULD, BUT DO NOT. THEIR VIBRATIONS VARY WITHIN THE BOUNDS OF THOSE ENERGY LAYERS WITHIN THE PHYSICAL MATRIX. THEY ARE ABLE TO REACH A DIFFERENT VIBRATION, YET ARE STILL HERE."

The book quickly shifts to even more exotic subjects, such as multi-dimensional worlds, astral planes, and karmic debts. At one point Mathes asked: "What can I learn about my prior lives? I'm especially interested in Biblical times." Mrs. Huett responded that Mathes once had been a Tibetan monk, named Twzen. "With the spelling of the name Twzen," Mathes wrote, "I felt a strange glow flood through my body." Mrs. Huett explained to Mathes that data on prior lives comes from Akashic Records, which are guarded by a person's "guides." When Mathes asked for the names of his guides, his question brought forth a scowl from Lenora. "Much later," Mathes wrote, "I discovered that the cause of her hang-up was bound up in the past. Lenora had innocently told some close friends of her newfound ability with telepathy and, when they tested her by requesting the names of former relatives, she had misspelled a few. Her close 'friends' had promptly called her a fake. Such mistreatment had caused Lenora no end of confusion and hurt," according to Mathes.

John Merrell told me that Cerny once admitted to him, during a conversation, that I had been "set-up" by prearrangement with Mathes. The Mathes letter of May 11, 1975, together with the contents of the Mathes book, offer evidence that the two men had a close friendship at the time of the KGO broadcast; yet each pretended to be unacquainted with the other. Art Finley, the talk-show host on the night of March 31, 1975, left the San Francisco area some time ago. Even if Station KGO were willing to expose the hoax on one of its current talk shows, how many of the original listeners would be tuned in?

One thing is certain. When the subject of UFOs comes up in conversation with those who heard the original broadcast, many may respond somewhat as follows: "Well, I don't know much about UFOs. But I do know that I heard a senior airline captain one night on the radio say not only had he seen a strange-looking disk-like object in broad daylight but also he had photographed it in color. Surely a senior airline pilot wouldn't tell a story like that on the radio if it weren't true!" Undoubtedly those hearing the story will be equally impressed and may even recount the incident later to friends.

7

Astronomers and UFOs

The Christian Science Monitor titled a story on April 27, 1977: "Probe UFO Riddle, Say Astronomers," while a *New York Times* article on March 17, 1977, was headlined: "Further Study of U.F.O.'s Endorsed in a Survey." The *National Enquirer* headlined an April 27 story: "Astonishing 80% of Astronomers Believe UFOs Should Be Investigated." If there are strange craft-like objects in our skies whose characteristics indicate they come from extraterrestrial civilizations, as most UFO enthusiasts claim, then UFOs should certainly be of keen interest to both professional and amateur astronomers who make up the membership of the American Astronomical Society (AAS). And if 11 percent of the general public has seen a UFO, as the 1973 Gallup Poll indicates, an even higher incidence of UFO sightings should be expected from astronomers, many of whom spend much of their time in "sky-gazing."

For this reason there was an air of great expectation among UFO enthusiasts when it became known that Dr. Peter A. Sturrock was polling the 2,611 members of the AAS on the subject of UFOs. Sturrock, a member of the AAS, is a highly respected astrophysicist at Stanford University's prestigious Institute for Plasma Research. The survey was Sturrock's own idea and AAS headquarters did not sponsor, nor participate, in the UFO survey but it posed no objection when he sought approval to make the survey.

The two-page questionnaire that Sturrock mailed to AAS members contained eleven multiple-choice questions that required no more than five minutes to complete. Each respondent was asked to give his name but was assured of anonymity in the subsequent published survey in order to elicit maximum participation and candor. Approximately 52 percent of the 2,611 members polled returned the questionnaire, which is a moderately good return for such a survey. But considering the potential significance of

57

extraterrestrial visitors to astronomers it is notable that 48 percent were not sufficiently interested in UFOs to devote five minutes of their time to the survey.

The key question, which was the cornerstone of the press release later issued by Sturrock through Stanford University, on which the news articles and headlines were based, was the following:

> Do you think the UFO problem (check one):
> (a) Certainly deserves scientific study   ( )
> (b) Probably deserves scientific study   ( )
> (c) Possibly deserves scientific study   ( )
> (d) Probably does not deserve scientific study   ( )
> (e) Certainly does not deserve scientific study   ( )

Curiously, this key question offers the respondent *three* choices that seem favorable to further scientific studies of the UFO problem, but only *two* choices that are opposed. However, if a respondent selected "possibly deserves scientific study," one could conclude that the respondent believed that possibly the problem does not deserve further study. But the press release issued by Stanford University, which my investigation showed that Sturrock had personally reviewed and approved, interpreted a choice of "possibly deserves" as being *favorable* to further UFO studies. It also is important to note that the question phrasing is based on "the UFO problem," and not "UFOs," per se. Thus, a UFO-skeptic might favor a study of why people believe, or want to believe, in UFOs without supporting further study of UFOs themselves, and certainly without believing that UFOs are of extraterrestrial origin.

One clue as to how such a loaded question found its way into the survey can be found in Sturrock's acknowledgements at the end of the formal report thanking those who helped him frame the questions. One of those was Dr. J. Allen Hynek, who has been characterized by *Oui* magazine as the "Galileo of UFO Studies." Another who assisted Sturrock in framing the questions was Dr. David Saunders, whose own book reveals him to be a staunch proponent of the extraterrestrial hypothesis. So far as I know, Sturrock did not enlist the aid of any experienced UFO skeptics in preparing his questionnaire, although he previously had corresponded with two such individuals: myself and the late Dr. Donald H. Menzel, a world-famous astronomer and former director of the Harvard Observatory.

Nor was Sturrock a newcomer to the field of UFOlogy. He already had organized two symposia on the subject. In both instances he had invited only those experienced UFOlogists who promote the extraterrestrial hypothesis, or even more exotic theories. There was a notable absence of experienced skeptical UFOlogists.

Returning to the all-important survey question, AAS respondents replied as follows: A total of 23 percent checked "certainly deserves," while another 29 percent checked "probably deserves" further scientific study. Another 27 percent checked "possibly deserves" while 18 percent checked "probably not" and three percent opted for "certainly does not." Thus 52 percent could be said to favor study of "the UFO problem," 21 percent were opposed and 27 percent were "possibly's." But the press release issued by Stanford University, after review and approval by Sturrock, began as follows: "A survey of trained observers of the skies, all members of the American Astronomical Society (AAS) indicates that most of them feel UFOs (unidentified flying objects) deserve further scientific study. Of 1,356 AAS members replying to a questionnaire from Prof. Peter A. Sturrock . . . , four-fifths feel that the UFO problem 'certainly . . . probably . . . or possibly . . . deserves scientific study' . . ." It was this press release that, understandably, generated the aforementioned headlines and similar ones in the nation's press.

Sturrock's survey can be criticized on another score: it provided no opportunity for AAS members to render a value-judgment. Although I doubt that most AAS members have an overwhelming interest in the diseases of snakes, I suspect that if they were asked whether they favored scientific study of arthritis in reptiles many would respond favorably. After all, what true scientist can be opposed to scientific study of any subject? Had Sturrock asked AAS members whether they favored scientific study of the UFO problem at the expense of study of pulsars, Black Holes or X-ray stars, we would have obtained a more meaningful measure of the depth of their interest, or curiosity, about UFOs.

Although the survey questions made no direct attempt to obtain a value-judgment of AAS members on further UFO research, the detailed survey report (which was not sent out with the press release) reveals, albeit unwittingly, that the nation's professional and amateur astronomers already had made personal appraisals. Although 53 of the AAS respondents indicated that they themselves had had what could be termed "UFO sightings," only seven of the 2,611 AAS members surveyed (including Hynek and Sturrock) indicated that they were actively working in the field of UFOlogy. *This indicates that barely one-quarter of one percent (0.27%) of the 2,611 AAS members believe the "UFO problem" is of sufficient importance to justify devoting their personal time to try to solve the issue.* This reveals much more than Sturrock's multiple-choice question as to how important the "UFO problem" appears to the nation's professional and amateur astronomers.

The explanation for this extremely low level of interest is revealed by responses to another question in the Sturrock survey. Each respondent was told to assume that a fellow member of the AAS had submitted a UFO sighting report and that the respondent had agreed to investigate it. But before launching the investigation, the AAS member was asked to indicate his estimate of the probability that the UFO report would prove to be explainable in terms of one (or more) of eight different possible causes. Six of these were terrestrial/prosaic causes, including a hoax or "some established but unfamiliar natural phenomenon such as ball lightning." A seventh possible trigger-mechanism for the report was "some other cause you cannot specify," while the eighth choice was "a technological device not of terrestrial origin," that is, an extraterrestrial craft. Respondents were asked to assign an estimated probability that the explanation for the UFO report from a fellow astronomer would turn out to be one or more of these eight possible explanations.

The collective view of all AAS respondents was that *the probability that the UFO sighting might involve an extraterrestrial craft was only three percent—the lowest figure offered for any of the eight options.* Collectively the respondents estimated that there was a four-fold greater probability (12%) that the incident would turn out to be a hoax! In other words, only three percent of the AAS respondents, or barely 1½ percent of the total membership, believe that there is the slightest chance that *any* UFO reports involve extraterrestrial visitors. Contrast this with the headlines generated by the Stanford University press release, such as the *National Enquirer*'s "ASTONISHING 80% OF ASTRONOMERS BELIEVE UFOs SHOULD BE INVESTIGATED."

In Sturrock's first questionnaire, he asked if the respondent had ever seen anything in the sky that he himself could not explain, or had ever obtained instrumental data related to the UFO question. Those who said they had then were sent another questionnaire to elicit details of the incident. From this Sturrock had obtained a total of 53 AAS-member visual-sighting reports. A few dated back many years, some to the respondent's youth. Additionally, there were several incidents that involved radio, radar, and photographic incidents. On the assumption that any AAS member who personally had experienced an unexplainable UFO incident would be sufficiently interested to participate in the survey, the 53 incidents correspond to only 2 percent of the 2,611 AAS members. Despite the fact that astronomers generally spend much more of their time in "sky-watching" than the general public, it is interesting to note that while the 1973 Gallup Poll indicates that 11 percent of the U.S. public has at some time seen something in the sky it could not explain, only 2 percent of the nation's astronomers have had such an experience. One explanation, as we shall see, is that many UFO reports from the public are triggered by bright celestial bodies that clearly would not confuse an astronomer.

Sturrock's survey reveals—not surprisingly—that AAS members who themselves have had unexplained sightings had done more extensive reading on the UFO subject and were more interested than those who had not had such an experience. Inasmuch as 99 percent of all UFO books and articles promote the extraterrestrial hypothesis, this means that AAS members who had themselves had UFO sightings had been exposed to the strongest possible evidence to support this view. Yet when these AAS respondents were asked to appraise the probability that what they themselves had seen might have been an extraterrestrial device, compared to the possibility that it might have a more terrestrial/prosaic explanation, they estimated that there was only a 5 percent chance that their own UFO might be an extraterrestrial craft, compared to 1½ percent of the total AAS membership's estimate of the probability that there are alien craft in our skies.

The collection of UFO reports submitted by AAS members, which form the bulk of the Sturrock survey report, are the most illuminating portion in my opinion. This is especially true of ten UFO reports that later proved to be "IFOs" — identified flying objects. For those UFO promoters who claim that reports from astronomers and other scientists are necessarily infallible in *all* details, the Sturrock report is an eye-opener. For example, one report came from an astronomer living near Tucson, Arizona, who described seeing something so "striking and unusual" for several minutes during the early evening of October 5, 1973, that he was prompted to write down his observations while they still were fresh and then to personally seek a possible prosaic explanation — something that most of the AAS respondents did not bother to do. This AAS member wrote Sturrock: "I am a professional astronomer, specializing in observational work, and have spent thousands of hours outside looking at the nighttime sky (both recently and for many years as a teen-age amateur astronomer)."

Quoting from portions of the astronomer's account of the incident, made shortly after the sighting:

> This report concerns a striking and unusual phenomenon which I witnessed for several minutes on the evening of Oct. 5, 1973 . . . The phenomenon was witnessed by at least one other person some miles distant, and may be related to a rash of "UFO" reports that have been occurring in recent weeks in the southern USA. Very near 8:00 P.M. Mountain Standard Time . . . I noticed a brilliant light in the sky seven degrees (plus/minus two degrees) north of west, about five to seven degrees high in the sky (rough estimate) . . . *I judged the distance of the light to be several miles away* . . . [emphasis added] . . . an independent report on the same phenomenon by an observer located approximately south of the position where I estimated the phenomenon to take place, confirms the location was where I judged it to be, approximately.
>
> The light was bright white, with perhaps a yellowish tinge, approximately stellar in appearance . . . and of roughly (minus) -6 magnitude . . . distinctly brighter than the planet Venus . . . within a few seconds . . . I became aware of a large "halo" . . . surrounding the bright light . . . . My distinct impression was that this halo erupted from the light itself in a kind of explosion or puff-of-smoke . . . within a few tens of seconds, at most, the bright light began to fade and transformed itself into an extended disk with soft edges, accurately estimated to be three moon diameters in size (1½ deg.). The transformation was completed in five to ten seconds. The disk was neither sharp-edged, nor was it a diffuse cloud . . . By this time the large luminous halo was no longer

visible . . . . The central disk, of whitish or possibly bluish hue, which was quite bright at first, gradually faded away in the course of at least five minutes (possibly as long as ten minutes). It did not change its size, sharpness, or position as it faded away. Indeed, the entire phenomenon was devoid of any translational motion [that is, the object seemed to hover motionless until it disappeared.] . . . I noticed an airplane flying . . . to the south of the phenomenon . . . and judged from its rate of motion that it might have been near the phenomenon at the time it commenced. My guess that it was something dropped from the airplane vanished as time revealed the phenomenon to be totally stationary in the sky . . . .

The astronomer's subsequent investigation revealed that this UFO was the fiery rocket exhaust from a giant USAF Titan-2 intercontinental ballistic missle that had been launched from Vandenberg Air Force Base, in California—more than 500 miles away! A USAF spokesman told the astronomer that ICBM launches made from Vandenberg shortly after dark often generated UFO reports from as far away as Oregon and New Mexico, the astronomer wrote Sturrock. After this puzzling UFO had been transformed into an IFO, this AAS member had the good sense to reread his original sighting report, to check on the accuracy of his powers of observation and recollections of a brief and unfamiliar event. Not surprisingly, he reported finding "several inaccuracies and inconsistencies." These, he observed, "are most readily explained as the usual difficulties of perceiving and remembering an unusual, rapidly changing phenomenon." Then he made an especially sage observation: *"This report . . . is perhaps typical of the reliability of a UFO observation by a trained observer."* [Emphasis added.]

But this was only a portion of the insight gained into the UFO phenomenon by this astronomer. Shortly after the original incident, and before an explanation had been found, the astronomer reported the incident to APRO, a large UFO organization based in Tucson. APRO assigned a scientifically trained investigator, a graduate student in astronomy at the University of Arizona, to investigate the incident. But when this APRO investigator later was informed that the incident was the result of the Titan-2 ICBM launch from Vandenberg, he *"was more prepared to believe that my report and others the same evening [from other area witnesses], were of a genuine extraterrestrial visitation rather than the more realistic Titan missile launch,"* according to the Tucson astronomer. [Emphasis added.]

The three-page press release that Stanford University sent out to the news media contained half a dozen capsule-summaries of some of the AAS-member UFO sighting reports that Sturrock had received—all of them mysterious, seemingly inexplicable. There was no mention of the Tucson astronomer's sighting, nor of his observation about the "reliability" of reports from trained observers. But the press release did include a statement volunteered by another AAS respondent: "It will indeed be fortunate if an increasing number of our scientifically trained people will admit that there exists a fascinating and as yet unexplained phenomenon worthy of careful study."

It now has been more than five years since the Sturrock AAS survey results were made public through the Sturrock-approved news release that stated that "most of them [AAS members] feel UFOs (unidentified flying objects) deserve further scientific study." During this period, the AAS has held ten of its regular semi-annual technical conferences, but not one of the many technical papers presented at these meetings has dealt with UFOs. Nor has there been any indication that members want the AAS to become involved in the UFO issue, according to an AAS official. Yet frequently I am told that "astronomers are really very interested in UFOs" by someone who recalls newspaper headlines that resulted from the press release Sturrock authorized.

8

An Intercontinental UFO

Mr. and Mrs. J. D. Chenoweth, who live in northern California, were driving to a wedding in southern California at the time an incident occurred, at around 7:30 P.M. on the night of February 19, 1976. Their car, headed south, was about 30 miles north of Bakersfield, when suddenly the ridges of the Diablo Mountains to the right were outlined in a bright orange glow, Mrs. Chenoweth told me in her letter of April 19, 1977.

> Then, shooting over the top [of the mountains] like a bullet, came a burnt-orange ball . . . [which] stopped in midair! . . . [The couple pulled to the side of Highway I-5 and watched the orange ball change into an arrow-shape.]
>
> Then, slowly, the "arrow" thing tilted to a 3 o'clock position and pointed west, northwest. And, incredibly, it began to *stretch* and *stretch* until its length was about six times the width of the spread-end of the "arrowhead." A few seconds later, a small burnt-orange ball . . . popped out of the tail of the "arrow" and simply hung in the air . . . . Then in just a few seconds, the small orange ball began to pulsate or blink, very rapidly—maybe fifteen or twenty times. Then, still blinking, it shot off to the north . . . while the glowing luminous arrow now developed a dark band at its center "waist" and began to slowly point in a 6 to 12 o'clock position . . . .
>
> We remarked what a beautiful sight it really was—like the result of some exquisite engineering . . . . As we continued to watch, we realized the thing had become more hourglass-shaped . . . . Both top and bottom ends were spread to about three times the width of its "waistband." . . . [As they watched, the object became enveloped in a sort of fog] . . . thicker luminous white cloud soundlessly blasted out of the two bottom legs of the slender "X" [that is, an hourglass shape]; then out of the top legs, but not simultaneously . . . the luminous cloud just hung there, brilliant against the black night sky. It was shaped like a headless ghost in shirt sleeves, with upraised arms, but got more and more transparent. The cloud hung there for a minute or two, then dispersed, disappeared and nothing was left: just the original black mottled sky

65

and the Western "star" [Jupiter] over the Diablo range. There was no sound, nor odor . . . .

When the couple arrived at Bakersfield a short time later and checked into a motel, they promptly wrote down their individual recollections of what they had seen. Mrs. Chenoweth said their descriptions "were almost identical," but she acknowledged that they differed in their estimates of the total duration of the incident. Following the incident, Mrs. Chenoweth read my book *UFOs Explained,* and she said she was writing in the hope that I might be able to offer an explanation for the incident. In a thoughtful attempt to ease the burden of my reply, she enclosed a separate "multiple-choice" reply sheet that I could use which included such possible explanations as "mass hallucination," "secret military contrivance," a launch of a missile or satellite from Vandenberg Air Force Base or "other."

During many years in the field of UFOlogy, I often have been approached—"challenged" might be more accurate—to explain personal UFO sightings. Usually the person involved does not remember the specific date of the incident and sometimes is unsure as to the month or year, which makes an investigation impossible. In some instances, where the details sound similar to another case, I may venture a tentative: "Well, from your description, it sounds as if it might have been . . . ." Often this hypothesis is rejected by the correspondent with an instant rejoinder: "No, it could not possibly have been . . . . I know what I saw. What I saw was a *genuine* UFO."

Mrs. Chenoweth's letter not only provided many useful specifics, based on notes made immediately following the incident, but its tone suggested that she truly wanted an explanation, and would be content to accept a terrestrial one. In my reply, I asked for a few additional details and requested a map of the area involved, including the direction she and her husband were looking at the time.

The important role of "Lady Luck" in uncovering prosaic explanations for UFO incidents is illustrated by this case. It was my good fortune that Mrs. Chenoweth's letter arrived shortly *after* I had finished studying the Sturrock report discussed in the previous chapter, on the UFO survey of AAS members, with its interesting incident involving the Tucson astronomer and the Titan-2 ICBM launch from Vandenberg AFB. After reading Mrs. Chenoweth's account, I got out a map of California and found that the Vandenberg missile test and satellite-launch facility was located approximately seventy-five miles southwest of her sighting.

This prompted me to make a telephone inquiry to the Air Force to determine if there had been any ICBM or satellite launches from Vandenberg on February 19, 1976. The next day I was informed that a Minuteman-2 ICBM had been launched on that date, at approximately 7:20 P.M., within ten minutes of Mrs. Chenoweth's estimated time of the UFO sighting. Mrs.

Chenoweth replied on April 26, with a map and a series of sketches (based on ones made shortly after the incident) which showed the curiously changing appearance of the object at various stages in the incident. She told me that she and her husband had been facing to the southwest throughout the sighting—the direction of Vandenberg AFB.

I decided that I would temporarily withhold my findings from Mrs. Chenoweth and would send her a portion of the Tucson astronomer's description of what he had seen, omitting his finding as to its cause, to ask if she found the astronomer's description to be similar to her own. She replied on May 5 with a very detailed analysis of the two reports, which prompted her to conclude that "what he sighted was not similar to what we saw." In certain respects this was understandable: the astronomer's "UFO" was a two-stage, liquid-fueled Titan-2, viewed from more than 500 miles away while Mrs. Chenoweth's "UFO" was a three-stage Minuteman using solid propellant and was seen from only 75 miles away.

In her reply, Mrs. Chenoweth mentioned that her brother had suggested that the sighting near Bakersfield might have been the result of a missile launch from Vandenberg. But she dismissed his explanation on the grounds that "I have *never* seen a launching look like that!" Presumably she was referring to manned space launches she had seen on television. I wondered if she would also reject my explanation of a Minuteman-2 launch.

On May 9, I wrote Mrs. Chenoweth to tell her of the Minuteman launch from Vandenberg. She replied on May 13 with a letter that began: "You have done me such a huge favor . . . . Thank heavens, inexplicable things have not arrived to taunt us from the heavens . . ." Her reaction stands in sharp contrast to many "UFO sighters," who will go so far as to sharply revise their original description of the incident after a prosaic explanation has been found in an effort to invalidate that explanation and to retain the distinction of "having seen a *genuine* UFO."

9

UFOs with a Message

In the summer of 1977, I received an interesting letter from William E. Bissonnette, of Bridgeport, Connecticut, who had recently finished reading *UFOs Explained* and was writing to describe several of his own UFO sightings, two of which had resulted in home-movies of the objects:

> Until a year or so ago, I guess my interest in UFOs was based on casual curiosity. I had read newspaper accounts and a book or two on the subject and had heard stories from relatives and friends who had claimed to see UFOs in the past. However, granting myself a slightly above average I.Q. (I am a member of MENSA*), I decided that these reports were distorted accounts of normal people seeing normal events under abnormal conditions. This is the way matters stood until a summer's evening in 1975 when a friend and I were standing out in a parking lot preparing to go to work when I noticed what appeared to be a dirigible flying in the almost darkened sky a few miles from us.
>
> I called the craft to my friend's attention and we watched it for a period of a minute or two. The craft made no sound and appeared to be of considerable size. It had white and red lights running the length of it on the bottom circumference. After watching it cross from left sky to directly in front of us, it started to move away from us. However, it did not make a turn to do so. Thus, even as it moved over the horizon, we still saw what we thought to be the side of the blimp. On several occasions since, my friend and I discussed this weird event and finally we reached the conclusion that it could not have been a dirigible as it would have had to turn to change direction and we would have seen the thing end on. We decided that what we saw was a UFO.
>
> During the course of the next year I thought little above this event. One evening while shopping in a bookstore I noticed a paperback book purporting to be based on the previously classified Project Blue Book data and reaching the conclusion that there were in fact legitimate UFO sightings. I read the

---

*MENSA is an organization of persons with significantly high I.Q.s, book and started thinking again about the incident mentioned. I called my friend again and we discussed what happened that night and I suggested that we should at least report it to someone. He laughed it off and said that unless we had photos of the thing, we would just be labeled crackpots . . .

A few days later, thinking about this, I loaded my Kodak available-light Super-8mm. movie camera with high-speed [ASA] 160 film and put it in the rear compartment of my stationwagon . . . determined that, if I ever saw such a thing again, I would get a film of it and that I would then either be able to deduce what it was or at least not be held up to ridicule for "seeing things."

About a month ago, around 7:30 P.M. , I took my six year old son for a ride down to the grocery store. Just as we started to drive down our street, my son asked me what that funny thing in the sky was. I looked up expecting to tell him it was a plane or helicopter when my eyes grasped the most spectacular sight I have ever seen. There in the sky over Bridgeport was the same, or similar, craft I had seen before. But it was even closer and lit up the night sky. Lights blinking on and off, banking and swooping around the city. I was dumbstruck for a second or two when I remembered the camera in the rear compartment. I stopped the car, ran to the back and pulled out the camera and started to shoot. I realized I was shooting straight into a street light that might be glaring so much as to ruin the shot so I moved out into a field and started to shoot again when my camera jammed! . . . By banging the side of it, I managed to get a few more feet of film . . . I recalled reading in various reports that mechanical failure of devices frequented the sightings of UFOs [that is, were caused by proximity of UFOs]. And I knew what I had seen was no aircraft. I . . . decided that I would not develop it [the movie film] as then the possibility of a hoax might crop up . . . .

The next evening about the same time . . . as I started down the street I saw the object again. Exactly where it had been the previous night. I stopped the car again and had the camera right by my side where I had left it. I jumped out and started shooting. This time the camera seemed to work fine and I shot at least 15-20 feet [of film] of the object . . . As I entered the town of Stratford . . . I saw the thing again! I pulled off an exit ramp and shot another 20 feet of film . . . I got back into the car and continued on to the job where I could hardly contain my emotions.

The only people I told about the sighting on the previous night were my housekeeper, my girl-friend and the friend who had seen the earlier sighting with me. When I arrived on the job, I took my friend aside and told him of the new sighting and that this time I had it on film. When I arrived home that evening, I started to tell my housekeeper about the new sighting and the film I had shot when she interrupted me to tell me that my girl-friend had called earlier in the night to ask her to tell me that she had been out with a friend that evening in a car and that she too had seen the UFO. My God, now I had confirmation of the whole thing. I had a film of it. I had additional witnesses . . . . There was now no question about any of it.

. . . just as I thought that at least UFOs were going to be proved beyond a shadow of a doubt, my housekeeper interrupted me to finish the story of my girlfriend's sighting. After sighting the thing, she gave chase after it and after several minutes managed to get directly under it for positive identification . . . .

The message she gave the housekeeper to give me was this: "Tell Bill that when you are directly under the thing and look up at it, it spells out: ANTHONY'S AUTO BODY — FREE ESTIMATES.

The UFO was an "advertising airplane," a small aircraft outfitted with hundreds of electric lights on a wire-screen to provide airborne sales messages!

On June 10, 1977, the *Washington Post* carried a short article reporting that a UFO had been sighted by a number of persons two nights earlier on the outskirts of the metropolitan area. One Maryland State Police officer described the object as resembling a "giant jellyfish." He was quoted as saying that the strange object had "disappeared in the southern portion of the sky after hovering for approximately five minutes." If, as one might expect, this law enforcement officer's word "hovering" meant precisely that, clearly this UFO could not possibly be a fixed-wing advertising aircraft.

But the next day's edition of the *Post* said that the UFO had indeed been identified as an advertising airplane. As a result of the previous article, the newspaper had received a telephone call from a Nadine Brown, who said "We are the culprits." She went on to explain that she and her husband operated an advertising airplane, a Cessna-150 with more than three hundred electric lights, controlled electronically to spell out sales messages. Mrs. Brown said: "You can see it from a long ways away, but you cannot read the message unless you are a quarter of a mile on each side of it." For observers watching from a greater distance and more oblique angle, she said, "you see a jelly fish sort of thing."

It was about 9:00 P.M. on the night of October 18, 1976, when Mrs. Robert G., of Everett, Washington, received an unexpected visit from her next-door neighbor who urged Mrs. G. to go outside and watch a giant UFO hovering over a not-too-distant shopping center. She did so and to her amazement saw an object that she later estimated to be 200 feet in diameter and disk-shaped. As she subsequently described the incident to a local newspaper reporter, Jim Casey of the *Everett Herald,* the object was silvery in appearance, seamless, with several tiers of windows that flashed multicolored lights. "It almost had a hypnotizing effect," she told Casey.

Mrs. G. located some binoculars for a closer look and later told Casey that she could see a short, ladder-like object extending from the UFO at a 45-degree angle. Using an inexpensive camera loaded with color film, Mrs. G. said she took four photos of the UFO. She called her husband, who had been working on his car, and he arrived shortly before the UFO headed off to the south and disappeared. Mrs. G. estimated that she and her neighbor had watched the object for approximately fifteen minutes before it flew away. She said she had called two nearby radio stations to try to report the

UFO sighting but neither was interested. Later, Mrs. G. made a clay model of the UFO—much like the hero did in the UFO movie *Close Encounters of the Third Kind,* which would be released more than a year later.

It was a few weeks later that Casey learned of the incident through a friend. Mrs. G. had not attempted to have her color film processed, preferring to maintain its integrity until it could be turned over to an interested, independent party. Casey had it processed but found that the film showed nothing but dark sky. When Casey published an article on the incident, on January 14, 1977, he said that Mrs. G. said she had had no prior interest in UFOs. But it was clear that her sighting had convinced her that she had been lucky enough to see an extraterrestrial spacecraft. "Everything about it was so abnormal from our technology," Casey quoted her as saying. "Whatever made this was very intelligent. Perhaps it was on some kind of a reconnaissance trip. It definitely wasn't something we made." Her husband added: "If people scoff, they scoff. I know what I saw."

I first learned of the incident in late 1976, when Casey called me to discuss the incident. We had met a couple of years earlier when he was a reporter for a Dayton, Ohio, newspaper and had interviewed me on the subject of UFOs. After listening to the account, I told Casey that I had mixed feelings. It struck me as curious that a giant UFO, which reportedly had hovered low over a shopping center for many minutes at a time when there should have been many witnesses had not generated a rash of other reports. But the fact that Mrs. G. had held back processing her film and thus could not know in advance what it might, or might not, show, suggested that the incident was not a hoax being perpetrated by Mrs. G. Casey sent me a copy of his January 14 article shortly after it was published. In his letter he noted that the article had prompted a local UFO investigator "associated with Hynek's center"* to interview Mr. and Mrs. G. for three hours. Casey said that the investigator later told him: "It's either the best sighting he's heard of or the biggest hoax."

On January 31, 1977, the *Everett Herald* carried a second article by Casey in which he reported that his first article had evoked reports from others who recalled having seen the strange UFO on the night of October 18. Also, Casey said, he had received calls from two local UFOlogists, Jerry Phillips, an Everett police dispatcher, and from Robert Gribble, a retired Seattle fireman. They told Casey that they suspected the UFO might have been an advertising airplane, a Cessna-150 owned by a Melvin Reynolds, which was based at the nearby Renton airport. This had prompted Phillips to call Reynolds, who had confirmed that his advertising plane had indeed been flying over the Everett area on the night of October 18, between 8:30 P.M. and 9:00 P.M.

---

*Dr. J. Allen Hynek's Center for UFO Studies (CUFOS), formed in late 1973.

Casey's article noted: "Although Gribble and Phillips both believe other-wordly spaceships have visited Earth, they're convinced that Reynolds' airplane was the cause of all the sightings, despite the discrepancies in descriptions." Phillips was quoted as saying: "Everybody is looking at this thing through their own eyes and describing through their own minds." Gribble added: "We're in a field where people see what they want to see."

And what was the reaction of Mrs. G. when Casey told her that her giant UFO appeared to have been simply a small advertising plane? "That's ridiculous," Casey quoted her as saying: "That's tommyrot about it being an airplane, which I know darn well it wasn't. I know that I wasn't looking at an airplane. . . . He [Phillips] won't convince me and neither will anyone else. It won't change the truth as far as I'm concerned." Mrs. G's reaction is quite common and raises an interesting question: Should her sighting be considered to be "explained" or "unexplained"? Must a UFO witness admit that her/his account was in error before a case can be considered to be explained?

There is no precise count of the number of advertising planes now operating in the United States and elsewhere. But Tom Foster, president of Nite Sign Inc., of St. Louis, Missouri, whose company developed and introduced a new computer-controlled system suitable for both helicopters and small fixed-wing aircraft in early 1978, told me that the company sold seventy systems during the first year. (They sell for approximately $7,000 and can earn their operators $400–600 per hour, according to Foster.) Before deciding to develop the new system, Foster said he made a market survey and concluded that approximately 125 systems had been produced previously by Night Light Corporation, which pioneered such systems, and Waugh Electronics Company.

Foster told me that he himself had been operating advertising airplanes since the mid-1950s, using systems produced by others, and that he knew from first-hand experience that they triggered UFO reports. "Even airline pilots would 'come unglued' . . . they would see this eerie-looking thing out on the horizon . . . I got reports of all kinds of crazy things," he told me. Foster added that his company's new system employs an improved design to better contain the "spill-light" on the side to reduce its distracting effect on the pilot, and this reduces the number of UFO reports generated. But he added that one of his Nite Sign systems sold to an operator in a South American country had created such a furor that "people almost ran into the jungle to escape, thinking the Lord had come." As a result, Foster told me, the government had banned further operation of advertising aircraft in that country. (A photograph of a Nite Sign installed on a helicopter is shown in Plate 1.)

One indication of the widespread use of advertising aircraft in the United States and the large number of UFO reports they generate is the fact that during a fifteen-month period, approximately 18 percent of *all* (day and night) UFO sightings reported to Hynek's Center for UFO Studies proved to have been generated by advertising aircraft. If you yourself have seen a mysterious lighted object in the *night* sky, seemingly doing things that defy explanation, the chances are better than one out of five that you were watching an advertising aircraft or helicopter.

There is little incentive for operators of such aircraft to publicize their operations widely in advance—in order to forestall generating UFO reports—in local news media, even if the latter were willing to do so, which is unlikely because the aircraft are competitors for advertising revenue. For if large numbers of people like to go outside and look at the night sky in the hope of seeing a UFO, this increases the number of viewers who will see the advertising message.

10

Extraterrestrial UFOs

UFOs are among the most popular type of copy for sensationalist tabloid newspapers, and so it was hardly surprising that the *Star* should send a two-man team in February 1976 to investigate reports that a UFO was hovering every night over the construction site for a large nuclear power plant being built in the vicinity of Apex, North Carolina. The first report had come in the early morning from six excited sanitation workers, who called the Apex police department to say that a UFO was hovering over the site. Then, around 5:00 A.M., a guard at the facility also had called the police to report a "strange object hovering right over our plant. It's shining a light on us. Bright as day it is here."

Officer Ross Denson jumped into his patrol car and drove over to investigate. Later, describing what he had seen to the *Star*'s reporter, Denson said: "It was about half the size of the moon, and it just hung there over the plant. Must have been there nearly two hours." With the dawn, the UFO vanished. The police also received a call from an air-traffic controller at the nearby Raleigh-Durham airport saying that he had spotted an unidentifiable blip on his radar scope—seemingly confirming the visual sightings.

The incident later was reported on February 17, 1976, in the *Star*, by reporter Paul Dougherty:

> Next night the same thing happened. The same vigil; the same indeterminate results. Wake County Deputy Sheriff Ron Stewart reported "a large lighted object. I observed it for about an hour." Auxiliary police officer Danny Mathews saw "five objects—they appeared to be burning. An aircraft came by while I was watching. They [burning objects] seemed to be 20 times the size of the plane." Wake County magistrate Phillip Castlebury, on his way to work about 6 P.M. Wednesday, saw an astonishing sight. "It was a rectangular object, looked like it was on fire . . . . We figured it [was] about the size of a football field. It was huge and very bright."

The two-man team from the *Star* arrived the same night and joined local residents at the nuclear construction site but there was no UFO. Those who had seen the UFO previously told the *Star* reporter to be patient, that the UFO normally appeared around 5:00 A.M. Sure enough, it did and the reporter and photographer jumped into their car and set off in pursuit of the UFO. But no matter how fast they drove toward the UFO, they could not seem to get any closer to it. Finally, they stopped the car so the photographer could try to take a picture of the UFO through his powerful telephoto lens. After viewing the UFO through the lens, photographer David Ranns commented: "Yep . . . that's the planet Venus all right." The *Star* team had just retired to their motel rooms when the phone rang. It was the Apex police reporting: "That thing's back." The *Star* team returned to the site, arriving as auxiliary officer Cecil Davis was commenting: "They saw the planet Venus, just like they did those other two nights."

Dougherty's subsequent article concluded:

> The dust settled slowly round the power plant and the Wake County UFO continued to rise majestically, bathing the still foliage in bright starlight . . . Next day, Federal Aviation Agency [Administration] supervisor Tony Loeb confirmed the Raleigh-Durham airport's unidentified radar blip, but added that these were sometimes caused by bird flocks, freak weather, and a variety of other conditions. The Naval Observatory in Washington likewise confirmed that Venus is indeed very bright at this time of year in southern skies, and does rise about an hour before the sun. They added that Jupiter is almost as bright around 6 P.M. in the evening (the time of the other sightings). Nearby Fort Bragg belatedly informed newsmen that there had been military exercises in the area, involving [burning] flares.

On the night of March 19, 1975, shortly after 9:00 P.M., three men living near Yakima, Washington, spotted a strange-looking UFO in the western sky and watched it for nearly forty-five minutes until it disappeared around 10:00 P.M. The incident was featured on the front page of the March 20 edition of the local newspaper—the *Herald-Republic*—which quoted one of the men as saying: "I never saw anything like it before." He described the UFO as being "cone-shaped" and said it had a "greenish-bluish light at the top and a sort of pale flame light at the bottom." The next day the newspaper revealed that the UFO had returned the next night at about the same time and had been seen by many more local residents before disappearing, again, around 10:00 P.M. One woman described the UFO as "a great big, huge light . . . like a bright round ball . . . with sort of streaks in it." Most of the time, she said, the UFO had "hovered" but occasionally it had "moved sideways."

On March 22 the newspaper reported that it had been "swamped by calls by people mystified and convinced they were seeing an alien craft from outer space." But one of these callers disagreed. He was Norman Steuart, an amateur astronomer, who not only had seen the UFO himself but was quickly able to identify it: the planet Venus, which was visible and very bright in the western sky between 9:00 P.M. and 10:00 P.M. Commendably, the *Herald-Republic* reported the UFO's identification on its front page, rather than burying the story elsewhere in the newspaper.

Bright celestial bodies have for more than thirty years been one of the principal trigger-mechanisms for generating UFO reports. During the more than twenty years in which the USAF investigated UFO incidents, it concluded that bright celestial bodies generated more than 10 percent of all reports, second only to meteor-fireballs. (During this time, there were few advertising airplanes in operation.) Investigations by Hynek's Center for UFO Studies show that more than 25 percent of all UFO sightings reported to CUFOS turn out to have been bright celestial bodies, according to figures given in its publication, *International UFO Reporter.*

There are both physiological and psychological reasons why bright celestial bodies so often seem, even to an intelligent observer, to be moving in a nonastronomical fashion and thus to be UFOs. One of these, first discovered by astronomers, is known to psychologists as "auto-kinesis," or the "auto-kinetic effect." The late Dr. Donald H. Menzel, former director of the Harvard Observatory, was the first to advance this explanation for the oft-mistaken identity. In the book *The UFO Enigma* (Doubleday, 1977), co-authored with Dr. Ernest H. Taves, a psychiatrist, Menzel wrote:

> If a subject is placed in a dark room and presented with a stationary pinpoint light source, the light will shortly seem to move—usually within five seconds. The nature of the motion varies from moment to moment and from subject to subject, but for almost everyone the light will seem to move. It may slowly swing through large arcs, it may more rapidly zoom and twist, or it may move rhythmically to and fro . . . . It should be said that the apparent movement perceived by the subject is not merely suggested or uncertain; it is very real. Many subjects flatly refuse to believe that the light is indeed stationary.

If the observer is in a moving automobile or aircraft, this auto-kinetic effect will be magnified.

This auto-kinetic effect, when combined with another that I have characterized as "deductive-psychological," makes it still easier to think a bright celestial body is a UFO. In the fall of 1973, during an appearance on a late-night "talk-show" on a Washington, D.C., television station, where viewers could telephone in, a woman called to describe how she and her husband had "chased" and "been chased by" a UFO on two successive nights earlier in the week. The woman's account and her voice indicated that she was an educated, intelligent person. She said that they had spotted the UFO near the eastern horizon around 9:00 P.M. while driving and that they had decided to try to get closer to the object for a better look.

But as they drove toward the UFO, it seemed to move away at the same speed so that no matter how fast they drove the UFO seemed to maintain the same separation. When they stopped the car, the woman said, the UFO also seemed to stop, that is, to hover. When the couple finally gave up and headed home, the woman said, the UFO turned and followed them, always maintaining the same separation distance. The next night, she reported, they again set out in the car to see if the UFO would return, which it did around 9:00 P.M. in the east, and the seemingly mysterious events of the previous night were repeated.

Beyond any doubt this UFO was the planet Mars, which then was at its closest, and brightest, proximity to earth (until the year 1986) and which rose in the east around 9:00 P.M. Once the woman and her husband began to suspect that the bright object was a UFO, the stage was set for self-delusion. No matter how fast or far they drove toward the bright light in the sky, it would appear to be the same size and brightness, that is, they would seem to be getting no closer to the object. Their logical deduction—if the light really was a UFO—was that the object was "pacing" them. When the car accelerated, clearly the UFO must have done the same. When the car stopped, the UFO must also have stopped and hovered. If this seems hard to accept, it should be noted that there have been many such reported incidents, some involving law-enforcement officers, who report chasing or being chased by a UFO that turns out to be Venus, Mars, or another bright celestial body.*

Even experienced pilots sometimes have difficulty in identifying a bright celestial body. For example, Dr. J. Allen Hynek wrote an article at a time when he was a UFO skeptic and a consultant to the USAF Project Blue Book. Published in April 1953, in *Journal of the Optical Society of America,* the article contains the following observation:

> And another sighting—in Northern Michigan—on July 29 of last year, a pilot chased a brilliant multicolored object close to the horizon, and due north. He flew at 21,000 feet, followed the object for over a half-hour but could not gain on it. Radar operator [in the aircraft] reported contact with the object for about thirty seconds. And ground control interceptor station reported blips too [on its radar]. In this case, it seems certain that our harried pilot was pursuing [the star] Capella! Capella was at lower culmination, that is, at the lowest point of its swing around the pole just skirting the horizon. I have seen it at that position myself in Canada, and can vouch for the fact that its blue, yellow and red twinkling can be spectacular.

In respect to Dr. Hynek's mention of radar blips, one of the ten UFOlogical Principles developed in *UFOs Explained* is: "Whenever a light is sighted in the night skies that is believed to be a UFO and this is reported to

---

*For other such incidents, see my *UFOs Explained*, Chapter 9.

a radar operator, who is asked to search his scope for an unknown target, almost invariably an 'unknown' target will be found . . ." (See Appendix A for these ten UFOlogical Principles.)

In the late spring of 1945, during the closing phase of World War II, Air Force flight crews flying B-29 night missions against Japan, from bases in the central Pacific, began to report that they were being followed by unknown aircraft equipped with a powerful searchlight. The B-29 crews suspected that the "searchlight aircraft" were designed to illuminate the B-29s so that Japanese interceptors could see and attack them. But, curiously, there were no interceptor attacks against the USAF bombers. Some B-29 gunners tried to shoot down the "searchlight aircraft," but without success. After several weeks of crew interrogation, intelligence officers noted that the "searchlight aircraft" always was reported to be on the right side of the B-29s as they approached Japan, that is, to the east, and on the return flight the mysterious craft always were off to the left, also to the east. This proved to be the vital clue, and the mysterious "searchlight aircraft" was promptly identified as the planet Venus, which was especially bright at the time.

Even an engineer trained in celestial navigation at the U.S. Naval Academy at Annapolis, who later would become president of the United States, can mistake a bright celestial body for a UFO. The incident occurred around 7:15 P.M. on January 6, 1969, shortly before a man named Jimmy Carter was to speak to the Lion's Club of Leary, Georgia. Carter did not make a formal report on the sighting until the fall of 1973, when the nation was experiencing a major "UFO flap." When Carter reported the incident to a UFO organization, he described the object as being "self-luminous" and "as bright as the moon." He said the UFO was hovering in the western sky at an elevation angle he estimated to be around 30 degrees.

The Carter sighting was painstakingly investigated by Robert Sheaffer*, whose job was made more difficult because Carter had erred by nearly nine months in trying to recall the date of his sighting. Sheaffer established the correct date from official Lion's Club International headquarters records and talked with Fred Hart, who had been president of the Leary chapter at the time. Hart, who was standing alongside Carter at the time of his UFO sighting, told Sheaffer he was not impressed with the UFO and was inclined to believe it might be a weather balloon or other prosaic object. Armed with the correct date, Sheaffer, who had studied astronomy at Northwestern University, checked astronomical tables for that date and time. He found that a very bright Venus was in the western sky at nearly a 30-degree elevation angle, just where Carter had reported seeing the UFO.

---

*Sheaffer, vice-chairman of the UFO Subcommittee of the Committee for the Scientific Investigation of Claims of the Paranormal, describes the incident in greater detail in *The UFO Verdict: Examining the Evidence* (Prometheus Books, 1981), Chapter 2.

11

Eyewitness Unreliability

Dr. J. Allen Hynek, who has spent more than thirty years in the field of UFOlogy and is considered by some—including many in the news media—to be the world's leading expert on the subject, claimed for many years that no useful insights could be gained from the study of UFO reports that proved to be IFOs (identified flying objects). For example, during congressional testimony on July 20, 1968*, Hynek said:

> I did not [as a USAF consultant]—and still do not—concern myself with reports which arise from obvious misidentifications by witnesses who are not aware of the many things in the sky today which have a simple, natural explanation. These have little scientific value, except perhaps to a sociologist or an ophthalmologist; it matters not whether 100 or 100,000 people fail to identify an artificial satellite or a high-altitude balloon.

I have long disagreed—strongly. UFO reports that prove to be IFOs show that intelligent people, including pilots, scientists, and law-enforcement officers, unwittingly embellish their accounts with inaccurate details and seeming cause-effects that are really unrelated. It follows logically that similar inaccuracies in other UFO reports may prevent their explanations. The problem is summarized in UFOlogical Principle 2, developed in *UFOs Explained:*

> Despite the intrinsic limitations of human perception when exposed to brief, unexpected and unusual events, some details recalled by the observer may be reasonably accurate. The problem facing the UFO investigator is to try to distinguish between those details that are accurate and those that are grossly

---

*This was a one-day "UFO Symposium" sponsored by Congressman J. Edward Roush (Dem—Ind.), at which not a single experienced UFO skeptic was invited to testify.

inaccurate. This may be impossible until the true identity of the UFO can be determined, so that in some cases this poses an insoluble problem.

In late 1976, a young man named Allan Hendry came to work for Hynek's Center for UFO Studies (CUFOS) as the managing editor of its publication, *International UFO Reporter,* and as the organization's full-time and principal UFO investigator. Hendry was a commercial artist and a recent graduate of the University of Michigan, where he had minored in astronomy, and thus had some training in scientific methodology. Although Hendry was a neophyte as a UFO investigator, he proved a fast learner.

For example, in a feature story published in July 1977 of *International UFO Reporter (IUR),* Hendry acknowledged the difficulty of sorting out IFOs from "true UFOs." He noted that people typically describe a UFO as being a domed disk, even when subsequent investigation reveals that what they saw was an advertising airplane or a bright celestial body. Hendry noted that such grossly distorted descriptions do not come from "an isolated fringe group, either. It obscures the objective judgement . . . of all of those typical, ordinary individuals, young and old, of all occupations, that are reporting these IFOs as UFOs, and are reporting them poorly," that is, inaccurately.

In the June 1978 issue of *IUR* Hendry returned to this crucial issue in an article entitled: "The Case For IFO Study: A Recent Example." After recalling his previous article that discussed "the problem of distorted observations," Hendry noted not only that "non-existent details" are reported but also that "false cause-and-effect assumptions about IFOs' motion and special effects" are reported by witnesses. Hendry commented that "it is obvious that any such exaggerated 'data' helps to disfigure the IFO's true identity and render identification more difficult. Deeper than this, however, are the implications—and portents—for those descriptions which we are forced to accept at face value . . . the true UFO reports for which we have no identifiable source." Clearly Hendry had learned more about the real UFO problem in less than two years than Hynek had in three decades.

Hendry illustrated the problem by describing a series of UFO sightings that had been reported to the Aurora, Illinois, police on the night of April 29, 1978, starting about 10:30 P.M. Hendry interviewed one couple involved, whom he referred to as "Mr. and Mrs. S.," who had reported a close-encounter with the UFO. Each of them drew sketches of the UFO and both showed the familiar disk-shaped object with a dome. The woman reported the UFO "was twirling like a carnival ride." Both witnesses agreed that the UFO was as large "as a football field," that is 300 feet in length, and reported that it was flying at treetop level when it passed over their car. When Hendry informed the couple that other witnesses had reported the same UFO to be only 25 feet in size, the couple "theorized that they may have viewed a 'mothership.'" The couple reported that the UFO had disappeared "in the blink of an eye" as it headed east. Because the couple said they heard no noise from the UFO they were certain it could not possibly have been an aircraft. After arriving home, Mr. S. went to a neighbor's house to report the UFO incident and in his eagerness "he tore the door off its latch and hinges," Hendry reported. The neighbor informed Mr. S. that the television set in his house had blanked out for two minutes, which Mr. S. attributed to the UFO.

Because Hendry had for two years received UFO reports from the Chicago area that turned out to have been triggered by an advertising airplane, he called Ad Airlines of Chicago. A company official told him that their airplane had indeed been flying in the vicinity of Aurora at the time of the rash of UFO reports on April 29. Hendry noted in his article that he had investigated some 300 UFO reports that turned out to have been generated by advertising planes and that in 91 percent of these incidents the witnesses reported that "no sound could be heard." Hendry suggested that this might be due to the slow speed at which advertising aircraft fly, so that their messages can be read more easily. This slow speed might also explain why observers often reported that the UFO seemed to hover in one spot. The two-minute outage of the neighbor's TV set had an equally prosaic explanation—a malfunction of the TV station's transmitter.

Hendry commented on the

> . . . distorted observations regarding "domed discs," "treetop heights," gigantic size estimates, claims of being deliberately followed in cars, false assumptions that the ad plane's sign [lights] turning-off *equated* to the "UFO" rushing away faster than the eye could follow, the causality attempted between the UFO and the TV interference, and most of all, the wholly unwarranted emotional reactions exhibited by the witnesses and the immediately, nearly universal conclusion that the ad plane was from outer space . . . . The key issue here is NOT that the sighting was "only an ad plane," because such a "solution" cannot in itself account for the independent witnesses' behavior and inaccuracies. I do not see this IFO as the "garbage" to be weeded out while the "real" UFOs are retained as "data," when there is a wealth of data present here about UFOlogy's old bugaboo: the reliability [that is, unreliability] of human testimony.

This was a remarkably wise and candid commentary that challenged Hynek's oft-stated position that IFOs should be discarded and ignored. Three months later, in the September 1978 issue of *IUR*, Hynek announced an important change in policy:

> For nearly two years we have, largely in the person of Allan Hendry . . . spent a great deal of effort and time . . . and money . . . in carefully checking *every* current report that came to our attention . . . . If the stimulus for a report was evaluated as an advertising plane . . . we got it straight from the ad

plane company by phone that they had had their plane at the reported spot and at the exact time of the sighting (not just "sometime that evening") . . . . And so with the other IFO (Identified Flying Objects) evaluations . . . . Now at the present time we wonder whether we have reached the point of diminishing returns. We have clearly established to our satisfaction that . . . *on the average 90% of the raw reports turn out to be IFOs.* [Emphasis added.] . . . 90% of our time was spent in tracking down the cause of reports that we were pretty sure, *on the basis of past experience,* were misidentifications of twinkling stars, planets, ad planes, etc . . . .

It is still essential that we be confident of our IFO evaluations, but perhaps too much space has been devoted in this publication in detailing IFOs—in presenting a monthly score [showing what percent of all UFO reports received proved to be IFOs]. This publication is a UFO reporter, not an IFO reporter. Henceforth, therefore, we shall present the overall results on IFOs . . . . Should anyone in the future—some sociologist perhaps—wish to study IFOs for their own sake (and much can be learned from IFOs about human behavior, the desire to believe, and wishful thinking), the material will be here in the files . . . .

There was another reason for de-emphasizing IFOs that Hynek did not mention: *an increasing percentage of the UFO reports submitted to CUFOS were turning out to be IFOs.* The 90 percent figure cited by Hynek was for the previous year—1977—and did not reflect the 1978 trends. For example, while the IFO percentage for January 1978 was 90 percent, the IFO figure for February was 98 percent, and the figure for IFOs in March was 99 percent. In April 100 percent of the UFO reports proved to be IFOs, while the figure for May was 95 percent. In June the IFO figure was 97 percent, and the figure for July (published in the September issue which announced the new policy) was 94 percent.

The most logical explanation for the rising percentage of UFO reports that became IFOs is that Hendry was becoming more experienced as an investigator. This closely parallels the experience of the USAF's Project Blue Book investigations, whose findings had been sharply criticized by Hynek. For example, in the book *The Edge of Reality* (Henry Regnery Company, 1975), co-authored with Dr. Jacques Vallee, Hynek charged that Project Blue Book "statistics, for instance, were really false. They boasted that they had only two or three percent unknown [that is, unidentified] . . . . But it wasn't two or three percent. It was twenty percent . . . ."

After the USAF Project Blue Book files were transferred to the National Archives in Washington, it became possible for anyone to purchase a microfilm copy of the complete files. CUFOS purchased a copy and Hynek, together with an unidentified staff member, "comprehensively re-evaluated all the cases" with the benefit of hindsight to see how many should be characterized as "identified," according to Hynek's subsequent book, *The Hynek UFO Report* (Dell Publishing Company, 1977). The results are interesting because of Hynek's earlier charge that there really were many more "unidentifieds" than the Air Force publicly admitted.

Hynek adopted the USAF procedure of excluding UFO reports where there was insufficient detail to permit analysis. After analyzing nearly 11,000 remaining UFO reports, Hynek concluded that there were 640 cases that should be characterized as "unidentified," that is, impossible to explain in prosaic terms. But his figure is *lower by 10 percent* that the 701 cases that the USAF itself characterized as "unidentified." Although Hynek's book devotes twenty-six pages to the chapter entitled "The Air Force Numbers Game," he never once mentions that his own figure of 5.8 percent unexplained cases is *lower* than the official USAF figures.

Hynek's retroactive analysis of Blue Book cases does provide valuable insights because it examines the occupational backgrounds of persons who submitted UFO reports that readily proved to be misidentification of prosaic objects. This is valuable because of the popular misconception, frequently promoted by Hynek himself, that pilots and technically trained persons are especially accurate observers and that their UFO accounts must therefore be taken at face value. This is denied by the results of Hynek's own analysis, shown in Table 11.7 of his book.

This table reveals that at least 88 percent of the UFO reports submitted by military pilots (single witness) were IFOs, and when there were multiple military-pilot witnesses, the misidentification percentage was only slightly lower—76 percent. Airline and other civil pilots proved even less reliable, according to Hynek's analysis, with 89 percent of the single-witness reports and 79 percent of the multiple-witness reports proving to be IFOs. For radar technicians, who presumably reported mysterious blips on their scopes, 78 percent of the cases turned out to have prosaic explanations, according to Hynek. Persons with technical training scored best according to Hynek's analysis, with 65 percent of the single-witness UFO reports proving to be IFOs and 50 percent of the multiple-technical-witness cases proving to be misidentifications.

In February 1975 CUFOS published a special report entitled *Police and the UFO Experience,* which highlighted some of the reports that had been submitted to the Center in 1974. The report said that 25 percent of the nearly 400 reports received had come *from law-enforcement officers who themselves had seen the UFO.* The report added: "Police-witnessed reports are difficult to discredit; police are trained to be accurate reporters of events and are proficient in observing and recording details." This CUFOS claim is disputed by an incident described on page 205 of Hynek's first book, *The UFO Experience* (Henry Regnery Company, 1972). On that page Hynek describes a rash of UFO reports submitted to the University of Colorado UFO investigating team by law-enforcement officers in Georgia in the fall of 1967. When the University of Colorado investigators flew to Georgia to investigate the UFO, which was returning nightly, they found it was Venus.

In describing the incident, Hynek wrote that the UFO "was most definitely
Venus! The latter case should be read by all UFO investigators. It is a fantastic example of how persuasive the planet Venus can be . . . . Police officers in eleven counties were 'taken-in' by this planet."

In 1979, Hendry published a book entitled *The UFO Handbook*
(Doubleday/Dolphin), which I would characterize as one of the best ever
published on the subject. It bears the subtitle: "A Guide to Investigating,
Evaluating and Reporting UFO Sightings." An equally appropriate subtitle
might have been: "The Education of a Disappointed Would-be UFO
Believer," for, as Hendry admits in the closing page of his book, "Personally, I *want* there to be anomalistic UFOs that defy the laws of physics . . . ."

Prior to joining CUFOS, Hendry's knowledge of the UFO question was
based on second-hand and third-hand accounts he had read in books and
periodicals. But as a result of the several years that Hendry spent with
CUFOS he became probably the world's most experienced UFO investigator. The book details the results of a fifteen-month period in which
Hendry investigated some 1,307 cases. He found prosaic explanations for
91.4 percent of the incidents, leaving 8.6 percent "unexplained." However,
of the 113 unexplained incidents, Hendry acknowledges that ninety-three of
them have *possible* prosaic explanations, leaving only 20 (or 1.5 percent of
the 1,307 incidents) that he characterizes as "strong reports with only a
minimal chance of a prosaic explanation."

I find it remarkable that Hendry, with his acknowledged bias in wanting
to discover anomalistic UFOs, was able to find prosaic explanations for
more than 91 percent of the incidents in the very limited time available to
him to investigate each case. During the fifteen-month period, CUFOS
received an average of nearly three UFO reports every day. If Hendry worked seven days per week for the entire period, without a single day off, and
ignoring the time required for him to write and publish *IUR* each month, he
would have been able to devote an average of less than three hours per case.
My own experience shows that a challenging UFO case may require many
dozens of hours of effort to find a prosaic explanation. Lack of sufficient
time can result in an unexplained case.

Although Hendry's book describes the many dozens of prosaic trigger-
mechanisms that generate UFO reports, there are only several brief
references to hoaxes. Hendry concludes that "hoaxes play a tiny role, either
in the thirteen thousand Air Force conclusions (0.9 percent) or in my own
collection." (The USAF found it awkward to accuse anyone of a hoax
without evoking protests from the person's congressman.) Hoax reports can
be the most time-consuming and challenging to unravel, as Hendry himself
reported in a so-called "close-encounter" case described in July 1978 in *IUR*
(but not discussed in his book). Two other incidents in which Hendry was
directly involved (recounted below in Chapters 24 and 31) suggest to me that
he had not yet fully developed his skills in spotting hoaxes.

In the final pages of Hendry's book, he admits that even "rigorous investigation" by itself is not always enough to find a prosaic explanation for some UFO cases. Sometimes the solution emerges as a result of "sheer luck," he acknowledges. After nearly two decades of UFO investigations, I strongly concur. But one is not always lucky, and thus some UFO cases that do have prosaic explanations remain unsolved.

In the introduction to the Hendry book, written by Hynek, he claims:

> Although I recognize the importance of finding out just to what extent misidentification, wishful thinking, emotions and hallucination enter into the UFO problem, I regretfully failed to make such a study. Allan Hendry is the first to attempt such an important evaluation . . . he has arrived at some very striking and unexpected results, and has exploded or thrown into serious question some of the "instinctive" conclusions of even very experienced UFO investigators, myself included.

With this strong endorsement by Hynek, it is useful to examine Hendry's final observations in the concluding chapter of his book. He writes:

> After examining 1,300 UFO reports firsthand . . . I still can not confidently draw the distinction between a "real" physical phenomenon and a complex misperception, a "real" physical CE III (Close Encounter of the Third Kind] and a sophisticated fantasy, a "real" physical-trace case and a false match of IFO and unrelated artifact . . . *never* does the evidence suddenly allow a burst of approval for even one UFO!

This prompted Hendry to ask the critical question:

> How can I be sure if my remaining "UFOs" aren't simply IFOs misperceived (sincerely) to the point of fantasy? The emotional climate about the subject (as revealed by IFOs) appears to be adequate to support such a hypothesis for a great many UFO situations, if not all . . . with our current inability to fully draw the distinction between real UFOs and IFOs, fantasies or hoaxes, coupled with a heated emotional atmosphere, I can only assert that it is my *feeling* that some UFO reports represent truly remarkable events . . . [But Hendry acknowledges that] while science may be initiated by feelings, it cannot be based on them.

In early 1981, barely four years after Hendry had joined CUFOS, he left to pursue another career outside UFOlogy, for a variety of reasons.

12

UFOs over SAC Bases

"UFO's vs. USAF—AMAZING (BUT TRUE) ENCOUNTERS" was the headline on the article published on December 10, 1978, by *Parade,* the syndicated Sunday supplement read by tens of millions of Americans. The article, by staff writer Michael Satchell, began:

> Shortly before 8 o'clock on a clear, crisp autumn night three years ago, a military police sergeant named Danny K. Lewis was on guard duty at the weapons storage area of Loring Air Force Base in Maine when he heard a whirring noise like that of an approaching helicopter. Lewis watched the peculiar lights of the machine as it lowered to within 300 yards of the weapons dump. He raised the alarm, the command post was alerted, additional security teams were deployed, and the control tower began tracking the craft on its radar. Loring, a bulwark of Strategic Air Command's (SAC) northern string of nine air bases, is home for the 42nd Bombardment Wing . . . . The strange craft, which displayed a white strobe and reddish-orange lights, flew over and around Loring for 90 minutes, tracked on radar or followed by observers who assumed it to be a helicopter from its noise . . . .
>
> The puzzling intrusion at Loring on the night of October 27, 1975, was the curtain raiser to a bizarre and still-unexplained series of incidents that unfolded over the next three and a half weeks at SAC bases at Loring, Wurtsmith AFB in Michigan and Minot AFB in North Dakota; at the Malstrom Minuteman ICBM base in Montana; at a half dozen missile launch control facilities throughout Montana; and at the NORAD long-range radar station operated by the Canadian Air Force at Falconbridge, Ontario . . . . *The full story of this UFO mystery has never been published before.* [Emphasis added.] It has been pieced together almost entirely from Air Force files—some classified and confidential, others declassified for release under the Freedom of Information Act. The bulk of the documents were obtained under the act by W. Todd Zechel of Citizens Against UFO Secrecy . . . and by the National Investigations Committee on Aerial Phenomena (NICAP) . . . .

89

Parade's claim that its account "has never been published before" was in error. Essentially the same story had been reported nearly a year earlier by the *National Enquirer,* on December 13, 1977, under the headline: "UFO SPOTTED AT NUCLEAR BASES AND MISSILE SITES." If *Parade*'s Satchell missed this earlier story there was less excuse for the *Washington Post,* whose Sunday edition carries *Parade,* to feature the same incident six weeks later on the front page of its January 19, 1979, edition in a staff-written article by Ward Sinclair and Art Harris.

From correspondence with Satchell, I learned that Zechel had been a major source of information for his article and that Satchell had been unaware of the earlier *National Enquirer* story. When I talked with Sinclair, he acknowledged that his story was based largely on material supplied by Zechel, who had been identified in the article as "a former NSA employe" [sic]. (My earlier investigation had revealed that this and other Zechel claims were spurious, as discussed in Chapter 31.)

During my conversation with Sinclair, he volunteered that he had read a number of UFO books, the most recent being one entitled *Aliens from Space,* but he had not read either of my two books on the subject. When I asked if he was aware that there was another viewpoint on UFOs, Sinclair replied: "Most definitely. I've seen you on television a number of times." Did he know that I lived in Washington? "I assumed you did," he responded. When I asked if he had considered calling me to see if I might be able to shed any light on the UFO incidents before writing the story, Sinclair responded: "No. In no way would I check with you. Why would I check with you? You've assigned yourself a credential that I have every right to be as suspicious of as Todd Zechel's credentials." But Sinclair earlier told me that he had talked with Zechel several times before writing his article.

Parade's Satchell offered a similar explanation for why he had not bothered to talk to an experienced UFO skeptic before writing his story: "You have become widely identified as a professional UFO debunker . . . I would regard you in the same light as a Hynek, or a Zechel, or an Acuff" [of NICAP]. But Satchell had talked to both Zechel and Acuff before writing his article.

The *Post*'s feature story was distributed through that newpaper's syndicated service and published in other major papers. When it appeared in the *News American,* of Baltimore, the story was headlined: "WHAT'S BUZZING OUR MISSILE BASES?" with a subhead that read: "The Air Force has been chasing UFOs. And they don't like talking about it."

The *Washington Post*'s article began:

> During two weeks in 1975, a string of the nation's supersensitive nuclear missile launch sites and bomber bases were visited by unidentified, low-flying and elusive objects, according to Defense Department reports. The sightings, made visually and on radar by air and ground crews and sabotage-alert forces,

occurred at installations in Montana, Michigan and Maine and led to extensive but unsuccessful Air Force attempts to track and detain the objects.

Air Force and Defense Department records variously describe the objects as helicopters, aircraft, unknown entities and brightly lighted, fast-moving vehicles that hovered over nuclear weapons storage areas and evaded all pursuit efforts. In several instances, after base security had been penetrated, the Air Force sent fighter planes and airborne command posts aloft to carry on the unsuccessful pursuit. The records do not indicate if the fighters fired on the intruders.* The documents also give no indication that the airspace incursions provoked much more than local command concern . . . .

The *Parade* article said:

> According to an Air Force information officer, there was no follow-up investigation and the overflights were not positively identified as either helicopters or fixed-wing aircraft. Asked how unknown aircraft could penetrate SAC bases at will for five nights, as they did at Loring and Wurtsmith, and hover within 100 feet of the nuclear weapons storage area—all without being identified or forced down—the Air Force spokesman said: "These bases have no air defense capabilities in peacetime."

Readers of the *Parade* or the *Washington Post* articles would not know that the portions quoted above contain some gross exaggerations. But most readers could easily conclude that either Soviet or extraterrestrial craft were brazenly penetrating airspace over some of the nation's most important military facilities and the U.S. Air Force was, seemingly, indifferent to the obvious implications of such intrusions. If *Parade,* the *Washington Post,* or the *National Enquirer* really believed what their stories implied, the USAF not only was derelict in its duties to defend the nation's airspace, but here was a coverup that dwarfed the Watergate scandal. It would have been an investigative reporter's dream. Yet none of these newspapers, nor any other news media that promoted the story, bothered to follow up on it, so far as I can determine.

Both *Parade* and the *Washington Post,* included in their articles a brief account of a seemingly mysterious UFO incident that had occured in the fall of 1976 in Iran, which involved two American-built F-4 fighter aircraft manned by flight crews of the Imperial Iranian Air Force. (This case will be covered in Chapter 14.) But neither article included an account of another incident that had occurred at another SAC base, during the same period as the other "UFO" incidents.

On November 3, 1975, at approximately 9:15 P.M. EST, unknown

---

*Had any of the fighter-interceptors fired weapons at the craft without first identifying them as hostile, it would have been a violation of USAF peacetime policies and certainly would have been noted in the official records.

persons penetrated the flight line at Grand Forks AF Base, in North Dakota, and fired small arms at SAC aircraft on the flight line, hitting two KC-135 tanker aircraft. Despite the efforts of security forces equipped with dogs, the attackers were not caught. A brief memorandum summarizing the Grand Forks incident, prepared in the Pentagon's National Military Command Center at 10:00 P.M. EST on November 3, was one of the documents released to Zechel on October 18, 1978, in response to his Freedom of Information Act request. Perhaps this incident was excluded because extraterrestrial visitors would not be likely to employ such "old-fashioned" weapons as small arms.

To understand how easy it is for aircraft based in the United States or Canada to overfly a SAC base, it is necessary to review briefly this nation's air-defense policy. In the late 1940s and early 1950s, when the major threat was the Soviet Union's growing fleet of long-range bombers, the USAF deployed a large network of air-defense radars. The network not only could detect enemy bombers approaching our borders but it also covered the interior to help direct USAF interceptors toward targets that managed to penetrate perimeter defenses. Additionally, the Army deployed a large network of Nike antiaircraft missiles, which were supplemented by longer-range Bomarc missiles operated by the USAF.

But by the mid-1960s, the major threat had shifted to intercontinental ballistic missiles (ICBMs), against which there was no effective defense. Pentagon strategists concluded that any Soviet attack would begin with an ICBM barrage that would wipe out any U.S. air-defense network, allowing bombers to penetrate later as a second-strike force. For this reason it was decided that defense funds could better be spent for our own ICBMs and submarine-launched ballistic missile forces as well as the SAC bomber fleet, to deter any enemy attack.

As a result, all of the nation's antiaircraft missiles were deactivated, except for a few in Florida, because of its proximity to Cuba, and in Alaska. Whereas the USAF operated forty fighter-interceptor squadrons in 1964, by 1979 the number had been slashed to only six. In 1979, the USAF was operating only fifty-four long-range air-defense radars, roughly one-third the number in use in 1964, and most of these covered the perimeter of the country to detect aircraft approaching over the oceanic routes that Soviet bombers might take. For airplanes based in the U.S. or Canada, that need not penetrate this peripheral radar fence, it is relatively easy to overfly a SAC base. It is even easier for a helicopter, which typically flies at a very low altitude where it is below radar coverage.

Loring AF Base, where the "UFO" incidents began, is located in northeast Maine, near Limestone, close to the Canadian border. Trying to piece together what occurred in late October 1975 from USAF and National Military Command Center documents released under the Freedom of Information Act is not easy. One reason is the poor reproduction of some of the original teletype messages from Loring, so that some words and numbers are indistinct on photocopies released under FOIA. Perhaps the best overall summary is contained in a memorandum, dated January 6, 1976, from Colonel William D. Myers, chief of security policy for the Stategic Air Command. The memo, prepared at the request of SAC's commander-in-chief, provides the following chronology:

SUBJECT: Unidentified Helicopter Sightings, Loring AFB

27 Oct. '75: Helicopter sighted flying over weapons storage area. Attempts to contact, negative results. 42BMW [42nd Bombardment Wing] Commander requested fighter coverage—request denied.

28 Oct. '75: 42BMW Commander requested and received helicopter support from Maine Army National Guard. Helicopter again sighted. Maine Army National Guard helicopter launched, but unidentified helicopter disappeared before acquisition. One and one-half hours later unidentified helicopter sighted again. Standby helicopter again launched, no contact made. Fighter launch again requested and denied. Local flight service inquired for possible identification, negative results. Radar contact on unidentified helicopter lost in vicinity of Grand Falls, N.B. [New Brunswick], Canada.

29 Oct. '75: Meetings with State Police, U.S. Border Patrol, Canadian authorities, OSI [USAF Office of Special Investigations] and National Guard—Plan and coordinate future actions. SAC/SP [SAC Special Police] message to all SAC northern bases advising of possible threat—advised to increase security during hours of darkness and review helicopter denial plans [that is, possible defense against helicopter intrusions.]

30 Oct. '75: Maine Army National Guard Helicopter replaced with Air Force helicopter from Plattsburgh. Placed on alert during hours of darkness.

31 Oct. '75: Several suspected sightings made—some visual sightings appeared to be substantiated by RAPCON [air base] radar. Alert helicopter launched—unsuccessful intercept.

1–8 Nov. '75: Alert helicopter and searchlight alert maintained during hours of darkness. No further activity reported or expected. All attempts to identify helicopter(s) throughout this period were negative. Although local USAF or Canadian authorities were unable to provide positive identification of helicopters the possibility exists that some type of game poaching or illegal smuggling across the borders not involving any threat to USAF resources could have been involved. At no time was the helicopter used in any manner which could have been interpreted as a hostile act against USAF resources.

The memo noted that there were no further intrusions after October 31. It discussed procedures that had been introduced to increase base security and added that if similar incidents should occur that *no* attempt would be made to shoot down the intruder "unless hostility is encountered."

There are some discrepancies in this summary memo in the dates of the late October incidents, judging from memoranda prepared in the National Military Command Center as messages were received from Loring. Based on these, made and dated at the time, it appears likely that the Loring request to use a locally based National Guard helicopter and the two early-morning sightings occurred on October 29, not October 28 as stated in the SAC Headquarters summary. But the significant point is that in every teletype message or memo of a telephone call, the unidentified craft was referred to as a *helicopter,* not a "UFO."

Several interesting conclusions emerge from study of all of these documents. Apparently Loring officials did not consider the first helicopter intrusion on the night of October 27 to be of sufficient significance to report it to the National Military Command Center in the Pentagon. Only when a repetition *seemed* to occur at approximately 1:00 A.M. EST on October 29, and again shortly after 3:00 A.M. EST, did Loring officials notify the Pentagon nerve-center. The documents indicate that Loring officials, understandably, took it upon themselves to dispatch the Maine Air National Guard helicopter to investigate the "intruder." Only later that same day did they decide to request Defense Department approval for future use of the locally based helicopter (subsequently replaced by a USAF helicopter) and to obtain approval to pursue the "intruder" beyond Canadian borders if necessary.

Several curious details on the October 29 incidents emerge from a study of teletype messages and documents originating at Loring. One is a statement in a teletype message from the 42nd Bombardment Wing, dated October 29, noting that "the unknown aircraft did not display lighting." My interpretation of this is that the "unknown aircraft" did not display *conventional* aircraft lighting, that is, red/green port/starboard lights and a rotating/flashing anti-collision beacon. But clearly the object must have been visible as a "light." Otherwise how would its presence have been detected? Even more curious is the statement that during the second incident on October 29, "ground personnel were able to direct the Air Guard helicopter to within 1,000 feet of the unknown aircraft with both helicopters in sight. *But visual acquisition [by the National Guard helicopter crew] was not made."* [Emphasis added.]

If the National Guard helicopter was within 1,000 feet of the unknown object—as it appeared to ground observers trying to direct the National Guard aircraft—and if ground observers could see both clearly from a much greater distance, why could not the National Guard helicopter crew see the "intruder"? One possible explanation is that in this particular instance the unknown object was a bright celestial body. If so, this could explain why the National Guard helicopter crew, searching for a low-flying aircraft, saw nothing while more distant ground observers concluded that the helicopter and the "UFO" were in close proximity.

If this seems far-fetched, consider the numerous reported UFO sightings that occurred barely two weeks later in the same area in the wake of U.S. and Canadian newspaper stories on the unidentified object over Loring. The base itself received a call during the early morning of November 16, around 2:35 A.M., from a deputy sheriff in nearby Carabou, reporting a mysterious light he had seen in the sky. When the base duty officer went outside, he too saw an object, estimated to be about two miles south of the base, *which he said looked like a helicopter.* But when he called the control tower, personnel there looked and concluded that the object was only a bright celestial body. About the same time, a U.S. Customs inspector in nearby Limestone spotted a bright light and reported hearing "a sound like a chopper" (helicopter). He later said the object had remained visible until around 6:00 A.M., when it disappeared to the southeast. These and other local UFO reports were carried on November 17 in the *Bangor Daily News,* which quoted the deputy sheriff as saying the UFO "seemed to have tremendous power when it moved." The Customs officer said the object moved both horizontally and vertically. The newspaper said Carabou police had received numerous calls between 1:00 A.M. and 2:00 A.M., roughly the same time as the October 29 sightings at Loring, and said the object had shown up on the Loring radar.

However, the next day the Loring public-information office said that the object had *not* been detected by the base radar. It added: "It is the opinion of a security policeman and a member of the radar approach control [RAP-CON] who both saw the bright light Sunday morning that it was a star or planet . . . ." On November 19 the *Bangor Daily News* revealed the trigger-mechanism for at least some of the many UFO reports in the area. Newspaper reporter Joan Brooks, after watching the so-called UFO herself, called Professor Clark Reynolds of the University of Maine at Orono, and he went outside to look for himself. From their two widely separated viewing locations, Brooks later reported, it was possible to triangulate and pinpoint the UFO's position more accurately. Reynolds quickly identified the UFO as Sirius, the "Dog Star," the brightest star in the sky. The newspaper article informed readers who wanted to see the "UFO" to "look low on the horizon to the southeast about 11 P.M. There it is in all its blinking splendor."*

---

*The public's awareness and interest in UFOs at this time had been heightened by a two-hour NBC-TV special shown in prime time on October 20, recounting the alleged UFO abduction of Barney and Betty Hill, and the widely publicized report that Travis Walton, of Snowflake, Arizona, was abducted by a UFO on November 5 and held captive for five days. (This case will be analyzed in Chapters 18-23.)

Returning to events at Loring on the night of October 29, I am not able to find any indication in the not fully legible telegraphic messages or in the NMCC memoranda that the "unidentified craft" showed up on the local base radar. Two nights later, on October 31, a bright light was sighted shortly before midnight at a location estimated to be about four miles northwest of Loring. About two hours later, a slow-moving target was detected briefly on the base radar and again the helicopter was dispatched to investigate but saw nothing. It should be noted that flocks of birds readily show up on radar and in late October migrating ducks and geese would be headed south. Following the October 31 incidents there were no more UFO/helicopter incidents at Loring.

If the lights observed on October 29/31 are explainable in terms of over-heated observer imaginations and bright celestial bodies, what about the first incident on October 27, where the object was reported to exhibit conventional aircraft lights and to have made sounds like those of a helicopter?

The batch of information on the Loring incidents released to UFOlogists included a memorandum that aroused my own interest. The memo, prepared by the 42nd Bombardment Wing's office of information, reported the highlights of a telephone call received on November 14, at 3:15 P.M., from Dean Rhodes, a reporter for the *Bangor Daily News*. The memo indicated that Rhodes had learned from Sheriff Francis B. Henderson, of Somerset County, Maine, that a helicopter bearing no external company identification had "dropped down in Rockwood," approximately 120 miles southwest of Loring, shortly after the late-October incidents at the air base. The memo indicated that the helicopter "appeared to have photo equipment on board. Could be that someone is taking photos of certain areas of Rockwood and Moosehead Lake for speculative purchasing possibilities." The memo noted that the helicopter operators had brought along their own fuel truck and maintenance personnel "despite availability of local services." The memo indicates that a copy of the information supplied by Rhodes had been passed along to the USAF Office of Special Investigations (OSI). But there is no indication in the released files that OSI ever investigated the "mysterious helicopter" that put in at Rockwood, so I decided to do so.

From the Sheriff's office I learned the name of the (former) deputy who was involved, Ivon Turmell, now postmaser in Rockwood. When I called Turmell, he told me that the red and white helicopter, built by Hughes Helicopter company, had created some talk in the small town, when it landed outside the Moosehead Motel and operated from this site for several days, taking off each morning and returning every night. When Turmell had called the owner of the motel out of curiosity, he learned that "the whole thing was very hush-hush," he told me, adding that the crew and maintenance personnel carefully avoided talking to other guests at the motel. At that point, Turmell said, he decided to ask his good friend George

Robbins, an experienced pilot, to "check things out." Later, when I talked with Robbins, he told me that he noted a special mount on the helicopter's landing skids which was designed to carry a large box. Its location suggested that the box might contain camera equipment for taking aerial photos and Robbins added that the crew carefully removed the box each night after landing. This, Robbins told me, suggested that they removed exposed film and reloaded the cameras for the next day's flight. When Robbins inquired of motel employees who might have talked to the helicopter crew to learn the purpose of the operation, he was told that the crew was very secretive and evasive.

Could Rockwood's "mysterious helicopter" have been the same craft that reportedly penetrated Loring's airspace on the night of October 27? If so, and if the penetration was unintentional due to a pilot-navigation error, the crew would have been reluctant to admit its role in the incident. Or the Loring intruder could have been a different helicopter, possibly one involved in illegal smuggling activities, whose crew would have good reason not to come forward and admit their involvement. After this initial incident had occurred, and Loring AFB personnel had been placed on alert to watch for possible future intrusions, bright celestial bodies and imaginations could explain the later incidents at the base.

More important, these several reported intrusions had served to generate a priority telegraphic message from Stategic Air Command Headquarters, from the chief of security policy, on October 29, alerting SAC bases to the possible threat of "helicopter assault," thereby setting the stage for "UFO" incidents that followed. This dispatch read as follows:

1. The past two evenings at one of our Northern Tier Bases an unidentified helicopter has been observed hovering over and in the near vicinity of the WSA [Weapons Storage Area]. Attempts to identify this aircraft have so far met with negative results.

2. In the interest of nuclear weapons security the action addressees will assume security option III during the hours of darkness until further notice . . . ."*

One of the SAC bases that received the preceding message, whose subject was listed as "Defense Against Helicopter Assault," was Wurtsmith AFB, Michigan, located near the shores of Lake Huron, across from the Canadian border. Less than 36 hours later, on October 31, at around 11:27 P.M. EST, a Lieutenant Colonel Giordano, senior controller at the Michigan base, called the Pentagon's National Military Command Center to report

---

*This contradicts the *Washington Post*'s claim that Pentagon documents "give no indication that the airspace incursions provoked much more than local command concern." At the time some radical groups protesting the war in Vietnam were resorting to violence and the use of explosives.

"an unidentified *helicopter* with no lights came over the back gate of Wurt-smith and *hovered over the Weapons Storage Area* and then moved on," according to an NMCC memorandum released to UFOlogists. [Emphasis added.] The memo states: "RAPCON [base radar] had it painted for a short time," that is, an unidentified target appeared briefly on the airbase radar. Seemingly, Wurtsmith had experienced an incident identical to that reported over Loring, which in turn had prompted the SAC Headquarters warning.

However, the NMCC memorandum indicates that approximately an hour later, at 12:30 A.M. EST, Giordano called to provide a significantly different account. Instead of a helicopter, the updated account said "an unidentified low flying aircraft came up over the back gate of Wurtsmith and was visually sighted in the vicinity of the motor pool. RAPCON [radar] showed several aircraft at the time, one near the WSA (there was no hovering as previously reported)." (Recall Satchell's *Parade* article, which informed readers that UFOs had hovered "within 100 feet of the nuclear weapons area at both Loring and Wurtsmith AFB.) This NMCC memo, based on information supplied by Giordano, continued:

> A [KC-135] tanker was dispatched and had visual and skin paint [radar contact] out over Lake Huron of a low flying aircraft (with lights on) heading SE at approximately 150 knots. Tanker reports that the aircraft appeared to be joined by another aicraft (with its lights on also). Tanker reports that both aircraft then turned out their lights simultaneously, as if on signal. Tanker lost all contact approximately 35 NM [nautical miles] SE of the base.

Still another version of the incident is contained in a brief telegraphic message from Wurtsmith, sent at 12:49 A.M. EST, also released to UFOlogists. It says:

> At 03:45Z [10:45 P.M. EST], CSC advised CP [command post] that the security guard at back gate spotted an unidentified aircraft flying low over the base at approx. 0320Z [10:20 P.M. EST]. Initial report to CP said that aircraft was also observed in the vicinity of WSA [Weapons Storage Area]. However, later reports said that aircraft observed may have been a KC-135 in the local traffic pattern. At 0330Z [10:30 P.M. EST] KC-135 said that they had skin painted on radar an aircraft 8½ miles NE of base *but could not spot the aircraft visually.* [Emphasis added.] At approx. 0350Z [10:50 P.M. EST] the KC-135 picked up the unidentified aircraft NE of the base at approx. 090/ZI on a visual sighting. KC-135 tracked the aircraft south to the Mich. thumb area and back north to the base area a number of times. Each time the KC-135 lost visual sighting. KC-135 landed when fuel approached minimums. Investigation in progress. Reports to follow as info is obtained.

The discrepancies in these several accounts indicate considerable uncertainty over precisely what had occurred and there are no followup reports in the released files to help resolve the conflicting details and ambiguities. However, it strikes me as curious that if there was indeed an overflight of Wurtsmith by an unidentified low-flying craft which was detected on the base (RAPCON) radar, that the unknown craft did not remain visible on the radar, enabling controllers to monitor subsequent movements. The reported visual and radar contact by the KC-135 crew occurred well within the sixty-mile operating range of an airport surveillance radar.

My investigation into the report by the KC-135 crew that the aircraft's own radar had detected "an aircraft 8½ miles NE of base," which the crew reportedly could not see visually, indicates that the target almost certainly was a large ship on Lake Huron, not a mysterious "UFO" or intruder aircraft for which the crew was searching anxiously. The reason is that the KC-135's radar, an AN/APN-59, is a pulse-type radar developed twenty years earlier solely for use as a navigation/storm-detection sensor. Such a radar could not possibly detect a low-flying aircraft, whose very weak echo would be masked by much stronger radar echoes from the surface below, although the radar would be able to "see" a large ship on the surface. It would not be until more than a decade after the APN-59 radar was designed and built that advanced "pulse-doppler" radar techniques would be developed for use in fighter-interceptor radars to enable them to spot low-flying targets against "ground-clutter" background.

According to the telegraphic report on the incident, the KC-135 crew did not make a visual sighting of what was believed to be the intruder-craft until 10:50 P.M. in the vicinity of the base. *This was thirty minutes after the security guard had reported seeing a low-flying aircraft* and there is no justifiable basis for concluding that whatever the KC-135 crew saw at 10:50 P.M. was necessarily the same thing reported half an hour earlier by the security guard. It is not clear what is meant by that portion of the message that says: "KC-135 tracked the aircraft south to the Mich. thumb [about sixty miles away] a number of times. Each time the KC-135 lost visual sighting." If the object was a low-flying aircraft cruising at 150 knots, as indicated in the NMCC memo, the KC-135 can fly at more than three times that speed at high altitude and should have had no difficulty in keeping pace. Rather, its problem would be in slowing down sufficiently to keep from overflying the other object.

But as this portion of the incident was described in the news media, the KC-135 simply could not catch up to the "mysterious UFOs." For example, the *Parade* article stated: "Meanwhile, Wurtsmith AFB in Michigan was visited by a similar craft [to the one over Loring] on the nights of Oct. 30 and 31 [actually the night of Oct. 30/31] with the flying machine making passes over the weapons storage area. An airborne tanker was sent up in pursuit, spotted first one, then two of the intruders flying in trail formation, *sometimes at high speeds, sometimes hovering.* [Emphasis added.] The tanker was never able to catch up with the objects." The *Washington Post's* account said: "The crew of a KC-135 tanker plane, already airborne [contrary to *Parade's* claim that it "was sent up in pursuit"], spotted the object near the base and attempted to give chase, *but couldn't keep up with it.*" [Emphasis added.] The story in the *National Enquirer* said: "It [UFO] was tracked by an Air Force plane on radar. Later, the plane's crew reported 'visual contact' with two UFOs. *But as the plane approached the UFOs they sped off.*" [Emphasis added.]

There are sufficient ambiguities and conflicts in the accounts of the incident to raise a question as to whether there actually was an overflight of Wurtsmith on the night of October 30 by a low-flying aircraft. Having personally seen thousands of aircraft on final approach to Washington National Airport from my own apartment window, I know that the aircraft appear from my viewing angle to "hover" for an extended period of time. Conceivably, the original security-guard report, which triggered the whole incident, could have resulted from his having seen one of several USAF aircraft then preparing to land, and his own heated imagination, which had been fired by the SAC Headquarters message calling for special vigilance against possible "helicopter assault."

Three nights after the Wurtsmith incident, as earlier noted, an NMCC memo states that at 9:15 P.M. EST, "a penetration of the flight line at Grand Forks AFB by unknown persons was reported." The memo adds: "At least two KC-135 aircraft were hit by small arms fire. Security forces with dogs are tracking the unknown attackers." Although the released files do not contain any further telegraphic messages to SAC bases from the chief of security police, in view of the incidents at Wurtsmith and at Grand Forks, it would be surprising if SAC Headquarters had failed to notify SAC-base security police of the incidents by telephone, urging still increased vigilance.

The incidents that followed several days later at SAC bases in the west are summarized in an NMCC memo, dated November 8, 1975. The memo indicates a call was received at 3:08 A.M. EST from the North American Air Defense Command (NORAD) command director reporting an incident that had occurred at 12:53 A.M. Mountain Standard Time:

> Malstrom AFB Montana received seven radar cuts on height-finder radar at altitudes between 9,500 ft. and 15, 500 ft. [that is, had observed targets on seven vertical scans of the radar]. Simultaneously ground witnesses observed lights in the sky and the sounds of jet engines similar to jet fighters. Cross-tell [check] with FAA revealed no jet aircraft within 100 NM of the sightings. Radar tracked the objects over Lewistown, Montana, at a speed of seven (7) knots. Two F-106 interceptors from 24th NORAD Region were scrambled at 0254 EST [12:54 A.M. MST] and became airborne at 0257 EST. At the time of the initial voice report personnel at Malstrom AFB and SAC [missile] sites K-1, K-3, L-3 and L-6 were reporting lights in the sky accompanied by jet engine noise.

Approximately half an hour later, NMCC received another call from NORAD reporting:

> Objects could not be intercepted. Fighters had to maintain a minimum of 12,000 ft. [altitude] because of mountainous terrain. Sightings had turned west, increased speed to 150 knots. Two tracks were apparent on height-finder radars 10-12 NM apart. SAC site K-3 reported sightings between 300 ft. and 1,000 ft., while site L-4 reported sightings 5 NM NW of their position. Sightings disappeared from radar at position 4650N/1090W (latitude/longitude) at a tracked speed of three (3) knots. [The NMCC memo indicates another call was received from NORAD headquarters about an hour later.] At 0405 EST [2:05 A.M. MST]: Malstrom receiving *intermittent* tracks on *both search and height-finder radars.* [Emphasis added.] SAC site C-1, 10 NM SE of Stanford, Montana, reported visual sightings of unknown objects. 0420 EST [15 minutes later]: Personnel at four SAC sites reported observing intercepting F-106's arrive in area; sighted objects turned off their lights upon arrival of interceptors, and back on upon their departure. 0440 EST [20 minutes later]: SAC site C-1 still had visual sighting on objects [sic]. NORAD stated that Northern Lights will sometimes cause phenomena such as this on height-finder radars, but their check with weather services revealed no possibility of Northern Lights.

The final telephone call from NORAD Headquarters noted on the NMCC memo, received at 5:22 A.M. EST, reads: "At 0405 EST [2:05 A.M. MST] SAC Site L-5 observed one object accelerate and climb rapidly to a point in altitude where *it became indistinguishable from the stars.* [Emphasis added.] NORAD will carry this incident as a FADE [radar target fading out] remaining UNKNOWN at 0320 EST [1:20 A.M. MST], since after that time only visual sightings occurred." This seems to indicate that NORAD had by now concluded that the "intermittent tracks" earlier reported on both the Malstrom search and height radars were caused by anomalous propagation conditions. (The still earlier very slow-moving radar targets could have been generated by birds.)

Valuable insights into the events of the early morning hours on November 8 emerge from a study of excerpts of the log kept by the command director at NORAD Headquarters, made available to UFOlogists under the Freedom of Information Act. This log notes that the two F-106 interceptors dispatched to investigate the radar/visual sightings "never gained visual or radar contact at any time," despite the fact that the aircraft radars are especially designed to detect other airborne objects. The log adds: "This same type of activity has been reported in the Malstrom area for several days although previous to tonight no unknowns were declared," that is, none were considered to be real unidentified targets. The reason is that *no unidentified targets had shown up on USAF/FAA radars, even briefly,* which is why the November 7 incidents had not been brought to the attention of the Pentagon. This emerges from study of pertinent extracts from the log of the senior director of the 24th NORAD Region, which was receiving the sighting report, also made available to UFOlogists under Freedom of Information Act requests. These are quoted below with time-of-occurrence changed from Greenwich Mean Time to local Mountain Standard Time:

3:35 A.M.: Received a call from the 341st Stategic Air Command Command Post (SAC CP), saying that the following missile locations reported seeing a large red to orange to yellow object: M-1, L-3, LIMA and L-6. The general object location would [appear] to be 10 miles south of Moore, Montana, and 20 miles east of Buffalo, Montana. Commander and Deputy for Operations (DO) informed.

5:03 A.M.   SAC advised that LCF [Launch Control Facility] at Harlowton, Montana, observed an object which emitted a light which illuminated the site driveway.

6:19 A.M.   SAC advised [that] K-1 says very bright object to their east is now southeast of them and they are looking at it with 10 x 50 binoculars. Object seems to have lights (several) on it, but no distinct pattern. The orange/gold object overhead also has small lights on it. SAC also advises female civilian reports having seen an object bearing south from her position six miles west of Lewiston.

6:27 A.M.   L-1 reports that object to their northeast seems to be issuing a black object from it, tubular in shape. *In all this time, surveillance [that is, radar] has not been able to detect any sort of track except for known traffic.* [Emphasis added.]

6:55 A.M.   K-1 and L-1 report that as the sun rises, so do the objects they have visual [that is, are observing visually].

7:29 A.M.   From SAC CP: *As the sun rose, the UFOs disappeared.* Commander and DO notified. [Emphasis added.]

The last two items, reporting that the UFOs rose in the sky as the sun rose, and with daylight the mysterious objects disappeared, confirm beyond any doubt that the mysterious lights were bright celestial bodies, as the earlier descriptions suggest. Venus was particularly bright at the time, rising about 2:30 A.M. local time. Obviously no celestial body ejects "a black object . . . tubular in shape," as one missile site reported. But as numerous cases already discussed here have demonstrated, erroneous details often creep into eyewitness reports. Considering that SAC Headquarters recently had alerted many of its bases to the possibility of "helicopter assault," security police and other SAC personnel could be expected to keep a very watchful eye for lights in the night sky—lights they might otherwise have ignored.

That even military observers can be misled by celestial bodies is documented in a book published in 1903, recounting an experience that involved a noted astronomer, Simon Newcomb, more than a century before the Montana "UFO" incidents.* In the book, *The Reminiscences of an Astronomer* (Houghton, Mifflin), Newcomb tells of his visit to Fort Snelling, Minnesota, where officers described the following:

> . . . a celestial phenomenon of a very extraordinary character which had been observed for several nights past. A star had been seen, night after night, rising in the east as usual, and starting on its course toward the south. But instead of continuing that course across the meridian, as stars invariably had done from the remotest antiquity, it took a turn toward the north, sunk toward the horizon, and finally set near the north . . . . My assurances that there must be some mistake in the observation could not be accepted, because this erratic course of the heavenly body had been seen by all of them so plainly that no doubt could exist . . . . The men who saw it were not of the ordinary untrained kind, but graduates of West Point, who, if any one, ought to be free from optical deceptions. I was confidently invited to look out that night and see for myself . . . .
>
> In due time the planet Mars was seen in the east . . . . "There it is!" was the exclamation . . . . Hour after hour passed, and as the planet went on its regular course, the other watchers began to get a little nervous. It showed no signs of deviating from its course. We went out from time to time to look at the sky. "There it is," said one of the observers at length, pointing to [the star] Capella, which was now just rising a little to the east of north; "there is the star setting." "No, it isn't," said I; "there is the star we have been looking at, now quite inconspicuous near the meridian . . . ." A very little additional watching showed that no deviation of the general laws of Nature had occurred, but that the observers of previous nights had jumped at the conclusion that two objects, widely apart in the heavens, were the same.

In view of the incidents that had been reported from Loring, Wurtsmith, and Grand Forks, the message from the director of SAC special police, and the numerous visual sighting reports during the early morning hours of November 7, 1975, from Montana missile sites, it is hardly surprising that security police and radar operators were energized to be even more vigilant the next night and during the early morning hours of November 8. This had resulted in similar visual sightings and a few intermittent radar targets, some of which could have been generated by migrating flocks of birds; however, they resulted in the incidents being reported to the NMCC in Washington. And since the bright celestial bodies, including Jupiter and Venus were still there on succeeding nights, it is hardly surprising that there were still more visual sightings on subsequent nights.

---

*I am indebted to David A. Schroth, of St. Louis, for bringing the Newcomb incident to my attention. Schroth is an associate member of the UFO Subcommittee of the Committee for the Scientific Investigation of Claims of the Paranormal.

Here are a few examples of the "UFO" reports on subsequent nights, taken from the log of the 24th NORAD Region. On November 8, at 8:05 P.M. MST, several missile sites reported seeing a bright yellow light, and fifteen minutes later another reported spotting an "orange white disc." But the NORAD report indicates that "surveillance unable to get height check," that is, the reported object did not show up on the height-finder radar. Another item from the report indicates that the FAA watch-supervisor reported that there were five airliners in the general area where the visually sighted object seemed to be located, but none of their flight crews reported seeing anything unusual, except for one United Airlines crew that reported seeing a bright meteor/fireball. Despite the lack of radar target, missile-site crews reported they could still see the light in the sky and it was "stationary." The next night there were several more visual-sighting reports, according to the same NORAD log. One, relayed through the SAC Command Post, was received at 6:25 P.M. MST: "Report UFO sighting from site K-1 around Harlowton area. Surveillance checking area with height finder [radar.]" Approximately half an hour later, the NORAD log notes: "Surveillance report unable to locate [radar] track that would correlate with UFO sighted by K-1."

At 4:25 A.M. MST on November 10, the NORAD log notes: "UFO sighting reported by Minot Air Force Station, a bright star-like object in the west, moving east, about the size of a car. First seen approximately 1015Z [4:15 A.M. Central Standard Time]. Approximately 1120Z [5:20 A.M. CST], the object passed over the radar station, 1,000 to 2,000 feet high, no noise heard. Three people from the site or local area saw the object." If the object that was reported to have passed over the radar station at 5:20 A.M. was in fact the same one that had been spotted to the west more than an hour earlier, this would rule out its being a celestial body. But as Newcomb's book shows, even West Point graduates can experience an "identity-transfer" from one object to another. The final entry in the 24th NORAD Region log, on November 19 at 6:27 A.M. MST, following a six-day lull in visual reports, noted that two military observers had reported seeing an "object traveling NE between M-8 and M-1 at a fast rate of speed. Object bright white light seen 45 to 50 sec. following terrain 200 ft. off ground . . . ." The description, plus the fact that the annual Leonids meteor shower was in progress and the earlier fireball report from the United Airlines crew, suggest that this UFO was also a fireball. It is possible that the object that passed over the Minot radar station was a fireball, but the available details are too sketchy to determine its identity with any certainty.

If the UFOs over the missile sites in Montana were bright celestial bodies, this could explain why observers reported that, when the F-106 interceptors arrived, the UFOs seemed to turn off their lights and to turn them back on when the jet aircraft departed. When the F-106s arrived, observers' eyes focused on the intense glow from their jet-engine exhausts, so that distant celestial objects would be much fainter and, comparatively, dark. When the jets departed, the observers' eyes had no bright, nearby distractions and once again focused on the bright celestial objects.

If the chain of events triggered by an unidentified helicopter's overflight of Loring AFB in late October, plus a justifiable SAC Headquarters dispatch warning of possible "helicopter assault" and alerting SAC bomber and missile-site personnel had made military personnel so edgy that bright celestial bodies seemed to be unknown flying objects, no one should be surprised. After all, CUFOS finds that one out of every four UFO reports it receives is triggered by bright celestial bodies, and the observers are under far less stressful conditions.

Nearly a quarter of a century earlier, on October 10–11, 1952, USAF personnel at weather stations at two bases in Maine, one of which later was renamed Loring AFB, reported a UFO they described as being a "circular orange object with four green lights." Fortunately the witnesses took azimuth and elevation-bearing measurements of the mysterious UFO, using theodolites, low-power telescopes employed to track weather balloons. These data were turned over to Dr. Hynek, then a consultant to Project Blue Book. Following his analysis, Hynek wrote on December 23, 1952, to Dr. H. M. Chadwell, of the CIA, a letter that concluded:

> In view of this strikingly close agreement in rates as well as general position in the sky, it would be an outrage to probability theory to consider that the object observed was anything other than the time-honored planet Jupiter.

13

UFOs over Canada

"FOR THE FIRST TIME EVER . . . AIR DEFENSE CHIEFS ADMIT: WE TRACKED UFO ON RADAR AND SCRAMBLED FIGHTER JETS TO INTERCEPT IT" read the headline on August 3, 1976, in the *National Enquirer*. The accompanying article described a UFO incident that had occurred near Sudbury, Ontario, just across Lake Huron from Wurtsmith AFB, on November 11, 1975. This was only a few days after the "UFO" sightings over SAC bases, which had not yet become known to UFOlogists or the news media. The *National Enquirer* quoted Lieutenant Colonel Brian Wooding, director of the 22nd NORAD Region control center as saying: "We get quite a few UFO reports but to my knowledge this is about the only one we've actually seen on radar and the only time we've gone to the point of scrambling interceptors." Clearly, the officer was not aware of the two F-106s that had been scrambled a few days earlier to investigate sighting reports in Montana.

Shortly after the *Enquirer* article appeared, I wrote to the public-information office at NORAD Headquarters, in Colorado Springs, to obtain the name of the commander of the Canadian radar station at Falconbridge, which had been involved in the incident, so I might obtain more first-hand information on the incident. Subsequently I received a letter from Colonel R. W. Buskard, one of many Canadian officers based at NORAD Headquarters, telling me that Major Robert Oliver, the officer who commanded the Falconbridge radar station at the time of the UFO incident, had since been transferred to Colorado Springs but was reluctant to discuss the incident further because he "has been subjected to a continuing stream of crank letters" since the *Enquirer* article was published. However, Colonel Buskard enclosed a two-page summary that Oliver had prepared in response to my query and asked that any further questions be routed through his office.

This authoritative summary revealed that the November 11 incident had been preceded by "an abnormal number of reports of sightings of unidentified objects in the sky" during the three weeks prior to the now-famous incident. This is not surprising, considering that a very bright Jupiter was visible beginning in the early evening and an extremely bright Venus rose shortly after 2:30 A.M. local time. On the night of October 20, NBC-TV, whose programs can be seen by Canadians living near the U.S. border, had rekindled interest in UFOs with a dramatic two-hour film recounting the alleged UFO abduction of Betty and Barney Hill.

At approximately 5:45 A.M., on November 11, the Falconbridge commander said he was informed that the station had received a number of UFO reports during the early morning hours. Oliver's summary stated: "All reports were similar in that three to four objects, described as bright, round objects with *no apparent velocity,* were sighted over the city of Sudbury," south-southwest of Falconbridge. [Emphasis added.] However, my own examination of some of these reports, passed on to NORAD Headquarters, shows that some observers reported only a single object. One observer said the object resembled a "bright star to naked eye, through binoculars it is spherical, rotating, approx. 100 ft. in diameter with an appearance similar to pictures of the moon. Also appeared to ascend and descend." Although the Falconbridge personnel had not previously noted any unidentified targets on their long-range surveillance radar, which is operated continuously, they decided to turn on their height-finder radar and look for targets to the south. In so doing they observed a target at a distance of about twenty-five miles south-southwest (direction of Sudbury), at an altitude of about 36,000 feet, moving slowly from west to east, according to Oliver.

His summary report said that station personnel, sent outside to watch the lights in the sky, reported that one of them "appeared to ascend at a high rate of speed. Simultaneously . . . the height finder reported a change in altitude [of radar target] . . . from 36,000 feet to 72,000 feet in a matter of two minutes." Although the visually observed objects disappeared shortly after daybreak, "at least two targets were carried by radar at reasonably high altitudes . . . into the afternoon," Oliver said. The Falconbridge commander discussed the persistent radar target with officials at both the 22nd and 23rd NORAD Regions and at approximately 1:00 P.M., the 23rd Region decided to dispatch two F-106 interceptors from Selfridge AFB, Michigan, to investigate. The aircraft were vectored to the vicinity of the radar targets in broad daylight but could see no craftlike objects — only high-altitude clouds laden with ice crystals that reflected sunlight. *Curiously, the lengthy* National Enquirer *article made no mention of this important detail.* Such clouds would return radar energy and produce blips on the Falconbridge height-finder radar.

Oliver's summary acknowledged that the lighted object reports received during the previous hours of darkness might have been generated by bright planets

> . . . combined with cold temperatures and light cloud conditions. This could also account for the illusion of movement and illumination. The radar sightings were never confirmed as definitely coinciding with the [location of] the visual sightings. Radar targets could have been produced by the phenomena of anomalous propagation (AP) not uncommon at that time of the year. The radar pattern that night suggested that AP was present in very limited amounts although the targets in question were distinct and separate from clutter and were not consistent with normal AP pattern.

After studying Oliver's report, I was curious to learn whether the target on the height-finder radar also had been spotted by the Falconbridge air-surveillance radar, whose coverage would extend far beyond Sudbury and up to at least 50,000 feet. If so, had both radars shown their unknown targets to be at the same bearing and range? Because the two radars operate at different frequencies, a "hard" target such as a metal craft would show up on both, while a "softer" target like an ice cloud, or anomalous propagation, might show a target on one radar but not the other. In my letter to Buskard raising this question, I noted that "it has been my repeated experience that once a radar crew has been told that there are unknown visual-objects in the neighborhood, they will invariably find 'unidentified' targets on the radar, and vice versa. In the excitement of the moment, the visuals and radar sightings will seem to confirm one another, even though the visuals and radar blips may be in quite different locations."

Colonel Buskard responded:

> No definite correlation with search [radar] data was obtained at any time for any of the reported targets. The two targets carried by radar were solely height-finder targets. The bearing and distance of [the radar] target only broadly correlated with the visually reported target. [Then, commenting on my observation, Buskard wrote:] My experience with radar, particularly with height-finders, would lead me to believe that even an experienced operator can have difficulty in correctly spot-lighting a target, and can see "ghosts" if the tension is high enough, but in this case there was more than one experienced observer. There is no suggestion that the radar sightings definitely coincided with the visual sightings. Given the civilian [observers] statement that the visual sightings were "southeast" of the city, and the look-angle difference between the visual reporters and the [Falconbridge] station itself, there could be a large variation in location between the two. There was no attempt at the station to triangulate the [visual] sightings with the radar data.

The *Parade* article by Satchell, after discussing the SAC bases and Falconbridge incidents, concluded: "What flew over the military installations during those 24 nights between Oct. 27 and Nov. 19 will probably never be fully explained . . ." I would agree fully if Satchell had appended: "to the satisfaction of those who want to believe in UFOs."

14

UFOs over Iran

The most useful account available of a now-famous UFO incident involving two Imperial Iranian Air Force (IIAF) jet fighters is a memorandum-for-the-record, signed by USAF Lieutenant Colonel Olin R. Mooy, executive officer to the chief of the U.S. Air Force section, Military Assistance Advisory Group (MAAG) in Tehran at the time, 1976. As Mooy later explained to me, Iranian officials had invited the USAF section chief to send representatives to attend a "debriefing" of one of the two flight crews involved in the incident. Mooy, along with Colonel Jerry R. Johnson, were assigned to the task. The memorandum-for-the-record, undated, reads as follows:

1. At about 12:30 AM 19 September 1976 the IIAF Command Post received a telephone call from the ADOC [Air Defense Operations Center] representative at Mehrabad [civil-military airport near Tehran]. He said that Mehrabad had received four telephone calls from citizens living in the Shemiran area saying that they had seen strange objects in the sky. One lady described them as a kind of bird, while another lady said, "Please tell this helicopter with a light on to get away from my house because I'm scared." (There were no helicopters airborne at that time.) The citizens were told it was probably stars.

2. The Command Post called Brigadier General Yousefi, assistant deputy commander of operations. After Yousefi talked to Mehrabad tower and determined Babolsar and Shahrokhi radars did not have the object [that is, no unidentified target on these air-defense radars], he decided to look for himself. He noticed an object in the sky similar to a star but bigger and brighter. [Note: the planet Jupiter was especially bright at the time.] He decided to scramble and [sic] F-4 from Shahrokhi to investigate. [Shahrokhi was an IIAF air base located approximately 130 miles southwest of Tehran.]

3. The F-4 took off at 01:30 AM and proceeded to a point about 40 NM

111

[nautical miles] north of Tehran. Due to its brilliance the object was easily visible from 70 miles away. As the F-4 approached a range of 25 NM he lost all instrumentation and communications (UHF and Intercom). He broke off the intercept and headed back to Shahrokhi. When the F-4 turned away from the object and apparently was no longer a threat to it the aircraft regained all instrumentation and communications.

4. A second F-4 was launched at 01:40 AM. The backseater [radar operator] acquired a lock-on at 27 NM, 12 o'clock high position [directly ahead and above] with the Vc (rate of closure) at 150 MPH. As the range decreased to 25 NM the object moved away at a speed that was visible on the radar scope and stayed at 25 NM.

5. The size of the radar return [echo-blip] was comparable to that of a [Boeing] 707 tanker [aircraft]. The visual size of the object was difficult to discern because of its intense brilliance. The light that it gave off was that of flashing strobe lights arranged in a rectangular pattern and alternating blue, green, red and orange in color. The sequence of lights was so fast that all colors could be seen at once.

6. The object and the pursuing F-4 continued a course to the south of Tehran, when another brightly lighted object, estimated to be 1/2 to 1/3 the apparent size of the moon, came out of the original object. This second object headed straight toward the F-4 at a very fast rate. The pilot attempted to fire an AIM-9 [infrared-guided] missile at the object but at that instant his weapons-control panel went off and he lost all communications (UHF and Interphone). At this point the pilot initiated a turn and negative-G dive to get away. As he turned the object fell in trail at what appeared the [sic] be about 3-4 NM. As he continued in his turn away from the primary object the second object went to the inside of his turn, then returned to the primary object for a perfect rejoin [that is, returned and merged with the primary object.]

7. Shortly after the second object joined up with the primary object another object appeared to come out of the other side of the primary object going straight down, at a great rate of speed. The F-4 crew had regained communications and the weapons-control panel and watched the object approaching the ground anticipating a large explosion. This object appeared to come to rest gently on the earth and cast a very bright light over an area of about 2–3 kilometers.

8. The crew descended from their altitude of 26M [26,000 ft.] to 15M and continued to observe and mark the object's position. They had some difficulty in adjusting their night visibility for landing so after orbiting Mehrabad a few times they went out for a straight-in landing. There was a lot of interference on the UHF [ultra-high-frequency air-ground radio] and each time they passed through a Mag. [magnetic] bearing of 150 degrees from Mehrabad they lost their communications (UHF and Interphone) and the INS [inertial navigation system] fluctuated from 30-degree to 50-degrees. The one civil airliner that was approaching Mehrabad during this same time experienced communications failure in the same vicinity (Kilo Zulu) but did not report seeing anything.

9. While the F-4 was on a long final approach the crew noticed another cylinder shaped object (about the size of a T-bird [jet-trainer aircraft] at 10 NM) with bright steady lights on each end and a flasher in the middle. When

queried, the tower stated there was no other known traffic in the area. During the time that the object passed over the F-4 the tower did not have a visual on it [that is, saw nothing], but picked it up after the pilot told them to look between the mountains and the refinery.

10. During daylight the F-4 crew was taken out to the area in a helicopter where the object apparently had landed. Nothing was noticed at the spot where they thought the object landed (a dry lake bed), but as they circled off to the west of the area they picked up a very noticeable beeper signal. At the point where the [beeper] return was the loudest was a small house with a garden. They landed and asked the people within if they had noticed anything strange last night. They [sic] people talked about a loud noise and a very bright light-like lightning.

11. The aircraft and the area where the object is believed to have landed are being checked for possible radiation. More information will be forwarded when it becomes available.

If the flight crew's report was accurate in all details, then clearly this UFO was outfitted with an exotic weapon that could induce electrical-electronic failure in a U.S.-built F-4 fighter aircraft (which is widely used by the USAF and the Navy), thus preventing the aircraft from firing its defensive missiles. Yet this posed a curious anomaly: If the UFO did indeed have such a remarkable defense at its disposal, why had it *seemingly* fired a rocket-missile against the F-4, which already had been rendered harmless? Did this indicate that UFOs suddenly had turned aggressive and hostile?

If there were any truth to the oft-repeated claims that the U.S. government has captured one or more flying saucers, or that the USAF/government really knows that UFOs are extraterrestrial craft, this Iranian incident should have generated an appropriate response. Presumably the USAF would itself have launched an all-out investigation, importing a team of specialists from the United States and the late Shah would have been asked to impose official secrecy to keep all news of the incident out of the press. *Yet none of these things happened.*

Mooy's memorandum-for-the-record was not even classified (that is, stamped "Top Secret") in the MAAG files. Later, when a copy was sent back to the U.S. and distributed to a number of agencies, including the CIA, State Department, and Pentagon, the memo was classified "Confidential"—the lowest security level. There was no followup investigation of the incident by the USAF or other MAAG personnel, according to Mooy. Nor were there any further MAAG dispatches on the subject from Tehran, although the incident was widely publicized in Iranian newspapers. Perhaps the best indication of how seriously the U.S. government was concerned over the incident and its implications is that a copy of the classified copy of Mooy's memorandum was leaked to NICAP soon after it was received in the U.S., and most of the memo was published in the November 1976 issue of its *UFO Investigator.*

My own investigation into the case did not get underway until the following summer. On July 10, 1977, I wrote to Major General Kenneth P. Miles, USAF, chief of MAAG in Tehran, enclosing a copy of the NICAP article and asking if he could supply additional information on the incident. My letter noted that my many UFO investigations showed the importance of obtaining first-hand information and added that I had yet to find a case that would prompt me to believe that any UFOs were extraterrestrial visitors. Miles replied on August 7, sending a photocopy of the unclasified Mooy memorandum, as well as several articles on the incident that had been published in Tehran's two English-language newspapers. Miles added: "I share your view that there is no evidence to suggest that the earth is being visited by extraterrestrial spaceships."

One of the articles, published on September 20, 1976, in the *Tehran Journal,* quoted a Mehrabad airport controller as saying that the UFO was flying at an altitude of about 6,000 feet over the southern part of sprawling Tehran, alternately flashing red, blue, and green lights. Yet Mooy's memorandum, based on information offered by the second F-4 crew, said the first F-4 had been 40 nautical miles *north* of Tehran when that airplane encountered mysterious electrical-electronic problems. The newspaper quoted controllers in the airport tower as saying that one of the pilots had seen a bright object separate from the UFO and fall into the hills below. The police had promptly been alerted and had made an all-night search of the area, apparently without finding anything UFO-related. The *Tehran Journal* said that ground observers in the area also had reported seeing a bright object flit across the sky or fall from the sky. The newspaper noted that there had been a rash of UFO reports from near Bushehr the previous May, and that a month earlier a man claimed that he had been "whisked aboard a flying saucer in the woods and carried off to Isfahan."

The next day (September 21), the *Tehran Journal* reported that a tape recording of one F-4 pilot's radio communications with the Mehrabad tower had been made available to reporters of the Persian-language newspaper *Ettela'at*. Quoting from the latter, the *Tehran Journal* identified the pilot as a Lieutenant Jafari, who was in command of the first F-4 involved in the incident. Based on these tapes the first F-4 flew over Tehran at the speed of sound (slightly under 700 mph.) and the pilot called the Mehrabad tower when he first spotted the UFO. Jafari described the UFO as being "half the size of the moon . . . It was radiating violet, orange and white light about three times as strong as moonlight." Although the pilot reported that he was flying at a maximum speed, he said that "on seeing him coming the UFO increased its speed," that is, he was unable to close on the bright light.

The Mehrabad tower told him to return to base if he could not close on the object and the pilot agreed to do so, but a few moments later he radioed: "Something is coming at me from behind. It is 15 miles away . . . now 10 miles away . . . now five miles . . . . It is level now, I think it is going to crash into me. It has just passed by, missing me narrowly . . . ." The newspaper said that "the disturbed voice of the pilot . . . then asked to be guided back to base. It was at this time that a second plane was ordered to take off." This account, based on a tape recording of pilot-control tower conversations indicates that there was not any mysterious malfunction of the electrical-electronics equipment aboard the *first* F-4, contrary to the account in the Mooy memorandum. The explanation for this discrepancy is that Mooy and Johnson sat in on the debriefing only of the second F-4 crew, and this misinformation must necessarily have resulted from the fact that the two crews had not had a chance to compare notes prior to the debriefing. It also is important to note that the glowing object that Lieutenant Jafari reported seeing was "coming at me from behind." Since he, presumably, was chasing the bright light in the sky at the time, which would have beed dead-ahead of him, the object coming at him from the rear seemingly was quite unrelated to the object he was chasing.

Continuing the *Tehran Journal* account, based on tape recordings of the tower's radio communications with the *second* F-4 pilot, "the pilot reported having seen the UFO and told the control tower that it had reduced speed. The pilot said the plane was working well and he was preparing to fire missiles at the UFO. After a moment's silence he said he had seen a 'bright round object, with a circumference of about 4.5 meters, leave the UFO.' A few seconds later the bright object rejoined the mother craft and it flew away at many times the speed of sound." There was no mention of an electrical-electronic failure aboard the second F-4, but if one *had* occurred, it would have interrupted radio communications with the tower. Nor was there any mention that an unknown object had been detected on the aircraft's own radar. (The Mehrabad radar was inoperative at the time.)

Tehran's other English-language newspaper, *Kayhan International,* published an article on the incident on September 21 that began:

> And now . . . the REAL story about that "UFO." Unfortunately, it's not quite as exciting as the tales we've been hearing over the last day or two about the bright light "thing" that allegedly had the audacity to chase two jets of the Imperial Iranian Air Force across Tehran. Nevertheless, the true facts as outlined by an official source yesterday still have the ring of science fiction about them. The source said individuals telephoned Mehrabad Airport's control tower to report a bright light in the night sky. Two jets were scrambled to investigate and one of the pilots reported seeing an object with a light so bright it illuminated the ground below. But the apparition soon disappeared and . . . that's it.
>
> The pilot did not report seeing red, blue and green flashing lights as the newspaper reports said. And most emphatically, said the source, it [UFO] did not switch round and chase the jets. The newspaper reports also said that when the object came to within five kilometres of the jets, all electrical appliances on the aircraft went out of action, they lost radio contact with the

ground and could not fire on the objects as they intended. Not so, said the official. The pilots made no attempt to open fire and at no time did the aircrafts' electronic gear fail to function. And since everything on the plane from controls to fuel pump is electronically operated, it's a little puzzling to figure out how the plane could possibly have kept in the air anyway. [Note: the aircraft has an emergency power supply to handle a few critical functions.]

The official summed it all up by saying the reports, which first appeared in afternoon papers on Sunday, were "exaggerated."* A reported verbatim conversation between pilot "J" and ground control, in which he reported the different lights and the chase, left the official "frankly puzzled." But he agreed that there was no apparent explanation for what the pilot DID see.

Despite this disclaimer from an unidentified "official source," it seems prudent to put more credence in the Mooy memorandum, since it is based on notes taken during the debriefing of the second F-4 crew, although it is clear from the Mehrabad tower tape recording that the second crew's account of what happened to the first F-4 contains serious errors.

Prior to writing to Major General Miles at MAAG, I contacted a friend in the aerospace industry who had made several business trips to Iran to try to sell equipment to the IIAF to seek his help in locating high-level IIAF officials who might be willing to assist in my investigation of the incident and to determine if there had been a followup investigation. This friend referred me to a USAF colonel, John Wilson, recently retired, who had been in Iran at the time of the incident, but Wilson could provide no further details. However, he suggested I write to Lieutenant General Abdullah Azerbarzin, who was IIAF's director of operations at the time of the UFO incident and had been promoted to vice-commander of the Imperial Iranian Air Force. (Subsequently I learned from Mooy that Azerbarzin had been present during the debriefing of the second F-4 crew.) On July 6, 1977, I wrote to Azerbarzin, saying that I was writing at the suggestion of Wilson, whom he knew. My letter noted that I was a UFO skeptic and asked if the IIAF had investigated the UFO incident further. Azerbarzin never replied.

Several months later, I met the Iranian ambassador in Washington, Ardeshir Zahedi, a very close friend of the late Shah, and we had exchanged letters on non-UFO matters. On November 29, I wrote Zahedi, enclosing a copy of my earlier letter to Azerbarzin, asking for the ambassador's assistance in obtaining more information on the UFO incident. Zahedi never replied. Early in 1978, I wrote to a young Iranian science

---

*On September 25, 1976, the *Tehran Journal* reported that *Ettela'at* offices "continued to be flooded with reports from people who claim to have seen flying saucers . . . . One man claimed yesterday that he had actually been kidnapped by strange beings, and taken inside a flying saucer . . . [the man], a researcher in Iranian history, said he had been reluctant to tell the story . . . because he thought people would make fun of him." The man described the UFOnauts as "two beings similar in shape to Egyptian mummies . . . ."

writer who had recently become a member of the Aviation/Space Writers Association (of which I am a member), seeking his help on the UFO investigation. My letter was returned, seemingly unopened, although I could not be certain of this. I also wrote to an astronomy professor at Tehran University, who had been quoted in a *Tehran Journal* article, suggesting that the UFO probably had a prosaic explanation, but I received no response.

Turning to American aerospace companies, I wrote to a technical representative in Tehran of McDonnell Douglas, which makes the F-4, but received no reply. A letter to the director for Middle East operations for E-Systems, Inc., in Tehran brought a brief response saying he could supply no more information than that contained in the NICAP account, which I had sent him. It was a frustrating business. On October 2, 1977, I telephoned Mooy, now a full colonel who had been reassigned back to the States, and he supplied a little useful background. He told me that the debriefing of the second F-4 crew had occurred on September 19. When I asked Mooy if USAF representatives in Iran had made any further investigation into the incident he replied: "There was no further action by the USAF." When asked if the IIAF had carefully checked the second F-4 to determine whether there had been any permanent damage to its electrical-electronic systems, he replied: "No, not that I am aware of. We [USAF] did not check it."

The January 31, 1978, issue of *National Enquirer* disclosed that the Iranian incident had been selected as the "most scientifically valuable UFO case" of the previous year by the tabloid's so-called Blue Ribbon Panel, consisting of experienced UFOlogists , many of them holding Ph.D.s. The article showed a photo of a smiling Ambassador Zahedi being presented with a check for $5,000, which was to be given to an Iranian charity because the F-4 crews were not allowed to accept it. Instead, the flight crews and a controller at the Mehrabad airport would receive commemorative plaques.

Dr. James A. Harder, one of the Blue Ribbon Panel members, was quoted as saying: "The case was particularly important because it provided evidence of long-range jamming of [interference with] fire control [weapons] electronics of the F-4." The newspaper said: "Earlier this year Lieutenant General Abdulah [sic] Azarbarzin . . . told the *Enquirer* that *virtually all* communications, navigation and weapons control systems aboard the *two* Phantom jets were jammed by the UFO." [Emphasis added.] The article, which gave a colorful but inaccurate, summary of the original incident, quoted Harder as saying: "You can always jam communications. But to jam the electronics of fire control within the plane is something that has not been firmly established before." Although Harder is a professor of civil engineering and not a specialist in military matters, he was quick to grasp the obvious import of what seemingly had occurred, if the second flight crew's account was accurate in *all* respects. Yet USAF officials on the scene, who should have been gravely concerned *if they accepted the IIAF crew's account at face value,* seemingly were oblivious to the matter.

If IIAF officials really believed that one of its F-4s, which might someday be needed to defend Iran from attack, had really been "zapped" by a UFO, causing electrical-electronic system outage, presumably the best experts available would be brought in to check the airplane to see if there had been any permanent damage. With that in mind, in late 1977, I contacted Westinghouse Electric, which produced the APQ-120 radar used in the F-4s, seeking to communicate with company tech reps who had been in Iran at the time of the UFO incident. It would be six months later before several Westinghouse field engineers would return to the States, enabling me to talk with them—and allowing them to speak candidly. They would provide valuable insights into the UFO incident—and the shortcomings of the Imperial Iranian Air Force.

The subsequent overthrow of the Shah and the departure of U.S. tech reps because of the wave of anti-American feeling, makes it doubtful whether any of the Westinghouse tech reps with whom I talked will ever return to Iran. Still, it seems wise not to use their names here, because of their candor. The Westinghouse tech rep who was stationed at Shahrokhi at the time of the incident, whom I shall refer to as TR-1, told me that only the second F-4 was briefly "quarantined" when it returned to the base by being placed in a remote revetment (designed to protect against surprise attack). This confirms that *only the second F-4 experienced any seemingly mysterious UFO-induced effects.* He told me that neither USAF specialists nor U.S. tech reps at Shahrokhi were even allowed to get close to the airplane, let alone being asked to check it over. Then, less than a week later, according to TR-1, the F-4 was returned to active duty, seemingly none the worse for its UFO encounter.

TR-1's superior (whom I will call TR-2), although based in Tehran, told me he was so curious about the incident that he personally investigated the matter as far as he could. TR-2 said that the IIAF's maintenance was so lax that it did not keep a running log of aircraft malfunctions and attempted maintenance fixes. However, the McDonnell Douglas tech rep at Shahrokhi was a very methodical person and kept his own private log, TR-2 told me. When this McDonnell Douglas tech rep managed to get close enough to the F-4 in the revetment to read its registration number and examined his own records, he had made a most significant discovery, TR-2 told me: *this F-4 had a long history of intermittent electric-power-system outages, which the IIAF maintenance shop at Shahrokhi had never been able to permanently cure.* This was confirmed by TR-1, who also told me: "The electrical shop at Shahrokhi was notorious for poor performance with respect to the other shops!"

During the course of TR-2's investigation, he told me that he had talked to Iranian maintenance crews to ask if they had checked the F-4 following the UFO incident. "They claimed that they did and that the only thing they found wrong was that one of the radios had some static in it," TR-2 told me. This is not an unusual complaint even for aircraft that have not had UFO encounters. Both Westinghouse tech reps told me they had been anxious to test their APQ-120 radar following the UFO incident, to see if it was performing properly. But they said the IIAF "did not allow any radar people, Iranian or otherwise," to check the system. However, about a month after the airplane was returned to service, TR-1 said, he was called in to perform some adjustments on the radar—indicating that at that time the radar was not operating completely satisfactorily. This could possibly explain the "UFO-blip" that was reported by the second F-4 crew, although another explanation would also emerge.

Thus, the second F-4's long history of electrical-power-system outages, involving an intermittent-type fault—admittedly difficult to isolate and fix—offers a prosaic explanation to the hypothesis that the aircraft was "jammed" by some emission from a UFO. *And this prosaic explanation also would explain why the Mehrabad airport's radio systems did not experience any UFO interference.*

The IIAF's reluctance to ask U.S. specialists to check the F-4 for permanent damage and the decision to return the airplane quickly to service suggests that the IIAF recognized that the electrical problems reported during the UFO incident might have a prosaic explanation, whose source was in the shortcomings of Shahrokhi's own electrical-maintenance shop. But these shortcomings were not something they would be anxious to bring to the attention of top IIAF officials in Tehran or the Iranian press.

Because none of the IIAF air-defense radars had reported a UFO-blip at the time the second F-4 reported seeing a UFO-blip on its much-less-powerful radar, I asked TR-2 about the skill-level of Iranian F-4 radar operators. He responded: "They are not too knowledgeable . . . . They are not really trained as radar operators or fire-control operators." He went on to explain that unlike the USAF, where airborne radar operators are trained exclusively for that function, in the IIAF the airborne radar operator typically was a junior-level pilot, whose principal goal was to "move into the front seat" as the aircraft's commander. Commenting on the second F-4's report that it had briefly locked onto a blip from the UFO, TR-2 volunteered: "He [radar operator] could have been in manual track or something like that and not really realized it."

One thing is evident: the second F-4 crew was clearly "rattled." This is obvious from their report that the target on their radar scope was at a range of twenty-five miles, but they were preparing to fire an AIM-9 air-air missile *whose maximum range is only a couple of miles.* (The AIM-9 is an infrared guided missile used for close-in dogfight combat.) Thus their missile could not possibly have reached the "target-blip" appearing on their radar. Later I would be told that this second F-4 crew had been awakened out of a sound sleep and dispatched on the UFO mission, so it is entirely possible that their judgments may have been clouded by not being fully awake.

TR-1 offered additional insights into the incident when he volunteered that F-4 flight crews "didn't do much night flying at Shahrokhi."* He said he had seen no night flights during his extended assignment at the base, other than the two F-4s that had been dispatched to chase the UFO. He added that flights sometimes were launched late in the afternoon with the planes returning around dusk. TR-1 told me: "It would have been very easy for something unusual to surprise them [the two F-4 flight crews]." If a USAF pilot experienced in night flying could mistake the bright star Capella for a UFO and chase it, as Hynek himself acknowledged some years ago, then an IIAF flight crew, awakened from sleep and dispatched into darkness with barely any training in night operations could certainly be victims of a similar misidentification.

As the pieces of the puzzle began to fall into place, a possible explanation emerged for my inability to enlist the aid of top IIAF officials in my investigation. The Imperial Iranian Air Force was the late Shah's pride and joy, and he had poured billions of dollars into providing it with the newest, most expensive American aircraft, such as the F-14. If the IIAF was having trouble keeping its older, less complex F-4s operational and if crew training in night operations was lacking, so that an F-4 pilot had tried to shoot down a celestial body with a short-range air-air missile, this would have been very embarrassing to IIAF officials—and to the Shah if it became public knowledge. This might also explain why USAF officials had not paid undue attention to the incident.

It would be far less embarrassing to settle for the original "UFO" explanation. After all, even the USAF had been forced to admit that it had encountered a few UFO incidents for which no prosaic explanation could be found. Instead of possible humiliation, the IIAF flight crews later would be honored for the best UFO case of the year by America's largest-circulation newspaper.

The foregoing does not, however, explain the first F-4 pilot's report of a missile-like object coming at him from behind (from the west) that passed overhead, nor the missile-like object reported by the second F-4 pilot that seemed to come from the UFO and which appeared to crash in the general vicinity of Tehran.

Less than a year earlier, on the afternoon of November 19, 1975, the pilot of an Eastern Airlines DC-9 flying south of Richmond, Virginia, enroute to Washington D.c., had radioed the Washington traffic-control center to report a close encounter with what appeared to be four "missiles or

---

*Subsequently this was confirmed to me by an official of another U.S. company with direct experience in Iran with the IIAF. He told me that the IIAF was considered "a flying country club for sons of rich families" and that the IIAF had no nighttime flying experience.

rockets." The fiery objects came out of the east, headed west, and were estimated by Captain C. S. Wilson to be only 2000 feet above the airliner and less than a mile in front of it. The pilot was quoted as saying: "I've never seen a salvo of missiles in flight, but by [sic] the pictures I've seen, this is what missiles could look like . . . ." But Captain Wilson sagely added: "I've been fooled many times by optical illusions . . . ."

The Federal Aviation Administration promptly launched an investigation to determine if any military aircraft in the area had inadvertently launched air-air missiles, but no military aircraft equipped with missiles had been aloft in the area at the time. Subsequently, based in part on the DC-9 flight crew's report that the objects "burned up after they passed us," the FAA issued a statement saying that the flaming objects were probably fragments of a meteor/fireball entering the atmosphere.

Intensely bright meteor/fireballs, with their long luminous tails of electrified air, are a major trigger-mechanism for UFO reports. In the late afternoon of June 5, 1969, jetliner flight crews of American Airlines and United Airlines and the crew of an Air National Guard jet-fighter, flying near St. Louis, Missouri, thought that they nearly collided with a squadron of UFOs coming out of the east. The objects proved to be a flaming meteor/fireball and smaller fragments flying in trail. Working from a picture made by an alert newspaper photographer in Peoria, Illinois, Alan Harkrader, Jr., and numerous ground-observer reports, it was possible to determine the trajectory of the fireball.* (Harkrader's photo appears in Plate 8.) This revealed that, despite the impressions of the experienced pilots flying near St. Louis, who believed that they nearly collided with the flaming objects, the fireball actually was approximately 125 miles to the north!

Because of the unusual appearance and brightness of fireballs, observers invariably estimate that the objects are much closer than they really are—especially at night. Even Hynek has acknowledged this. In an article published December 1967 in *Playboy* Hynek wrote: "Pilots have been known to swerve their planes violently when they suddenly encounter a very bright meteor they think is on a collision course, but which later proves to have been 50 to 100 miles away."

Is it possible that the missile-like objects reported by both of the Iranian F-4 pilots, and the glowing objects reported by ground observers near Tehran to have fallen from the sky or flitted across the sky, might have been meteor fireballs?

Flaming objects, whose descriptions sound like fireballs, were reported by many observers to the west of Iran that same night. Shortly after the 2:10 A.M. take-off of a TAP (Portuguese) jetliner from Lisbon, which was heading for Africa, the crew reported seeing a flaming object, with

---

*For a more detailed account of the St. Louis incident, see *UFOs Explained,* Chapter 5.

"streamers of fire," coming out of the west. Although the crew estimated that the fiery object came within several hundred yards of their aircraft, this estimate could be in error by more than a hundred miles if the object were a fireball, as the St. Louis incident demonstrated. At about the same time, another TAP crew flying 600 miles to the east reported seeing a very bright light zip past from west to east.

The very same night saw a rash of reports from Morocco of what was described as a luminous object giving off a trail of bright sparks — a description characteristic of a fireball. The object was reported to be coming out of the west or southwest on a northeasterly heading, similar to the trajectory reported by the two TAP flight crews. The time of the sighting, according to one report from a police officer, was approximately 1:15 A.M. Although Portugal and Morocco are in the same time zone, if the former were using Daylight Saving Time and the latter were not, a question I was not able to resolve several years later when I launched my investigation into the Iranian incident, then the object reported by the TAP crews was almost certainly the same flaming object reported out of Morocco.

But the flaming object, or objects if not one and the same, would *not* coincide with the timing of the missile-like objects reported by the two Iranian F-4 pilots, which would have occurred several hours earlier. However, the sighting reports from the TAP flight crews and from Morocco suggest that there was more fireball activity that night than normal. Although fireballs can occur at any time, they are most frequent during meteorshowers. By a not-so-curious coincidence, two meteor showers were under way and at their near-peak activity on the night of September 19: Aquarids and Southern Piscids.

Since the Iranian flight crews were attempting to intercept an unknown object that conceivably could be a Soviet MIG-25 on a covert reconnaissance mission and since there had been several such incidents earlier, the crews would be under considerable stress. And if they saw meteor fireballs zipping across the sky, they could, quite understandably, conclude that these were rockets or missiles which the unknown object was firing at them. As UFO investigator Hendry has acknowledged, during the excitement of a UFO incident, observers often deduce a cause and effect where none actually exists.

Under such stressful conditions, even experienced flight crews become unreliable observers, as psychologist Robert Buckhout noted in his article dealing with the unreliability of eyewitness testimony published in the December 1974 issue of *Scientific American:* "Research I have done with Air Force flight crew members confirms that even highly trained people become poorer observers under stress . . . ." The second F-4 crew admitted that they were experiencing "some difficulty in adjusting their night visibility," according to Mooy's report, and they had difficulty attempting a landing at Mehrabad Airport, despite its modern lighting-landing aids.

It might seem difficult to accept the idea that the F-4's power system chanced to malfunction when the aircraft "passed through a Mag [magnetic] bearing of 150 degrees from Mehrabad," as the crew reported, to explain the loss of radio communications and the erratic operation of the F-4's inertial navigation system. But it seems to me equally unlikely that a UFO would decide to "zap" the F-4 *only* when it was on one specific bearing relative to the airport. The F-4 crew report that an airliner approaching Mehrabad at the same time experienced a communications failure seems mysteriously related to the F-4 problems. But whereas the F-4 experienced malfunctions of many of its avionic systems—indicating electric-power-system problems—the airliner seemingly experienced trouble only with one piece of radio equipment. The fact that airliners carry duplicate, or triplicate, sets of radio and navigation equipment on board reveals that they occasionally experience outages of such equipment due to quite natural causes.

The F-4 crew reported that the day after the UFO incident, while they were aboard a helicopter being used to search a dry lake bed for the bright object the crew thought had landed there, the helicopter picked up "a very noticeable beeper signal." This seems especially mysterious, considering that the UFO was no longer visible. Mooy offered a prosaic explanation. He noted that large military transport aircraft, such as the USAF's C-141, are equipped with an emergency locator radio beacon, which is designed to eject automatically if the airplane should crash. The radio beacon is ejected with sufficient force that it will fly clear of the aircraft for survival and is rugged enough so that when it hits the ground the beacon still can transmit a beeping signal for several days to enable search-rescue aircraft to locate the downed airplane. Mooy told me that there had been some problems with these emergency locator beacons being ejected during flight if an airplane encountered severe turbulence, and that turbulence often was experienced over the mountains near Tehran.

Despite the difficulties of obtaining first-hand information from IIAF officials on the prize-winning "UFO" incident, it is possible to come up with prosaic explanations for the incident and to conclude that the bright starlike object, as it was described by Brigadier General Yousefi, was a celestial object, perhaps the bright planet Jupiter. Certainly the second flight crew's description sounds like many other UFO reports, where the object proved to be a bright celestial body, and this would explain the F-4's inability to "close" on the object.

If the prosaic explanation seems strained, consider the alternative: that the "UFO" was an extraterrestrial spaceship with the remarkable ability to *selectively* disable *many* avionic systems on the F-4, *only* the radio equipment on an airliner, without causing *any* interference in any IIAF air-defense radars or the Mehrabad radio equipment. Despite this remarkable defensive capability, the "UFO" decided to fire an "old-fashioned" rocket-missile at the second F-4, which missed the airplane and landed on a dry lake bed *without* causing an explosion. And the next morning this rocket-missile mysteriously disappeared, leaving behind only a mysterious beeping radio signal, similar to that emitted by crash locator beacons.

15

Delphos

In the spring of 1977, the *Reader's Digest* assigned one of its senior editors, Ronald Schiller, to write an article on UFOs. The experienced journalist, having no prior expertise on this subject, set out to educate himself by reading several books, including *UFOs Explained*. Then he toured the country to interview the recognized leaders and "experts" in UFOlogy. These included APRO's international director, James Lorenzen, and APRO's director of research, Dr. James A. Harder; MUFON's director, Walter Andrus; John Acuff, then head of NICAP; GSW's William Spaulding; and both Hynek and Hendry of CUFOS. Schiller also interviewed Dr. Peter A. Sturrock, who had made the UFO survey of astronomers; Stanton Friedman, a one-time nuclear physicist who earned his living as a pro-UFO lecturer; and Ray Stanford, director of Project Starlight, which operates a facility near Austin, Texas, intended to attract UFOs (so far without success) and to obtain hard data on their characteristics. To obtain the views of UFO skeptics, Schiller talked with Robert Sheaffer and me. (Dr. Donald H. Menzel, a famous astronomer and UFO skeptic had died a few months earlier.)

During Schiller's travels he talked with ten UFO proponents and only two skeptics, but when his article was published in November 1977 in *Reader's Digest,* a number of UFO proponents charged that he had been "brain-washed" by the skeptics.

Schiller asked each UFOlogist to list what he considered to be the three outstanding cases, incidents that defied explanation in prosaic terms. (I declined, saying I would be accused of picking "easy-to-explain" incidents.) Later Schiller told me that he was surprised to find such wide differences of opinion as to which were "strong cases" and which were "weak." He said that one case endorsed strongly by several UFOlogists would be characterized as "quite unimpressive" by others. (I too had been surprised by strongly divergent opinions when I first entered the field in the mid-1960s.)

Despite this, Schiller came up with three UFO cases which, he told me, were endorsed by a majority of the ten UFOlogists. All ten had nominated at least two of the three cases, but not always the same two.

The trio of outstanding cases that emerged from Schiller's survey include two "close-encounter" incidents and a third involving an alleged abduction in which the "victim" was missing for five days, setting a record for "UFO abduction" incidents. The trio is distinguished by the fact that each previously had been selected as the most outstanding UFO case of its year by a so-called Blue Ribbon Panel of experienced UFOlogists to receive a monetary award by the *National Enquirer*. The first of the three involved a reported UFO "landing" on a farm near Delphos, Kansas, on the night of November 2, 1971, in which the UFO seemingly left behind a strange deposit that reportedly had deleterious effects on the principals involved. The second incident involved an Army Reserve helicopter flying near Mansfield, Ohio, on the night of October 18, 1973, in which the UFO seemingly exerted mysterious forces on the helicopter and "blacked-out" its radio communications. The third incident involved the alleged abduction of Travis Walton on the night of November 5, 1975, in front of six witnesses. (All three cases will be analyzed.)

The Delphos case would not have attracted national attention—inasmuch as the report came from one teenage boy—were it not for the crude horseshoe-shaped ring of white material found on the ground where the youth, Ronald Johnson, said he had seen a UFO hovering and for the mysterious properties reportedly exhibited by the white residue. The incident was investigated in great detail by Ted Phillips, of Sedalia, Missouri, who specializes in such "physical-trace" UFO cases on behalf of Hynek's CUFOS. At Hynek's request, Phillips visited the farm of Durel Johnson, situated less than a mile northeast of Delphos, on December 4, 1971, barely a month after the UFO incident, to investigate and obtain samples of the white residue. Phillips returned again on January 11, 1972, and a third time with APRO's Dr. Harder. The Johnson farm quickly became a Mecca for UFOlogists. One who made a thorough investigation was Clancy D. Tull, a Kansas City lawyer (since deceased). Stanton Friedman visited briefly when he went to nearby Concordia College for a lecture. I spent February 28, 1973 in Delphos.

As the Johnson family described the incident to Phillips during his first visit, Mr. and Mrs. Johnson had gone inside after dark to have dinner and young Ronald was to join them when he finished tending his sheep. But they had finished dinner around 7 P.M., when Ronald came running in to say he had seen a flying saucer hovering in a grove of trees several hundred yards behind the house. The youth said he heard a rumbling noise, looked up and there about fifty feet away he saw a mushroom-shaped object which he said had *paralyzed and blinded him* until it finally flew away, heading south past the Johnson house towards Delphos. Mr. and Mrs. Johnson told Phillips that at first they did not believe the boy's story, but finally went outside to see for themselves. Mr. Johnson said that once outside he had seen the UFO "right up between those trees by the road," only a couple hundred feet away. This was not consistent with Ronald's account that he did not regain his vision and run into the house for "what seemed like several minutes," by which time he said the UFO already was "in the sky." Pro-UFO investigators were not bothered by this inconsistency, nor the fact that the youth's description of the UFO's shape and sounds were at variance with the silent, saucer-shaped UFOs most often reported.

The Johnsons told Phillips that they then walked back to the grove of Chinese elm trees, where Ronald said he had seen the UFO and that as they approached this area "they saw in the darkness a glowing circle. The soil surface was glowing a bright grey-white. Portions of the nearby trees glowed also." Seemingly the mysterious visitor from another world had left behind visible evidence confirming Ronald's story. The terrifying prospect that this "glow" could have been some deadly radiation might have prompted most persons to keep a safe distance from the area and to call in local law-enforcement officers. But not the Johnsons, according to their story.

The family not only proceeded to walk right up to the "glowing ring" but both Mr. and Mrs. Johnson said they reached down and touched the white crystalline material on the ground, which they said was not even warm. At that point, Mrs. Johnson later claimed she felt a "numbing in her fingertips," and rubbed them against her leg to knock free the material, only to find that "her leg also became numb," Phillips was told. Mr. Johnson said he too had experienced a numbness in his fingers. Mrs. Johnson said that the numbness in her fingers persisted for about two weeks, preventing her from taking the temperatures of patients in a rest-home where she worked. (But, curiously, she did not promptly report her ailment to a resident physician.) Ronald said his eyes were bloodshot for several days and that he later suffered headaches.

Under the circumstances, one could forgive the Johnson family if they had panicked that night, gotten into their car and driven to the nearby Delphos hospital for emergency treatment. But instead, the entire family exhibited remarkable "cool," according to their account. Mrs. Johnson, despite the reported numbness of her fingers, returned to the house to get a Polaroid camera and came back to photograph the glowing ring. Meanwhile, Mr. Johnson and Ronald drove into Delphos, not to seek medical aid but to visit the local newspaper office, to invite its editor to come out to the farm. But as editor Williard Critchfield of the Delphos *Republican* later explained to me, when Durel and Ronald arrived, he was "on deadline" and decided that it was more important to get his weekly newspaper printed on schedule than to take off twenty minutes to visit the Johnson farm to see the mysterious after-effects of the reported UFO visit.

The following day, after having had the opportunity to consider the terrifying implications of what allegedly had occurred the previous night, the

Johnsons still did not seek medical aid. Instead, Mr. Johnson drove into Delphos to have lunch at the town's major restaurant, near the newspaper office, where editor Critchfield usually ate. He was not there at the time, but one of his reporters, Mrs. Lester (Thaddia) Smith, was, and she had heard of Johnson's visit the previous night. So she went over to talk to Johnson and was invited to come out to see the UFO site. A short time later, Mrs. Smith and two members of her family visited the farm to see the irregular horseshoe-shaped ring, which measured about 7½ feet in diameter. She noted that the center area and the area surrounding the ring were very muddy as a result of recent rains, but the ring itself was dry and very light in color, compared to the dark ground. (See Plate 6.)

Her keen reporter's eye spotted a dead tree just south of the UFO site, and she asked Mr. Johnson if the tree had been standing prior to the UFO incident, and he said that it was (indicating it had been knocked down by the UFO). The UFO site is surrounded on three sides by trees, so that a UFO would have had to approach from the south, over a low hog shed, and the dead tree would have been directly in its flight path. This prompted Mrs. Smith to write, on November 4, 1971, in the *Republican:* "A dead tree in the path of the flight, either when landing or take-off, was crushed to the ground [by the UFO] . . . ." This was a logical conclusion, if Johnson's statement was true that the tree had been standing prior to the night of November 2. But if the tree had been knocked down by a UFO as it approached from the south, or as it departed to the south (as Ronald had reported), the fallen tree should have been lying in an north-south direction. Instead, it was oriented in an *east-west* direction, as shown in a photograph taken by Mrs. Smith and in other photos taken later that same day by a local law-enforcement officer. Furthermore, none of the early investigators who examined the fallen tree were able to see any impact marks on its trunk.

Mrs. Smith later told me that she had urged Mr. Johnson to report the UFO incident to local law officials, but that he had declined her suggestion. So she herself alerted the sheriff's office and later that afternoon Sheriff Ralph Enlow, a deputy, and a Kansas State highway patrolman visited the site to take photos and soil samples from the mysterious ring. Enlow subsequently told me that he too noted that while the soil inside and outside of the horseshoe-shaped ring was very muddy, the ring itself was relatively hard and dry. This provided useful insights. If the ring had been created by a UFO, then prior to the UFO's arrival the entire area must have been very soft and muddy. If a visiting UFO had touched down on the ground, it should have left an indentation that would have been visible. Yet the Enlow photos, made less than twenty-four hours after the reported incident, do not show any indentations. Small twigs lying atop the whitish ring show no signs of bearing a heavy weight or of being exposed to high temperatures. (UFO-lecturer Friedman would later speculate that the whitish material had been produced by intense heating caused by microwave radiation from the UFO.)

If a UFO had visited the Johnson farm, clearly it must have hovered for the duration of its stay and the whitish material was something emitted by the UFO, possibly its propulsion system. Yet this hypothesis has serious flaws. One is that traces of the whitish material were found *beneath* the ring's surface down to a depth of at least eight inches. Another flaw emerged from Tull's careful on-site investigation. If a UFO had emitted the white substance, traces of the material should have been found atop the low hog shed over which the UFO passed as it arrived and departed. Yet when Tull examined the roof of the shed, he found none. *Nor did Tull, or other investigators, report finding any trace of the whitish crystalline material anywhere except in the irregular horseshoe-shaped ring.*

Another curious anomaly was the Johnsons' claim that the ring had glowed brightly in the dark, as did the trunks of some nearby trees, which seemingly had been photographed by Mrs. Johnson. During my own investigation, Mr. Johnson invited me to come in and view some of these Polaroid color prints, which he assured me had all been taken in total darkness and which showed how "the whole placed glowed up." The first print clearly showed a golden-glow from the trunks of trees near the ring, but it was obvious that the photo had been taken in late afternoon and that the golden glow was coming from the setting sun—which explained why all of the tree trunks glowed on their *western* sides even though that side faced *away from* the ring. When I challenged Johnson's claim that the photo had been taken in "pitch dark," he finally conceded that he might be wrong and brought out the one that Mrs. Johnson had taken on the night of the UFO incident.

The ring was clearly evident and the photo had been taken at night, beyond any doubt. Johnson agreed to allow me to photograph this print. Later, when I showed my photograph of Mrs. Johnson's picture to Robert Sheaffer, an expert on analysis of UFO photos, he quickly concluded that her picture had been made using a flashlamp and that the ring "glowed" due to flashlamp light being reflected from its whitish surface. This was obvious, Sheaffer pointed out, because those parts of the ring that were nearest the camera/flashlamp were much brighter than those parts of the ring several feet away. This was confirmed by the "glow" from a stick, close to the camera, which glowed more brightly than any part of the ring.

Although the Johnsons claimed that the ring and tree trunks had glowed for several days, Sheriff Enlow told me that the residue samples he had taken less than twenty-four hours after the incident had never shown any fluorescent characteristics when he had viewed the samples in darkness. Nor had Phillips or other investigators reported seeing fluorescence in the samples they had taken a few weeks later. The only independent corroboration came from Mrs. Smith, who returned to the Johnson farm on the night of November 3 and reported that the ring glowed faintly. When I had asked Mrs. Smith if the moon had been bright on the night of her visit, she said that she thought it had not, because it had been very dark in the grove of trees. But my subsequent check with an almanac showed that there had been a full moon on the night of her visit. Moonlight reflecting off the whitish residue on the ring could readily account for its faint glow.

At one point in my interview with Durel Johnson he unwittingly provided an opportunity for me to check on whether he liked to spin tall tales. He told me that all of his mail "that comes from any distance at all" was being "censored right in here at the [Delphos] post office." When I probed for more details, Mr. Johnson told me that the local post office was slitting open his mail with a razor blade, reading its contents, and then resealing the envelope with a piece of tape. Johnson offered to show me samples of this alleged censorship but after a brief search he gave up, saying his wife had put the letters away. When I asked if he had protested this illegal invasion of privacy to his local postmaster, he said he had not. Upon returning to my home in Washington, I made a copy of my taped interview with Johnson in which he had made these serious allegations and brought the matter to the attention of the Delphos postmaster, who promptly turned the matter over to the regional postal inspector in Kansas City. On August 14, 1973, the postal investigator wrote me to say that a full investigation revealed "there were no grounds for the allegation." I was not surprised at this finding, nor that Johnson had become accustomed to dealing with UFO investigators for whom no tale, no detail, is too incredible. Nor was it surprising that Durel Johnson is well liked, and respected, by those in the Delphos area who know him.

In reporting on the Delphos case in *UFOs Explained,* published in late 1974 after the incident had been selected to receive the first *National Enquirer* best-case prize of $5000, I concluded that the incident was a hoax. The glowing-ring photo taken by Mrs. Johnson had, beyond all doubt, been made with a flashlamp and Mrs. Smith's confirmation was the result of light from the full moon reflecting off the whitish material in the ring. I wrote that my investigation prompted me to "believe that the irregular horseshoe-shaped ring had been there *prior* to November 2, 1971, when the UFO was alleged to have come. Phillips' report that he had found traces of the white material many inches below the surface suggested that the ring might have been there for months or years before the November 2 date."

This prompted me to speculate that the irregular ring might have resulted from a circular livestock feeder or watering trough. Tull had taken samples of the whitish residue and had them analyzed. The analysis showed a great deal of organic material, he told me. Later, Friedman had an analysis made of samples taken from the ring and from the surrounding area, which showed the soil from the ring itself had nearly four times the salinity of the surrounding area. This analysis also revealed that the trace-element concentration of zinc in the ring sample was more than a hundred times that of the surrounding area. In my book I wrote: "*One possible explanation* for this very high zinc content is that the ring had been produced by an animal feeder constructed from galvanized iron which contains zinc to protect it from rusting. It would also explain the high content of iron oxide reported by Tull." [Emphasis added.]

On May 27,, 1973, the *National Enquirer* announced that its Blue Ribbon Panel had selected the Delphos incident for its first $5000 prize award. The incident was called "a major scientific mystery—the most baffling case the panel encountered in a full year of investigation." For the next several months, the Johnson family basked in the light of international fame in the world of UFOlogy. Then, on October 11, 1973, the limelight shifted many hundreds of miles to the south to Pascagoula, Mississippi, where two men—Charles Hickson and Calvin Parker—claimed they had been abducted and taken aboard a flying saucer for a physical examination. The Pascagoula incident occurred at a time when a major "UFO flap" was under way in the United States. Overnight, Hickson and Parker became the new UFO celebrities, appearing on network TV news and talk shows—treatment that had not been accorded the Johnson family. A week later, the Army helicopter UFO encounter near Mansfield, Ohio, became front-page news, and some of its crew members also appeared on network TV talk shows. UFOlogists focused their attention on new heroes with far more exciting tales to tell.

By a curious coincidence, exciting events were happening again on the Johnson farm, as the family recounted to reporter Jim Suber of the *Salina* [Kansas] *Journal* when he visited the Johnsons in the fall of 1974. According to Suber's subsequent article on Ooctober 13, 1974, in the *Journal,* the Johnsons claimed the UFO had returned. Ronnie had rushed into the house one evening shouting, "I told you it was coming back again." When Mr. and Mrs. Johnson hurried outside, they told Suber, "It was the same one, or one just like it. It circled the same spot where it was before, then circled the house and took off east." Although the incident allegedly occurred during broad daylight, there were no reports from others in the Delphos area to confirm the Johnsons' tale.

The Johnsons told Suber that Ronnie had acquired "psychic powers" as a result of his original UFO encounter. Beyond predicting that the UFO would return a second time, "just days after the second sighting, Ronnie begged his other sister-in-law not to drive to Salina. She did anyway and was involved in an accident." Although in the youth's original report of his first UFO sighting he had not gotten closer than 50–75 feet from the hovering UFO, in the wake of the claims of the two men from Pascagoula that they had been taken aboard their UFO for physical examination, Mr. Johnson suggested that Ronnie might also have had a similar experience. Suber quoted him as saying: "The scientists who were here believe he [Ronnie] was examined by whoever was on the thing [UFO]."

Suber wrote that the Johnsons told him that the brief UFO visit in 1971 seemed to have made two-thirds of their prize-winning sows barren, but had just the opposite effect on their young sheep. Ronnie explained that "his ewes were just ready to lamb when the UFO came," Suber wrote. "Just six months and 50 pounds later, the new lambs [themselves] gave birth to tiny lambs, none of which lived. The six-month-old lambs had not been bred," according to Ronnie. Mr. Johnson reported that neither one of his two wrist watches would operate for more than two days and that a Salina jeweler could find nothing wrong with them. None of these mysterious after-effects were reported to me when I visited the Johnsons a year after the original UFO incident, nor have I read of them in the reports of other visiting UFOlogists.

Finally, the Salina newspaper said that Ronnie reported having an en-counter with "the wolf girl," said to be a creature about three feet tall with wild, blond hair, wearing a torn red dress, that reportedly had been sighted by others in the Delphos area. Ronnie was quoted as saying: "When it ran, it got down on all fours and ran away faster than anything human can run." The Salina article concluded: "Ronnie cannot say if the UFO and the creature are related. But he does say the UFO is coming back." I received the Salina newspaper article from Ralph Enlow in early 1975, after he had retired from the sheriff's office. He wrote that the new sheriff had solicited his ideas for handling the "wolf girl" reports and Enlow said he suggested the use of a lie-detector [polygraph] test. Enlow added that Ronnie and others had declined to take such a test and "there have been no further [wolf girl] reports."

In 1975, Dr. Jacques Vallee, long-time UFOlogist and friend of Hynek, published his third book on the subject—*The Invisible College* (E. P. Dutton). Vallee disclosed that he had obtained a sample of the white crystalline material from the UFO ring, which he sent to a biological laboratory in France (where Vallee was born and raised.) This laboratory, Vallee revealed, finally had managed to identify the whitish material as "vegetal in nature . . . an organism of the order of the Actinomycetales, which is an intermediate organism between bacteria and fungus . . . . It is often found together with a fungus of the order of the Bacidiomycepes, which may fluoresce under certain conditions. *This fungus can cause a cir-cular pattern to be visible on the surface of the ground.*" [Emphasis added.]

This substantiated my earlier published conclusion that "the irregular horseshoe-shaped ring had been there prior to November 2, 1971, when the UFO was alleged to have come." But Vallee concluded that the French laboratory analysis served to "destroy the 'explanation' of the case put forth by Philip Klass in his book *UFOs Explained*, where he claimed the substance was produced by the urine of sheep feeding from a circular device." (I had offered this only as "one possible explanation.") Despite the prosaic ex-planation for the ring of whitish material, Vallee still did not consider the possibility that the incident might be a hoax. Instead he admits to being puzzled only by "the coincidence of this fungus ring with the observation made by the Johnsons." In other words, Vallee is puzzled by the coincidence of why a visiting UFO would choose to hover over an existing fungus ring!

At the 1981 MUFON symposium, held in Cambridge, Massachusetts, Phillips presented a paper on "physical-trace" cases, where the UFO seemingly leaves behind physical evidence of its presence, on which he is considered an international authority. In addition to presenting summary data on such incidents, Phillips offered an updated report on the Delphos case, including portions of an interview with Mrs. Johnson when he returned to Delphos on April 15, 1978 — his fifth visit. Phillips described the results of a number of different laboratory analyses of the whitish material. Among those who were willing to express an opinion, the prevalent view was that the material was a fungus. Phillips acknowledged that the reported glow could have resulted from the full moon at the time that others witnessed the ring, whose illumination would have been reflected from the whitish material, as I had earlier suggested.

Phillips briefly mentioned the fallen tree, which would have been in the flight path of the alleged UFO and included a sketch showing the UFO striking the tree as it departed in a southerly direction. *But he did not mention the absence of impact marks on the tree or the fact that it was lying in an east-west direction.* Phillips also reported that the Polaroid camera used by Mrs. Johnson to take the photo showing the "glowing" ring on the night of the incident had a separate flash attachment that "must be attached to the camera and the cord plugged into the camera," and he quoted Mrs. Johnson as having "stated that the flash was not on the camera at the time the photograph was taken."

But Phillips did not explain why these seemingly mundane details were important. They indicated that Mrs. Johnson was not telling the truth. Phillips had been much more candid five years earlier, on April 11, 1976, when he discussed the Delphos case during a talk before the UFO Study Group of Greater St. Louis. David Schroth, who was in the audience, tape-recorded the talk and later supplied me with a partial transcript.

In St. Louis, Phillips said: "We do have a photograph taken on the night of the observation by the Johnsons, of what they claim is the glowing ring. But the problem there is that Mrs. Johnson swears she didn't use a flash, and it's obvious from the picture [that] she did use a flash." Phillips is himself a professional photographer and thus understood the point raised by Sheaffer about the light intensity from a nearby stick in the photo as quoted in my book. Phillips admitted in his St. Louis talk that "I've always held this case in very high esteem . . . because we've done so much work on it. And boy, if it turns out to have a natural explanation, I'll never sleep again."

The Phillips MUFON paper, as later published in the Conference Proceedings, concluded with what he calls "Statements Pertaining to the Credibility of the Johnson Family," offered by four Delphos residents who had become involved in the case. All of them, including Sheriff Ralph Enlow (now deceased) spoke well of the Johnson family, as did Enlow and others with whom I talked during my visit in 1973. I have no doubt that they are basically good and honest people. Yet there is evidence that sometimes they, like other fundamentally honest people, can shade the truth. After Sheriff Enlow had read my analysis of the case, he wrote me on January 22, 1975, to say that "your conclusions bear out my suspicions."

When the *National Enquirer* announced that the Delphos incident had been selected for its first outstanding-UFO-award of $5000, the tabloid quoted Dr. Hynek as saying: "The Panel chose the Johnson case because of the great number of individual items of 'strangeness' involved which remain unexplained even after a long series of chemical, optical, electronic and other physical tests carried out by eleven university and private laboratories." The article concluded: "Dr. Hynek emphasized that the panel carefully investigated the possibility of a hoax but are [sic] completely satisfied that the sighting was real."

16

Army Helicopter Encounter: 1

The Army helicopter UFO incident that occurred shortly after 11:00 P.M. on the night of October 18, 1973, near Mansfield, Ohio, at the time of a major "UFO flap" in the U.S., has become a classic case. If all of the seemingly mysterious events reported by the helicopter crew actually were caused by the unknown object, then the incident would defy explanation in earthly or prosaic terms. Nor is there any reason to suspect that the incident might be a contrived hoax. But there are numerous uncertainties over what actually happened during the brief, frightening encounter. Thus it is useful to examine the first public report on the incident, which appeared in a Cleveland newspaper, *The Plain Dealer,* on October 21, less than three days after the encounter. It was written by newspaper reporter John P. Coyne, who mentioned in his story that he was a second cousin to the helicopter pilot.*

> A crew of four aboard an Army helicopter enroute to Cleveland narrowly missed a midair collision with an object described as "unlike anything produced on earth," it was revealed yesterday. Military and federal aviation officials are puzzled over the incident.
>
> The occurrence involving experienced aviators, comes in the midst of a growing number of reports in recent weeks of unidentified flying objects [many of which were in Ohio]. An Army captain and three reservists aboard a Huey [Bell UH-1H] helicopter said the unusual event happened Thursday night as they were returning from a flight to Columbus, where they had gone for physicals.
>
> Capt. Lawrence J. Coyne, 36, who told the story to Federal Aviation Administration officials, is commander of the 316th Medivac unit based at

---

*Important details in the following and other early accounts which would later become contentious or crucial are italicized. This does not represent italics in the original.

135

Cleveland Hopkins International Airport. He said his craft was flying at 2,500 feet [above sea level] *about 10 miles east of Mansfield* when the crew chief, Spec. 5 Robert J. Yanacsek, 23, reported a red light about five miles to the east. At first, the crew thought it was a radio beacon. [There are several tall radio-TV towers with red warning lights to the east.]

Seconds later, Yanacsek yelled, "The light is moving. It's coming at us. It's on a collision course." Coyne, a verteran of 19 years of military flying, grabbed the controls from his copilot, Lt. Arriggo D. Jezzi, 26, of Sandusky. "It looked like a fighter plane coming straight for us," Coyne said. "I took immediate evasive action. I cut the power and dropped into a shallow dive. We dropped through 2,000 feet, and it was headed right for us. We braced for impact."

Coyne said when the helpcopter reached *1,500 feet,* the approaching craft [UFO] *appeared to stop momentarily about 500 feet above the helicopter* and banked to one side. "We never saw anything like it before," Coyne said. "It was unreal. It was unlike anything produced on earth—a cigar-shaped craft with a glowing steady red light on its leading edge. A hull was at the very top of it and a green light emitted from the rear of the craft filled our cabin with a green glow. It was eerie."

Coyne said the strange craft *hovered over the helicopter only a few seconds.* He glanced at the altimeter and noticed the helicopter had risen from *1,500 feet to 3,000 feet* "although none of the crew members felt the gravitational pull normally felt when a helicopter rises. We felt a bounce and then the other craft took off to the northeast,"* Coyne said. *Seconds later the craft disappeared.*

The helicopter crew, by now fearful, tried to radio Mansfield Airport, but got no response. *The unusual communications blackout lasted about 10 minutes* until they finally got through to Akron-Canton Airport. The story told to [by?] Coyne was verified by the other members of the four-man crew. Each of the men described the incident as unlike any experience he has had. Coyne, who previously had steadfastly believed that all UFO sightings could be explained, found no rational explanation for this sighting . . . .

Pilot Coyne's next public recounting of the incident occurred shortly afterward, on November 2, when he was a guest on ABC-TV's "Dick Cavett Show." Coyne said:

> In the vicinity of Mansfield, Ohio, my crew chief observed a light on the east horizon. By the way visibility was 15 miles on that night and the sky was clear. There was a normal amount of [air] traffic. And he notified me of a bright red light on the horizon. I told him to keep an eye . . . on it, check it out, and he stated that it looked like an obstruction light on top of a radio tower.
>
> *About a minute later* he said that the red light was pacing us, paralleling us at our speed. Our altitude was 2,500 feet and we were on a heading of 030

---

*This is believed to be an error either by reporter Coyne or by pilot Coyne, who in subsequent accounts reported that the UFO flew off to the northwest.

[NNE]. Our airspeed was 90 knots . . . . *About a moment later* he said the light was converging on us on a collision course. I looked to my right through the right window and I observed the light coming at a very fast speed, in excess of 600 knots.

Now in Mansfield you've got a National Guard F-100 fighter base there and we had Mansfield tower on frequency. I contacted Mansfield tower. They acknowledged our identification and [I] requested to know whether they had any aircraft in the vicinity that night, flying in excess of 600 knots, which below that altitude is a "no-no." There was no acknowledgement of our transmission. I immediately put the collective [pitch control] down and got the helicopter to descend. And the aircraft wasn't moving fast enough to get out of the way, so I put the aircraft in about a 20-degree angle of dive to get out of the way [using the cyclic pitch control]. And by then— *it was a matter of 10 seconds*—the light was upon us. I could see it coming. It looked like a torpedo coming at us.

The flight medic [Sergeant John Healey], the crew chief and I, all three of us, observed it closing, converging from the east directly toward the ship [helicopter]. So we left 2,500 feet, we passed through 2,000 [feet] and we're around *1,700 feet,* and it was still coming at us, so we braced for impact. Nothing happened. We looked up and there was this object, *right over us, stopped.* The best way I can describe the object is it was approximately 50 to 60 feet long, was about as big as our aircraft. The leading edge of the craft was a bright red light. The trailing edge of the craft had a green light, and you could delineate where the light stopped and the grey metallic structure—you could see because there were reflections of the red and the green off the structure itself. It—the trailing light on the aft end of the craft [UFO] swung about 90 degrees and came on the helicopter, because it came *on the upper Plexiglass and flooded the cockpit with a green light* . . . the instrument lights, the red lights that are utilized for night flying were just blurred out with green. Everything was green in the cockpit for about a couple of seconds.

And this only existed *for two or three seconds* because we all saw the craft *hovering over us.* But it moved out of my field of vision and the copilot and flight medic [sitting on the left side] still had visual contact with the craft. I, *immediately,* handling the controls of our aircraft, looked back at our altimeter. *We were at 3,500 feet* climbing at 1,000 feet per minute. No power. We were supposed to be going down [descending] but we were going up.

When Cavett asked if the helicopter was "being sucked, drawn, or magnetized, or what?" Coyne replied: "I really don't know. It was *just a matter of seconds.* We were [had been] at 1,700 feet and then we were at 3,500 feet climbing a thousand feet per minute with no power, I mean the collective [pitch control] was down and I was in a shallow dive. At this time the craft [UFO] continued west. The copilot and flight medic observed its departure. It slowly accelerated. It continued on a westerly heading, cleared the Mansfield airport and turned to a northwest heading. And the flight medic stated that the green light was then [had turned] white, and on the northwest heading it did another 45 [degree] up and off the earth."

When Cavett asked if Coyne had been able to photograph the object, he replied: *"There wasn't any time."* When Cavett then asked, "All this happened in how long?" Coyne replied, *"in about a minute's time."* Later, Coyne said:

> . . . as close as it [UFO] passed to us, there was no turbulence, no vortex. There was no engine sound. We felt the G-forces [gravity] as we began descending, but we had no feeling of our climbing a thousand feet a minute until I observed the altimeter . . . . Another thing is that radio contact—*there was no radio contact established until five or six minutes later.* I had the co-pilot changing the [radio] frequencies, calling Mansfield tower, Mansfield radio, Cleveland radio, Columbus radio. We were going through the radio panel quite fast [changing frequencies]. And when you change frequencies you do hear the channeling tone and the radio was functioning, except that when you keyed the mike there was no keying sound, even though we transmitted.

When Cavett asked, "That equipment was out of commission then?" Coyne replied, "No, the equipment was functioning, but we just couldn't transmit or receive. We finally got ahold [sic] of Akron-Canton approach [control] about *six to seven minutes later* but the keying sound was back again." When Cavett asked if Coyne could offer any explanation for this extended radio blackout following the UFO incident, the pilot replied: "No, no explanation." Coyne said that when he finally reached Cleveland that night, he had "related my story to the [Federal Aviation Administration] flight service station." He said he also had checked with the Cleveland radar operators to see if they had spotted the UFO but was told that the helicopter had been flying too low at its distance from Cleveland for it, or the UFO, to have been seen on the Cleveland radar.

My own interest in the case was sparked when a member of the helicopter crew, John Healey, and I, among others, met in New York City on November 1, 1973, to tape a TV program on UFOs for David Susskind. The following night I watched Coyne on the Cavett show and this further sparked my interest. On November 5, I called Lawrence Jenkins, a watch supervisor in the Cleveland tower, to ask if the FAA had any report on the incident. Jenkins read to me, and I tape-recorded for accuracy, a report that had been written by another watch supervisor, Emil Emery, during the early morning hours of October 19, recounting information supplied by pilot Coyne shortly after he had landed in Cleveland.

Emery's report read as follows:

> Last evening the pilot of an Army copter based on the west side [of the Cleveland airport] called after landing to express his thanks for expeditious handling. He sounded emotionally shaken, unsure of what report he would make on what occurred on a flight near Mansfield. He indicated he would call the Flight Standards district office in the morning. At 03:25 [Greenwich Mean

Time/11:25 P.M. EDT], Akron-Canton approach control affected a radar hand-off with Army copter 15444. His position seven miles southwest of Sharon at 2500 [feet] MSL [mean sea level]. On initial contact, the pilot advised *low fuel,* wanted to land as soon as possible. The aircraft was cleared direct to the [Cleveland] airport. Approximately 04:15 [GMT], I received a phone call from Capt. Coyne, the pilot of the aircraft, thanking us for the [special] handling and to relate *a strange event which resulted in his critical fuel situation.* He said that *he was over the NDB* [airways nav-aid] at Mansfield, *planning to land at Mansfield for fuel,* at 22:30 EDT, altitude 2500 MSL.

An aircraft [UFO] with a strange red light at the nose, or front, was approaching at high speed. *He quickly put his copter in auto-rotation* to avoid collision. Total crew on the copter was four. All saw the strange craft in good visibility as the craft passed at about 500 feet. It was described as being as big as the copter, but circular or round shape. Absolutely no wings and made no sound at all. No internal lighting. No rotation [anti-collision] beacon. No white tail light. Just a soft red light in front and a green light in the rear. The craft had no windows. Its speed was estimated at 600 knots and was approximately at the same altitude [as the helicopter]. The pilot stated that *he was so frightened* that he just wanted to leave the area immediately and head for Cleveland *without refueling* [at Mansfield airport].

It is understandable that Coyne originally planned to land at the Mansfield airport prior to the UFO encounter to refuel, because as copilot Jezzi later recalled, the low-fuel warning light came on before they reached Cleveland and when they touched down there was less than ten minutes worth of fuel remaining. It is surprising that Coyne did not remember to refuel during the layover in Columbus. The UH-1H can carry enough fuel for roughly 3½ hours of flight, and the flight from Cleveland would have consumed nearly half of a full tank of fuel. What is also surprising is that Coyne attempted to blame his critical fuel situation on the UFO encounter, according to Emery's report. During the time that Coyne was descending to avoid a possible midair collision, the helicopter would have been consuming *less* fuel than under normal, level-flight conditions. And if the helicopter's subsequent seemingly mysterious climb was due to some strange suction force exerted by the UFO, and if the helicopter controls were still set for auto-rotation as Coyne recalled, fuel consumption also would have been *less* than for a normal, uneventful flight. Thus the helicopter should have consumed *less,* not more, fuel because of the UFO incident.

Coyne and his crew submitted an official report on the incident to his commanding officer in Columbus on November 23, 1973, barely a month after the encounter. Key portions of this report are as follows:

The reported incident happened as follows: Army helicopter 68-15444 was returning from Columbus, Ohio, to Cleveland, Ohio, and at 2305 hours [11:05 P.M.] east, southeast of Mansfield Airport in the vicinity of Mansfield, Ohio, while flying at an altitude of 2500 feet and on a heading of 030 degrees, SSG

Yanacsek observed a red light on the east horizon, 90 degrees to the flight path of the helicopter. *Approximately 30 seconds later,* SSG Yanacsek indicated the object was converging on a midair collision heading. Cpt. Coyne observed the converging object, took over the controls of the aircraft and initiated a power descent from 2500 feet to 1700 feet to avoid impact with the object. A radio call was initiated to Mansfield Tower who acknowledged the helicopter and was asked by Cpt. Coyne if there were any high performance aircraft flying in the vicinity of the Mansfield Airport, however there was no response received from the tower. The crew expected impact from the object instead, the object was observed to *hesitate momentarily over the helicopter* and then slowly continued on a westerly course accelerating at a high rate of speed, clear west of Mansfield Airport, then turn 45 degree heading to the northwest. Cpt. Coyne indicated the altimeter read a 1000 fpm. [feet per minute] climb and read 3500 feet with the [helicopter] *collective [control] in the full down position.* The aircraft was returned to 2500 feet by Cpt. Coyne and flown back to Cleveland, Ohio. The flight plan was closed and the FAA Flight Service Station notified of the incident. The FSS told Cpt. Coyne to report the incident to the FAA GADO office at Cleveland Hopkins Airport . . . .

It is interesting to note that Coyne did not mention the low-fuel situation, nor was there any mention of a blackout of radio communications following the UFO encounter. The official report, concluded with a statement that it had been "read and attested to by the crew-members" and was signed by each of them. This official report was considerably more restrained than Coyne's account to *The Plain Dealer* and on the "Dick Cavett Show."

If the recollections of Coyne and his crew were accurate and if the helicopter's change from a steep descent to a climb and the seeming blackout of radio communications were caused by the high-speed object that passed overhead, it would be impossible to explain this UFO in prosaic terms. The only plausible explanation would be that it was a craft from a distant world with technology far more advanced than our own.

But my long experience in investigating UFO incidents—like that of Allan Hendry—has demonstrated that seemingly mysterious side-effects often are unrelated to the UFO, even though they seem to be UFO-induced in the excitement of the moment. Experiments conducted by psychologists who specialize in human perception have shown that persons who observe brief, unexpected events later can be grossly inaccurate in describing what occurred, especially when the observer is under stress. Certainly Coyne and his crew, fearing a midair collision with an unknown high-speed object, were in a high-stress situation.

Psychologist Robert Buckhout, author of an article published in December 1974 in *Scientific American* entitled "Eyewitness Testimony," offered the following commentary: "An observer is less capable of remembering details . . . when under stress . . . . Research I have done with Air Force flight crew members confirms that even highly trained people become poorer observers under stress . . . . *Time estimates are particularly exaggerated.*" [Emphasis added.]

On the night of November 26, 1975, a senior American Airlines pilot, Captain Guy Ely, suddenly found himself in a stressful situation, facing the prospect of a midair collision with a TWA jetliner because of an error by an FAA traffic controller. When the potential conflict was discovered, Captain Ely received a cryptic radio message instructing him to descend immediately—a message that instantly conveyed that there was danger of a midair collision. During the next thirty seconds the stress-level for this airline flight crew was comparable to that experienced by Coyne and his crew as they watched the UFO approach. The airline incident was investigated by the National Transportation Safety Board and included testimony by Captain Ely, a pilot with more than 21,000 hours flight time acquired over a quarter of a century. In the NTSB's subsequent report on the incident it noted that this experienced pilot *"can not remember the exact sequence of his observations and actions during the short time in which the traffic conflict materialized and was avoided."* [Emphasis added.] If this senior airline captain, far more experienced than Coyne, admitted he was unable to recall precisely what occurred, and the sequence of events, during this high-stress situation, certainly Coyne could be expected to have similar difficulties.

One indication that Coyne had differing recollections of what had transpired during his own high-stress encounter emerged during my three telephone interviews with him on January 3, 1974, on January 15, and on January 23. During our first conversation I asked Coyne how long a time had elapsed from the moment he recalled looking at his altimeter and noting he was at 1700 feet as the helicopter descended, until he again looked and saw that the altitude was 3500 feet and increasing. Coyne replied: "I would guestimate, oh, I don't know. I'd say a matter of seconds." But three weeks later, on January 23, when I posed the same question, Coyne replied: "Oh, I wouldn't know. It is pretty hard to guess. I'd be guessing now by this time, but I would say maybe thirty seconds, maybe thirty to forty seconds."

During our first interview, when Coyne recounted the incident, his report closely followed the versions reported earlier. He said that when he noticed the altimeter was reading 3500 feet, "the first thing I did was pull the collective [control] back up again, and then push it down, and then pull the cyclic [control] aft to reduce my speed." Later, when I transcribed the tape recording of our conversation, I puzzled over Coyne's statement, because pulling back on the collective was precisely *the opposite of what an experienced pilot should have done to halt the climb and level off.* It was as if an experienced driver seeking to avoid a stalled car on the right-hand lane were to turn right instead of turning left.

I raised this question again when we talked on January 23 by asking what he had done when he noticed the helicopter was at 3500 feet and climbing. Coyne replied: "I pulled the collective up." Then, recognizing the incongruity of his statement under the circumstances, Coyne added: "The collective was in the bottom position," that is, for an auto-rotation descent. When I replied that his action seemed strange because pulling back on the collective would "cause you to climb more," Coyne responded: "Right. But I noticed we were climbing with a bottomed collective and I wanted to see if I could stop the climb so I pulled the collective up." Coyne said that then there was "a slight bump . . . . Then I pushed the collective down and we started to descend."

If some mysterious suction force generated by the UFO was responsible for the helicopter's change from a dive to a climb, *the curious thing is that this mysterious suction force disappeared as soon as Coyne discovered his helicopter was climbing and took steps to level off.* Coyne never claimed that he had to fight a mysterious force. It seems strange that the UFO would know to turn off its suction force at the very moment that Coyne first attempted corrective measures.

A more prosaic explanation emerged after I discussed the incident with several helicopter pilots. One was Dave Brown, then Washington Bureau Chief for *Aviation Week and Space Technology* magazine. Another was a representative of Bell Helicopter Corporation, which produces the UH-1H, Dan Tisdale, a former Marine Corps helicopter pilot with 3000 flight hours in copters. Brown suggested that Coyne might unconsciously have pulled back on the collective control, perhaps as he leaned back in his seat to view the UFO passing overhead, knowing that the midair collision threat had passed. Tisdale agreed that this seemed a likely possibility.

When I examined an aeronautical chart for the Mansfield area and converted Coyne's reported altitudes from their mean-sea-level reference to actual helicopter height above the terrain below, the results were quite revealing. Nearby Mansfield airport is nearly 1300 feet above sea level. Thus, when the helicopter altimeter showed 1700 feet, the helicopter was *only approximately 400 feet above the ground* and was, by Coyne's account, descending at 2000 feet per minute. Having escaped a midair collision, *the helicopter would crash into the ground below within 12 seconds unless Coyne quickly pulled back on the collective control.* It was a clear night so Coyne and Jezzi could see the terrain below coming closer — fast. (During my first interview with Coyne he had volunteered that the helicopter had come "awful close to the ground.") *There would be no purpose, no need, for Coyne to look at his altimeter at that instant, for it could tell him nothing about his terrain clearance, which now was the critical parameter.* A brief look out the windshield would tell him all he needed to know: Pull back the collective before you crash! Only much later, after the helicopter had safely climbed out of danger, would there be any reason for Coyne to look at his altimeter to see whether he had climbed back to his original cruise altitude. At that point, still in a state of shock, Coyne could be forgiven if he had forgotten that he earlier had pulled back on the collective.

The basic issue then is whether Coyne behaved instinctively as an experienced pilot should and pulled his helicopter out of its perilous dive. Or was Coyne so mesmerized that he was oblivious to the impending crash into the ground within a few seconds and the crew was saved by a "kindly UFO" that somehow knew that Coyne was being derelict in his responsibilities, and so the UFO turned on a "suction force" to save the crew from disaster. I prefer to believe that Coyne behaved properly as one would expect an experienced pilot to do, and that he can be faulted only for fuzzy recollections of what occurred in precisely what sequence during those brief moments of extreme stress. Most UFO proponents prefer the alternative explanation.

If the helicopter's climb was caused by some mysterious suction force exerted by the UFO, which would have been pulling the aircraft upward while its rotor blades were angled to provide a descent, this would have caused severe strains in the rotor blades. For this reason I asked Coyne if his helicopter later had been examined for possible damage. Coyne told me: "We had the mechanics go over it with a fine-tooth comb," adding that they "checked the structure, the blades, everything . . . I had five mechanics check it. And I had an FAA-certified airframe and engine inspetor check it, using a magnifying type [Magnaflux] device, looking for any structural damage. *There was none."* The fact that there was no structural damage offers convincing evidence that Coyne's helicopter had been operated entirely within normal, expected conditions.

A prosaic explanation for the radio communications "blackout" emerged after I made a few distance measurements on the aeronautical chart for the Ohio area and made a few calculations. The reason that radio contact with Cleveland, Columbus, and the Akron-Canton airports could not be established immediately after the so-called UFO encounter was that the helicopter was too distant and at too low an altitude for its signal to be received, which Coyne would have recognized under less stressful conditions. To confirm this explanation, I asked Coyne to conduct an experiment on his next flight to Columbus. I suggested that in the vicinity of Mansfield he fly at an altitude of around 2500 feet MSL and that he try to make radio contact with the airports at Cleveland, Columbus, and Akron-Canton. When we talked next on January 23, I asked how the experiment had gone. Coyne told me that he had *not* been able to reach any of the three airports, which confirmed my hypothesis.

This, however, did not explain why the helicopter had been unable to make contact with the nearby Mansfield airport following the incident. After determining that the UH-1H was equipped with a Model 807A radio transceiver, built by Wilcox Electric Co., I talked to one of its engineers — Robert Piper — to learn more about the radio's characteristics and limitations. I learned that the radio was a relatively old design that could require up to five seconds to retune from one frequency to another. I recalled Coyne's statement on the "Dick Cavett Show" that the copilot had been "changing frequencies . . . going through the radio panel quite fast." In those anxious moments, perhaps he had not waited the full interval required for the radio to retune. Another possible explanation is that the Mansfield tower has only one controller on duty after 11:00 P.M. If the helicopter called while the controller was talking to another aircraft, he would not reply, expecting Jezzi to call back a few moments later, by which time the copilot was trying to call one of the other three airports, far beyond line-of-sight communications range.

Still another possible explanation is that because the crew was not accustomed to landing at Mansfield, they might not have selected the correct frequency. (Many months later, under much more relaxed conditions when Coyne was being interviewed by a UFO investigator, he had great difficulty remembering the Mansfield-tower frequency.) However, this hypothesis is at variance with Coyne's early statements that immediately after he grabbed the controls from Jezzi and put the helicopter into a steep descent to avoid a midair collision, Coyne says he called the Mansfield tower to ask if the UFO might be an Air National Guard jet fighter based at that airport. Coyne claimed that Mansfield briefly acknowledged his first call, but when he asked about other traffic, he got no reply. If Coyne's recollections are correct, this would indicate that the crew had selected the correct Mansfield frequency. But several days later, when Coyne called the Mansfield tower and they checked the tape recordings that are made of all incoming/outgoing radio calls, *they could find no record of even the first Coyne call on the night of the UFO encounter.* It also strikes me as odd that during the brief interval when Coyne was maneuvering his helicopter while keeping an eye on the fast-approaching object, that he would even bother to call the airport to ask if the object was one of their aircraft. Coyne's recollections on this point also seem to be flawed, suggesting that the call was made *after* the UFO had passed overhead and there was no acknowledgement.

While the foregoing indicates that the mysterious side-effects were not related to the UFO, it sheds no light on what the object might have been. But this does open the door to consideration of a prosaic explanation for the UFO itself. From Coyne's description and one supplied by flight medic Healey during a long interview in New York, it occurred to me that the object might have been a meteor-fireball. As noted earlier, in 1969 experienced flight crews aboard two jetliners and an Air National Guard jet fighter, *in a broad daylight incident,* had mistaken a glowing fireball and its flaming fragments, with their long luminous tails, for a squadron of UFOs that had seemed close enough to pose a collision threat to the aircraft. Yet in reality, the flaming meteors were more than one hundred miles away. Even Dr. Hynek, in an article published in the December 1967 issue of *Playboy,* acknowledged: "Pilots have been known to swerve their planes violently when they suddenly encounter a very bright meteor they think is on a collision course, but which later proves to have been 50 to 100 miles away."

If the UFO was a fireball, this would explain several curious aspects of the incident. As the fireball passed overhead, its intensely bright light would stream through the green-tinted windows over the pilot's and copilot's heads [See Plates 7 and 8], flooding the cabin with green light — exactly as the crew had reported. And this illumination could persist for several seconds because of a fireball's long luminous tail, which can extend for hundreds of yards, even miles. Later, when the crew tried to reconstruct what had occurred, they would recall the several seconds during which the cabin had been flooded with green light. This could prompt them *to deduce* that the UFO must have halted briefly in its high-speed flight to hover overhead. When the fireball moved on to the west, where it would be seen through clear white side windows, the long luminous tail would appear white, exactly as the crew had reported.

Prior to my first conversation with Coyne, I had called Dr. David D. Meisel, director of the American Meteor Society, which collects meteor-sighting reports, to ask if he had received any from central Ohio for the night of October 18. Meisel said he had not, but expressed interest in learning more about the Mansfield incident that had occurred during the peak of the Orionids meteor shower, which he said produces a lot of fireballs. Meisel told me that the Orionids meteors come out of the east, which matched the direction of the Mansfield UFO. When he asked me at what time the incident occurred, I replied that it was around 11:05 P.M. By a not-so-curious coincidence, the Orionids shower typically begins around 11:00 P.M.

During my first conversation with Coyne, I had described the "UFO squadron" incident near St. Louis in 1969, explaining that the objects had proved to be a fireball and flaming fragments. Then I informed Coyne of the information obtained from Meisel, indicating that the direction and timing of his "UFO" could have been a fireball from the Orionids meteor shower that was under way at the time of the incident. Coyne responded: "Well, that would sound like a logical explanation." I said that I was not attempting "to deprive you of your sighting," and Coyne responded: "No, it sounds good." At that point I did not pursue the full implications: that if the object was a fireball, then Coyne's recollections, widely reported in the news and on television, must necessarily be flawed. Less than three weeks later, Coyne would discover for himself that the seemingly mysterious radio blackout had a prosaic explanation.

During our third conversation on January 23, Coyne told me that he had received a call from Dr. Hynek, who would visit him the next day for a first-hand investigation, because the incident was under consideration for the *National Enquirer*'s best-case award. I decided it would be interesting to compare my findings with those of the man who is so often hailed as one of the world's leading UFO experts.

At the time, I was almost finished writing *UFOs Explained,* but decided to include a chapter on the Mansfield incident. Before the book went to press in late spring, the Coyne/Mansfield case had been selected as the best of 1973 and the four-man crew had been awarded a $5000 prize. My chapter on the case concluded: "Now that the Mansfield incident has been selected as the best UFO case of 1973 by the *National Enquirer's* panel of experts, and the four-man crew is $5000 richer as well as being internationally famous UFO celebrities, it will not be easy for them to accept the explanation that the UFO was merely a bright fireball, that the seemingly mysterious behavior of the helicopter was due to the unconscious, instinctive reactions of well-trained pilots, and that the seemingly curious behavior of the radio was due to quite normal causes." This would prove to be prophetic, as we shall see in the following chapter.

17

Army Helicopter Encounter: 2

In the spring of 1976—roughly a year after publication of my prosaic explanations for the Mansfield/Coyne helicopter incident—Dr. Hynek decided that the incident needed a more thorough investigation. Mrs. Jennie Zeidman, of Columbus, Ohio, was asked to conduct the new investigation. She and Hynek had worked together on UFO matters in the early 1950s when Hynek was a faculty member at Ohio State University and Zeidman had been a research assistant in the astronomy department. The results of Zeidman's investigation, which sharply challenged my conclusions and confirmed Hynek's original findings, were published by CUFOS in a 122-page report in the spring of 1979.

The Ziedman/CUFOS report contains portions of a verbatim transcript of a tape-recorded interview with Coyne by Hynek on January 24, 1974, in which Coyne described radio-communication difficulties experienced on the night of the UFO incident. Although this interview occurred less than twenty-four hours after Coyne had told me of the results of the experiment he had conducted at my suggestion, which confirmed my hypothesis that the reason radio contact could not be made with the three Ohio airports was that the helicopter was too far away and too low in altitude, there is no indication that Coyne even mentioned the experiment to Hynek. If Coyne ever discussed these experiments with Zeidman during her six subsequent interviews with him, there is no evidence of it in the tape transcripts she chose to include in her CUFOS report.

Instead, Coyne focused on alleged communications difficulties in reaching the nearby Mansfield tower as the UFO approached, rather than the post-encounter "blackout" Coyne had stressed in the original *Plain Dealer* interview, on the "Dick Cavett Show," and in earlier conversations with me. Coyne claimed that the Mansfield tower had acknowledged his first radio call as the UFO approached but not subsequent transmissions.

But he admitted that when Mansfield controllers, at Coyne's request, played back tape recordings of *all* incoming and outgoing radio communications during the night of the UFO incident, *they could find no recording of Coyne's two calls or any acknowledgement by the tower, indicating that Coyne's recollections of this part of the incident were in error.* When Zeidman interviewed copilot Jezzi, he indicated that he was not convinced that the radio-communications problems were related to the UFO, and he noted that radio outages were not uncommon because of poor-equipment maintenance.

During Zeidman's 1976 inverview with Coyne, he casually mentioned that the helicopter's magnetic compass had begun to spin erratically as the UFO approached, *something he had never before mentioned, even in his official Army Reserve report.* Further, Coyne claimed, *the compass had continued to spin even the following day.* He said it had been replaced, but so far as the transcript shows Coyne never thought to ask for a follow-up report on what strange malady had been induced in the compass by the UFO. Zeidman speculates that the compass malfunction might have been caused by a strong pulsating magnetic field emitted by the UFO. But she acknowledges that another, separate magnetic sensor for the helicopter's gyrocompass showed no evidence of UFO-induced damage.

When Zeidman later interviewed Jezzi, he told her that the "mag compass never worked" properly *prior to the UFO incident,* a statement that Coyne later challenged. Jezzi added that when a new compass was installed, *it too behaved erratically,* which Coyne confirmed. The problem finally was traced to a faulty installation, Coyne told Zeidman, but he did not elaborate. If Coyne originally believed that the erratic magnetic-compass behavior was induced by the UFO, it seems strange that he did not mention it on five previous occasions: when interviewed the next day by his cousin for *The Plain Dealer* article, on the "Dick Cavett Show," during any of my conversations with him, during the original Hynek interview, or in his official report. Not until more than two years later—*after* my own prosaic explanation had been advanced—did Coyne remember to bring up the compass troubles. If the compass malfunction was attributed to the UFO, this would seem to rule out my hypothesis that the glowing object was a meteor-fireball.

Transcripts of tape-recorded interviews with Coyne in the CUFOS/Zeidman report also reveal ambiguities in his recollection of the position of the collective pitch control during the helicopter's descent. During Coyne's January 24, 1974, interview with Hynek, he said that the helicopter was "in autorotation, a controlled autorotation." This would confirm Coyne's initial recollection that he had pushed the collective control *all the way forward/down.* In this extreme position, the engine is declutched from the rotor blades, which continue to rotate due to airflow. Yet during Coyne's 1976 interview with Zeidman, he offered conflicting statements. At

PLATE 1: Nearly one out of every five UFO reports submitted to the Center for UFO Studies proved to have been generated by an advertising aircraft, such as the one shown, with strings of lights that spell out a messsage to people almost directly beneath. But to observers at a distance, such craft are easily mistaken for a glowing UFO that can suddenly disappear when the lights are turned off. (See Chapter 9.)

PLATE 2: In early January 1975, many people living in New Jersey reported seeing a glowing UFO flying low over the Hudson River near New York City. This UFO was a small, twin-engine aircraft, equipped with a floodlight to illuminate its tail, manufactured by Devore Aviation, that was being photographed against a Manhattan backdrop from another aircraft for sales-promotion purposes.

PLATE 3: Giant balloons that carry scientific experiments to extremely high altitudes, as well as ordinary weather balloons, generate a number of UFO reports. The balloon shown, several hundred feet in diameter at an altitude of 95,000 ft., reflects sunlight after the sun has set and surface observers are in darkness.

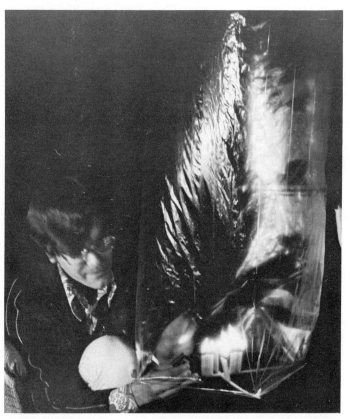

PLATE 4: Hot-air balloons, often constructed by ingenious teen-agers as a hoax, are among the most difficult UFO reports to explain. Some even are outfitted with battery-operated flashing lights, or flares that burn free and fall to earth.

PLATE 5: Passengers on this Scandinavian Airlines System jetliner saw a glowing UFO (arrow) that seemed to be following the aircraft until it mysteriously disappeared. This "UFO" was a Sub-sun, a reflection of the sun off a very thin layer of ice crystals. When the aircraft flew beyond this meteorological condition, the glowing light naturally disappeared.

PLATE 6: Durel Johnson, a farmer living near Delphos, Kan., stands on spot in grove of trees where his son claimed to have seen a mushroom-shaped UFO hovering on the night of Nov. 2, 1971, while pointing to a tree branch he claims was damaged by the UFO. This case was selected as the most impressive of 1971 by a panel of experienced UFOlogists and the Johnson family won a $5,000 prize. In Chapter 15, the author discloses many discrepancies that prompt him to conclude the case is a hoax.

PLATE 7: An Army/Bell Helicopter UH-1H, similar to the one shown above, was involved in another prize-winning UFO incident that occurred near Mansfield, Ohio, on the night of Oct. 18, 1975. In Chapters 16-17, the author discusses results of his investigation that indicate the incident is explainable in prosaic terms and that the bright, glowing high-speed UFO was a meteor-fireball from the Orionids meteor shower under way at the time. There are numerous instances of experienced pilots mistaking a meteor-fireball for a UFO, even in broad daylight. For example, on June 5, 1969, two experienced airline crews and a military jet-fighter pilot, flying near St. Louis, Mo., mistook a fireball and its flaming fragments for a squadron of UFOs. The fireball was photographed by an alert newspaper photographer, Alan Harkrader, Jr., and is shown below (Plate 8). Although incident occurred in daylight, the background is dark because Harkrader intentionally reduced the camera lens aperture for an optimum-contrast picture of the fireball. If the Mansfield, Ohio, UFO was such a fireball, light from its very long luminous tail passing through green-tinted overhead windows *(arrow)* would explain the crew's recollection that the object bathed the inside of the cockpit with green light and that it seemed to "hesitate momentarily."

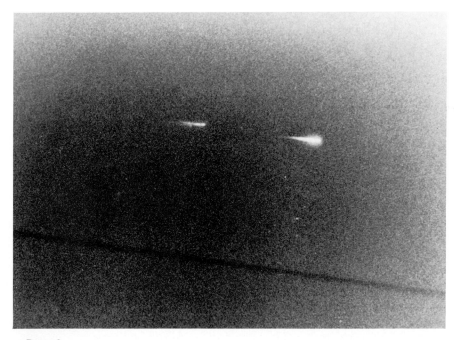

PLATE 8.

5 Witnesses Pass Lie Test While Claiming . . .

Arizona Man Captured by UFO

By TONY BRENNA, JOHN M. CATHCART, CHRIS FULLER, PAUL JENKINS, NICK LONGHURST, ROBERT G. SMITH and JEFF WELLS

In one of the most baffling cases ever recorded, a young laborer was taken aboard a UFO — in full view of six terrified co-workers — and held for five days.

The stunned witnesses readily agreed to take lie-detector tests. Five passed, proving they were telling the truth. The sixth was so nervous that the results of his test were inconclusive.

The abducted man, 22-year-old Travis Walton of Snowflake, Ariz., suddenly disappeared when struck by a dazzling ray from the strange hovering, saucer-shaped object, his fellow workers told police and The ENQUIRER.

In gripping detail, the witnesses described the chilling incident:

Dwayne Smith, 21: "It was a spaceship, there's no doubt of that — and Travis went on it. He got out of our truck, walked toward it — and just vanished!"

Kenneth Peterson, 25: "I saw a bluish light come from the machine and Travis went flying — like he'd touched a hot wire."

Alan Dalis, 21: "It sent out a blue ray, and the last we saw of Travis was his silhouette outlined, arms outstretched. We couldn't believe what was happening — the horror was unreal!"

Mike Rogers, 28: "We were all scared! We couldn't think of any other explanation except that Travis had been

SKETCH of hovering UFO drawn by Mike Rogers and Dwayne Smith.

tree trimmers were heading home at dusk along an isolated mountain road. Crew member Dwayne Smith said they were about 12 miles from Heber when they suddenly spotted the saucer hovering in a clearing beside the road.

"I was numb with disbelief — and terrified!" said Smith. "The UFO was smooth, and was giving off a yellowish-orange light."

just vanished! Mike Rogers, who was driving the truck, screamed 'Shut the door!' and gunned past the saucer.

"When we could see the saucer wasn't following us, Mike stopped the truck and we all got out, shouting and screaming at each other with fear in our faces and terror in our hearts. Then we saw a flash in the trees, and figured the saucer was leaving.

"We went back to the spot where the saucer had been . . . but Travis was gone. He went on the spaceship, there's no doubt of that.

"We went and reported what had happened. We didn't expect anyone to believe us, and nobody did — until we took lie detector test."

Because Walton wasn't able to recall all the details of his amazing experience, The ENQUIRER arranged for him to

Dr. Harder that as he approached the craft for a closer look, he was hit by something and suddenly everything went black.

"When I woke up, there was a strong light in my eyes and I had problems focusing. I was panicked because there was a terrible pain in my head and chest," he told Dr. Harder.

"My mind cleared a little and I thought I was in a hospital. I was lying on a table on my back, and these figures were standing over me.

"It was weird. They weren't human — they were creatures.

"They looked like well-developed fetuses to me — they were about 5 feet tall and wore tight-fitting tan-brown robes. Their skin was white like a mushroom and they had no clear features. They made no sounds.

"Their faces had no texture or color, and there was no hair. Their foreheads were domed and their eyes were very large. They had long fin-

EXPERTS QUIZ abducted man, Travis Walton (center). At left is Dr. Jean Rosenbaum, at right Dr. James Harder.

SHERIFF Marlin Gillespie: "I'm sure they saw UFO."

ing aboard the craft — and his description of the creatures he saw fitted the description given by Walton.

"There's been no publicity

PLATE 9: The *National Enquirer* feature article on the Travis Walton "UFO abduction" incident stresses that five of his six associates passed a "lie-detector" test but fails to inform readers that Walton himself failed a lie-detector test given by the most experienced polygraph examiner in Arizona, John J. McCarthy. The test by McCarthy was given several weeks earlier and had been arranged by the *National Enquirer* whose reporters were present when McCarthy reported the test results.

PLATE 10: Travis Walton, who was "missing" for five days and claims to have been aboard a flying saucer, had a long-standing interest in UFOs, as had other members of his family. According to the psychiatrist who interviewed Walton shortly after he reappeared, Travis had told his mother, Mrs. Mary Kellett, a few weeks before the incident that if he was ever abducted by a UFO she should not worry because he would return safely. (See Chapters 18-23.)

PLATE 11: Travis Walton's mother, his older brother, Duane, and his wife pose alongside the "slash pile" where Travis reportedly was "zapped" by an intense beam from a hovering UFO. The day after the incident, law-enforcement officers scrutinized the slash-pile but found no evidence of intense heat or burning. In a tape-recorded interview while Travis was still "missing," Duane said he was not at all concerned for Travis's well-being and that he wished he were with his brother to share the experience. (See Chapter 18.)

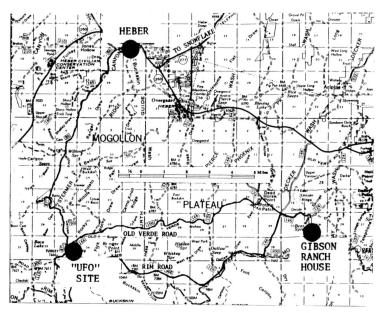

PLATE 12: Map shows proximity of the Gibson ranch house to the site of the alleged abduction and to Heber, where Travis Walton finally reappeared shortly after midnight on Nov. 11. The Gibson family allowed Mrs. Kellett and her family to stay in a mountain ranch-house during summer to escape the heat of Snowflake. Although first snows occasionally fall in late October, Travis's mother was still living in the Gibson ranch-house on Nov. 5, the time of his alleged abduction. But immediately afterward, she returned to Snowflake. Mrs. Richard Gibson reports that members of the Kellett/Walton family sometimes played practical jokes on the Gibson family prior to the UFO incident. (See Chapter 21.)

PLATE 13: Gas station on the main street of Heber from which Travis Walton telephoned his family shortly after midnight (Nov. 11, 1975). When his brother and brother-in-law drove to Heber, they found Travis collapsed in a pay telephone booth *(arrow)*.

PLATE 14: The Gibson ranch-house, where Travis's mother was living at the time of the UFO incident. When a law-enforcement officer and Mike Rogers, Travis's boss, drove over to inform Mrs. Kellett that her son reportedly had been "zapped" and abducted by a UFO, she took the news quite calmly, according to the officer, as did Travis's sister when they drove back to Snowflake. During the five days that Travis was missing, none of the law-enforcement officers searched the Gibson ranch-house because their initial suspicions were that Travis might have been the victim of foul play at the hands of his work-associates. On one occasion, a law-enforcement officer said he planned to search the Gibson ranch-house, but Duane's brother offered to do so and his offer was accepted. The author believes that the Gibson ranch-house served as a night-time hideout for Travis Walton.

PLATE 15: The most experienced polygraph examiner in Arizona, John J. McCarthy, examines the original charts from the lie-detector test he gave to Travis Walton shortly after he reappeared. McCarthy's conclusion was: "Gross deception." Beyond failing the test, McCarthy detected that Travis was holding his breath in an effort to "fool the machine." (See Chapter 20.)

PLATE 16: Tom Ezell, one of Arizona's leading polygraph examiners, disavowed a lie-detector test later taken by Travis Walton, given by one of Ezell's employees, who concluded that Travis was telling the truth about his alleged abduction. Ezell disowned the tests because his former employee had allowed Travis to "dictate" questions he would be asked, which is contrary to established procedures, and because the resulting charts were inconclusive.

Grand Forks Herald

PLATE 17: Deputy Sheriff Val Johnson examines the damage to the patrol car he was driving near Warren, Minn., on the night of Aug. 27, 1979, when he claims he collided with or was attacked by a UFO. The cracked windshield and one broken headlight, together with the two bent antennas *(arrows)* seem to indicate impact with some physical object. Yet, when the antennas were examined under a microscope, there was *no evidence of impact* and the residue of dead insects still was present at the bends. (See Chapter 24.)

Safe Air Ltd.

PLATE 18: A British-built Argosy aircraft of this type, flown by Safe Air Ltd. and carrying a television crew headed by Quentin Fogarty, was involved in one of the best-documented UFO incidents of all time while flying from Wellington, New Zealand, to Christchurch and returning to Blenheim, Dec. 30-31, 1978. The slightly more than eight minutes of film of UFOs was shot from the crowded cockpit, mostly through the windows visible on the right side of the aircraft. (See Chapters 25-27).

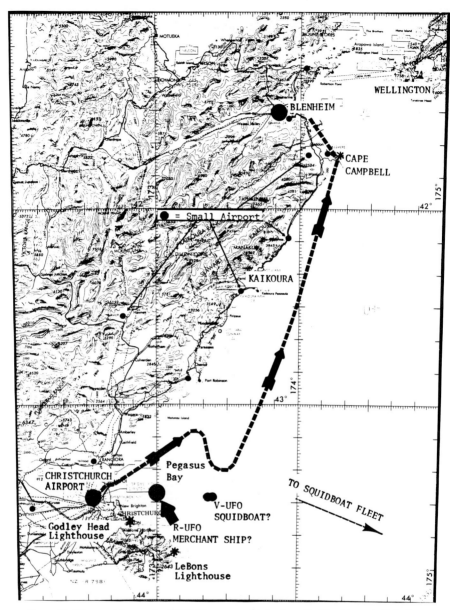

PLATE 19: The most impressive UFO films were obtained on the Northbound flight from Christchurch. Shortly after takeoff, a very bright light was spotted to the right of the aircraft and the pilot, Capt. William Startup, also noted a large blip in roughly the same direction on his airborne radar scope, prompting him to conclude that the radar blip (R-UFO) was coming from the visible UFO (V-UFO). About 40 miles Northeast of Christchurch, the pilot decided to turn toward the V-UFO to obtain a closer look, and cameraman David Crockett went below to get a telephoto lens. Shortly after Crockett returned and installed the new lens—incorrectly, as it turned out—the pilot suddenly decided to head back to Blenheim. The author believes that the radar blip came from a large merchant vessel in Pegasus Bay and that the bright light came from a Japanese squidboat that carries intense illumination to attract squid from the ocean bottom—a squidboat that had departed Wellington earlier and had listed its destination as Pegasus Bay.

PLATE 20: Japanese squidboat, photographed from the surface, with a string of intense lights, typically 4,000 watts each and approximately 50 in number, used to attract squid. Note illumination of the water produced by intense light.

PLATE 21: Capt. Startup later took photos of two Japanese squidboats from the Argosy cockpit while in flight at a range of about 30 miles, and these are superimposed below a projection of the bright V-UFO filmed east of Christchurch for comparison. If the V-UFO was a squidboat, it would have been approximately 30 miles away at the time, but the aircraft would have been at a lower altitude than when the pair of squidboats later was photographed.

PLATE 22: The TV crew's excitement was spurred by reports from the Wellington traffic-control center that its radar was showing mysterious blips whose source was unidentified. Sometimes the crew could see flickering lights in the general direction of the reported radar blips; sometimes they could not. But even when the unknown radar blips were reported to be almost directly ahead of the aircraft's flight path, the pilot never evidenced any concern over a possible mid-air collision, nor did he ever ask the Wellington controller to vector him out of the way of the unknown blips. Subsequent investigation showed that the Wellington radar, whose antenna is located at a 1,700 ft. altitude, is very prone to spurious targets and even can "see" ships at sea and moving trains on the surface. When New Zealand government scientist William Ireland visited the Wellington center a few days later, its radar frequently showed spurious blips, such as the one that Ireland photographed *(arrow)*. Spurious blip shown is off the west coast of South Island (whose outline is displayed to left of blip), in roughly the same area where blips intermittently appeared during the night of Dec. 30-31, 1978.

one point he said the "collective was bottomed," which would mean the craft was in autorotation. But a few moments later Coyne said, "It was a powered descent, not an autorotation." This would mean that the collective was not quite "bottomed."

As Coyne recalled the incident for Hynek during their initial interview, Coyne said that *shortly after the UFO had passed over the helicopter* and headed west, he had looked at his altimeter and discovered the aircraft was at 3500 feet and climbing 1000 feet per minute. In 1976, after Coyne had had the opportunity to consider my own hypothesis, he told Zeidman that *while the UFO still was in view to the west,* he had looked down and seen that the helicopter was at 3500 feet and climbing. If Coyne's recollections were collect, the helicopter had suddenly changed from a 2000-feet-per-minute descent (using Coyne's own figure) to a 1000-feet-per-minute climb. Yet despite what would have been a relatively high-G maneuver, none of the crew members recall sensing these acceleration effects in their bodies. Had the helicopter changed from a steep descent to a climb in a matter of several seconds, it certainly should have been felt by the crew members. And it should have caused structural damage to the blades.

Although Zeidman accepts as "gospel" most of Coyne's recollections of what transpired during the UFO encounter, she concluded that he is wrong about the time-interval between the instant when he said he looked and saw the altimeter indicating 1700 feet and later when he again looked and saw the helicopter was at 3500 feet and climbing. Zeidman concluded that for the helicopter to have experienced an 1800-foot change in altitude (at a climb-rate of 1000 feet per minute) would have required 1.8 minutes. I fully agree. But despite questioning the accuracy of Coyne's recollections under stress on this key issue, Zeidman then accept's Coyne's recollection that after watching the UFO depart the "first thing" Coyne did was to look at his altimeter, which reportedly read 3500 feet altitude.

If Zeidman is correct, this necessarily means that Coyne spent 1.8 minutes watching the UFO after it had passed overhead and no longer posed a collision threat, and completely forgot that his helicopter would crash into the ground in less than twelve seconds unless he pulled it out of its dive! She accepts Coyne's explanation that "the reason I didn't crash into the ground was because I could *see* the ground." (The ability to "see the ground" is hardly protection against crashing into it.) Coyne continued to insist that the helicopter controls remained in a position calling for a steep descent, although the helicopter was only a few hundred feet above the ground, until 1.8 minutes later, when Coyne remembered to look at his altimeter.

When Zeidman and Hynek jointly interviewed copilot Jezzi on February 12, 1977, she asked if he believed that Coyne might have been responsible for the helicopter's climb. Jezzi replied: "I don't know. Larry said: 'Son-of-a-gun, it pulled us up.'" Inasmuch as Coyne was Jezzi's commanding officer and a more experienced pilot, Jezzi would probably be reluctant to challenge

Coyne's views. Jezzi noted that he no longer had his hands on the helicopter controls, but he added that "climbing is something that occurs somewhat easily in a helicopter if you're not paying attention." According to Coyne, he was focusing his attention on the departing UFO, but surely even an inexperienced pilot would not ignore the impending crash into the ground, which Coyne emphasized that he could see.

When Hynek asked Jezzi to try to recall what the crew had talked about just after the incident, the copilot remembered that they had discussed the UFO's colorations and shape, speculated on what it might have been, the fact that "we almost got killed" and then about the seemingly mysterious change from a dive to a climb. Curiously, none of the crew thought to express gratitude to the UFO for having pulled the helicopter out of its death dive, when Coyne forgot to do so and spent 1.8 minutes gawking at the departing UFO — *if* Coyne's recollections on this key issue are accurate.

During one Zeidman interview with Coyne, he expressed the view that the UFO intentionally had tried to ram the helicopter and to "kill us." But if that was the UFO's intent, why did it change objectives and pull the helicopter out of its death dive? And how did the UFO know the precise instant that Coyne would discover the helicopter was climbing and activate his controls to halt the climb so that the UFO could instantly turn off its mysterious suction-force? All of these conflicting issues disappear if one assumes that Coyne behaved exactly as a competent, experienced pilot should, but later had trouble recalling precisely what had occurred during those high-stress moments. Even Zeidman concedes that Coyne's recollections of events are flawed, when she concludes that 1.8 minutes transpired between the times that Coyne viewed his altimeter.

Zeidman's assumption that Coyne's recollections are flawed on one important detail, but otherwise are completely accurate, enables her to conclude that the glowing object remained within view of the crew for *approximately five minutes,* and that this long duration rules out any possibility that the object might have been a meteor-fireball. If her five-minute figure were correct, I would agree.

In dismissing the fireball hypothesis, Zeidman's report states that fireballs "rarely last more than ten seconds." She acknowledges that an extremely slow fireball, with a velocity of only twelve kilometers per second, theoretically might be visible for 110 seconds, but adds that "theory and reality are not always compatible." Zeidman concludes that *under the most favorable conditions,* a fireball could not be visible for more than *"30 to 40 seconds."* These conclusions, she notes, are based on extensive consultations with Hynek and another professor of astronomy, at Ohio State University.

Seemingly Zeidman was not aware of a very large fireball that streaked across the Rockies on a south-north trajectory in mid-afternoon on August 10, 1972. Because the fireball passed over popular tourist areas, a number of persons managed to photograph the fireball. One of these was James M. Baker, vacationing with his wife in the Grand Tetons of Wyoming, who saw the fireball and photographed it with a 35mm. still camera. A few seconds later, his wife Linda aimed her Super-8mm. movie camera at the fireball and managed to obtain *twenty-six seconds* of color movies of the fireball before it disappeared behind some broken clouds and the mountains. Had the incident occurred over flat terrain, with a cloudless sky, and had Mrs. Baker been aloft in a helicopter, she would undoubtedly have obtained enough footage to disprove Zeidman's contention that a fireball cannot possibly be visible for more than thirty to forty seconds.

Because the August 10 fireball was a relatively large meteor, generating considerable heat as it entered the atmosphere, the object was detected and recorded by an infrared sensor aboard a Defense Department meteorological satellite which, fortuitously, was overhead at the time. From data obtained from this satellite and ground-based sightings (and presented in the July 1974 issue of *Sky and Telescope* magazine), scientists were able to calculate that this fireball initially entered the atmosphere with a velocity of 10.1 kilometers per second, or roughly 20 percent slower than Ziedman's "slowest fireball." Its velocity accelerated due to earth's gravity, and scientists concluded that it finally skipped back out into space rather than burning up. In contrast to Zeidman's statement that bright fireballs can have a path length no more than approximately 300 kilometers, scientists concluded that the August 10 fireball had a path length of 1500 kilometers, or five times the maximum figure cited by Zeidman. *Transit time was 101 seconds.*

Returning to Zeidman's conclusion — derived from calculations based on the flight crew's time-estimate recollections that the glowing object was continuously in view for approximately five minutes — her figure differs sharply from the one given by Coyne himself only two weeks after the encounter when he appeared on television. At that time, Coyne estimated that the entire incident from start to finish had occurred *"in about a minute's time."* When Jezzi was interviewed in 1977, he estimated that he had watched the UFO for a period of thirty to sixty seconds.

Any effort to estimate the total duration of the incident should take into account the caveat provided by psychologist Buckhout in his *Scientific American* article, describing his experiments with highly trained USAF flight crews. Recall that he found that under high-stress conditions "time estimates are particularly exaggerated." Evidence of this can be found in the widely differing time estimates by members of the helicopter crew. For example, in the report that Coyne wrote and submitted to his commanding officer, he said the glowing object appeared to "hesitate momentarily" over the helicopter. But the Zeidman report quotes Yanacsek as saying the object "just stopped, for maybe 10 to 12 seconds, and I mean *stopped.*"

Even under conditions where there is no threat to the observer, but the phenomenon is unfamiliar and the incident is relatively brief, there is a wide disparity in observer time estimates, as shown by an incident that occurred on the night of March 3, 1968. At that time, a Russian rocket reentered the atmosphere, breaking up into a string of fiery objects. The USAF received many dozens of eyewitness reports, a few from persons who said they had seen a giant saucer-shaped UFO with illuminated windows. Analysis of all reports on the incident in which the observer *volunteered* an estimate of the duration of the sighting shows the following:

1. 15 percent estimated the sighting lasted less than fifteen seconds.
2. 8 percent estimated the sighting lasted more than five minutes.
3. 25 percent estimated the sighting lasted less than thirty seconds.
4. 25 percent estimated that it had lasted for more than two minutes.

This shows why it is risky to place too much credence in the accuracy of time estimates from observers of unusual, unexpected, and brief events, even when they are not under stress. One indication of the stress-level in the helicopter during the UFO encounter was Jezzi's comment that "all hell broke loose in the cockpit. Everybody was starting yelling and screaming . . ." Zeidman quotes Yanacsek as denying Jezzi's account, claiming that the crew was "under emotional control."

It is possible to make an independent appraisal of the time involved for one significant segment of the total encounter from the fact that the helicopter was cruising at 2500 feet, until Coyne put it into a dive and his recollection that the altimeter read 1700 feet only a moment before the UFO passed overhead, indicating an 800-foot descent. Only two weeks after the encounter, during Coyne's appearance on the "Dick Cavett Show," he said: "I put the collective down . . . the aircraft wasn't moving fast enough to get out of the way, so I put the aircraft in about a twenty-degree angle of dive [using cyclic control] . . . by then this — *it was a matter of 10 seconds* — light was upon us." Several days later, Coyne was interviewed by United Press International, whose account of the incident quoted Coyne as saying: "It [UFO] came *from the horizon to our aircraft in about 10 seconds.*" [Emphasis added.]

At the helicopter's original cruising speed of ninety knots (103 mph.), a twenty-degree angle of dive corresponds to a descent rate of approximately 3100 feet per minute, or slightly more, taking into account the helicopter's increased speed due to the dive. Actually the maximum descent rate would have been even higher because the helicopter's collective pitch control was all the way forward, greatly reducing rotor-blade lift. (When I asked Bell Helicopter, which designed and built the UH-1H, what descent rate could be expected with both the collective and cyclic pitch controls in the full forward position, a company spokesman told me it would be nearly 4000 feet per minute.) If one uses a very conservative 3100-feet-per-minute figure as an average for the full 800-foot descent, this segment of the incident would have occurred in approximately fifteen seconds, close to Coyne's own ten second figure given on television and during his interview with UPI.

But Zeidman concludes that the 800-foot descent required approximately thirty-six seconds. On October 25, 1978, I wrote to her, challenging that figure, based on data supplied by Bell Helicopter. I proposed that this important issue be resolved scientifically by asking Coyne to conduct an experiment using his UH-1H, with a four-man crew, to replicate the original UFO-encounter conditions. Coyne then would push both the collective and cyclic controls full forward/down and Zeidman could then photograph the vertical velocity indicator in the cockpit to resolve the issue. When nearly two months elapsed without a reply, I wrote to Zeidman on December 16, again suggesting the experiment. *She never responded.* But a few months later, when her CUFOS report was published, it contained her original thirty-six second figure.

It is much more difficult to estimate the time that elapsed from the beginning of the incident until Coyne initiated his evasive maneuver. According to the first account in *The Plain Dealer,* when Coyne's recollections were freshest, he said that Yanacsek "reported a red light about five miles to the east . . . . Seconds later, Yanacsek yelled, 'The light is moving. It's coming toward us.'" When Coyne appeared on television two weeks later, he reported: "My crew chief observed a light on the east horizon . . . I told him to keep an eye on it, check it out, and he stated that it looked like an obstruction light atop of a radio tower. About a minute later he said the red light was pacing us . . . . About a moment later he said the light was converging on us on a collision course." But in Coyne's official report, written a couple of weeks later, he altered his time estimate: "Yanacsek observed a red light on the east horizon, 90 degrees to the flight path of the helicopter. Approximately 30 seconds later, SSG Yanacsek indicated the object was converging . . . ."

During the interview with the copilot, Jezzi recalled: "There was a mention of a red light on the horizon . . . and the conversation was that it looked like a radio tower, but it wasn't flashing, *and then a few seconds later* [Yanacsek] said, 'No, it's not a radio tower, it appears to be moving.' The next comment I heard was 'It's coming toward us' and very shortly thereafter . . . Coyne took over the controls . . . ." The longest time estimate came from Yanacsek, who said he had watched the then distant red light for more than a minute before he even mentioned it to Coyne, thinking it was an aircraft too distant to pose any threat because he didn't want "to bother" Coyne. (This is curious, inasmuch as Jezzi was flying the helicopter and Coyne's role would be to look for other traffic that might pose a threat.)

Based on the foregoing, Zeidman concludes that the UFO probably *was in view for nearly two minutes before Coyne decided to take evasive action*—which would clearly rule out any possibility that the object might have been a fireball. Her figure depends heavily on Yanacsek's estimate, even though the report shows that his ten-to-twelve-second estimate of how long the object allegedly hovered over the helicopter is much longer than that of Coyne and Jezzi. Zeidman fails to consider the possibility that the red light that Yanacsek initially observed to the east, where there are a number of radio/TV antenna towers as well as two major airways, might have been the warning light atop one of the towers or the red light on the left wing of a northbound aircraft flying on one of the two airways. Since the red light, according to Yanacsek, initially seemed too distant to pose any possible threat, he might have briefly diverted his eyes from the original red light, then have had his attention attracted by the apparent movement of a fireball coming out of the east. In the excitement of the moment he could easily conclude that the fireball was the object he had been watching earlier. *If so, then the "UFO" itself would have been in view for only a few seconds prior to Yanacsek's warning* of a potential mid-air collision threat to which Coyne quickly responded. In this event, the elapsed time between Yanacsek's sighting of the glowing object coming toward the helicopter and the time when the helicopter had descended to 1700 feet, would have been *no more than thirty seconds.*

There remains the question then of how long the object remained in view after it had passed over the helicopter. Copilot Jezzi and flight medic Healey, sitting on the left side of the helicopter, would have had the least-obstructed view as the object departed to the west. Jezzi described this final phase of the incident as follows: "I just saw it go away and disappear." But it will be recalled that he later estimated that the total time interval that he had watched the object approach *and* depart was thirty to sixty seconds. (Sitting on the left side, Jezzi would have had a more restricted view as the object approached.)

Flight medic Healey, also sitting on the left side of the helicopter behind Jezzi, estimated that the total incident had lasted approximately four minutes—two minutes until the object passed overhead and two minutes until it disappeared to the west, according to the Zeidman CUFOS report. But when Healey and I talked in New York City, less than two weeks after the encounter, he told me that the entire incident had occurred in "about two minutes," or half the figure given several years later to Zeidman.

If the object was a fireball burning up as it entered the atmosphere, its luminosity would decrease, so that it would be visible to the crew for a shorter time interval as it departed to the west than as it approached. And if the UFO was not really the same red light that Yanacsek originally spotted to the east from which he had briefly diverted his gaze because it seemed to pose no threat, then the total time the object would have been visible to the crew would be something less than twice the approach-segment earlier calculated, *or less than one minute.* This estimate closely matches Coyne's original figure given on the "Dick Cavett Show," as well as Jezzi's own estimate. And the figure is well within the time limits of a fireball.

Perhaps because Zeidman recognizes that her five-minute time estimate is a questionable basis for rejecting my fireball hypothesis, her report stresses recollections by several crew members that the UFO had a craftlike appearance. Coyne's formal report included a sketch of a cigar-shaped object with a shallow dome atop, which Coyne indicated was a "grey metallic hull" that he estimated to be between fifty and sixty feet long. Yanacsek said the UFO emitted a white light that illuminated its tail and "gave definite proof . . . that it was something solid, something solid and metallic." Three years after the incident, Healey described the UFO as a "solid metal thing, with no rivets or seams." However Jezzi did not recall seeing "a body to it at all . . . . The only thing I recall seeing was a white light, a very bright, intense white light on the aft portion of the object . . ." That would be an excellent description of the long luminous tail of a fireball during atmospheric entry.

If the light from the object was as bright as Coyne, Jezzi, and other crew members reported, they would have been blinded momentarily *and unable to make out any shape or mechanical features—even if the object had such features.* (If anyone doubts this, he or she should stand near a four-lane highway at night to see if he or she can identify the type of automobile that is passing while caught in the glare of the automobile's headlights.) Furthermore, since the UFO passed over the helicopter, as Coyne repeatedly emphasized in his early accounts, Yanacsek and Healey, sitting in the rear, would not have been able to see the object directly through the two forward-located overhead windows, so their subsequent descriptions of the object's shape and mechanical configuration almost certainly are based on Coyne's initial description. The reports that the UFO appeared as a white light as it departed to the west, where it was viewed through the white side windows, while the cockpit was bathed in green light when the object was overhead, where its illumination would pass through the green overhead windows, are all consistent with the fireball hypothesis. And its long luminous tail, which could illuminate the cockpit for several seconds with green light, would explain why the crew later deduced that the object seemed to "hesitate momentarily" overhead.

In Zeidman's determined effort to rule out the fireball hypothesis, she notes that if the UFO were a fireball there should have been numerous other eyewitness reports, yet there were not. This ignores the fact that the Mansfield encounter occurred shortly after 11:00 p.m. in a relatively rural area, when there would be few potential observers outside. Two nights later, the crew of a United Airlines jetliner flying approximately 150 miles east of Mansfield, reported seeing a fireball from the Orionids shower. This incident occurred approximately two hours earlier (9:07 p.m.), in the vicinity of Pittsburgh, Pennsylvania, a large metropolitan area. *Yet there were no other reports of the October 20 fireball submitted by other flight crews or by ground observers.*

On August 19, 1976, nearly three years after Coyne reported the incident, the *News Journal* of Mansfield published a feature article on the incident, including Coyne's sketch of the object, announcing that the head of a small Ohio UFO group was searching for persons who might have seen the helicopter-UFO encounter. Within several days, Warren Nicholson, director of the Civil Commission on Aerial Phenomena (CCAP), received a telephone call from a 16-year-old youth who claimed that he, his mother, and three younger siblings, had witnessed the Coyne-UFO encounter. The August 25 edition of the *News Journal,* reporting on the new development, quoted Nicholson as saying that the stories recounted by the family were "a bit disjointed" but that CCAP would try to piece them together into a composite story. Nicholson was quoted as saying that some of the discrepancies in the family's account and the details recounted by Coyne and his crew might be due to the nearly three years that had elapsed since the incident occurred.

On November 22, 1976, I called Nicholson to discuss the "new witnesses" and tape-recorded our conversation to assure that I got the facts straight. Nicholson admitted that he himself was "curious why they had never said anything" publicly about having witnessed the famous UFO incident, until he had issued a request via the Mansfield newspaper. But Nicholson seemed satisfied with the explanation he was given by "Mrs. C.," who insists on anonymity. Nicholson told me that Mrs. C said "they drove home and told their neighbors and they just laughed at them because there had been quite a few [UFO] sightings in that area at that time. And so they figured, well, if our neighbors won't believe us, we aren't going to tell anybody else."

Examination of the Mansfield newspaper during the middle and late part of October 1973 reveals that the area had indeed experienced a rash of UFO reports. For example, two days before the Coyne event the October 16 edition of the *News Journal* carried a story headlined: "UNIDENTIFIED FLY-ING OBJECTS SIGHTED OVER MANSFIELD, ASHLAND." The October 19 edition carried another feature, under the headline: "MANSFIELD, ASHLAND AREA PEOPLE GO ON UFO BINGE," reporting that two sheriff's deputies had chased a UFO about 9:00 P.M. on October 18, the night of the Coyne incident. The October 22 edition of the *News Journal* carried more area UFO reports, including a brief account of the Coyne incident, under the headline: "STATE PATROLMEN WATCH FOUR UFOS." On October 24 there was another story under the headline: "MORE UFO REPORTS RECEIVED BY POLICE." The next day's paper carried still another story, headlined: "CITY'S UFO SPOTTERS SEEING SOMETHING UP THERE—BUT WHAT?" Although numerous local citizens were willing to risk possible ridicule to report their UFO sightings, Mrs. C. and her family remained silent.

Then, on November 4, the *News Journal* carried a major feature on the Coyne incident under the headline: "CHOPPER PILOT FILES OFFICIAL REPORT ON ENCOUNTER WITH UFO OVER MANSFIELD." If Mrs. C. really had witness-ed the helicopter encounter as she later claimed, she no longer had cause to fear ridicule because her story would have been supported by four respected members of the Coyne helicopter crew. Yet Mrs. C. and her family remained silent—for nearly three years. I found this highly suspicious, but it did not seem to bother either Nicholson or Zeidman, who devoted considerable space in her CUFOS report to the story of Mrs. C. and her family.

The account in the CUFOS report is based on tape-recorded interviews by both Zeidman and Nicholson. It quotes Mrs. C. as saying that the family saw the incident as they were driving home on the night of October 18, around 11:00 P.M., headed east and approaching the Charles Mill Reservoir, a manmade lake approximately five miles southeast of the Mansfield airport and approximately two miles southeast of the NDB non-directional beacon mentioned earlier. According to Mrs. C.'s story, the near-miss occurred while the helicopter was directly over the reservoir. But this contradicts Coyne's statement to FAA controller Emery, immediately after landing at Cleveland, that the UFO incident occurred as the helicopter was "over the NDB beacon at Mansfield" where Coyne was "planning to land . . . for fuel." Coyne's statement, made while the incident was still fresh in his mind, would have put the helicopter *at least two miles west* of where Mrs. C.'s family claimed the encounter happened. Coyne's report to the Cleveland FAA confirms his statement to me on January 3, 1974, that he normally used the Mansfield beacon for navigation because it put out a strong signal and was conveniently located.

If Coyne was preparing to land and refuel at Mansfield, as he told the FAA and as his very low fuel supply demanded, he would have been guilty of sloppy navigation to have flown over the reservoir when he intended to turn west after passing the radio beacon and land at the airport. The airport was plainly visible.

Zeidman quotes Mrs. C. as saying that the UFO encounter lasted so long that there was time for her to stop the car and let several children get out to watch, for an interval that she estimated as "not over a couple of minutes." Then, according to their account, the family got back into the car and headed *east,* only to find that the UFO was following them, that is, had reversed its high-speed westward flight and now was flying east for more than a minute, Nicholson told me. Yet none of the helicopter crew ever reported that the UFO had reversed direction and flown eastward for more than a minute.

When Zeidman asked Mrs. C. why she had not reported the incident before, Mrs. C. explained that she was having domestic problems and did not want to "make waves." Furthermore, Mrs. C. said, until her son Charles read the August 19, 1976, article in the *News Journal,* "they had no idea *where* to report it," according to Zeidman. Apparently it never occurred to Mrs. C. to report the incident to the local newspaper, which had been filled with numerous UFO reports from other local citizens. Zeidman was satisfied with Mrs. C.'s explanation. I am not.

In my letters of October 25 and December 16, 1978, to Zeidman, proposing that Coyne run an experiment to determine the UH-1H's descent rate with both its collective and cyclic-pitch controls all the way forward/down, I also proposed that Mrs. C. undergo a polygraph test, dealing solely with her story about having witnessed the Coyne helicopter encounter. Zeidman never replied to these suggestions.

In the closing pages of the Zeidman/CUFOS report, she writes: "This report offers only a presentation of the facts and my unswerving conviction that we are being confronted with new empirical data which deserve the serious attention of both behavioral and physical scientists." Earlier, in the chapter entitled "Conclusion," Zeidman writes: "The possibilities that the object was either a meteor or a high-performance aircraft have been considered at length and have been shown to be untenable."

On October 18, 1977, exactly four years after the Coyne helicopter encounter, almost to the hour, a very large fireball from the Orionids shower came out of the east, as had the Mansfield UFO, on a westerly trajectory several hundred miles to the south. Because the time was 8:15 P.M., and the trajectory was over more populated areas, there were numerous ground-observer reports. While this anniversary incident does not resolve the basic question of whether the Mansfield UFO was a fireball, it does refute the claim made by Zeidman, attributed to Hynek, that the Orionids shower "does not produce fireballs at all." ("Major Coyne and the UFO: The True Story," by Jennie Zeidman, *Fate*, August 1978.)

Meanwhile, Coyne has become an international celebrity in the world of UFOlogy. On November 27, 1978, he was one of three pro-UFO persons invited to address the United Nations' Special Political Committee on the subject of UFOs. The other two speakers were Hynek and his long-time UFO associate, Dr. Jacques Vallee. The presentation had been arranged by Sir Eric Gairy, then prime minister of the Caribbean-island state of Grenada, who had long urged the United Nations to sponsor a global UFO investigation. (Within several months Gairy would be overthrown and his successor, Maurice Bishop, publicly accused Gairy of practicing witchcraft. Following Gairy's overthrow, a search of his home disclosed "a room apparently used for witchcraft, with pieces of animals and what looked like dry blood in one corner," according to Bishop.)

Coyne, now a lieutenant colonel in the Army Reserve, briefly recounted the Mansfield UFO incident, but with additional changes from his original accounts. Many of these changes supported Zeidman's claim that the object could not possibly have been a fireball. For example, in sharp contrast to earlier statements, he told the UN that it was "several minutes" after Yanacsek spotted a red light to the east before he reported it to Coyne, and "several minutes after that" before Yanacsek warned that the object was on a collision course. But later Coyne admitted that "trying to recall time in terms of minutes or seconds at the point of interception . . . was ridiculous." For the first time, Coyne claimed that while he was diving to avoid the UFO he also was trying to "select a field site for an emergency landing." If the helicopter was over the large manmade lake as Mrs. C. claimed, this would be a risky landing spot.

But Coyne cautiously qualified his earlier claim that he had not been responsible for the helicopter climb by saying, "I had not during any time to my recollection increased power . . . ." Then he added a new detail, designed to defeat my explanation: "I looked outside to the ground and could see that the helicopter was in fact climbing and rechecked myself to see if I had moved any controls." *Yet in all of Coyne's early accounts he emphasized that he had not been aware that the helicopter was climbing until he looked at his altimeter and vertical velocity indicator.* And, to my knowledge, he had never before claimed that he had "rechecked myself to see if I had moved any controls."

Coyne told the UN committee: "Mr. Chairman and members of this committee, there was no change in the controls or power setting. They were still set for a 2000-foot-per-minute descent, even though the helicopter was climbing at 1000 feet per minute with the object [UFO] still positioned *in front of the aircraft* . . ." In front? Coyne had repeatedly stressed in earlier statements that the UFO was *over* the helicopter. And a couple of sentences after saying the UFO was in *front* of the helicopter, Coyne told the UN that "the object momentarily was *over* the helicopter and could be observed through the *top* plexiglass which is green in color." [Emphasis added.]

But the most significant point is that in Coyne's UN statement he claims that the UFO still was directly in front of his helicopter when he noted that the helicopter was at 3500 feet and climbing. Yet when I talked with Coyne on January 23, 1974, barely three months after the incident and asked how long an interval elapsed between the time that "the bright object passed overhead before you looked down at the altimeter and vertical-velocity indicator and saw the 3500 feet and 1000 feet per minute," Coyne replied: "I'd be guessing now by this time. I would say maybe thirty seconds, maybe thirty to forty seconds." But nearly five years later his account had changed and his recollections were unqualified.

Before thanking Gairy's delegation for the opportunity to appear before the UN, Coyne concluded: "As a result of my experience, I am convinced this object was real and that these types of incidents should require a thorough investigation. It is my own personal opinion that worldwide procedures need to be established to effectively study this phenomena through an international cooperative effort."

When I read a published version of Coyne's statement before the UN committee, I recalled his response nearly five years earlier to my suggestion that the UFO might have been a meteor-fireball: "Well, that would sound like a logical explanation." During our first interview, Coyne had volunteered: "I don't believe in UFOs and space monsters and all this kooky stuff, because I don't believe they exist." But that was before Coyne had become an international UFO celebrity and his encounter had become a classic case for the UFO movement.

For Coyne, for Hynek, and for Zeidman there can be no turning back now. For them and for many other UFOlogists, what happened near Mansfield, Ohio, on the night of October 18, 1973, will always remain inexplicable in prosaic terms and, therefore, convincing evidence that extraordinary craft are operating in our skies.

18

Travis Walton's UFO Abduction

Until the mid-1960s—nearly two decades into the UFO era—there were no U.S. reports of persons who claimed to have been abducted and taken aboard a flying saucer against their will. Back in the early 1950s, religious cultist George Adamski coauthored a book in which he claimed that he had frequently accepted invitations to visit a giant "mother-ship," populated by handsome Venusians, Martians, and Saturnians. Adamski claimed his gracious extraterrestrial hosts had flown him past the backside of the moon, then hidden to terrestrial observers, where he reported seeing snow and tree-covered mountains as well as cities and UFO landing strips. But most serious UFOlogists rejected Adamski's tale even before mid-1966, when American Lunar Orbiter satellites began to return photos of the backside of the lunar surface that showed none of the things that Adamski had reported seeing.

Then, in October 1966, *Look* magazine published a two-part series on a Portsmouth, New Hampshire, couple—Barney and Betty Hill—suggesting that they had been abducted five years earlier and taken aboard a flying saucer, where they were given a physical examination by strange-looking creatures. The articles, and a subsequent book, were written by John G. Fuller (who later would write books about a "psychic surgeon" who allegedly could remove diseased organs from the body without making a physical incision and about the ghosts of an Eastern Airlines flight crew, who allegedly haunt its aircraft.)

During the nearly two decades since the Hills' story emerged, approximately two hundred persons have come forward with similar stories of "UFO abductions," usually claiming that they too were examined by curious UFOnauts. But in each of these incidents the "victim" did not report the incident until hours, weeks, months, or even years after the event allegedly occurred—until November 5, 1975, when a curious incident occurred near

161

Heber, Arizona. Travis Walton was the first "UFO abductee" to be reported to law-enforcement officers while the "victim" was still missing. It would be five days before Travis would reappear, making it the longest "UFO abduction" on record. Additionally six other persons, members of a timber-cutting crew, reported that they had witnessed the initial part of the incident.

The Travis Walton case was thoroughly investigated by APRO, the Tucson, Arizona, UFO group headed by Mr. and Mrs. L. J. Lorenzen, who have been active in the field of UFOlogy for more than a quarter of a century. In recent years, APRO has focused much of its efforts on "UFO abductions" and thus presumably has acquired expertise in such investigations. When the Lorenzens were interviewed for an article published in August 1977 in *UFO Report* and were asked "What's the most impressive UFO case you've ever investigated?" Mrs. Lorenzen replied: "I'd say the Travis Walton incident." Her husband did not disagree with her choice.

In the late spring of 1976, after the Walton incident had been selected as the most impressive UFO case of 1975 by a Blue Ribbon Panel for a prize by the *National Enquirer,* the case was strongly endorsed by individual members of the panel. Dr. James A. Harder, APRO's director of research and a professor at the University of California at Berkeley, said: "Beyond any reasonable doubt, the evidence is as valid as any that would be accepted in an American criminal court." Dr. Leo Sprinkle, University of Wyoming, said: "The evidence is very strong. It's a solid sighting in terms of witnesses, the number of witnesses, and the investigation of them by polygraph." Dr. Frank Salisbury, another panel member, from Utah State University, was quoted as saying: "Thanks to the many witnesses and the polygraph examinations of those witnesses, we have pretty good reason to take the Walton case at face value."

Thus the Travis Walton incident stands not only as the best of the "UFO abduction" cases but it also offers a good means of assessing the investigative modus operandi of some of the nation's leading UFOlogists.

Walton, age 22 in 1975, was a member of a seven-man crew headed by Michael H. Rogers, age 28. The crew was thinning and stacking timber in the Turkey Springs area of the Sitgreaves National Forest, located in the mountains of east-central Arizona. As Rogers described the incident in a tape-recorded interview three days later, the crew had quit work around dusk, at about 6:00 P.M., on Wednesday, November 5, 1975, was heading up a rough logging road for the ride back home to Snowflake, roughly forty-five miles away, via the small village of Heber. Allen Dalis, age 21, sitting in the rear of the truck, reportedly was the first to see a yellowish glow through the heavy timber. When the truck reached a clearing, both Dalis and Travis Walton, who was sitting in the front seat next to the door, reported seeing a saucer-shaped object hovering less than one hundred feet off the road, directly over a "slash-pile" of cut timber. Rogers said the object was about fifteen feet in diameter and "looked like a flying saucer . . . something I'd seen pictures of . . . ."

Travis reportedly yelled for Rogers to stop the truck, but before he could do so young Walton opened the door, leaped out and ran toward the UFO, disregarding warnings from the other crew members. As Travis neared the object, suddenly there was a brilliant flash of blue-green light, like an explosion or stroke of lightning, which "blew him back ten feet," according to Rogers, who said he panicked and drove off in haste, leaving Travis to his fate. After reaching a point that Rogers estimated was about a quarter of a mile away, he stopped the truck. After much discussion, and after observing a streak of light that suggested the UFO had departed, Rogers said it was agreed that they would go back to rescue Travis. But upon returning to the site, they could find no trace of Travis.

Finally Rogers drove into Heber, a thirty-minute trip, and a crew member called Undersheriff L. C. Ellison around 7:45 P.M. at his home. He agreed to meet them in the village. As Ellison later recalled (for me) his first meeting with the group, the officer said "they seemed pretty upset. They said: 'We don't think you're gonna believe us, and maybe we'd just better go on and forget it.' I said: 'Hey, you called me up and got me down here, you'd better have something to tell me.'" After listening to the story, Ellison called his superior, Navajo County Sheriff Marlin Gillespie, at Holbrook, about thirty miles northeast of Heber. Gillespie and his deputy, Kenneth Coplan, promptly drove to Heber. Three of the crew members refused to return to the site to search for Travis and used the Rogers truck to drive back to Snowflake. But Rogers, two other crew members, and the three law-enforcement officers returned to the site and spent several hours searching in vain for young Walton.

Shortly after midnight Gillespie decided to abandon the search until daylight and to notify Travis's next-of-kin. Travis's mother, Mary Kellett, whose home was in Snowflake, spent the summer months living in a small ranchhouse owned by the Gibson family of Heber, which was located about fifteen miles away from where the UFO incident reportedly had occurred. Although it was early November, and the first winter snows were expected momentarily, Mrs. Kellett was still living in the Gibson ranchhouse. Rogers offered to direct Coplan to the ranchhouse, and the two of them set off to break the tragic news to Travis's mother. They arrived around 1:30 A.M., Coplan told me. "When Rogers told the mother what had happened, she did not act very surprised," according to Coplan. "She said, 'Well, that's the way these things happen.' Then Mrs. Kellett proceeded to tell about Duane [her oldest son] seeing a UFO several years before at the ranch. Then she said another UFO came by and that both she and Duane saw it."

Mrs. Kellett did think that she ought to inform her daughter, Mrs. Grant Neff, who lived near Snowflake, and Duane, who lived in Glendale, a suburb of Phoenix. Since the ranchhouse had no telephone, this meant driving to Snowflake. Because Mrs. Kellett said she did not like to drive at night, Rogers offered to drive Mrs. Kellett in her car while Coplan came along in his. They arrived around 3:00 A.M., Coplan later told me, awakened Mrs. Neff, and broke the tragic news to her. Coplan said that Mrs. Kellett calmly announced that "Travis is gone," and when her daughter asked where, the mother replied: "A flying saucer got him." Coplan told me that he was surprised also at how calmly Mrs. Neff took the word that her young brother had been abducted by a UFO. Mrs. Kellett then telephoned Duane and asked him to come. He arrived in Snowflake around 7:00 A.M., Thursday, November 6.

By mid-morning on November 6, a party of nearly fifty people, including law-enforcement officers, Forest Service personnel, and volunteers were searching the Turkey Springs area for Travis or his remains. Curiously, considering the explosive force of the blue-green beam that reportedly had "zapped" Travis only a few hours earlier, there was not a shred of physical evidence to support the story. The officers could not find any blood, any shreds of clothing, nor any evidence of intense heat on the slash-pile of dry timber and pine needles over which the UFO reportedly had hovered.

Late in the afternoon the law-enforcement officers were surprised when, according to Coplan, "Mrs. Kellett finally came up and said: 'I don't think there is any use of looking any further. He's not around here. I don't think he's on this earth." On this basis, Gillespie told the volunteers they could abandon their search, but he and a few associates continued the effort the following day, November 7, without finding a single clue. At one point the law-enforcement officers talked about going over to the Gibson house where Mrs. Kellett had been living but which she now had vacated, to see if Travis might be there. But Duane Walton offered to drive over to look for Travis and did so, Coplan told me. In response to my question, Coplan said that to the best of his knowledge, none of the law-enforcement officers ever searched the Gibson house to see if it might have been used as a hideout for Travis.

At that stage, the officers were more concerned over the possibility that Travis might have been the victim of foul play at the hands of his crew mates and that the UFO story had been concocted as a cover. A similar concern was expressed by Travis's own brother Donald, whose initial reaction was that the UFO story was simply a cover for foul play. On the evening of November 7, Sheriff's Deputy Glen Flake, of Snowflake, visited Rogers to say that he understood that the crew had volunteered to take a polygraph test, which Rogers confirmed. On that basis, Flake asked Rogers to have the crew come to Holbrook early Monday morning, November 10, for polygraph tests that would be given by C. E. Gilson, of the Arizona Department of Public Safety, in Phoenix. Rogers agreed.

Early the next morning, Saturday, November 8, Rogers and Duane Walton drove to Holbrook to complain to Sheriff Gillespie because he was not continuing to search for Travis. Gillespie, understandably, was surprised because the earlier search had been abandoned at the suggestion of Mrs. Kellett herself. But he quickly assembled another search party, which included a helicopter, and by late that afternoon the effort was under way again, with Duane flying aboard the helicopter. The sheriff would have been even more surprised at the demand for a new search effort had he been able to eavesdrop on an interview that took place at the UFO site at around 6:00 P.M. Saturday evening. The interviewer, veteran Phoenix UFOlogist Fred Sylvanus, tape-recorded the sixty-five-minute conversation with Rogers and Duane Walton, and a copy of the tape was later supplied to me by William Spaulding, of GSW. If Rogers and Duane really believed that Travis had been zapped by a UFO three nights earlier, for all they knew he might now be on a spaceship headed back to the UFOnauts native planet, where he might be dissected like a frog in a biology class, or stuffed and placed in a museum. Almost certainly Duane would never again see his young brother alive again. Or, if the UFO had dumped poor Travis from the craft over the Sitgreaves National Forest, predators would almost certainly be chewing at his body by that time.

Yet never once during the sixty-five-minute interview did either Duane Walton or Rogers express the slightest concern over Travis's well-being. Quite the opposite! Nor did Rogers ever voice any regret that he had decided to drive off and abandon his good friend Travis, leaving him to a supposedly strange fate. When Rogers described the appearance of the UFO to Sylvanus he never once used words like "frightening" or "ominous." Instead, Rogers said the UFO was "really kind of pretty . . . it was really beautiful." But it was the comments volunteered by Travis's brother Duane, who had functioned as a father to Travis because of Mrs. Kellett's two ill-fated marriages, that really surprised veteran UFOlogist Sylvanus. For example:

SYLVANUS: Anything else you can tell us, Duane?

DUANE: No, other than I don't believe he's hurt or injured in any way. [He'll] be back sooner or later, whenever they get done doing what they're doing.

SYLVANUS: You feel he will come back?

DUANE: Sure do. Don't feel any fear for him at all. Little regret because I haven't been able to experience the same thing. That's about it.

SYLVANUS: You feel you just miss him and he'll come back.

DUANE: He's not even missing. He knows where he's at, and I know where he's at.

SYLVANUS: [Very surprised] You know where he's at?

DUANE: He's not even missing. He knows where he's at, and I know where he's at.

SYLVANUS: Well, where do you feel he is?

DUANE: Not on this earth.

SYLVANUS: You don't think he's on this earth?

DUANE: I sure don't. It's ridiculous for man to assume that he's the only civilized technological society in the universe . . . . It's ridiculous. [The UFO] people aren't here to make a war or they'd have destroyed us a long time ago.

SYLVANUS: Have either one of you fellows read much about flying saucers?*

ROGERS: A little.

SYLVANUS: How about you Duane?

DUANE: As much as anybody.

SYLVANUS: Well, some have read a lot and some have read a little.

ROGERS: I'm not a fan, or I wasn't until now.

DUANE: I don't follow it like I do a lot of things. But it's there. I know it's [UFOs] real. It's *not* a [natural] phenomena. I've lived with it for the past ten or twelve years. *I've been seeing them all the time.* It's not new to me. It's not a surprise.

Nor was Duane surprised that Travis, reportedly, had run under the UFO despite the warnings from his terrified friends. This was all part of a long-standing plan between the two brothers, he explained.

DUANE: Travis and I discussed this many, many times at great length and we both said that [if either ever saw a UFO up close] we would immediately get as directly under the object as physically possible.

SYLVANUS: If you saw one you would get underneath it?

DUANE: *We discussed this time and time again!* The opportunity would be too great to pass up . . . and whoever happened to be left on the ground—if one of us didn't make the grade—to try to convince whoever was in the craft to come back and get the other one. But he [Travis] performed just as we said we would, and he got directly under the object. And he's received the benefits for it.

SYLVANUS: You hope he has!

Listening to the foregoing portion of the tape-recorded interview, it is clear from the tone of Sylvanus's voice that he is much more concerned over Travis's well-being than either Rogers or Duane Walton. The interview concluded with the following exchange.

SYLVANUS: Anything else you'd like to add?

DUANE: Nothing other than I don't feel any fear for his life. He's not in any danger. He'll turn up sooner or later, whenever they are ready, or whenever he's ready.

SYLVANUS: Do you know that he's definitely . . .

---

*Many experienced UFOlogists are suspicious of reports from persons with a long-standing interest in UFOs.

DUANE: [Interrupting] *Having the experience of a lifetime!* I don't think he's in any danger at all. He'll turn up. All I can say is that I wish I was with him.

SYLVANUS: Can you give me any basis for this feeling? I'm not trying to ridicule, don't misunderstand.

DUANE: Oh no. Everybody in my family . . .

ROGERS: [Interrupting] Long-time consideration of the idea.

DUANE: [Continuing] We've paid a lot of attention to it. We've lived with it [UFOs] for ten years. The fact that they are here and *we see them quite regularly.* And they don't kill people. They don't kill people! That's not why they're here . . . . It's just that he's gone. And he's had an experience of a lifetime. And all I wish is that I was there, at any cost.

Had Sheriff Gillespie been able to eavesdrop on this interview, undoubtedly he would have cancelled the expensive search effort the following day, Sunday, November 9. But the search got under way Sunday morning and continued until late afternoon, when Duane informed the sheriff that his mother once again recommended terminating the effort. And so the law-enforcement officers and other members of the search party returned to their homes, allowing the village of Heber to return to its somnolent pre-UFO-incident status.

The next morning, November 11, Rogers and the other five members of his crew showed up at Holbrook to take polygraph tests administered by C. E. Gilson. Because the major concern at that point was that Travis might have been murdered by one or more members of the crew, three of the four "relevant" questions used by Gilson dealt with whether Travis had been seriously injured or killed by one or more members of the crew. The fourth relevant question, which Gilson later told me was added at the last minute, asked: "Did you tell the truth about actually seeing a UFO last Wednesday when Travis Walton disappeared." Unfortunately, it did not ask whether the subject had seen Travis being "zapped by a UFO."

All six members of the crew answered "No" to the first three questions and all answered "Yes" to the one UFO-related question. After analyzing the polygraph charts, Gilson concluded that five of the six men were truthful. But he concluded that the test results were "inconclusive" for the sixth man, Allen Dalis, who reportedly had been the first to see the UFO. Gilson gave his findings to Gillespie verbally on the evening of November 11, and put them into a formal written report two days later. In this report Gilson said: "These polygraph examinations prove that these five men did see some object that they believe to be a UFO and that Travis Walton was not injured or murdered by any of these men, on that Wednesday (5 November 1975). If an actual UFO did not exist and the UFO is a manmade hoax, five of these men had no prior knowledge of a hoax. No such determination can be made of the sixth man whose test results were inconclusive."

Within hours after Gilson concluded his testing, Travis Walton reappeared in Heber, and called his sister's home from a pay-telephone booth. Unresolved at that point was the question of whether Travis really had been abducted by a UFO or was involved in a hoax. Had Travis reappeared in New Zealand or in Denmark, for example, without a passport or travel funds, there could be scant possibility of a hoax. But invariably "UFO abductees" reappear close to where the incident was alleged to have occurred, and Travis Walton was no exception. Heber is approximately fifteen miles from the spot where the UFO was reported to have zapped Travis, and roughly the same distance from the Gibson ranch, where Mrs. Kellett had spent the summer months and where she still was staying, despite the fact that the first winter snows could arrive at any moment. (She did return to Snowflake immediately after the UFO incident.) Clearly, the Gibson ranchhouse could have provided a handy hideout for Travis during his five-day absence. (A map of the area is shown in Plate 12; the Gibson ranchhouse in Plate 14.)

19

Travis Returns

It was shortly after midnight when Travis called his sister's home and her husband, Grant Neff, answered. Travis's voice sounded so befuddled, Neff later said, that he first thought the caller was an intoxicated hoaxer and so he started to hang up until Travis screamed his identity and begged for help. Travis was calling from a pay-phone at the Enco gas station in Heber. Neff then drove to nearby Snowflake to inform Mrs. Kellett (who had no phone) and to pick up Duane so the two men could drive to Heber. They found Travis collapsed on the floor of the phone booth.

When Travis had called collect, the telephone operator had obtained his name so she could ask the other party if they would accept the charges. When Travis gave his name, the operator recognized the importance of the call, and she remained on the line long enough to hear Travis ask that his family come to Heber to get him. The operator later decided she should inform Sheriff Gillespie, who in turn called Sheriff's Deputy Glen Flake, in Snowflake, to ask him to get dressed and drive to the outskirts of town to watch for a car bringing Travis back.

But by the time Flake got to the edge of town, Neff and Duane Walton already had returned with Travis. By this time it was around 2:00 A.M. Flake then decided to drive to Mrs. Kellett's home, where he noted that the lights were on but the shades were drawn. Outside the house Flake saw a man siphoning gas from one car to another. The man was Duane Walton, who explained to the officer that he had to get back to Phoenix and had forgotten to buy gas while the local stations were open, so he was siphoning fuel from his brother-in-law's car. Flake made no mention of information obtained through the telephone operator, who asked that her action be kept secret because it was a technical violation of telephone-company policy. Flake did not inquire about the activity in Mrs. Kellett's house at this late hour or ask to go inside. And Duane, who barely forty-eight hours earlier

had been pounding the desk in the sheriff's office, demanding another costly search effort, did not tell Flake that Travis had returned and was inside
the house.

Upon returning with Travis to Snowflake, Duane had insisted that
Travis strip off all his clothes to stand "inspection." *He found no bruises,
no burns, no evidence of physical injury,* except for a small red scab-mark
on the inside crease of the right elbow. Duane's subsequent actions suggest
that he may have suspected that the reason for Travis's "befuddled" state of
mind was that he was under the influence of drugs. If that were the case, the
drugs could have been administered aboard the UFO, *if the abduction story
were true.* (Later Travis publicly admitted to having "experimented" with
pot, "uppers," and LSD in what he called his "early wild years.")

Duane concluded that despite the lack of any evidence of physical in
jury, Travis was sorely in need of medical attention. But he decided against
going to the closest doctor in Show Low, some twelve miles away. Instead
Duane decided to drive Travis to Phoenix. They set out shortly after law-
enforcement officer Flake departed and arrived at Duane's house in Glendale, near Phoenix, shortly before 7:00 A.M.

After arriving home, Duane called William Spaulding, of Ground
Saucer Watch, who lives in Phoenix. He had met Spaulding several days
earlier when the GSW official visited Heber for an on-site investigation into
the incident. At that time Spaulding told Duane that if Travis should return,
that GSW could provide specialists for his examination. Spaulding also had
told Duane to be sure to obtain a urine specimen promptly in case there
should be any speculation that Travis "was off on a drug-trip," Spaulding
later told me. After Duane called, Spaulding arranged for the Waltons to
visit a "Dr." Lester Steward, a hypnotherapist who runs a school of hypnosis in Phoenix. But when they arrived at Steward's office and saw the sign
on the door, Duane's first words to Steward were that Travis needed a
medical examination, complete with laboratory tests, and was not yet ready
to undergo regressive hypnosis to probe his memory of the events of the
past week.

Steward later recalled that Travis "seemed very confused" and sat with
his head in his hands, letting Duane do most of the talking about what
allegedly had transpired aboard the UFO. Steward later told me he first
believed that Travis's behavior was the result of his traumatic experience
aboard a UFO. But as time passed, Travis seemed to emerge from his state
of depression, reminding Steward of drug addicts with whom he had worked. As time passed and the office became warmer, Travis rolled up his
sleeves and Steward said he noticed the red mark at the crease of the elbow
that Duane had spotted a few hours earlier. Steward made several telephone
calls, attempting to arrange for medical-laboratory tests for Travis. Finally,
Duane became impatient with the delay and the two men left, to return to
Duane's home.

Shortly after arriving back in Glendale, Duane began to receive telephone calls from reporters who had heard reports that Travis had returned. Duane acknowledged that Travis had been found but said that he was then undergoing medical tests in an unnamed hospital in Tucson. APRO's Coral Lorenzen, having heard this cover story, checked with all the Tucson hospitals and found the story was spurious, prompting her to suspect that Travis was in Glendale with Duane. She called, explained APRO's sympathetic views on stories of UFO abductions, and asked if APRO might be of assistance. When Duane said that Travis was sorely in need of a medical examination, Mrs. Lorenzen offered to send a doctor to Duane's house within a matter of several hours, an offer that Duane promptly accepted.

Shortly after 3:00 P.M., on Tuesday, November 11, Dr. Howard Kandell and Dr. Joseph Saults, both APRO members, arrived at Duane's home for what must have seemed to the two doctors to be a historic moment — the opportunity to give a physical examination to a man who, reportedly, had been aboard a UFO for five days. They brought along a camera and a tape recorder, *but Duane flatly refused to let them use either,* Kandell later told me. Further, Duane asked that the doctors limit themselves to a cursory examination and not to ask Travis for any details of his UFO experience, and the doctors complied. Kandell told me that Travis would reply cryptically to questions "but he really did not expound on anything voluntarily."

Kandell said that Duane gave him a urine specimen, which he said was the first voided by Travis after his return. Subsequent laboratory analysis of this specimen showed no traces of drugs, but it revealed something else that Kandell found perplexing. He explained to me that "if a person goes without food or water for more than a day or two, your body starts to break down its own fat. The waste product . . . is a substance that is excreted in the urine, called acetone. So that if a person has been without nutrition for a period of four or five days, you would expect to see acetone in his urine." *Yet the lab analysis showed no such acetones in the specimen that Duane claimed had been the first voided by Travis after his return.* Travis later would claim that he weighed himself the night he returned and found that he had lost ten pounds during the five-day absence. When I asked Kandell if it would be possible to determine whether the specimen had come from Travis or from another male, he said that there was no way to determine who had voided the specimen.

Kandell said he also noted the small mark in the crease of Travis's right elbow "which was compatible with a puncture wound such as when somebody takes blood from you . . . . I came across this in the course of my examination and asked him if he knew how he got this. And he said no, he hadn't noticed it before." This is curious because the mark reportedly had been observed earlier both by Duane and by Steward. Months later Travis would suggest that the "puncture wound" had been caused by a thorn acquired during timber-thinning operations nearly a week earlier. Yet Kandell told me that the wound appeared to be only from twenty-four to forty-eight hours old.

Shortly after Mrs. Lorenzen had made arrangements for Kandell and Saults to examine Travis, she received a telephone call from the *National Enquirer,* which also had heard of Travis's return. It was seeking APRO's appraisal of the case. Mrs. Lorenzen suggested that Travis and Duane be "sequestered" in the nearby Scottsdale Sheraton Inn, because he was too disturbed to tell his story to the news media. The *National Enquirer* agreed to underwrite the expense in return for getting an exclusive story on the incident.

About the same time, Duane decided that he ought to inform Sheriff Gillespie that Travis had returned. But when he telephoned the law-enforcement officer, he said was calling from Tucson where Travis had entered an unnamed hospital for a physical checkup. Several hours later Duane called again to revise his story, saying that he and Travis were in a private home near Phoenix. As Gillespie later recalled the incident for me, "I told him I need to talk to Travis, and he said, well, Travis is not available. And I said, well, you need to make him available so I can talk to him." Duane finally agreed and Gillespie made the four-hour drive to Glendale, arriving around 11:00 P.M. on Tuesday night, November 11 — nearly twenty-four hours after Travis had first called from Heber.

Gillespie told me that he found Travis lying on a sofa in Duane's living room. The sheriff had brought along a tape recorder but told me that "they made an almost insistent request that there be nobody else around, *and no recordings.*" Gillespie told me that Travis spoke "in a very low tone of voice. I talked to him quite a while, asking him numerous questions and had him relate his story." Travis volunteered to take a polygraph test within several days, and so when Gillespie returned home he made arrangements for the lie-detector test to be given in Phoenix on Friday, November 14.

By Wednesday, November 12, Duane and Travis had moved to a suite at the Scottsdale Sheraton Inn to escape the news media and Travis's return was making headlines across the nation, even overseas. The *Arizona Daily Star,* of Tucson, headlined its story: "MAN SAYS BROTHER SPENT 5 DAYS ON UFO." The article quoted Duane as saying: "He was on a UFO for five days and did have some contact with alien beings. *I'm not a UFO buff and neither is my brother.* I'm convinced he's telling the truth. He's never lied in his life, never even played a practical joke." [Emphasis added.] The article said that Duane had told Deputy Sheriff Coplan: "He [Travis] had a great experience" and that his brother only wanted a brief rest before making a full report on his remarkable experience. The article said that Travis would hold a press conference in Phoenix on Friday—the same day he was scheduled to take the polygraph test. The following day, Travis secretly visited the office of Dr. Kandell for a more detailed examination that included analysis of a blood sample, which revealed nothing unusual.

On Thursday, November 13, APRO's James Lorenzen drove to Phoenix, where he was met by APRO's director of research, Dr. James A. Harder, who had just flown in from San Francisco. The two proceeded to the Scottsdale Inn for their first meeting with the Waltons. They were joined by a crew of reporters from the *National Enquirer.* The mood must have been a festive one for both APRO officials and the *Enquirer* reporters because they had exclusive access to the principal involved in one of the most dramatic UFO incidents on record.

Because the whereabouts of the two Walton brothers was secret, the news media peppered Sheriff Gillespie's office with its queries. One telephone call came from a London newspaper reporter. Another from a woman who said that her child had just been abducted by a UFO! An AP dispatch from Holbrook indicated that the sheriff's office had some doubts about Travis's abduction claims. It quoted Deputy Sheriff Coplan as saying that Travis had volunteered to take a polygraph test "after he has had a chance to recuperate" and that the test would be given Friday or early the following week. The sheriff's office was being intentionally vague because Duane had asked for secrecy.

But Travis did not show up on Friday, November 14, for the scheduled polygraph test or for a press conference. The explanation later offered by APRO, in the November 1975 issue of *The APRO Bulletin* was: "The press literally laid siege to Duane's home and were camped at the building where the test was to be administered and Duane did not feel his brother was ready to face the press." This is a curious explanation inasmuch as Travis already was talking to the press—a team of reporters from the *National Enquirer,* a publication that readily accepts tall UFO tales. If the Waltons were concerned about reporters "camped at the building where the test was to be administered," Duane could have called Gillespie to ask that the polygraph examiner discretely come to the Scottsdale Inn. But he did not.

That night, the Waltons, APRO officials, and the *National Enquirer* reporters convened in the home of Dr. Kandell, who, understandably, was eager to learn more about Travis's experience. APRO's Dr. Harder attempted to hypnotize Travis, to see if he was susceptible to hypnosis, and found that he was, Kandell later told me. While Walton was under hypnosis, Harder asked him a few questions about his experience aboard the UFO. "We spent about two hours chatting about the incident," Kandell later told me, before the party broke up and the Waltons returned to the hotel.

The next morning, Lorenzen called Dr. Jean Rosenbaum, a psychiatrist who lives in Durango, Colorado, and invited him and his wife Beryl, a psychoanalyst, to fly to Phoenix to help APRO appraise the veracity of Travis's story. The Rosenbaums arrived in Phoenix during the early evening of Saturday, November 15, and spent the next several days there interviewing Travis. On Sunday, Dr. Rosenbaum invited a prominent Scottsdale psychiatrist, Dr. Warren Gorman, to meet and talk with Travis. During the

Rosenbaum's visit they watched as APRO's Harder used hypnotic-regression on Travis in an effort to enhance his recall of events that alleged-ly had occurred during his UFO experience. Subsequently Dr. Rosenbaum told me that Harder's questions during hypnosis were "loaded." While the psychiatrist said he believed that Harder "did this unconsciously," he said that Harder would guide Travis by asking: "Didn't you feel this, or that?" Beryl Rosenbaum agreed that Harder "is a very 'suggestive hypnotist.'"

In my later discussions with Dr. Rosenbaum, I asked whether Travis had at any time mentioned a strong prior interest in UFOs. The Durango psychiatrist replied:

> Everybody in the family claimed that they had seen one . . . he not only comes from a "UFO-family," but from a "UFO-culture." Everybody in that area of the country sees UFOs all the time. And his brother had seen one a week or two before, and his mother had seen some. Everybody in the family had seen some and he's been preoccupied with this almost all of his life . . . . *Then he made the comment to his mother just prior to the incident that if he was ever abducted by a UFO she was not to worry because he'd be all right.*" [Emphasis added.]

When I asked: "There's no doubt in your mind that he, his mother, and his brother were UFO enthusiasts?" Dr. Rosenbaum replied: "Oh for sure. They talked about it all the time."

After spending several days with Travis, Dr. Rosenbaum said that he, his wife, and Dr. Gorman, concluded that "he [Travis] really believes he was abducted by a UFO. But my evaluation of the boy's story is that . . . it was all in his own mind. I feel that he suffered from a combination of imagina-tion and amnesia, a transitory psychosis—that he did *not* go on a UFO, but simply was wandering around during the period of his disappearance. But I'm unable to account for five witnesses having [telling] the same basic story and passing lie-detector tests about it."

When I talked with Dr. Rosenbaum a few weeks later he told me:

> My conclusions are that he [Travis] really believes this happened to him, that he's not lying, but that he underwent a mental aberration, a severe mental aberration . . . . [Travis had] undergone a considerable life crisis in the past year, details of which I cannot go into, and this [UFO incident] was the culmination of that life crisis. As far as we are concerned . . . he really believes it happened. *We know it didn't.* It is accountable as a mental aberration, of which I have seen a lot.

The life crisis to which Dr. Rosenbaum referred subsequently was made public in a UFO magazine. Travis's father reportedly had abandoned his family when Travis was only eighteen months old. Later Travis's mother had remarried and the family had moved to Phoenix, but two years later her new husband had abandoned the family and they had moved back to a relatively impoverished life in Snowflake. Travis's own father had twice tried to establish ties with Travis, but a year before the UFO incident the father had died, plunging Travis into an extended period of depression.

Dr. Rosenbaum's explanation seemed flawed on several counts. First, it did not account for the stories told by Rogers and five other crew members that they had seen a UFO "zap" Travis with an intense blue-green ray that sent him reeling. If Travis simply had been wandering around the woods for five days, without nourishment, why were there no acetones in the urine specimen supplied by Duane to Dr. Kandell? And if this specimen had not really come from Travis, then Duane was resorting to trickery, which would suggest that even he suspected the incident might be a hoax.

A book published on the incident, *The Walton Experience* (Berkley Publishing Corp., 1978), which gives Travis Walton as its author, quotes a statement issued by Dr. Rosenbaum that says: "Our conclusion—which is absolute—is that this young man is not lying—that there is no collusion, no attempt to hoax . . . ." But the book omits Dr. Rosenbaum's other conclusion: that Travis actually "did not go on a UFO."

On Saturday, November 22, eleven days after Travis reappeared, the public had the first opportunity to hear him tell his story of what allegedly had occurred during his experience aboard a flying saucer, when he was interviewed on Phoenix television station KOOL by reporters James Ryerson and Charles Diamond. Diamond began by inviting Travis to "publicly recount your story from the time you were driving in the truck."

> WALTON: Well, the first part has been told [previously] by all the [other] witnesses. Ah, but I'll recount my view of that. Ah, we'd just finished working, because it was getting dark. We packed up to leave and we all got in the truck and we were riding up the road. And we looked off to the right side of the road and I saw a glow that I thought was [pause] a sunset, or something. I was about to comment when we came past the thicket that we were looking through to where we could see more clearly, and we saw a UFO hovering in the air, about thirty yards off to the side of the road. Everybody started yelling and they stopped the truck. I wanted to get a closer look and, ah, I got out of the truck and I started over there. Everybody was yelling to come back, to stop. I stopped and looked back. Somebody called my name and I turned back around and it [UFO] started to make a noise and started to move and I took one step. I crouched down behind the log that was there and just as I started to raise up—I was just going to stand up—I didn't have any intention of going any closer, but it was just as if I was struck. It was a kind of a physical blow. It just knocked me back. I don't remember seeing any flash of light or anything like what they described. I just lost consciousness. When I regained consciousness I was looking up at a light shining down on me from the ceiling. I could tell I was laying [sic] up on a bed or a table or something, because the ceiling was close. I was in a lot of pain. I couldn't quite bring myself totally awake.

RYERSON: What type of pain? What parts of your body?

WALTON: Ah, it was kind of like my head, but just all over. I can't describe it. And [pause] I believed that I was in the hospital and I was looking up at the ceiling. And I didn't make any attempt to move because of the pain I was in. But I felt something laying [sic] across my chest. And I looked down and it was sort of a flat thing that kind of curved across like that. And I couldn't focus my eyes very well. But I looked beyond the top edge of the thing that was laying across me and I saw two men leaning, leaning over me. They were a lot like men, ah, ah, they were a lot like men, but they weren't quite human.

DIAMOND: What did they physically look like?

WALTON: They were, they had kind of underdeveloped features, and no hair of any kind. And they were dressed in a kind of brownish-orange.

DIAMOND: About how tall were they?

WALTON: They were [pause] slightly shorter than myself.

RYERSON: What type of clothing was their dress?

WALTON: It was sort of a loose coverall. I didn't see any buttons or anything like that. But I, being in so much pain, and everything, I didn't, I didn't even think. I just lashed out and knocked them back. I could see that there were two on the right side and one on the left. I [pause] jumped into the corner.

DIAMOND: Did you actually strike them? Did you actually touch them when you lashed out?

WALTON: Yes, I did. I kind of hit these two with the back of my arm, and they fell back real easily.

DIAMOND: Did it feel like hitting a person would?

WALTON: Yes, they seemed light, like they weren't heavy. But I, I couldn't stand up very well. I, ah, I, ah, I leaned against—there was a bench across the back wall—I say the back wall, I mean there was only one door. And I grabbed up a tube, a clear piece of glass, or something, and I tried to break off the end to get something sharp to defend myself with. But they didn't try to approach. They just kind of put out their hands like that. [Long pause] I was leaning—I couldn't stand up very well—*and I was bleeding very heavily.** And they didn't try to approach or anything. They just left. They just ran out real fast. And I was alone there for several minutes and I couldn't catch my breath. It was very hot. And I was afraid they'd come back. And so I, I left. They'd gone. There was a corridor outside and they went to the right so I went to the left.

RYERSON: You went through the door?

WALTON: Yes, there was no door. It was just a hole, a doorway.

RYERSON: An opening?

WALTON: And I, it was a curving hallway. It curves to the right. And there was another door with no doorway. It was just a hole. And I went into a room there and . . .

DIAMOND: [Interrupting] Had you gone very far, a very far distance at that point?

---

*No evidence of blood was found on Travis's clothing, nor did subsequent medical examination reveal any external or internal source of heavy bleeding.

WALTON: It was only about thirty feet, or forty feet. I don't know. Not very far. No, not even that far. I don't remember. It was a very narrow corridor. And it was dimly lit everywhere. And I went into this room that you could see *out* [of]. *You could even see the stars* back through the wall I just came through. It was—I could still see that there were walls—but I could see the stars at the same time.

RYERSON: And they didn't look like windows?

WALTON: No, it wasn't like that. And there was nothing in the room but a chair with some controls and knobs and things. I was just, kind of, I was, I was hysterical. I was frantic. And I just moved around in there for a while. And I started fooling with the buttons there.

DIAMOND: Did you sit in the chair?

WALTON: Yes, I did later. At first I just touched it. I didn't think that I should be [pause]. I was afraid I'd mess something up and that somebody would come. And, ah, I heard somebody come in, and I turned around, and it was a man, just like, just like people. I mean he wasn't like the other creatures, or whatever, at all. He looked just like you and I, except he had a helmet on, a sort of a clear helmet.

DIAMOND: And he had hair and everything?

WALTON: Yes. I, I started babbling questions to him, and I ran over there, and he wouldn't, he wouldn't answer me. He just took me by the arm and wanted me to go with him. I thought maybe he can't hear me through the helmet. So we went out through the door, down to the right and out to the left. There was a small room there. It had doors on it, and it was kind of like an air-lock. It was just a small room with nothing in it. And then there was a door that went outside. And it was a ramp that went down, and it was cool outside. It was, I could feel a wind. There was a draft, or something. It was a large room that this thing was sitting on the floor in there. And it was shaped like the drawing that they [Mike Rogers] made, like the thing [UFO] we saw the first time, only bigger. *And there were two other things in there, other UFO-looking things, looked like flying saucers,* kind of, except that they were rounded and oval-shaped, and they were really shiny, like, ah, chrome. It was, it was a big room, like there was a lot more rooms in there. And there was a curved ceiling. It curved this way, and it had flat ends to the room. I came out of the door, out of the first ship, facing this way, and there was a doorway across in the, the far wall. He led me across there and through that doorway, down a hallway to a room, and I'd had a burning in my chest, and it was starting [pause], I felt better. [Pause]. I was trying to get this man to tell me what, what, you know, *I asked him if he was from earth* and just anything I could think of. And he wouldn't answer. [Emphasis added.]

DIAMOND: Was he expressionless? Did he have any expression on his face?

WALTON: No, he looked friendly. He gestured and smiled. But there were no words.

DIAMOND: In this place that you were in, could you see out at all?

WALTON: No, there was no way out there.

RYERSON: So you were going from one ship [craft] to another? Was that essentially it?

WALTON: Yes. This must have been inside of a larger building or ship. I don't know if it was a large ship or a building. I never felt any motion or anything. It was just like being in a large building all the time. Everything solid. I was led down the hallway. The man sat me in a chair and in a room with three other people that were like himself. They were dressed in blue. And he went out—there was a door on the other side—he went through. And I sat in the chair and I tried to get the people to talk to me that were there. And they didn't have things [helmets] on their heads and so I thought that maybe they could hear me. But they wouldn't answer either. There was [sic] two men and a woman in the room after the first man left. A man and a woman came from around the table and they each took me by the arm and they led me over to the table, and got me up on the table. And finally, I don't know why I should cooperate with them. They put a deal over my face—it was kind of like an oxygen-mask thing. It was kind of clear plastic and it had a round, black thing on it about that big, just attached to it. I looked up at the ceiling, which was just all solid light. There wasn't any light fixture or anything, but light in the room coming from the ceiling. And that was the last I remembered. I went to sleep. Until I woke up, I was laying [sic] on the pavement. It was very cold. I woke up suddenly and I looked up the roadway. I was laying outside. It was night. And I could see a light on the bottom of a flying saucer that looked just like the rounded ones that were inside there. And it was very shiny. But the only light came out of the bottom, but, and that went off, and it went straight up, just really fast. [Pause] Just without a sound.

DIAMOND: What were your feelings at that point? Were you still in pain? Did you know where you were?

WALTON: I didn't know where I was immediately, but I recognized the roadway. And I could see a light down the hill, so I ran down that way. And it was about a mile or half a mile to Heber. And I ran down to the phone booth that is by the gas station there, and I called my brother-in-law. And I don't know what I said, I was, I was, hysterical. And he answered and said, "Who is this?" And I tried to tell him, and he said, "I think you've got the wrong number." And he started to hang up and I screamed at him that it was me. And so he, he stopped and he said, "Okay, I'll get somebody to come, to come and get you." And I hung up and I just couldn't stand up anymore and I just sat down there [inside the booth].

DIAMOND: Were you in physical pain?

WALTON: No, not at the time. I didn't feel any more pain. I was just so weak I couldn't stand up. I was extremely thirsty. And I haven't been able to make any purpose out of that, or anything. But that's the way it happened.

RYERSON: A question that's been bothering a lot of people, Travis: Why didn't you bring your story to the [news] media?

WALTON: Well, they, my family, ah, ah, told me about the news people and all the people that were crowding around and I was in no condition to talk to anybody, especially, you know, a mob of people like that. I just couldn't handle it.

At this point in the program, APRO's James Lorenzen was introduced, and Ryerson asked him if Travis's reluctance to submit to news-media questioning was typical for such UFO incidents. Lorenzen replied: "It is in some cases, yes. I can vouch for what he said because when I saw, first saw, Travis he was in a very unsettled state and, ah, he was really in no position to fend questions or to respond." Later in the interview, the following exchange occurred:

> DIAMOND: Could you tell us what kind of testing that Travis has undergone, what the results were of that, and what the plans are for the future?
>
> LORENZEN: Well, I can do this generally. We had him checked by a couple of M.D.'s, and they ran some tests . . . and this completely does away with the idea that there was any drug involvement that some people have brought up . . . . And he's been, ah, ah, interviewed at great depth by some very well-respected psychiatrists. And they have concluded that he is not a party to any hoax, and that he's telling the truth . . . . [Lorenzen failed to add that the psychiatrists also were firmly convinced that Travis had not really been taken aboard a UFO and that he was simply fantasizing.]
>
> DIAMOND: What other kinds of tests would he be going through in the future?
>
> LORENZEN: Well, see, ah, we're really sort of past the testing stage in a sense. In other words, from now on I think you'd more, I think you'd be more likely to call it research. We hope to have this memory, the blocked memory relieved so that we can get a full account of what happened. [Although Travis had been absent for five days, the events he described could not have occupied more than an hour or two.]
>
> RYERSON: Why not the polygraph test? This has been a major criticism.
>
> LORENZEN: All right. Because a lot of people have criticized it [that is, Travis's failure to show up for the scheduled polygraph test]. Because they think polygraph is a lie-detector, because it's called that. But it's not. And Travis was under that impression too. He was anxious to take a lie-detector, or polygraph, test. *I advised him not to, and several other people advised him not to,* because what it actually measures is stress. And questions about stressful memories would bring stress reactions, just as well as anything else. So it would have been meaningless to have him take that test at that time. It could have been—in fact one of the psychiatrists say it would have been a disaster for him to take it at the time. It would have created a lot of false impressions. [Emphasis added.]
>
> DIAMOND: How would you explain the other six witnesses taking a [polygraph] test and having passed it then?
>
> LORENZEN: Well, their memories, of course, are not blocked. They remember what happened. It wasn't the same sort of stressful situation that Travis has obviously gone through.

Lorenzen was withholding a key fact—that Travis had taken a polygraph test in secret, administered by John J. McCarthy, the most experienced and one of the most respected examiners in the state of Arizona. Lorenzen himself had made the arrangements for the test and had been informed of the results immediately after the tests were completed. Travis had flunked the lie-detector test—badly.

20

Polygraph Tests

The initial reactions of major UFO organizations to the Walton story were mixed, even before they learned of the secret McCarthy polygraph test. GSW's Spaulding called the case a hoax. NICAP, one of the most conservative of the UFO groups at the time, expressed doubts as to whether the case was authentic. MUFON straddled the fence; its first account of the case in its monthly publication concluded: "Because of inconsistent factors, it is impossible to determine whether the case is authentic or a hoax." APRO's conclusion was that "the Travis Walton case is one of the most important and intriguing in the history of the UFO phenomena."

On the afternoon of February 7, 1976, APRO announced that it had new evidence to support its position: Travis and Duane Walton both had taken polygraph tests in Phoenix, arranged by APRO, and both had passed, according to examiner George J. Pfeifer, then employed by Tom Ezell and Associates, a respected organization. The first detailed account of these tests appeared in *The APRO Bulletin,* dated December 1975, but which obviously had not been published until late February 1976.

The first of nine relevant (test) questions that Travis was asked was: "Before November 5, 1975, were you a UFO buff?" He had answered "No," and Pfeifer concluded that he was telling the truth. This contradicted extensive indications that Travis, Duane, and their mother had had a long-standing interest in UFOs. In the tape-recorded interview with Fred Sylvanus, on November 8, Duane said, "We've paid a lot of attention to it [UFOs] . . . we see them quite regularly." And Duane had described his pact with Travis that if either ever got the opportunity to go aboard a UFO he would try to get the UFOnauts to pick up the other brother. "We discussed this time and again," Duane told Sylvanus. When Deputy Sheriff Coplan and Mike Rogers had driven over to inform Mrs. Kellett of the incident, she had told him of her own and Duane's frequent UFO sightings.

181

Dr. Rosenbaum, who had spent several days talking with Travis, had told me that "he comes from a 'UFO-family. . . . They talked about it [UFOs] all the time. When I had asked Dr. Kandell if Travis or Duane had mentioned a prior interest in UFOs, the physician replied: "They admitted to that freely—that he was, you know, a 'UFO freak', so to speak . . . he had made remarks before that if he ever saw one he'd like to go aboard." Yet when Travis was tested by Pfeifer and was asked if he was "a UFO buff," he had answered "No" and Pfeifer's appraisal of the polygraph chart was that Travis was being truthful. This aroused my suspicions about the test.

During my earlier investigation into the Pascagoula, Mississippi, "UFO abduction" incident, I had acquired some understanding of the use of the polygraph. I had learned that the value of any polygraph test is determined principally by the skill and experience of the examiner, both in framing the relevant questions and in interpreting the complex charts of the test-subject's heart-beat/pulse, respiration, and perspiration that are produced by the polygraph machine. For this reason it was important to determine the credentials of Pfeifer, the man who had tested and passed Travis and Duane Walton.

Whenever possible, I try to conduct my UFO investigation interviews after formal working hours so as not to interfere with a person's work and my own. But when I tried to obtain Pfeifer's home telephone, I was told that it was "unlisted" and could not be given out. This left me no choice but to call Pfeifer at Tom Ezell and Associates, which I did on March 13, 1976. Ezell himself answered and told me that Pfeifer no longer was employed by his company. Ezell said that Pfeifer originally had given up his own private practice to work for Ezell and Associates about a month before giving the Walton tests and that Pfeifer had left, by mutual consent, a few weeks after the Walton tests to again set up his own practice.

Ezell told me that APRO's representative, Dr. Harold Cahn, had tried to call Pfeifer at his original business number and had been referred to his new place of employment. Pfeifer had told Cahn that he should make arrangements with Ezell, which he had done. Ezell told me that he himself had been out of town on the day the tests were given and had since been too busy to examine Pfeifer's polygraph charts to make his own appraisal. But he offered to do so and suggested I call him back in about ten days.

On March 22, when I called Ezell back, he told me he had gone over Pfeifer's charts and that *in his opinion it was impossible to tell whether Travis and Duane Walton were responding truthfully to the test questions.* Further, Ezell said, Pfeifer had noted on the charts that he had allowed Travis to "dictate" some of the test questions he would be asked. This, Ezell said, was a violation of basic principles of polygraphy. He explained that the test-sponsor or subject could outline the general area to be probed, but the examiner ought to frame the relevant questions using proven polygraph techniques. (Ezell had taken his own training at the highly respected Keeler Polygraph Institute, in Chicago, graduating in 1971. He had served as a polygraph examiner for the Phoenix Police Department until 1974, when he left to set up his own company. His earlier experience with the Phoenix Police Department had included a stint as an investigator on its homicide squad.)

Ezell confirmed our discussion in a letter dated March 29 which said: "Upon review of this examination, I find that to me it is not acceptable. In the first place I would not be a party to an examination in which the subject *dictated* the questions to be asked. . . . Because of the dictation of the questions to be asked, this test should be invalidated. Also, upon examining the resultant charts, I find that I cannot given an opinion one way or another," that is, whether the subjects answered the test questions truthfully or not.

During my March 22 conversation with Ezell, I asked him about the statement contained in *The APRO Bulletin* (December 1975), saying that Pfeifer "is a licensed and experienced polygraph operator." Ezell told me that the state of Arizona did not then require polygraph examiners to be tested and licensed, although he and others were actively pushing the legislature to pass such a law. As for APRO's claim that Pfeifer was an "experienced" examiner, Ezell told me that Pfeifer then had been practicing for only two years. (Pfeifer later would confirm this.)

Near the end of our first (March 13) conversation, Ezell casually dropped a bombshell: "Let me give you a little information that might help you. Walton was also given another examination before George [Pfeifer] gave him one." When I asked who had given this heretofore secret test, Ezell replied: "I believe by a Jack McCarthy, who I would say is one helluva good examiner, in Phoenix." Considering that McCarthy was Ezell's competitor, his unsolicited endorsement was strong praise. Ezell added that he suspected that APRO had contacted Pfeifer to conduct a polygraph test "because I don't think McCarthy passed him." He added: "McCarthy is well thought of in APA [American Polygraph Association] circles." Ezell had learned of the earlier test from Pfeifer, who in turn had learned of it from APRO officials.

I asked Ezell how a relatively inexperienced examiner like Pfeifer could pass Travis Walton, knowing that such a respected and experienced examiner as McCarthy had flunked him. Ezell replied: "Perhaps George is like a lot of examiners . . . always looking for one big break. Knowing this [Walton case] is a national deal, perhaps George could see his name emblazoned in neon lights." (Within a month after the Walton tests were made public, Pfeifer *was* a UFO celebrity and set up his own office.)

Subsequent investigation revealed why John J. McCarthy elicited such praise from a competitor. He had been trained at the Army's polygraph school, then located at Fort Gordon, Georgia, which is recognized as the top polygraph-training center in the world. After leaving the Army,

McCarthy had passed the rigorous licensing examination given by the state of Illinois and for nearly twenty years he had practiced in Phoenix, making him the senior examiner in Arizona. McCarthy had qualified as an expert witness in the Superior Court of Maricopa County (Phoenix) and as a result of his participation before the Arizona Supreme Court, expert polygraph testimony for the first time had been accepted as admissable evidence in any criminal trial in Arizona.

My first telephone call to McCarthy on March 15 could not have come at a more fortuitous time. A few days earlier a friend in Flagstaff had sent McCarthy a newspaper article telling of the results of Pfeifer's examination of Travis and Duane Walton. This friend was not aware that McCarthy had earlier tested Travis and had concluded that he was not telling the truth about the UFO incident, but the friend knew of McCarthy's keen interest in all matters dealing with his profession. McCarthy and his wife had chanced to see Travis tell his story on TV station KOOL on November 22 and had heard APRO's Lorenzen say that three psychiatrists had "concluded that he [Travis] is not party to any hoax. And that he's telling the truth." But Lorenzen had made no mention of the McCarthy polygraph test. It certainly must have rankled McCarthy later to read that a polygraph test given by a relatively inexperienced examiner seemingly had endorsed the authenticity of the "UFO abduction," when McCarthy's own examination indicated quite the opposite.

After introducing myself to McCarthy, telling him of my investigation into the Walton incident and the fact that I was skeptical about UFOs and "abduction cases," I observed: "Now maybe you can guess why I am calling." McCarthy replied: "I've got a pretty good idea." I mentioned that Ezell had told me that he understood that McCarthy had earlier tested Travis, and McCarthy acknowledged that he had. When I asked for McCarthy's conclusions, he replied: *"Gross deception!"*

McCarthy told me that he had first been approached by Lorenzen, who had obtained his name from an APRO member in Phoenix who had once used the services of McCarthy's Arizona Polygraph Laboratory. Lorenzen had called on Friday, November 14, the day that Travis had decided not to appear for the test scheduled by Sheriff Gillespie. Lorenzen then had introduced APRO's Harder and bowed out of the conversation, while Harder briefed McCarthy on the incident. Harder told McCarthy that he had subjected Travis to regressive hypnosis the night before, prompting the experienced examiner to ask if Travis would be under the influence of post-hypnotic suggestion during the test, which could affect its results. Harder said that Travis would not be under such influence. McCarthy said he asked Harder if he believed that Travis was mentally and physically able to take a polygraph test and Harder said he was. Harder explained that Travis was being sequestered at the Scottsdale hotel and insisted that McCarthy not reveal in advance that he had been asked to test Travis or to disclose his whereabouts. McCarthy agreed.

McCarthy arrived at the hotel shortly after noon where he was met by Harder and two reporters from the *National Enquirer,* Paul Jenkins and Jeff Wells. A photographer also was present and McCarthy was asked if he had any objection to having his picture taken after the tests for use in a subsequent article, to which the examiner agreed. While Harder and the reporters went out for lunch, McCarthy listened to tape recordings Harder had made earlier in which Travis described his alleged UFO experiences, to enable McCarthy to prepare his test questions. It was shortly after 2:00 P.M. when McCarthy was introduced to Travis, and the two retired to the hotel suite where McCarthy had set up his polygraph machine.

During the lengthy pre-test discussion, intended to acquaint the examiner with the subject's background and to bring out any incidents that are *unrelated* to the issues to be probed during the test but which might cause undue stress, McCarthy asked Travis if he had ever used drugs. Travis admitted that he had earlier tried marijuana, "speed," and LSD. When Travis was asked whether he had ever been arrested, he acknowledged that he had been involved in the theft of payroll checks five years earlier and subsequent forgery of those checks.* Finally, McCarthy went over each of the test questions he would ask, which is standard procedure to assure that the subject understands each question and is able to answer each with an unequivocal "Yes" or "No." After reviewing one of the questions, "Have you acted in collusion with others to perpetrate a UFO hoax?", McCarthy decided to ask if Travis knew the meaning of the word *collusion.* When Travis revealed that he did not, McCarthy explained, "That means acting in concert with somebody else, one or more people to perpetrate a hoax . . . . Just like you acted in collusion with this friend of yours to burglarize the office, steal the checks, and forge them, right? That's collusion . . ."

After the test began, McCarthy asked several non-relevant questions, such as Travis's last name, whether or not he was born in Phoenix, went to school in Flagstaff—questions to which there would be no motivation to lie and which could provide a benchmark stress-level for comparison with the relevant questions. Additionally, McCarthy used the "intentional falsehood" technique to assure that Travis did respond significantly when telling a lie. McCarthy had prepared slips of paper, each containing a

---

*On May 5, 1971, Travis Walton and Charles Rogers, Mike Rogers' younger brother, had pleaded guilty in the Navajo County Superior Court to the following charge: "On or about the night of February 18, 1971, they broke into the office of the Western Molding Co., with intent to steal and did steal therefrom a quantity of Western Molding checks and on the 19th day of February filled out said checks payable to a fictitious person and signed the name of Robert W. Gonsalves, thereby to cheat and defraud." After the defendants agreed to make restitution of the funds, they were placed on a two-year probation. On August 3, 1971, having lived up to the terms of probation, they were allowed, under Arizona law, to "cleanse the record" by appearing in court and pleading "not guilty" to the original charge.

different single-digit number from which he asked Travis to select one while the examiner turned his head away. Then McCarthy told Travis to answer "No" to each question asked about what digit was on the selected piece of paper. McCarthy asked if Travis had selected the number three and he answered "No." Then the number five? Two? Six? Four? McCarthy, after looking at the polygraph chart, observed: "Okay, on here you're a good reactor. You picked the number six, right?" Travis acknowledged that McCarthy was correct. McCarthy explained that this procedure was used "to determine whether or not your, any anxiety you have or apprehension or anything else that you have [is] adversely affecting your responses."*

McCarthy and Travis emerged shortly after 4:00 P.M., after more than two hours together, and the experienced polygraph examiner announced his findings: "Gross deception," based on Travis's responses to nine relevant questions dealing with the alleged UFO incident. Furthermore, McCarthy said he found evidence that Travis intentionally was holding his breath before answering certain relevant questions in an attempt to "beat the machine," as McCarthy phrased it.

The *National Enquirer* reporters adjourned to another room for private discussions, while APRO's Harder called Lorenzen to inform him of the test results. Shortly, the *National Enquirer* representatives emerged with a hastily typed "secrecy agreement," which they asked McCarthy to sign. The agreement was so hurriedly drafted that it was erroneously dated February 15, 1975, nine months before the test was actually given, which clearly invalidated the agreement. McCarthy was asked to prepare a formal written report and send it to John Cathcart, associate editor of the *National Enquirer* at the tabloid's headquarters in Lantana, Florida, and to mark the envelope "Private and Confidential." There was no further talk of McCarthy posing for pictures with Travis and the polygraph machine.

The next day, November 16, McCarthy typed up his formal report and sent it to *National Enquirer* headquarters. The report concluded: "Based on his [Travis] reactions on all charts, it is the opinion of this examiner that Walton, in concert with others, is attempting to perpetrate a UFO hoax, and that he has not been on any spacecraft." If McCarthy assumed that the *National Enquirer* and APRO now would quietly abandon their support for the Walton incident, he underestimated the reluctance of a sensationalist tabloid and a major UFO group to give up a "hot case." Exactly one week later, when McCarthy and his wife saw Lorenzen on the local television program, he began to suspect what the future held. And several weeks later the *National Enquirer* published its full-page account of the Walton incident under the headline: "5 WITNESSES PASS LIE TEST WHILE CLAIMING

---

*APRO tape-recorded the McCarthy test. A verbatim transcript is contained in the book *Abducted* by Coral and Jim Lorenzen (Berkley Publishing Corp., 1977).

. . . ARIZONA MAN CAPTURED BY UFO," without any mention of the Mc-Carthy test. Then in February the media reported that both Travis and Duane had passed a polygraph test given by Pfeifer. Still McCarthy held his tongue until March 15, when I called and said that Ezell had told me that McCarthy had tested Travis several months earlier.

At that moment, McCarthy had faced a difficult moral issue as well as one reflecting on the professional standing of polygraphy. McCarthy opted to reveal the truth. Less than a week later, on March 21, I discussed the Walton case with APRO's Lorenzen by telephone, including the Pfeifer-administered polygraph tests. Without revealing what I had just learned about the earlier McCarthy test, I asked Lorenzen: "Do you know if Travis has taken any other polygraph tests?" Lorenzen replied: *"No, never."* I decided against revealing that I knew this statement was false.

Several weeks later I talked with Pfeifer by telephone, having learned from Ezell that he now was operating under the business name of Associated Polygraph. When I asked Pfeifer if it was true that "Travis came in with a list of questions that he wanted you to ask him, that he had framed the relevant questions," Pfeifer admitted that "theoretically that's correct." He went on to explain that "he and I sat down together and we discussed the incident and I solicited his questions, or questions to be used, beside some questions I wanted myself." When I asked if this was standard polygraph procedure, Pfeifer replied "Yes." But when I challenged his reply by noting that I had talked with other examiners who told me it was "not standard procedure," Pfeifer responded: "Well, like I wouldn't say no. But we don't have a standard situation here either." When I asked "in what respect," Pfeifer replied: "Well, how many times do people claim that they've been picked up by a UFO?"

In other words, Pfeifer admitted that he had departed from proven polygraph procedures, tested over many years, but he attempted to justify it on the grounds that traditional practices were not valid if the object of the test was to assess whether Travis was telling the truth about being abducted by a UFO.

During our conversation I learned of another curious aspect of the Pfeifer tests, one unknown to Ezell. Pfeifer told me that when APRO's Lorenzen called him to arrange for the examination he had asked for a test of only *one* of the Walton brothers. *Not Travis, but Duane.* There had not been any mention of the possibility that Travis was to be tested until *after* Pfeifer finished with Duane and had announced to Lorenzen and others in the APRO party that Duane had passed his test. *Only then did Lorenzen introduce Pfeifer to Travis and ask if he might also be tested.*

Several months later, when I exposed this curious aspect of the tests, Lorenzen had a ready explanation: "We needed to test Duane to examine whether there had been a conspiracy. I didn't feel there could have been a hoax without Duane being involved. As for not telling Pfeifer about Travis, he was still on the road from his home [in Snowflake] and we weren't sure he was going to make it, so we didn't want to bother Pfeifer with it until he [Travis] arrived." Since Travis was making the four-hour long drive from Snowflake solely to take a polygraph test, it seems strange that Lorenzen would not at least have mentioned this to Pfeifer in advance to be sure the examiner would have time to test Travis if/when he arrived in Phoenix. Another possible explanation for not mentioning a polygraph test for Travis in advance is that APRO did not want to risk a repetition of its earlier experience with McCarthy until its officials had had the opportunity to evaluate Pfeifer using Duane as a guinea pig.

When I apologized to Pfeifer for taking his time during working hours, adding that he probably was bothered a good deal by people wanting to talk about the Walton case, he replied: "I enjoy it." He expressed regret that he had not been able to meet with Dr. Hynek, CUFOS director, when he had visited Phoenix. But Pfeifer explained that Hynek's visit occurred on the same night that APRO had brought in Travis's mother for a polygraph test, which she too had passed, he said, except for one question.

During Hynek's visit in late March he interviewed Travis. Later Hynek had been interviewed by the local press, resulting in an Associated Press dispatch that began: "A leading national authority on unidentified flying objects said yesterday there is 'no substantiation' for allegations of a hoax made against a young Arizonan who said he was abducted by a UFO last year. Dr. J. Allen Hynek, a Northwestern University astronomer and head of the Center on [sic] UFO Studies, said he had interviewed Travis Walton and believes he is 'not hoaxing.' He also said Walton had successfully taken a lie detector test three weeks ago . . ."

Increasing doubts about the Pfeifer polygraph tests arose in my mind when I talked by telephone with Duane Walton in late April, before I made public the "secret" McCarthy test. One of the relevant questions that Duane had been asked during his test was: "Would you lie to help Travis in this matter?" Duane had answered "No" and Pfeifer concluded that Duane had responded truthfully.

Yet when I asked Duane: "When did Travis first take a polygraph, or lie-detector, test," he had replied: "I don't know. I don't have the foggiest notion. I know that he and I took one together recently," that is, the Pfeifer examination. Then I asked: "Had he taken any polygraph test before that?" Duane replied: "I don't have the foggiest notion. I really don't know." Yet Duane had been present in the Scottsdale hotel suite and had talked to McCarthy about Travis shortly before he had been tested. *And when McCarthy reported his findings, Duane had been "furious," McCarthy told me.*

Also it was a matter of record that Duane had lied to Sheriff Gillespie when he first called to report Travis had been found and had told the Sheriff that Travis was in a Tucson hospital undergoing medical tests when actually he was with Duane in Phoenix. While Duane's protective instincts were understandable, clearly he had told a falsehood during the Pfeifer tests, which the examiner failed to detect. Later when Pfeifer tested Mrs. Kellett, one of the relevant questions was, "Have you yourself ever seen a flying saucer?" She answered "No" and Pfeifer concluded she had answered truthfully. Yet the record shows that Mrs. Kellett repeatedly claimed to have seen UFOs on numerous occasions.

By late May when I talked with C. E. Gilson, who had given the polygraph tests to Mike Rogers and other crew members, Gilson had begun to have some second thoughts about his initial appraisal and public misinterpretations of his earlier comments. Gilson said that "our sole purpose" in giving the test was "to determine whether or not there had been a crime committed," that is, whether Travis had been the victim of foul play. The one UFO-related question asking if crew members had seen a UFO the night that Travis disappeared "does not make it a valid test as far as verifying the UFO incident. I wish these people out here would realize that, but there's no way you can even get them to listen to you," Gilson told me.

Gilson also had second thoughts about the test of Allen Dalis, whose charts he originally had characterized as "inconclusive." Gilson said that during interviews with the news media, Dalis had described the UFO in great detail, but during the pre-test discussion with Gilson, Dalis changed his story, claiming he had been so frightened that he had "ducked down in the seat and didn't see any blue-green flash," the examiner told me. "So he wasn't even being truthful to start with; what he originally claimed he saw he [later] admitted to me he didn't see any of it." (Dalis later would figure in a surprising development to be discussed in Chapter 22.)

21

Best Case of 1975 Award

As my own investigation continued and my suspicions of a hoax continued to grow, the question arose of possible motives. The most obvious, but difficult to prove, was the multi-thousand-dollar award offered each year by the *National Enquirer* for the most impressive case of the year, with a prize of $100,000 then being offered for "positive proof" of extraterrestrial visitors. Because the *National Enquirer* is prominently displayed at the checkout counter of most supermarkets and the prize-winning case is featured each year on the front page, it would be surprising if the Waltons were not aware of the prize money, considering their long-standing interest in UFOs.

But another possible motive emerged from my study of the Sylvanus tape-recorded interview of November 8 with Mike Rogers and Duane Walton. At one point in the interview Rogers said: "This contract we have [with the U.S. Forest Service] is seriously behind schedule. In fact, Monday [November 10] the time is up. We haven't done any work on it since Wednesday because of this thing [UFO incident], and therefore it won't be done. I hope they take that into account—this problem." Rogers' statement suggested that his default on the contract was at least partially the result of the UFO incident, which might be considered the sort of "act-of-God" extenuating circumstance included in such contracts.

However, I discovered that Rogers had been seriously behind in his contract long before the UFO incident when I talked with the Forest Service contracting officer, Maurice Marchbanks, at Springerville, Arizona, and his work-site inspector, Tom Hentz. Rogers had received a contract to thin out the Turkey Springs area more than a year before, on June 26, 1974, when he submitted a low-bid of only $27.40 per acre. The Rogers bid was less than half the price quoted by another bidder and 27 percent below that of another. Under the terms of the contract, Rogers had two hundred working days to complete the thinning of 1277 acres, which later was reduced to 1205 acres without a corresponding reduction in contract time. Contract completion for such work is specified in terms of working days to allow for bad weather and the long winter in the mountains, which typically begins in late October or early November and extends into May, preventing thinning operations during this period.

Rogers was slow in getting under way, Marchbanks told me after examining his records; he did not begin work until six weeks after receiving the contract. By early August of 1975, the two hundred working days had expired and Rogers had completed only about 70 percent of the job, leaving 353 acres yet to complete. To avoid default, Rogers had requested and been granted an eighty-four working-day extension to November 10, 1975. The basis for this extension, Marchbanks explained to me, was that during the initial year Rogers had averaged four and one-fourth acres per working day. If he could have maintained this average, he should have been able to finish the Turkey Springs job by November 10, barring an early snowfall. But Rogers would be penalized $1.00 per acre for work performed during this extension, reducing the price to $26.40 per acre. If Rogers originally had underestimated the difficulty of the job, as his failure to finish on schedule suggested, then he and his crew would fare even worse at the new reduced price.

Under standard Forest Service contracting policy, the agency withholds 10 percent of a contractor's earnings until the job is completed satisfactorily. If a contractor should default, then the job is put out for new bids. If the new low-bidder's price is higher than that of the defaulting contractor, then the latter's "10 percent retention fund" is used to make up the difference, with the defaulting contractor getting the net balance. Thus Rogers faced serious problems if he failed to finish the remaining 353 acres by November 10. He could, of course, seek another contract extension and it might be granted, but there would be another reduction in payments. Even more serious, the first winter snows could arrive at any moment, making it impossible to complete the Turkey Springs job until the following May or June. This would mean that Rogers and his crew could not collect more than $2500 in retention funds until the following summer, leaving them hard-pressed for money to carry them through the long winter.

The only alternative open to Rogers was to default on his contract and hope that the replacement bidder's price would not drain his own retention-fund too seriously. But Rogers already had defaulted on an earlier contract and a second default would not help his reputation with the Forest Service or enhance his prospects of getting future contracts. Rogers could have avoided having to choose between these two equally unattractive alternatives if his crew had been able to average four and one-fourth acres per day during the three-month extension. But by October 16, 1975, less than four weeks from the November 10 deadline, Rogers had used up roughly 80 percent of his contract-extension time and had completed only 37 percent of the remaining 353 acres. By mid-October it was obvious to Inspector Hentz that Rogers could not possibly complete the Turkey Springs job before the contract deadline, Hentz later told me, and he had so indicated in his report to Marchbanks.

On October 20, four days after Hentz's adverse report to Marchbanks, Rogers felt obliged to write his contracting officer as follows:

> I am writing to tell you personally of our progress on the Turkey Springs thinning. I cannot honestly say whether or not we will finish on time. However, we are working every day with as much manpower as I can hire. I will not stop work until the job is finished or until I am asked to stop. I have had considerable trouble keeping a full crew on the job. The area is very thick and the guys have poor morale because of this. I have had to break in several green men. We will keep working and trying hard.

Marchbanks later told me he had taken Rogers' hard-luck story at face value. It would be several months later before Marchbanks would learn, as a result of my investigation, that he had been grossly misled by Rogers as to why he was running so far behind schedule.

On October 20, 1975, the same night that Rogers sat down to write to Marchbanks, NBC-TV televised a two-hour special on UFOs. The dramatic Hollywood-produced film told the story of Betty Hill and her late husband Barney, who had claimed that they were abducted by strange-looking creatures and taken aboard a flying saucer for a physical examination—*a story similar to one that Travis Walton would tell several weeks later.* Rogers later acknowledged that he "did watch the first part of it. But then I turned it off because it was boring. I just was not all that interested in UFOs before this thing happened," according to the book *Ultimate Encounter* by Bill Barry (Pocket Books, Simon & Schuster, 1978). Rogers' claim of disinterest in UFOs is contradicted forty-one pages later in the same book where crew member John Goulette is quoted as saying that during the brief time he had worked for Rogers "UFOs came up [that is, were discussed] maybe three times at the most. Mostly it was just Mike [Rogers] and Travis arguing about what would make them fly."

The "UFO-abduction" incident occurred relatively early in the NBC program, which Rogers acknowledges that he saw. To a man facing two unattractive alternatives on his Turkey Springs contract, the account of the Hills' "UFO-abduction" could easily suggest a third alternative. If a member of the Rogers crew were to be "abducted" by a UFO near the Turkey Springs work-site, the other members could hardly be blamed if they were too frightened to return to the site. The Forest Service just might consider this to be an "act-of-God," which would result in contract termination; Rogers could collect his retention-fund, but without having another contract-default black mark against his record. Also, the incident might win the *National Enquirer*'s best-case award of from five to ten thousand dollars.

Fortunately for Rogers, he had a crew member sufficiently familiar with UFOs so that he could concoct a story about his experience aboard a flying saucer. Even if Marchbanks did not "buy" the UFO-abduction incident and did not treat it as an act-of-God, Rogers would be no worse off than if he simply waited until November 10 for a standard default termination, which now was inevitable. And even if Marchbanks decided on a conventional default termination, the *National Enquirer* might still select the case for a prize, and the incident might be turned into another Hollywood-movie-for TV, with the proceeds shared among the crew.

As I reviewed all of the evidence turned up by my investigation, one thing was quite obvious: *If the incident was not a hoax, then the UFO had behaved as if it were following a script carefully prepared by Mike Rogers and Travis Walton.* For example, the incident had to occur close to the Turkey Springs work-site so Rogers later could claim his crew would not return to work and he could not complete his contract. That remote locale also offered the advantage that there would be no other witnesses to dispute the tale. Were such an incident to occur many miles away from the work-site, it would deprive Rogers of his excuse for terminating work.

Had Travis been as frightened by the alleged UFO as Rogers claimed he and all other crew members were, then Travis would have stayed in the truck and no abduction could have occurred. Fortuitously, Travis was so eager to get a ride in a UFO that he would disregard his own safety and warnings of his associates to jump out of the moving truck and run under the UFO. If Travis had not been seated next to the door, his exit would have been blocked by one of the other terrified crew members and the abduction could not have occurred.

If the "UFOnauts" had simply dragged or carried Travis aboard in the manner reported by other "abductees," Rogers and his crew might have rescued Travis. Instead, the UFO allegedly had "zapped" poor Travis with a beam of light so powerful it had knocked Travis back, causing Rogers to panic and drive off. If the powerful UFO had interfered with the truck's ignition, as is sometimes claimed in other close-encounter cases, Rogers could not have driven off and the crew might have rescued Travis. The UFO's beam seemingly was explosive in its force, knocking Travis unconscious so he could not remember how he was taken aboard, but the beam was so gentle and harmless that it left no burn or bruise marks on Travis's body when he was examined a few days later, and there were no burn marks on the dry timber near where Travis had been standing.

There seemed to be too long a string of "remarkable coincidences" for the UFO abduction to be true. I found it more plausible that the incident was a hoax.

Mrs. Richard Gibson, of Heber, Arizona, also suspected a hoax, based on numerous hoaxes perpetrated earlier by Mrs. Kellett and members of her family. The ranchhouse in which Mrs. Kellett was living at the time of the UFO incident was owned by Mrs. Gibson's father-in-law, who let Mrs. Kellett use it without charge as a summer home. Despite this generosity, Mrs. Gibson told me that her family was the victim of numerous pranks and hoaxes. On one occasion, "they called the ranch and said somebody has killed a whole bunch of your cows. They are dead all over the meadows up here. So we went running up there to see . . . and there wasn't one dead cow . . . . It was a complete hoax." Mrs. Gibson said, "Another instance that happened last May 17 [1975] . . . the mother [Mrs. Kellett] called and said, 'Your tank-dam is washing out and you're going to lose all your water.' . . . we got out there and the tank-dam was exactly the same as it ever was . . . . So it's been just instance after instance that these things have happened."

By early June 1976, after five months of investigation, I concluded that the time had come to make public my findings, including the "secret" McCarthy polygraph test results, Ezell's disavowal of the Pfeifer tests, the shortcomings in those tests that I had uncovered, and Rogers' possible motivation for staging such a hoax. Copies of my seventeen-page White Paper, dated June 20 and summarizing my findings were supplied to the *Arizona Republic,* a Phoenix newspaper; to *The Star,* a tabloid competitor of the *National Enquirer;* to NICAP, GSW, MUFON, and APRO.

On July 6, the *National Euquirer's* July 13 edition hit the stands announcing that the Travis Walton case had been selected as the most impressive UFO incident of 1975 after having been "exhaustively investigated." A $5000 prize was awarded and divided among the crew members. The *Enquirer* reported that "Walton, his mother and brother, as well as his six companions, were subjected to 'lie-detector' tests—and, without exception, were found to be telling the truth." There was no mention of the earliest test given by McCarthy, which Travis had flunked. The article contained strong endorsements from members of its Blue Ribbon Panel of expert UFOlogists that had selected the Walton case:

• Dr. James A. Harder: "Beyond any reasonable doubt, the evidence is as valid as any that would be accepted in an American criminal court."

• Dr. Frank Salisbury: "It's probably one of the most spectacular abductions that has ever been reported anywhere . . . . Thanks to the many witnesses and the polygraph examinations of those witnesses, we have pretty good reason to take the Walton case at face value."

• Dr. R. Leo Sprinkle: "The evidence is very strong. It's a solid sighting in terms of witnesses, the number of witnesses and the investigation of them by polygraph."

• Dr. J. Allen Hynek (a former panel member): "I talked with Travis

Walton and he seems to me to be straightforward. Of course I was impressed by the polygraph tests on the others, and I would stress that above all."

Less than a week after these ringing endorsements, the July 12 edition of the *Arizona Republic* became the first publication to reveal the highlights of my investigation of the Walton case. The article, headlined "POLYGRAPH TEST FAILURE REVEALED: HOAX CHARGED IN TALE OF UFO ABDUCTION," was written by Richard Robertson, a "stringer" who also was editor of the *Payson Roundup* and who earlier had investigated the Walton incident for an article for his own newspaper. Being a good reporter, Robertson had contacted Rogers to obtain his response to my charges, which Rogers dismissed as "ridiculous." Robertson wrote that Rogers "denied he was having financial problems with the contract . . . was within two weeks of completing the job at the time of the alleged UFO sighting."

Robertson's article said that "the seven woodcutters have written a letter to Klass challenging his allegations. In the letter, they propose another series of lie-detector tests be administered to them . . . . if they fail the tests, they will pay the costs of the tests, and if they pass, Klass will pay, Rogers said. He also said the results would be made public." Before writing the article, Robertson had called me to get my reaction to the "challenge." I told him I had not yet received any letter from Rogers but that I would be "delighted to accept the challenge," a quote that he included in his article.

The Star, after receiving my paper on the case, had sent a reporter to Arizona to check my facts. The tabloid later published its own conclusions in a two-page feature in the August 10 edition under the headline: "WOODCUTTERS FOOLED THE WORLD, SAY AVIATION AND LIE-DETECTOR EXPERTS." The article said that when Travis was asked about the McCarthy test results he responded: "I was in a very emotional state when I returned, and the psychiatrist connected with APRO and the *Enquirer* advised me against taking a polygraph test so soon. What's important is that I passed the later test."

The wire services, which had carried numerous stories on Walton's alleged abduction, his return, and the Pfeifer polygraph test which Travis had "passed," ignored my newly released disclosures on the incident, as did the *Enquirer.* NICAP promptly published highlights from my White Paper, offering its own appraisal that "the indications are that a hoax has been perpetrated." GSW, and later MUFON, also published all of my material. It was late September before APRO members received the July 1976 issue of *The APRO Bulletin,* informing them that my White Paper had been published.

APRO admitted that it had withheld information on the McCarthy test, but explained:

. . . initially, the *Enquirer's* insistence in [sic] confidentiality was tied to their interest in protecting their story and the agreement was made between McCarthy and the *Enquirer* that results of the test would be their property . . . . When the validity of the test results were [sic] over-ruled by the other experts consulted, there was, of course, no point in [APRO] requesting its release since it had then become useless information from a scientific standpoint.

APRO claimed that "three psychiatrists who examined Travis *on the same occasion* declared the test to be meaningless because of Walton's state of mind and the circumstances under which it was given." [Emphasis added.]

APRO members could easily conclude from this that Dr. Jean Rosenbaum and his two associates had been present at the time McCarthy gave the polygraph test, when in fact the Rosenbaums did not arrive in Phoenix until several hours *after* the test was completed. If Travis was showing signs of stress by the time he met with the psychiatrists it should not be surprising. His attempt to pass his first polygraph test, administered by Arizona's most experienced examiner, had failed. Before taking the test, he had signed a standard "Polygraph Examination Statement of Consent," which acknowledged the test-subject's right against self-incrimination but which also said that "any statement made by me may be used as evidence against me in subsequent judicial proceedings." Travis knew that Sheriff Gillespie had threatened legal prosecution in Navajo County if the UFO incident proved to be a hoax and that barely five years before he had appeared in the same Navajo County Court to plead guilty to a burglary and forgery charge.

Having failed to convince McCarthy of the UFO-abduction story on the afternoon of November 15, Travis now had to try again, this time to convince Dr. Rosenbaum and his two associates. Little wonder that Travis was showing signs of severe stress. Dr. Rosenbaum told me that APRO did not inform him that Travis already had taken, and flunked, the McCarthy test. Rather he said he was asked if Travis was in shape to take a polygraph test and the psychiatrist recommended against it.

APRO also charged that McCarthy was "unbelievably incompetent. In his pre-test interview with Travis and in the framing of questions he broke some of the most elementary rules of the polygraphic profession." To support this charge, APRO noted that relevant questions must be phrased so they can be answered with an unqualified "Yes" or "No," and it claimed that the first test question violated this principle. The question was: "Were you actually taken aboard a spacecraft on November 5th?" APRO claimed that "Travis was 'boxed in.' The question forced him to speculate since the information required to answer the question was not in his memory."

This is nonsense, as the transcript of the McCarthy test, later published on pages 177-178 in the Lorenzens' book, reveals. During the pre-test discussion with Travis, McCarthy said: "All right, from all the intelligence we've gathered from, ah, Dr. Harder and the other gentleman, you are convinced that you were taken aboard a spacecraft?" Travis replied,

"That is correct." Later, McCarthy went over each question with Travis before beginning the formal examination to assure that Travis felt able to answer each with a simple "Yes" or "No." During this pre-test run McCarthy asked: "Were you actually taken aboard a spacecraft near Heber on November 5?" and Travis replied "Yes" without hesitation.

APRO charged that the next question was flawed for the same reason: "Were you actually aboard a spacecraft from the 5th of November to the 10th of November?" APRO said that "Travis had repeatedly emphasized that he did not know where he was and that of the five-day period, he remembers at the most, two hours. There is no way that Travis, whether he said 'yes' or 'no' could have passed the first two questions." (Recall Travis's description of the strange-looking creatures allegedly seen in the UFO and later of having seen several flying-saucer type of craft in what seemed to be a large hangar.) APRO concluded its criticism of McCarthy's test in the following words: "Describing this test as meaningless . . . is really being too kind. It was badly botched by the tester. Sometimes long years of experience can serve to crystallize bad habits."

Some months later, after the Arizona legislature had passed a law requiring that all polygraph examiners be licensed, four of the state's most respected practitioners were appointed to the Arizona Polygraph Licensing Board. Two were polygraph examiners employed by state agencies. The other two were John J. McCarthy and Tom Ezell; this fact offers an independent appraisal of McCarthy's expertise and standing.

APRO's article concluded by noting that "Rogers, Walton, and the other woodcutters have challenged Klass: they will each take another test *with an expert that Klass finds acceptable* if he will pay for it providing they pass—otherwise it will cost him nothing. Klass is still equivocating on this one." [Emphasis added.] This was a grossly inaccurate description of my response to the offer made by Rogers and his crew, as will be documented in the next chapter.

On July 11, I decided to call Mike Rogers. Initially he was reluctant to talk to me on the grounds I would "twist" whatever he said. I replied that I was tape-recording our conversation and would send him a copy of the tape (which I did); later I would discover that Rogers also was recording our conversation.

Rogers claimed that the Turkey Springs job "was the best contract I've ever had . . . I made a better profit on it than any contract I'd ever had to work on." He assured me that there would have been no need for him to concoct a UFO hoax "because even if I was in trouble on a contract, all I would have had to have done was to have gone to the contracting officer and say, 'Hey, I'm in trouble on this contract . . . what can we work out.'" At first Rogers denied he had been hard-pressed financially and needed the 10-percent retention funds to carry him through the long winter, as suggested in my paper. But when pressed, he admitted that he had had to use food stamps for several months until his contract was terminated for default and he received his retention funds.

Rogers acknowledged that he had been counting on getting retention funds "to carry me through the winter. And that's why I was in a financial bind this winter . . . if this thing [UFO incident] hadn't happened out there, in two weeks or maybe three weeks . . . we would have had that job finished and I would have gotten over $3000 in retention, which would easily have held me over the winter until the spring. That was my plan." I challenged Rogers' claim that if the UFO incident had not occurred he could have finished the Turkey Springs job within two or three weeks. I reminded him that during the first three months of his contract extension (August 4 to November 5), he had been able to complete only 115 acres.

Rogers attempted to justify his earlier claim and went on to explain that his work-rate would increase sharply "because I had no other contracts at that time. Everything else was finished. The reason that was the only amount of acreage that had been accomplished on that job during that amount of time was because I had two other jobs going besides that one [at Turkey Springs]." Rogers unwittingly had let the cat out of the bag. The reason he was seriously delinquent at Turkey Springs was that he had been working on two other jobs. If the Turkey Springs contract was yielding Rogers a "better profit" than on any previous contract, as he claimed, why had he put his crew to work on other jobs? When I sought to learn more about these other jobs Rogers became secretive. One, he indicated, was a "lopping job" (cutting off the tops of felled timber) for Western Pine Company of Snowflake, while the other was for another Forest Service contractor whom Rogers refused to identify.

When I asked Rogers if contracting officer Marchbanks had been aware of his other two jobs, he replied: "They knew about the lopping job. They didn't know about the subcontract I had [with another Forest Service contractor]." When I asked whether Rogers had any objection to my checking with Marchbanks to see if he knew about the lopping contract, Rogers replied: "Of course he knew about the lopping contract." When Rogers again assured me that he could have completed the remaining 238 acres at Turkey Springs within three weeks because his crew had been "averaging fifteen acres per day" just before the UFO incident, I told him I intended to check Marchbanks and Hentz to see if they confirmed his claim. He replied: "It doesn't make any difference to me what their opinion is." Then he warned me "not to say anything too derogatory . . . because it will make a lot of people mad." Near the end of our long, rambling conversation, I asked Rogers about his new polygraph challenge. He declined to discuss it over the telephone, but said it would be mailed to me shortly.

The next morning, on July 12, Rogers drove sixty-four miles to Springerville to be there when the Forest Service contracting office opened. Rogers had apparently decided to inform Marchbanks about the real reason for his delinquency on the Turkey Springs contract. When I called Marchbanks, he told me that Rogers was sitting in his office. The contracting officer said he had been completely unaware of Rogers' lopping contract until Rogers had informed him that morning. Marchbanks still was not aware of Rogers' second job for another Forest Service contractor until I mentioned it.

Marchbanks clearly was embarrassed that someone else had uncovered facts that should have been known to a Forest Service contracting officer, and Hentz, who had known of Rogers' lopping job, had failed to mention this in any of his periodic reports on the Turkey Springs contract.

Rogers' claim that his crew had been averaging fifteen acres per day just prior to the UFO incident proved false when Marchbanks examined his official records. One field report, dated October 16, 1975, showed that Rogers had completed only fifteen acres during the two previous weeks. And the last inspector's report, dated October 28 (barely a week before the UFO incident), showed Rogers had completed only four acres during the previous twelve-day period—nineteen acres in four weeks. Yet during our conversation the previous night Rogers had said, "We were moving at about fifteen acres per day."

As for Rogers' claim that he could have completed the remaining 238 acres within two or three weeks if the UFO incident had not occurred, the Forest Service records showed that on January 6, 1976, after Rogers was terminated, the remaining work was awarded to low-bidder John Hammond. It was not until April 26 that weather conditions enabled Hammond's crew to begin work, and it had required forty-two calendar days—six weeks—to finish the job. Hammond had lost only four days due to bad weather, quite a different situation from the one that Rogers faced the previous November. Marchbanks told me that the first snowfall sometimes came as early as October and that the Turkey Springs area "was one of the heavier snowfall areas." Our July 12 conversation concluded with Marchbanks again stressing that "I was not aware of it" [that is, Rogers' moonlighting activities].

On July 18, I again called Rogers to say that I had not received his written offer for a new series of polygraph tests, and he assured me that it would be mailed shortly. Later, when I chided Rogers for failing to tell Marchbanks about both of his moonlighting jobs, he told me that "before you called him on the phone, he [Marchbanks] happened to listen to that whole, entire telephone conversation, which I had taped." If Marchbanks had heard Rogers' tape recording of the telephone conversation of July 11, it was surprising that the contracting officer was not aware of both outside jobs because Rogers and I had discussed them several times during our conversation.

Later that day I called Marchbanks at his home to resolve this curious contradiction. He told me that both he and an associate, Dennis Allen, had listened to the Rogers tape recording but they had heard nothing about a second moonlighting job, only references to the lopping contract. When I asked Marchbanks whether Rogers had played the entire tape recording, he replied: "Well, a lot of it you couldn't even understand. There was something wrong with the tape, a lot of it. I mean a minute here, or a minute there. And he [Rogers] tried to say something was wrong with the tape recorder." What a curious coincidence that something apparently went wrong with Rogers' tape recorder every time he and I discussed his second moonlighting job. (It brought to mind the equally curious coincidence of the eighteen-and-a-half minute blank spot on one Nixon White House tape.)

Marchbanks himself commented that "Mike was sitting there at my desk, and he heard me tell you that I had not heard about the other contractor, and Dennis heard it." Yet Rogers had not spoken up to remind Marchbanks that he had heard references to this second outside job on the tape recording. I sent Marchbanks an "unexpurgated" tape recording of my telephone conversation of July 11 with Rogers.

During the early phase of my investigation into the Travis Walton case, after learning that the Walton family had a long-standing interest in UFOs, I had first suspected that members of the family might have been the architects of an abduction hoax. But by late July 1976, especially after the incident of the "flawed" Rogers tape recording and his deception of the U.S. Forest Service, my suspicions began to shift to Rogers.

22

Intentional Deception

It was not until July 19, 1976, that Rogers sent me the long-awaited "challenge" for a new series of polygraph tests. His long, rambling letter included a bitter tirade against me, which was understandable since my efforts had forced Rogers to confess the real reason for his Turkey Springs delinquency to Marchbanks a week before. Rogers distributed his letter widely, sending copies to reporter Richard Robertson and the heads of many UFO organizations. My copy was sent by registered mail, and it was nearly noon on Saturday, July 24, before I received the letter.

Rogers set ten conditions for the retests and demanded that I accept all of them. Most were acceptable. For example, he stated that the tests should be given by "a mutually acceptable examiner of high standing and proper credentials." I was also willing to accept his condition that if all of the subjects should pass the new tests I would pay their total cost as well as travel expense and loss-of-pay for the test subjects. If any of the subjects failed to pass, Rogers said I would be "reimbursed." But there was no provision for how the expense would be divided if any of the tests turned out to be "inconclusive."

Rogers said the "examiner will be provided with copies of this challenge and of APRO's written report on the Travis Walton case and of Philip Klass's seventeen page written report, to familiarize the examiner with the areas from which to formulate questions, so that it will be unnecessary for any of the parties involved to suggest questions." This too was acceptable and would avoid the issue that had tainted the Pfeifer tests of the two Walton brothers. Rogers said that "Travis Walton, Duane Walton, and Mike Rogers *must* be retested . . . at least three of the other five witnesses must be tested, all five if possible. Travis's mother is also willing to be retested."

Another requirement was that prior to the test, I must sign a notarized statement "that states that you [Klass] accept our subsequent passing of these tests to be positive proof of the truth of our experience with a UFO and, when we pass, that you will make public retractions of all accusations of a hoax . . . ."

This condition was not acceptable, because not even the most experienced polygraph examiner would claim his test results offered "positive proof." Controlled tests have demonstrated that polygraph tests by experienced examiners are correct more than 90 percent of the time, but not 100 percent. If polygraph tests could provide "positive proof," they could replace long, judicial proceedings. (Curiously, Rogers did not volunteer to issue a public statement admitting the incident was a hoax if one or more of the test subjects failed the retests.)

Another item was sufficiently ambiguous that it could cause problems. This was his condition that if I did not "arrange for the retesting to take place . . . within thirty days, it will constitute a refusal of our challenge." If it should take longer than thirty days to work out a satisfactory agreement for the retests and to find a competent, mutually acceptable examiner who could find time to come to Arizona and conduct the lengthy series of tests, then I would be charged with default.

Finally, Rogers demanded that my "acceptance or refusal of our challenge must be sent by registered mail to the Snowflake address given below and postmarked no later than twenty-four hours after receipt of this challenge. If you do not reply within that twenty-four hours . . . it will constitute refusal of our challenge." *This was a surprising condition if Rogers and associates really were eager to take a new series of polygraph tests.* By the time I read the letter, my nearby Post Office had closed for the weekend and the twenty-four-hour ultimatum would expire before the Post Office reopened on Monday. I decided to telephone Rogers to say that I was eager to proceed with the retests, that most of his conditions were satisfactory, and to ask that the deadline be extended to Monday noon.

Rogers was not at home when I called, but his wife said he would call me when he returned, which he did later that afternoon. After the initial greeting, the following conversation ensued:

> ROGERS: First of all, I'd like to tell you that this call is being recorded.
> KLASS: Good. I'm doing the same on this end.
> ROGERS: Now what I want to ask you is, have you received our letter?
> KLASS: I just received it this noon. I had to pick it up at the Post Office because, of course, it had to be signed for.
> ROGERS: Right. It's a registered letter.
> KLASS: Right, and . . .
> ROGERS: (Interrupting) Have you got time this day, today, to reply?
> KLASS: I'm going, yes, I'm going to give you a qualified statement on the phone.
> ROGERS: No, I can't accept that, because I'm not in a position where I can. This is not my capacity, the letter said . . .

KLASS: (Interrupting) Well, let me, may I read my statement?

ROGERS You reply to, by registered mail. Your reply has no significance over the phone.

KLASS: You will receive, you will receive a written response.

ROGERS: Okay. Now the thing I'm replying to here, the reason I'm calling you is because the letter said to reply within twenty-four hours, now, right? Now we are holding you to that unless, because being Saturday, if there's no way that you can, because it being Saturday.

KLASS: Well, I'm glad you suddenly thought of that because I think it unlikely that I could get the Postmaster General to open up the Post Office . . . . But now would you (let me read my prepared statement) . . .

ROGERS: Okay, well, what I'm going to say about that is this. Now, like I said, *I can't receive any reply over the phone. It has no significance!*

Once again I tried to read my brief prepared statement, and again Rogers refused, whereupon he hung up and terminated the conversation. About an hour later, Rogers called back and apologized for having hung up on me. He then offered to let me read my brief statement, but I told him that since he had agreed to extend his deadline that I would reply in writing and this would be sent by registered mail before Monday noon. We then had a long rambling conversation in which I stressed that most of his conditions were satisfactory and that I felt that we could work out a satisfactory compromise on those that were ambiguous or flawed.

After our conversation ended, I decided to replay my tape recording of it. In doing so, I discovered that in my haste to connect the recorder when Rogers unexpectedly called back, I had plugged the telephone pick-up into the wrong "jack." As a result, the recording contained none of Rogers' comments but thanks to a built-in microphone, the tape did contain all of my statements and replies to Rogers. Because he had made several interesting disclosures during this second conversation, I called Rogers back and explained that my telephone pick-up had been connected to the wrong jack. Rogers laughed and asked "since when," and I replied "since the beginning"—meaning since the beginning of our *second* telephone conversation. Rogers again laughed and replied, "Oh really."

When I tried to ask Rogers a question, he replied:

> Have you got your tape machine running right [correctly] now? I realize that all our previous conversation was a bunch of bickering and you didn't seem to really want to understand all that much. I'll just make this final statement to you, like I said a while ago. We want you, *we're giving you 'till noon Monday to give us a reply.* We expect you to reply "yes" or "no" to our challenge by noon Monday. *If you do not reply by noon Monday* we will consider that you are not accepting our challenge and that will be reported to the [news] media. And that's it. [Emphasis added.]

Rogers then terminated the conversation by hanging up.

Rogers did not keep his word and wait to receive my response, which was sent by registered mail Monday morning, July 26. Instead, on Sunday, July 25, Rogers distributed a press release that alleged: "Mr. Klass essentially rejects our challenge! He flatly refused to sign the statement agreeing that the new tests would be proof of truth when passed. He said he could not meet some of the other conditions of acceptance . . . in a recorded telephone conversation on July 24 . . . ."

Yet during our first conversation on July 24 Rogers had repeatedly refused to let me read my prepared statement saying I eagerly accepted his challenge in principle. Recall that Rogers had told me: "Your reply has no significance over the phone."

Yet within twenty-four hours Rogers had written a press release claiming I had rejected polygraph retests based on our telephone conversation, without waiting to receive my written response. I can only conclude that Rogers believed that I had no tape recording of *either* of our first two telephone conversations, when in fact I had a full record of the first and a record of everything I had said during the second. Based on Rogers' misunderstanding of what I had on tape, Rogers decided that he could issue an erroneous press release without fear of contradiction. (I was quickly learning much about Rogers' modus operandi.)

The press release said: "If Mr. Klass honestly believed we are not telling the truth he should have had no problem in accepting our challenge." The press release concluded: "However, when we receive his letter we will make the effort to send him a second, more lenient challenge, in the hopes of getting him to accept."

The letter that I mailed Monday morning began:

> I eagerly accept in principle your proposal that you, the other six members of your crew, and Duane Walton, undergo a new polygraph examination to be given by an experienced examiner who is mutually acceptable to both of us, as soon as the necessary arrangements can be worked out, and that the full results and charts of the tests be made public. Further, I agree to pay the costs of tests for each subject, who in the opinion of the selected examiner, truthfully answers all relevant questions. Additionally, for those subjects who meet this criterion, I will pay their cost of travel to the examination site, at 15 cents/mile, as well as reimburse each for loss of pay involved if they must be absent from work for the tests.

My letter, dated July 24, discussed the few conditions proposed by Rogers that were ambiguous or inappropriate and said that within ten days I would send him a revised proposal

> . . . incorporating most of your ten principles with the required clarifications to assure there is an unambiguous meeting of minds on the arrangements. Inasmuch as you took ten days to formulate and execute your letter-challenge, it

seems only fair that I be given ten days to formulate my formal response and more precise terms of the agreement. There will be no deadline for your response, with the thought that both of us are desirous of reaching prompt agreement to proceed with the re-tests.

On August 1, I sent Rogers my counterproposal. It suggested that the polygraph examiner be a full member of the American Polygraph Association and have at least ten years of field experience. It also provided that each test-subject would provide a urine-sample, to be voided in the presence of the examiner or a designated representative, which would be analyzed by a qualified laboratory to check for "the possible presence of drugs that might have been taken to defeat the intent of the test," and that any drug traces found for a test-subject would cause the test to be treated as "failed" regardless of the charts. Also, to assure prompt payment of the selected examiner, for urine tests, and for travel pay I suggested that both Rogers and I set up an escrow fund of $2000 in a recognized financial institution. (APRO later would agree to supply the funds for Rogers' escrow account.)

It was two weeks later before Rogers replied, in a letter dated August 16, saying that it was

> . . . necessary that we remind you that *you* are not challenging *us*. *We* are challenging *you* . . . However, in our efforts to be honest and fair in getting you to respond to our challenge to have us retested, we will consider your suggestions. It is very likely we will include every one of them in our new, more lenient challenge . . . We will cover everything in our second and final challenge, which you must accept or reject with no further quibbling . . .

The day after Rogers' reply, August 17, APRO's James Lorenzen wrote to Cleve Backster, head of the Backster School of Lie Detection, in San Diego, indicating that the APRO official, on his own initiative, had selected a polygraph examiner to give the proposed new test series. Lorenzen sent me, and many others, a copy of this letter, which he said was intended to confirm "todays [sic] phone conversation for the record," with Backster about the Travis Walton incident and the proposed retests. Lorenzen wrote: "I don't know how familiar you are with the work of our organization or the Travis Walton case but the enclosed copies of our publication should set the stage for what I am going to discuss."

Lorenzen's letter explained how he had happened to write and call Backster on August 17:

> Last Thursday (August 12) I participated in a television program in Phoenix in which this matter was discussed. As sometimes happens in situations of this sort the discussions continued after the show was over. *During that discussion, Mr. Jack McCarthy of the Arizona Polygraph Laboratory suggested your name as that of an authority in the polygraph field who might be willing to*

come to Phoenix and settle this matter. McCarthy also furnished your address and phone number, arriving in today's mail. Mr. McCarthy (one of the examiners who tested Walton) expressed great respect for your ability and reputation. I have checked with George Pfeifer (the other examiner who tested Walton) and have received the same reaction from him. Travis Walton, who was on the same TV program . . . expressed willingness to undergo further testing if you will agree to do it. [Emphasis added.]

I volunteered to be the one to initiate contact with you . . . thus my phone call and this letter . . . . By this letter I am acknowledging your willingness to perform the suggested testing and your quote of $350.00 per day plus expenses to come to Phoenix and test the principals and (by copy of this letter) I will inform the other interested parties asking only that *if any decide to correspond directly with you on this matter that they furnish this office a copy of said correspondence.*" [Emphasis added.]

Judging from the letter, Rogers apparently believed that the conditions I had proposed on August 1 were reasonably satisfactory. Although I was surprised that Lorenzen would initiate discussions with the prospective polygraph examiner without first obtaining my approval, if Backster had been recommended by McCarthy, as Lorenzen claimed, he would appear to be qualified.

What I did not know at the time, and would not discover until mid-November, nearly three months later, was that *Lorenzen previously had talked with Backster about the Walton case on August 9, three days before the TV discussion in which Lorenzen falsely claimed that Backster's name had been suggested by McCarthy! Lorenzen's letter of August 17 was intended to deceive me into thinking that Backster had been proposed by McCarthy on August 12 and into believing that the very first Lorenzen conversations with Backster had occurred on August 17.*

Lorenzen, having held secret phone discussions with Backster, was now anxious to ensure that there would be no others; in his letter of August 17, he requested: "if any [interested parties] decide to correspond directly with you on this matter that they furnish this office a copy of said correspondence." On August 22, I wrote to Backster, sending him copies of my June 20 White Paper, a supplemental report on Rogers' work for and problems with the Forest Service, and a copy of my recent correspondence with Rogers seeking to work out mutually acceptable conditions for the retests. I concluded my letter by saying that after allowing time for Backster to study the enclosed material, I would telephone him. In keeping with Lorenzen's request of August 17, I sent copies of my letter to APRO and to Rogers.

My letter to Backster prompted Lorenzen to write him on August 31, expressing concern over

. . . a potential problem area, that is, Klass' offer to "chat with you by telephone." I can foresee a situation where [if] Travis' test came out unfavorably to him, he would then claim that Phil had influenced you against him in off-the-record conversations. To guard against such eventuality I suggest that any such conversations be recorded "for-the-record." This rule should apply to anyone who contacts you by telephone in this case, including myself.*

I fully supported this caveat because the new tests needed to be arranged and given so that the results would be above any possible criticism. But Lorenzen expressed a different concern: "these proposed briefings . . . could easily become special pleadings . . . could become a waste of your valuable time. It is my understanding that your [Backster] method of testing eliminates the subjectivity from the polygraph process; therefore it would not matter what your predisposition, if any, is on this case." This was a curious claim for Backster to make, and for Lorenzen to accept, unless Lorenzen already had reason to think that Backster might have a "pro-UFO" bias.

On August 28, Rogers called me to complain about my having written to Backster and my plans to talk with him by phone, even though I had sent him a copy of my letter to Backster. Rogers accused me of "jumping the gun," saying "in our proposal we said that there should be no verbal exchange with the examiner." Rogers indicated that he had some hesitancy about accepting Backster "because he was suggested to us by McCarthy," and then he asked, "Did you put McCarthy up to suggesting Backster to us?" I assured him that I had not. Later in our conversation, I learned that Rogers already had talked with Backster "to check on him," without informing me.

Within a few minutes there was a curious change in Rogers' attitude toward Backster. Whereas Rogers first seemed reluctant to accept Backster because "he was suggested to us by McCarthy," very shortly Rogers was pushing me hard to say that Backster was acceptable to me. At one point Rogers said: "Well, I suppose that we could agree on Backster . . . I assume that by this letter that you're with him, that you would as soon have him." I replied that since Lorenzen and Rogers both had had the opportunity to talk with Backster that I should have the same opportunity "before I give a final go-ahead." Rogers replied, "I assumed from your letter that you were kind of suggesting him, or affirming him." I responded, "I was simply indicating that I certainly have no objection to him [at this stage] and he seemed to have good qualifications." Later when I replayed the tape recording of this conversation with Rogers I was troubled by the curious change in his attitude toward Backster that occurred within a few minutes—and without any prodding by me.

A few weeks later I gained new insights into the man whom Lorenzen

---

*Later, when I asked Lorenzen for a copy of the tape recording of his August 17 conversation with Backster, he told me he had not made a recording.

and Rogers were so eager to select to perform the new polygraph tests. I happened to find a newspaper clipping from the January 29, 1975, edition of the *Washington Star-News* (a year and a half earlier). The article reported a sharp debate at the New York City meeting of the American Association for the Advancement of Science between Backster and a panel of biologists over whether house plants have feelings and extrasensory perception (ESP). In 1968, Backster had conducted tests using a polygraph machine that he claimed showed that plants reacted electrically to indicate discomfort when they witnessed the death of brine shrimp being dropped into boiling water. The article quoted plant physiologist Edgar L. Gasteiger, University of Missouri, as reporting he had conducted similar experiments but was "unable to confirm Cleve Backster's observations . . ." Dr. John L. Kmetz, Science Unlimited Research Foundation, of San Antonio, also reported that he had attempted to repeat Backster's earlier experiments, with Backster's assistance, but had not been able to confirm earlier reported results.

Subsequently I contacted Dr. Kmetz and learned that the foundation for which he worked had been created in 1972 "because of our funder's interest in the Backster plant work." When the test results failed to confirm Backster's findings, Kmetz informed me, Backster had tried to prevent Kmetz from presenting his contradictory results at the AAAS meeting.

Later I came across an interview with Backster that had been published on April 18, 1972, in the *Washington Post*, which quoted him as saying: "I also found that whenever I talked about my office plant, no matter what part of the country I was in, the plant would show a corresponding [electrical] reaction on the charts, at exactly the moment I was talking about it." The article said: "Backster, who said he has received little criticism from anyone about his theories, said that plant perception could someday be used to thwart airplane hijackers by keeping a plant at the gate to sense bad intentions." Yet in the field of polygraphy, Backster is considered quite knowledgeable; he was one of a handful of specialists invited to testify June 4–5, 1974, at hearings held by the Government Operations Committee.

Rogers' next letter, written September 18, was much more conciliatory than that of August 16. Where the latter had said that I must accept his "second and final challenge . . . with no further quibbling," his September 18 letter admitted that "we now feel that you were justified in refusing [to sign the original challenge] . . ." Rogers even said there would be no need for me to issue a notarized statement admitting the polygraph retests provided "positive proof" of the UFO incident. Then Rogers added: "In our recent telephone conversation [August 28] we accomplished a major step by reaching *agreement in selecting an examiner. We agree that Cleve Backster does indeed seem to be the man for the job . . . . Like you we believe he will be competent and unbiased in his administering of the examinations.*"

Inasmuch as Rogers had initiated the August 28 telephone call, I felt certain that he had tape-recorded it. If he had listened to the tape after our conversation, as I always did, he would have known that *I had not agreed to Backster's selection*. I had made it clear that I would not make any decision until after I had had the opportunity to talk to Backster. It was not until more than two weeks later, during the evening of September 14, that I had been able to talk with Backster, and I had not talked or written to Rogers since my phone conversation with Backster. The revised Memorandum of Agreement for the retests that Rogers enclosed with his September 18 letter suggested that he did not really believe that I had agreed to the choice of Backster, inasmuch as the agreement contained a blank space for the name of the selected examiner to be typed in.

Rogers' revised Memorandum of Agreement was not significantly different from the one I had proposed six weeks earlier. He had added several new provisions that were acceptable in principle but which were carelessly phrased. For example, he had added the proviso: "No personal contact will be made between Klass or his representative(s) and any of the Test Subjects, either prior to, or during the testing series." As written it meant that were I to call Rogers a few days before the retests were scheduled to assure that all was in readiness, this call would amount to my violation of the agreement. My original Memorandum of Agreement proposed that Travis, Rogers, and all crew members be tested—but not Duane or Mrs. Kellett, since they had not been directly involved in the original incident. If all the principals passed, or if all of them failed, the tests of Duane and Mrs. Kellett would be of no import; it seemed better for the polygraph examiner to focus his available time on the principals. But in Rogers' September 18 letter, he insisted that Duane and Mrs. Kellett also be tested.

I replied on September 25, proposing clarification of the language in some of the new proposals. He replied on October 8 with a letter that was conciliatory in tone, saying that my "re-draft contains some useful clarifications and changes, but it contains some slight ambiguities and contradictions." Rogers continued to press for retest of Duane Walton and Mrs. Kellett.

The original challenge of July 19 had not been signed by two crew members, Allen Dalis and Dwayne Smith. But during our August 28 conversation, Rogers *said he finally had been able to locate Dalis and Smith and that both had agreed to take new polygraph tests*. Still, he had not confirmed this in writing.

By late September I had good reason to believe that Dalis would not be available for retests; he had been committed to the Arizona State Penitentiary to serve three five-year concurrent sentences for armed robbery. I had learned this from GSW's Spaulding, who sent me copies of Maricopa County Superior Court records; these indicated that Dalis had pleaded guilty to committing the felonies to support his hard-drug habit and that he had been in and out of correction centers repeatedly during his troubled youth. Dalis had been incarcerated in the Maricopa County jail in Phoenix since June 22, awaiting trial. If Rogers had talked with him, as he had claimed during our August 28 conversation, Rogers had good reason to know that Dalis would not be available for retest.

It occurred to me that this might explain why Rogers now was pressing so hard for retest of Mrs. Kellett and Duane, to set the stage later for a compromise in which they would be withdrawn if I agreed that Dalis need not be retested. In my letter of October 13, responding to Rogers' letter of October 8, I pressed him "to produce written evidence that all seven members of the crew are willing and able to undergo retest," without revealing what I had learned about Dalis' incarceration.

While we seemed to be making progress toward resolving the relatively few differences that remained for the retests, I began to feel increasingly uneasy over Rogers' repeated attempts to get me to accept Backster as the polygraph examiner. As I reviewed correspondence and a tape of our August 28 conversation, I was struck by the curious change in the tone of Rogers' letters since Lorenzen had first proposed Backster in his letter of August 17. In listening to the tape of my first, and only, conversation with Backster on September 14, I realized I had forgotten to ask about his prior interest in UFOs. Hence, I wrote Backster on October 12 to explore this issue, sending a copy to Lorenzen and Rogers. I posed four questions:

> 1. Prior to the August 17, 1976, telephone call from L. J. Lorenzen, referred to in his letter of that date, how would you describe the extent of your interest in the subject of UFOs?
> 2. As of August 17, 1976, were you a member of any UFO group such as APRO, NICAP, GSW, or MUFON, or had you previously been a member?
> 3. Had you talked or communicated with L. J. Lorenzen at any time prior to the telephone call referred to in his letter of August 17?
> 4. Prior to August 17, 1976, had you discussed the Travis Walton "UFO abduction" incident with any of the persons involved, including Walton himself, Mike Rogers et al., or with any of the three polygraph examiners [McCarthy, Pfeifer or Gilson], who by then had become involved in the incident?

Backster responded promptly on October 18. Before answering my questions, Backster said such issues could not possibly affect the outcome of an ethical polygraph examination and that both sides should be free to talk with him because such discussions could not possibly influence the results of his tests. As for his prior interest in UFOs, Backster said he had an "inactive interest not involving belief or disbelief—only open-mindedness." He said he had not been a member of any UFO group. On the question of conversations with Lorenzen, Backster said there had been none "prior to *August 1976*," although my question had been phrased: "Prior to August *17, 1976* . . ."

In response to my last question, Backster said that he had participated in a polygraph seminar in Phoenix on April 10–11, and "I believe I was introduced to Mr. George Pfeifer" and that he had been told that Pfeifer had run tests on Travis and Duane Walton. Backster added that "I may have had a telephone conversation with George Pfeifer some time in July." Further, Backster said, he had known McCarthy and Gilson, the latter having been trained at Backster's own school. Following Lorenzen's August 17 letter, Backster said that McCarthy had sent him material on the Walton case.

Backster's account of having been introduced briefly to Pfeifer during his April visit to Phoenix conflicted with what Pfeifer had told me when I interviewed him on April 27, barely two weeks after Backster's visit. Pfeifer volunteered that "he [Backster] and I had a *long* conversation [about the Walton case] at a symposium here in Phoenix not long ago, and he is very interested in this."

On October 21, I wrote Backster again asking if he had had any communication with Lorenzen or other APRO representative prior to August 17, and whether his account of being introduced briefly to Pfeifer meant that the two men "did not have extensive discussions of the Walton case." Backster answered on October 27 with a cryptic response that urged me to reread his October 18 letter "more carefully." Backster refused to say whether he had talked with Lorenzen prior to August 17 and said "if you as a writer wish to establish more exact chronology I suggest that you contact the other parties."

I replied on October 30, pointing out that "if one accepts your statement at face value [that neither side could possibly influence the results of the tests] then clearly there is no good reason why you should not have answered my questions forthrightly and fully." Pointing out that I was one of two major principals who needed to agree on a polygraph examiner "whose neutrality and objectivity must be far removed from any taint of suspicion," I said: "it seems to me that I have every right to try to determine for myself whether the polygraph examiner first suggested by one of the protagonists on August 17, 1976, had an involvement and/or discussion of the Walton case with any of the several other principals prior to the Lorenzen telephone call of August 17, 1976."

I added: "Obviously I cannot agree to retain the services of a polygraph examiner who himself resorts to falsehoods or is evasive in answering questions which he himself has stated to be of no great importance." I concluded by asking Backster to reconsider and to "respond fully and forthrightly to my several questions." *Backster never replied.*

Lorenzen, who had received copies of the exchange with Backster, wrote me on November 5, accusing me of trying to "find an excuse to back out" of the retests. He charged that the issues I had raised with Backster were "another attempt to be disruptive and thus to prevent the testing from ever coming about." After a lengthy attack on me for daring to raise the issues, Lorenzen made a startling admission: "Bob Greber, a graduate of the Backster school, had recommended Mr. Backster to me and I made an exploratory contact with him by telephone on August 9, 1976, to feel him out on the UFO subject generally and question him concerning the special techniques he had developed." Lorenzen went on to say that although he already had talked to Backster by the time of the TV show on August 12, "I did not volunteer Backsters [sic] name on August 12 because I wanted McCarthy's recommendation to be entirely spontaneous."

Later I checked with McCarthy and he flatly denied having suggested Backster in the discussions at the TV station. McCarthy said that someone else had suggested Backster as an examiner for the retests and that Lorenzen then had asked McCarthy about Backster's credentials. McCarthy said he had responded that Backster was an experienced and well-known examiner.

Many months earlier I had been surprised when I had asked Lorenzen if Travis had taken any polygraph tests prior to the one given by Pfeifer, and the APRO official had replied: "No, never." But I was shocked at the secret, under-the-table discussions between Lorenzen and Backster, and by Lorenzen's attempt to deceive me into thinking that the first discussion had occurred on August 17. Clearly Rogers had been a party to this deception, as evidenced by his repeated attempts to get me to say that I would accept Backster. Backster himself knew that Lorenzen's letter of August 17 was an attempt to cover up the earlier conversation of August 9, as evidenced by his subsequent reluctance to respond forthrightly to my questions. Regardless of Backster's standing in the field of polygraphy, he was not acceptable to me for the retests.

On November 11, I wrote to Lorenzen, with copies to Backster and Rogers, denouncing his attempted deception. My letter concluded:

> Under these circumstances, *Mr. Backster is not now satisfactory to me* for the proposed retest of Rogers et al. Had the circumstances been the reverse, I have no doubt that you would have reached the same conclusion.
>
> Before any steps are taken to find a mutually satisfactory examiner for the retest, I urge that you and Rogers et al. agree to an above-board procedure, such as that proposed in my November 6 letter to Rogers [to be discussed in Chapter 23], copy of which was sent to you. Under this proposed procedure, none of the principals on either side of the controversy will approach or hold discussions with any other prospective examiner until the other side has been informed and gives approval.
>
> I hearby swear that I have not to date discussed with any polygraph examiner the matter of the retest except for Backster, following receipt of your August 17 letter, and McCarthy, who obviously is not himself a candidate for the retest.
>
> *Let me emphasize as strongly as possible that the foregoing should not (repeat not) be construed by you and your associates as indicating any desire to withdraw or back-out from the proposed retest of Rogers and the other six members of his crew.*

But if you agree to an above-board no-secret-discussions with any prospective polygraph examiner for the retest, I caution you that I will not tolerate any violation of such an agreement.

Lorenzen never replied to my letter, nor was there any response from Backster. In mid-November of 1979 Backster was a featured speaker at a three-day UFO conference held in San Diego; he briefly discussed his involvement in the Walton case. Backster told the audience that I had disqualified him for the retest because I "found out" that Backster "was open-minded and then decided that that would never do."

23

Ultimatum

Mike Rogers' response to the disclosure that Lorenzen had resorted to deception to prevent me from finding out about his earlier talks with Backster provided additional insights into Rogers' sense of fair play. I wrote to Rogers to say that because of Backster's lack of candor about the secret talks with Lorenzen, he was not acceptable to me for the new polygraph tests. But I added that there were many other experienced polygraph examiners in the United States who should be

> . . . mutually acceptable in terms of his neutrality on the UFO issue. *But it is essential that there not be any secret contact or discussion with any prospective examiner about conducting said test, by any of the principals (Klass, Rogers et al., Lorenzen, Pfeifer or McCarthy). Any such discussions shall begin only after both sides have been fully informed in advance that such contact is planned, and a tape recording of all discussions with such prospective examiner shall be made and supplied to both parties to this controversy.*

I asked that Rogers and Lorenzen, who was sent a copy, agree in writing to these conditions. Rogers replied on November 12, making a counter-proposal that would allow Backster to give the test, unless I could get the American Polygraph Association's Ethics Committee to certify that he was "incompetent and/or dishonest." (At the time Backster was a member of the board of directors of the APA.) When I refused to accept this proposal, Rogers shifted to another. In Rogers' letter of December 9, he claimed that Lorenzen's improprieties were not grounds for rejecting Backster because *"Jim Lorenzen is not a principal of this challenge-agreement. You cannot reject Mr. Backster on the basis of independent actions of persons who are not principals of our challenge-agreement.* Lorenzen's conversations with Backster could only be considered 'under the table' if Lorenzen was bound by the challenge-agreement. But he is not."

217

It was true that Lorenzen was not a signatory to the proposed retest agreement. But he and APRO would lose many hundreds of dollars and much prestige if Rogers and his crew failed the new test. If Lorenzen was only a "disinterested party," as Rogers now was attempting to claim, why had Lorenzen initiated discussions to arrange for Backster to give the new test and why had Rogers never criticized him for getting involved? In Rogers' letter of December 9, he concluded: "You are a free man Mr. Klass. You can be as honest or dishonest as you choose to be . . . . *If you cannot prove Mr. Backster to be dishonest or incompetent, you cannot rightfully reject him. We await your decision."*

In my reply of December 16, I challenged Rogers' claim that Lorenzen's attempted deception could be ignored on the grounds claimed and denied that I had ever stated in writing, or orally, that I had accepted Backster for the retest. (Even had I done so prior to discovering Lorenzen's attempted deception, surely I would be entitled to change my mind when I found that Backster was cooperating with Lorenzen to try to maintain that deception.) I concluded my letter by asking if Rogers believed "there is no polygraph examiner in the entire United States who is competent to give you an unbiased test, except Backster." And I asked Rogers if he now refused to undergo new polygraph examinations "unless that test is given by Cleve Backster?"

It would be five months before Rogers would respond, for reasons I would not discover until the spring of 1978. On May 16, 1977, he finally replied that the new test had to be given by Backster unless I could convince the American Polygraph Association to issue a statement saying that Backster "is incapable of administering polygraph examinations to the Test Subjects that would be both competent and honestly performed." Less than a year earlier, Rogers had announced that he and his crew were eager to take a new polygraph test. But months of negotiations had shown that he was only willing to do so if the test was given by Backster—a man whose tests with a polygraph machine prompted him to believe that house plants have extrasensory perception. Rogers' letter demanded that I accept his latest "challenge" as written within ten days: *"Anything less than this will constitute a public decline of our challenge."* He sent copies to the leaders of numerous UFO organizations.

My reply of May 29 was a seven-page letter that summarized our many months of negotiations to try to arrange mutually acceptable conditions for the new test. My letter concluded:

> I am anxious to proceed to try to devise fair and equitable ground rules for such a test, ground rules that are fair and equitable *to all parties involved*. If you yourself share this intent, you will return to the format of the near-agreement that we had reached in mid-October . . . And you will give up your determined efforts to have the retest conducted by Cleve Backster. I set no ultimatum-like time limit for your response, because 10 months already have

elapsed and the most important consideration is that the tests *be given under the most rigorous possible conditions so that the results shall have maximum possible credibility and acceptance.*

Rogers replied by a letter dated June 11 but not postmarked until June 16. He said, "The definition of a challenge is not 'an equitable agreement,' as you would prefer. A challenge is a *challenge.* You have failed to accept ours—pure and simple." I replied on June 25, saying that "you and your associates are not willing to undergo new polygraph tests administered by a mutually acceptable examiner of unquestionable integrity and reputation . . . *If you should ever change your mind, rest assured that I will be eager to participate and to hear from you."* Rogers never replied.

Because Rogers had distributed widely his final "challenge" of May 16 to major UFOlogists, I sent these same persons copies of my letter of May 29, which summarized the whole sordid affair of Lorenzen's use of deception to lure me into accepting Backster for the new tests, and Backster's lack of candor in disclosing the secret talks in responding to my questions. I had expected that at least a few of the UFO-movement leaders would respond with expressions of disapproval of such trickery. But only GSW's Spaulding did so.

Dr. J. Allen Hynek, one of the UFOlogists who received copies of my letter, appeared with Travis Walton a short time afterwards on ABC-TV's "Good Night, America." After Walton had described his alleged experiences aboard the UFO, Hynek was asked, "What do you think of Travis's story." Hynek replied:

> Well, I think that the—he underwent, I understand, a Minnesota Multiphasic Personality Inventory and passed it with high colors. It showed that he was no psychotic, or was not given to deception. But what I've always felt about this case—I've divided it into two parts. One is the first part involving all seven [members of Rogers' crew], and they took lie-detector tests and passed them. It fits a pattern, see. If this were the only case on record then I would have to say, well, I couldn't possibly believe it. But at the Center for UFO Studies now we have some two dozen similar abduction cases currently being studied. *Something is going on!*

A week earlier, in preparation for the show, a representative of ABC-TV had called James Oberg, in Houston, Texas, to invite him to appear on "Good Night, America" with Hynek and Walton. Oberg is a computer-systems analyst by profession, a freelance writer, and a skeptical UFOlogist. When he was told that Walton would be the principal guest, Oberg advised the ABC-TV representative that he ought to invite me instead because I had spent more than a year investigating the Walton incident. Oberg was told that Hynek had refused to appear on the program if I were invited and had suggested Oberg instead. Because Oberg was unable to take time to go to New York for the program, he suggested that ABC call Robert

Sheaffer, another UFO skeptic, who lived in the Washington, D.C., area. When ABC called Sheaffer and told him that Walton would be the featured guest, he too urged that I be invited. After he also was told that Hynek would not appear if I were invited, Sheaffer accepted.

It was not the first time that I had been denied the opportunity to present my views because of Hynek's refusal to appear if I was a guest. And so on May 31, 1977, I wrote Hynek to complain about "your continuing efforts to stifle my opportunity to present the 'other side' of the UFO issue. This is neither fair-play nor in the scientific tradition." Hynek never responded.

APRO's endorsement of the authenticity of the Walton case continued. The April 1977 issue of *Official UFO* magazine carried the second of a two-part series on the incident, written by Oberg. (His first article had presented the highlights of my findings on the case, and the second offered Jim Lorenzen the chance for rebuttal.) When Oberg asked Lorenzen if he were "willing to stake your reputation as a UFO investigator on the authenticity of this case," Lorenzen replied: "I don't stake my reputation on any case. *I would stake my reputation on the way I conducted this case.*" [Emphasis added.]

Several months later, an interview with Lorenzen was published on July 23, 1977, in the *Tucson Daily Citizen.* He was quoted as saying: "I think that he [Walton] is describing a real experience to the best of his ability . . . I believe he was transported aboard some sort of craft. *No one has come up with an alternative workable hypothesis.*" [Emphasis added.] In the August 1977 issue of *UFO Report* magazine, Mr. and Mrs. Lorenzen were interviewed by Jerome Clark, a well-known writer in the UFO field. When Clark asked Mrs. Lorenzen, "What's the most impressive UFO case you've ever investigated," she replied, "I'd say the Travis Walton incident." Her husband added: "It's been very illuminating to observe the extent to which skeptics like Klass will go to defeat an idea that threatens them."

APRO and others who accept the Walton story argue against its being a hoax on the grounds that the crew members had no binding ties of friendship that could motivate them to remain tight-lipped. That is not true. For example, Travis and Mike Rogers' younger brother had been involved in the burglary-forgery incident five years before, and after the incident Travis married Rogers' sister. Crew-member Allen Dalis, who went to jail for armed robbery, had been married to the sister of John Goulette, another member of the crew.

But the principal motivation for holding their tongues was Sheriff Gillespie's threat to prosecute if the incident turned out to be a hoax. The prospect of winning prize money from the *National Enquirer* offered added incentive against loose talk. And after crew members had shared the prize money, they might worry about the prospect of being charged with obtaining money under false pretenses if a hoax were revealed.

The following year, after Bill Barry's book on the incident was published (May 1978), I first learned from the book that one crew member, Steve Pierce, had confronted Rogers with the fact that he was considering repudiating the incident. This had occurred in late 1976, about the time Rogers suddenly lost interest in continuing negotiations for the retest. Clearly Rogers feared that at least one member of his crew would fail the test, regardless of who was selected as the examiner.

Barry's book quotes Rogers as saying: "Steve told me and Travis that he had been offered ten thousand dollars just to sign a denial. He said he was thinking about it . . . So I told him, 'Then you'll spend the money alone, and you'll be bruised.'" The latter suggests that Rogers was threatening Pierce with physical harm if he recanted. Barry hints that I had made the alleged $10,000 offer through Sheriff's Deputy James Click, of Taylor, Arizona, who had befriended young Pierce in the months following the UFO incident. Had Barry checked with me, I would have assured him that I had never made such an offer to Click or to anyone seeking to "buy-off" a member of the Rogers crew. In fact, until I read Barry's book, I had never heard of Click. However, because of what I read in Barry's book, I did call Click on May 27, 1978. With his aid, I was able to locate Pierce, who then lived in Ft. Worth, Texas.

On June 11, 1978, Pierce, who was seventeen at the time of the UFO incident, told me that the Rogers crew usually quit work around 4:00 P.M. to drive back to Snowflake, but on the day of the UFO incident they had stayed two hours later; thus it was dark when they got ready to leave. Pierce told me that Travis did not work at all during the day of the UFO incident because he claimed to be ill. During the afternoon, Mike Rogers had disappeared from the work site for about two hours. But I could not gain any meaningful details about what had transpired.

When I told Pierce that I believed the UFO-abduction story to be a hoax, he replied: "Me too. If I could ever *prove* it was a hoax I'd damn sure do it." But clearly it would be one young man's word against those of the other crew members. And Pierce could end up, as Rogers had phrased it, being "bruised."

24

A UFO Attack?

A historic event in the annals of UFOlogy seemingly occurred shortly after midnight on August 27, 1979, when Deputy Sheriff Val Johnson reported that his patrol car had been attacked by a UFO. The residual damage offered convincing evidence that the reported UFO could not have been a bright celestial body, a meteor-fireball, a weather balloon, or an advertising aircraft.

The incident occurred in northwestern Minnesota, not far from the town of Warren. At 2:19 P.M. Johnson radioed in to report: "Something just hit my car. I don't know how to explain it. Strange . . . . Something attacked my car. I heard glass breaking and my brakes lock[ed] up and I don't know what the hell happened." The officer requested assistance and Deputy Sheriff Greg Winskowski was dispatched to his aid. When he arrived he found Johnson's car, a Ford LTD, at right angles to the road blocking the opposing lane with tire skid marks stretching for nearly one hundred feet.

Johnson said he had been driving west on Highway 5 when he spotted a bright light that seemed to be coming from a wooded area about two and a half miles south along nearby Highway 220. He said he turned south on Highway 220, accelerating to a speed of about 65 mph. Johnson said he suspected the bright light might be an aircraft because there had been instances of smugglers using aircraft to bring drugs over the nearby Canadian border. But, curiously, Johnson did not radio in to report such a potentially hazardous mission. After covering about a mile and while still more than a mile from the wooded area, Johnson said the bright light suddenly seemed to zoom toward his car at a very high speed. Later he said he recalled seeing the blinding light rushing toward his car, heard the sound of breaking glass, and then he lost consciousness. He said he had no recollection of applying the brakes despite skid marks that extended for nearly a hundred feet. He estimated that the incident had occurred at about 1:40 A.M., indicating that

223

he had been unconscious for nearly forty minutes before calling to report the incident.

Johnson told Winskowski that when he had regained consciousness his head was against the steering wheel. A small red mark on Johnson's forehead seemed to suggest that his loss of consciousness was due to his head hitting the wheel. Johnson was not wearing his seatbelt at the time, despite the high speed of his vehicle. The officer did not complain of a severe headache, although Winskowski later reported that he seemed to be in a state of mild shock. An ambulance was dispatched to pick up Johnson, and about 4:00 A.M. he was taken to a hospital in nearby Warren where he was examined by Dr. W. A. Pinsonneault. Johnson did complain about discomfort in his eyes and the doctor noted a minor irritation, administered some medication, and Johnson then went home to sleep.

A member of the sheriff's department drove the patrol car back to Warren, where it was inspected and the following damage was noted:

> • The cover-glass on *one* of two headlights on the driver's side was broken, but there was no damage to the adjacent headlight, *nor was there any damage to the metal ring that held the broken cover-glass.*
> • The windshield was severely cracked in front of the driver's seat, suggesting it had been struck a heavy blow in several locations.
> • The red plastic cover-glass on *one* of five lights atop the forward portion of the roof had a small puncture in it, *but there was no damage to any of the other four lights.*
> • There was a small circular dent on the top of the hood; its appearance suggested it could have been made by hitting the hood with a hammer.
> • A radio antenna located immediately aft of the rotating red beacon atop the roof was bent back at an angle of approximately 60 degrees, with the bend located a couple of inches above the top of the red beacon.
> • Another antenna for Citizens Band installed on the car's rear trunk had its upper tip bent back at an angle of nearly 90 degrees, *but this bend was many inches higher than the 60-degree bend in the forward antenna.* A third antenna, for a standard car-radio receiver, located on the passenger's side fender was *undamaged.*

Later it was discovered that both the car's electric clock and Johnson's mechanical wristwatch were running fourteen minutes late, although Johnson said he had set both for the correct time when he went on duty.

If Johnson's story of how the damage had occurred was true, there is no possible prosaic explanation. When I first read the news accounts of the incident, I was struck by a number of similarities between Johnson's story and the UFO encounter of the hero while driving his truck in *Close Encounters of the Third Kind,* the movie that had attracted such large audiences a little more than a year before the incident in Minnesota. Curiously, *Johnson claimed that it never occurred to him that he might have had an encounter with a UFO* until Sheriff Dennis Brekke suggested that possibility and decided to call Hynek's Center for UFO Studies, which brought Allan Hendry to the scene to investigate the case.

Hendry published a two-part series on the incident and the results of the CUFOS investigation in *International UFO Reporter (IUR)* in the autumn of 1979. In the first article (Sept./Oct.) Hendry wrote: "Prior to this first sighting of his life, he [Johnson] was rather indifferent to the whole subject." But in an interview with reporter Debra Stone of the *Minneapolis Star,* September 11, 1979, Johnson was quoted as saying: "I had an open mind [about UFOs] prior to the occurrence and I still do. I read a couple books about them [UFOs] but I've read a couple books on any number of subjects. I wasn't any more interested in that than anything else."

Subsequently I talked with several people who had worked with Johnson in earlier years, when he was a tool-and-die maker; all of them spoke well of Johnson. When I asked George Erickson if Johnson had shown any interest in UFOs at that time, he replied: "We used to talk about them . . . but it wouldn't be any more than he would talk about anything else . . . just in a normal conversation." Another former co-worker, Glen Meyer, told me that Johnson occasionally mentioned UFOs. He told me that at one time, when there were reports of cattle being mutilated by UFOs, Johnson had suggested "setting up a UFO watch." When I asked Meyer if Johnson was the sort of person to play jokes on his associates, he replied: "I don't know if you'd call him a 'practical-joker.' He did like to pull tricks on a guy once in a while . . . like maybe hide your coffee cup on you." But he added: "As far as we know, he's never told us any untruths."

Hendry conducted a rigorous investigation of the incident. For example, he arranged for Meridan French, a windshield expert from the Ford Motor Company, to visit Warren to inspect the fracture patterns in the windshield. French's conclusions, published in the November *International UFO Reporter,* were that the fractures were "the result of mechanical forces rather than thermal stresses . . . there was no evidence of unusual heat." One of four cracks, French concluded, could have been made by "a rubber-headed hammer . . . [or] with a blow from the side of a tightly-closed fist." Another, he noted, showed the glass was "severely crushed in a small, roughly circular area as though impacted by an extremely hard object" French concluded that "all cracks were from mechanical forces of unknown source."

In Hendry's initial report on the case, he noted that both the roof-top and trunk-mounted antennas were spring-loaded at the base so that "if you grab the antenna and bend it, it simply arches over and snaps back again." Thus, if some object had hit this antenna shortly after impacting the windshield, the spring at the base of the antenna should have allowed it to give with the impact and then snap back undamaged. Yet the top of the roof antenna had been permanently bent on a 60-degree angle and the one on the trunk was bent 90 degrees. Hendry noted another oddity: "the large 'bubble' lamp [with the rotating red beacon] is just inches in front of the [roof] antenna, and is virtually the same height as the location of the bend, but it is unscathed." (Some of the car damage is shown in Plate 17.)

When several engineers in the materials-testing laboratory of Honeywell volunteered to examine the two bent antennas, they discovered another curious anomaly. *There was absolutely no evidence of physical impact on either of the two bent antennas. Nor was there any evidence of extreme heat.* The bodies of dead insects that earlier had impacted against the two antennas were still covering the antennas. When the Honeywell engineers ran "hardness tests" on the antennas in the vicinity of the bends, they found no significant softening of the metal. It retained its original qualities of "spring temper" steel, Hendry reported in *IUR*.

In investigating the fact that both Johnson's mechanical wristwatch and his car's electrical clock were running fourteen minutes late, Hendry investigated the possibility that this might have been caused by an intense magnetic field from the UFO. It is known that when the metal elements of an automobile body are stamped out, they retain a portion of the prevailing earth's magnetic field so that similar models made during the same year will have similar "magnetic fingerprints." Thus, if the reported "time-lag" in the Johnson watch and in the Ford LTD patrolcar clock were caused by an intense magnetic field from a UFO, that should also have changed the magnetic-fingerprint of the patrol car. A portable magnetometer was used to map the magnetic field of the patrol car and an identical model. Hendry reported the tests revealed "no significant deviation" between the two, which ruled out the prospect that an intense magnetic field from a UFO had somehow stopped both Johnson's watch and the car's clock for the identical fourteen-minute period, after which both had resumed normal operation.

If the reported intense illumination from an unidentified craft contained strong ultraviolet radiation, this could explain the eye irritation that Johnson reported. But when tests were conducted on the windshield glass, Hendry reported, it showed that the vinyl layer used in the laminated glass "completely blocks out UV [ultraviolet] . . . Furthermore, Johnson's eyeglasses should have provided him additional protection . . ." Hendry also noted "the lack of sunburn on Johnson's face."

Approximately ten hours after the incident, after Johnson awoke, he was taken to Grand Forks, North Dakota, for examination by Dr. Leonard Prochaska, an ophthalmologist, who reported: "There was no sign of any disease or damage to either eye at that time. There was a mild conjuctival irritation."

The hard physical evidence leaves only two possible explanations for this case. One is that Johnson's car was attacked by malicious UFOnauts, who reached out and hit one headlight with a hammerlike device, then hit the hood and windshield, then very gently bent the two radio antennas, being careful not to break them, then reached inside the patrol car to set back the hands of the watch on Johnson's arm and the clock on the car's dashboard. These UFOnauts would then have taken off Johnson's glasses, aimed an intense ultraviolet light into his eyes, and replaced his glasses, while being careful not to shine ultraviolet on his face.

Or, the incident is a hoax. There simply are no other possible explanations. Nor are there any nearly identical incidents in more than thirty years of UFO reports.

After reporting the results of the CUFOS investigation, Hendry noted that some persons had suggested that Johnson undergo regressive hypnosis "to see if he was 'taken on board a spaceship to be used for breeding purposes.' Still others insisted that a polygraph test was just what he needed to undertake! How easily laymen can prescribe ill-explored and controversial techniques." Hendry was on sound ground in rejecting the use of hypnosis as a "magic truth serum." But it is surprising that Hendry lumped hypnosis and polygraph tests into the same category. Especially since Hendry later informed me that he himself had proposed that Johnson undergo a polygraph test and that Johnson had refused.

What was Hendry's reaction to Johnson's refusal to take a polygraph test? In the November *IUR,* Hendry wrote: "Johnson's personal reaction to such suggestions [polygraph test and hypnosis] is a firm one: he does not want to become a sideshow for the benefit of other people's 'morbid curiosity.'" Yet Johnson was willing to journey to New York to appear with Hendry on ABC-TV's "Good Morning, America" to describe the incident.

Hendry concluded: "Since he enjoys the trust of his employer, he feels no obligation to 'prove' his experience to others . . . an attitude which *IUR* feels lends still further to his credibility." In other words, Hendry believes that Johnson's unwillingness to take a polygraph test provides convincing evidence that the incident is not a hoax. On the "Good Morning, America" show, Hendry characterized the incident as "one of the most important [UFO cases] we have."

25

UFOs over New Zealand: Prelude

The best-documented UFO incident of all time occurred off the east coast of New Zealand, beginning shortly after midnight on December 31, 1978. The documentation includes a little more than eight minutes of 16 mm. color film showing lights plus a tape-recorded commentary, both made from a four-engine Argosy cargo aircraft under the command of an experienced pilot, Captain William Startup. There also is a tape recording of flight-crew radio communications with an air-traffic controller during portions of the incident, and a tape recording of the flight crew's recollections made several days later. At times, mysterious blips appeared on the display of an air-traffic control radar near Wellington, on the southwestern tip of New Zealand's North Island, and an unidentified blip appeared briefly on the Argosy's own airborne radar.

The incident has undergone more rigorous investigation than any other in the history of UFOs, principally by Dr. Bruce Maccabee, who has publicly stated that he is "convinced that there is something real and new behind the UFO phenomenon," a pro-UFO view he held long before the New Zealand incident. Maccabee is a physicist employed by the U.S. Navy, near Washington, D.C., but his UFO activities are not sponsored by the government, although he did use Navy facilities to analyze the New Zealand films.

This incident might seem to qualify as the most impressive UFO case of all time, considering that there were five observers, and that their observations seemingly were confirmed independently by radar and on movie film, making this a "radar-visual-photographic" case. Yet, as has been shown in earlier chapters, things are not always as they first appear to excited participants in a UFO incident.

Many UFOlogists are not impressed by UFO reports that involve lights at night ("nocturnal lights"), especially when the lights remain essentially motionless, as in this incident, because they usually have prosaic explanations.

For example, of the 1103 nocturnal-light cases investigated by Allan Hendry of CUFOS, 93 percent were found to have prosaic explanations. Of the remainder, only 1 percent were classified as "best nocturnal lights" that seemed to defy an earthly explanation.

This very high percentage of explainable "nocturnal lights" indicates why most UFOlogists are not impressed by such a report — unless the UFO's presence seemingly is confirmed by radar. Yet those with extensive expertise in radar know that radar is far from infallible.

Under certain atmospheric conditions, such as temperature inversions that occur more frequently during the hot summer months, the energy from an air-surveillance radar can be deflected downward so that the radar briefly "sees" ships at sea or automobiles, producing spurious blips that resemble airborne targets. Such spurious targets have been a problem ever since radar was invented and are known as "angels." Radar designers are still trying to devise corrective measures to filter out such spurious returns, although very recent systems are less prone to "angels." One characteristic of radar "angels" is that they usually appear briefly in one geographic location, then disappear as atmospheric conditions change, only to reappear at a different location.

Many UFOlogists lean on a curious sort of logic when they boast that a visual UFO sighting was confirmed by radar. If the bearing of a nocturnal light, which usually can be only crudely estimated by the observer, seems to be in roughly the same direction as an unidentified blip on the radarscope, this seems to confirm the presence of an unidentified craftlike object. But if the radar operator reports an unidentified blip in a direction where the observers do not see any light, that is of no importance because it is assumed that the UFO decided to turn off its lights. (This assumes the UFO's lights are simply ornamental and not associated with its propulsion system.) If observers see a light where the radar operator cannot find a blip, that too is inconsequential because it is assumed that the UFO simply decided to make itself invisible to radar energy. (This assumes a UFO can make itself visible or invisible to radar as it wishes and that somehow the UFO knows that its presence is being monitored both by a radar operator and by other observers.)

An even more remarkable manifestation of this curious logic was encountered twice during these New Zealand incidents, during an Argosy's southbound flight to Christchurch, when the traffic controller at Wellington reported that his radar showed an unidentified blip flying alongside the Argosy, which also was within range of a similar radar at Christchurch airport. But the Christchurch radar showed only the Argosy — no UFO. Rather than conclude that there might be something amiss with the Wellington radar, Maccabee prefers to believe that the UFO had the ability to make itself visible to the Wellington radar to the north, while simultaneously making itself invisible to a very similar Christchurch radar to the south.

This best-documented of all UFO cases might never have occurred except for the fact that Quentin Fogarty, a TV reporter from Channel "O" of Melbourne, Australia, was vacationing in New Zealand during the Christmas holidays, and there was little exciting news during this period. When TV producer Leonard Lee read press accounts of nighttime UFO sightings by flight crews of Safe Air Ltd., a cargo airline, that had occurred on the night of December 20–21, he called Fogarty to ask him to hire a crew to make a minidocumentary on the incident. Fogarty made arrangements with David Crockett, a professional cameraman, and his wife Ngaire, an experienced tape-recorder operator. Fogarty arranged to interview Vern Powell, one of the Safe Air captains, and Wellington traffic controllers, and then to fly aboard a Safe Air Argosy from Wellington to Christchurch, retracing the flight path of Powell during his recent UFO encounter.

The interview with Captain Powell went well, as Fogarty later described in an article published in December 1980 in *Fate* magazine. "Powell proved to be an ideal subject, articulate and obviously delighted with all the attention," Fogarty wrote. "He told me of his longtime interest in UFOs and said that for 36 years he had searched the skies but to no avail. Naturally he was thrilled that at long last his patience had been rewarded . . . He was due to retire in a few months and his chance of an aerial encounter with a UFO would then be gone."

The prelude to Powell's encounter had occurred around midnight on the night of December 20–21, when several observers at a Royal New Zealand Air Force base near Blenheim (about fifty miles southwest of Wellington, on the northeast corner of South Island), spotted what seemed to them to be unusual lights to the southeast. They called the Wellington traffic-control center to see if there were any unusual targets on the Wellington radar.

The Wellington radar antenna is located atop a mountain, at 1700 feet elevation, to give it an unobstructed view over mountainous terrain in the area. But this has proved a mixed blessing, because, from this high elevation even under normal atmospheric conditions, the radar antenna illuminates objects on the ocean's surface. As a result, even under normal conditions the Wellington radar can "see" ships at sea and even echoes from moving trains on South Island.

To help filter out unwanted targets, including buildings and mountains (known as "ground clutter"), the Wellington radar, like most air-surveillance radars, is equipped with a "moving target indicator" (MTI) designed to filter out fixed and slow-moving targets to avoid distracting controllers. When the MTI is functioning properly, no stationary targets should be displayed, nor slow-moving objects, such as birds. But even a properly functioning MTI cannot filter out spurious targets caused by atmospheric conditions if the speed of winds aloft and the target exceed the selected lower limit. The Wellington radar MTI filters out only objects whose velocity is less than fifteen knots.

Around midnight that December, before receiving a call from one of the observers at Blenheim, Wellington controller Andrew Herd and associate John Cordy had spotted as many as five radar blips that did not correspond to any known aircraft traffic, Herd later recalled. He said the radar blips "moved slowly and aimlessly" and that the blips would disappear from one location, then suddenly appear elsewhere—characteristic of "angels" induced by atmospheric conditions found most frequently during warm summer months. (Late December in New Zealand corresponds to late June in the Northern Hemisphere.) Controller Cordy later acknowledged: "We were not too bothered about these targets as radar does sometimes show these spurious echoes."*

Upon receiving the call from an observer in the Blenheim tower reporting seemingly unusual lights, two of which had merged into one which was now moving *north*, Cordy examined his radarscope and found one unidentified blip in the vicinity of the reported light(s), but the radar blip was moving *south*. Later, when the Blenheim observer reported the light had disappeared, Cordy reported that his unidentified radar blip was still present. Still later, when the Blenheim observer said a bright light had reappeared, Cordy observed not one large blip but numerous small targets.

Shortly before 1:00 A.M., the Wellington controllers noted what they called a "persistent target" that seemed to be moving southeast at about 120 knots. But after several minutes the blip stopped moving and remained stationary for forty minutes despite the fact that the MTI—if functioning properly—should have filtered out all non-moving targets. When the controllers asked the flight crew of a Safe Air Argosy headed for Blenheim if they could see any craft in the vicinity of two of their unidentified blips, one was identified as a ship at sea while the other could not be viewed because of cloud cover.

At about 1:00 A.M., another Safe Air Argosy had departed Blenheim, headed south to Christchurch. Its pilot was Captain John Randle, who himself had seen the seemingly mysterious lights to the east while waiting for his flight at Blenheim; his co-pilot was Keith Heine. According to Captain Startup's book, Randle "had an open mind [to UFOs]. He was interested because he had previously seen two or three objects which could have been UFOs but were later satisfactorily explained. However, he has many friends he consders to be reliable who have seen unusual things which could not be explained."

The Wellington controllers alerted Randle to try to identify the source of one of their unidentified radar blips, but its location was too far from his position. Shortly after passing Cape Campbell, about twenty-five miles

*From *The Kaikoura UFOs,* by Captain Bill Startup with Neil Illingworth (Hodder and Stoughton, 1980).

southeast of Blenheim, Randle and Heine saw lights in a location near where Wellington's radar showed unidentified blips, but they later acknowledged that it was very difficult to distinguish these lights from ground lights usually seen in the same area. Later in the flight Wellington controllers alerted the flight crew that it had unidentified radar blips in the vicinity of the aircraft, but the crew saw nothing visually although the aircraft's radar did show a blip briefly. (This could have been a ship.) Later the aircraft radar detected another target that appeared to be a ship.

The Argosy landed at Christchurch and departed at 3:10 A.M., headed north for Auckland. At approximately 3:25 A.M., shortly after reaching cruising altitude of 12,000 feet co-pilot Heine observed a very bright light directly to the east. As Heine later described this observation to Startup:

> The thing that struck me most about it was its intensity. It was a very bright light, considerably brighter than Venus is when we see it . . . . There was no indication of shape, but it had a gold-ambery tinge around the edge and this wasn't constant. This tinge was fading out until it was just a pure white light . . . . It was in sight for three to five minutes and I couldn't see any movement. It remained stationary in relation to the position from which we first saw it and thus gradually went out of sight behind us as the aircraft travelled north . . . . The light was very strange. I can't recall seeing anything like it in the sky before . . . or anywhere else, either.

The flight crew reported this brilliant UFO to the Wellington controllers, who in turn relayed it to the crew of another Safe Air Argosy, then heading south to Christchurch. This flight, with Captain Vern Powell in command and with Ian Pirie as co-pilot, had departed Blenheim at 3:14 A.M. Prior to departing they had heard about the visual UFO reports and the mysterious blips on the Wellington radar, so they were not surprised when they were asked to call Wellington via radio to try to identify some of the unknown blips on the radar.

At 3:25 A.M., roughly the same time as the northbound Argosy under Captain Randle first spotted the bright light to the east, Powell and Pirie flying south also spotted what almost certainly was the same UFO. In Startup's book, Powell described the UFO in these words: "We looked and there we saw a massive big light hanging in the sky. There was cloud beyond it and also between us and the light. At times the cloud was obscuring our vision, but the light was so bright we could see a reflection on the cloud. It changed colour; sometimes red, but mostly a brilliant white."

When Powell and Pirie first spotted the brilliant UFO, it was slightly ahead of the aircraft's left wing and the aircraft was flying a south-southeast course, which meant the UFO was to the east. For the next ten to twelve minutes, the UFO seemed to maintain a constant bearing at or near the Argosy's own altitude. And Wellington reported that its radar showed an unidentified blip that seemed to be pacing the aircraft.

When the Argosy reached Kaikoura-East, roughly halfway between Wellington and Christchurch, the aircraft came within range of the Christchurch radar, which is similar but slightly less powerful than the one at Wellington. Although the Wellington radar, located at 1700 feet altitude, showed a "UFO-blip" was pacing the Argosy as it turned at Kaikoura-East, *the Christchurch radar showed only the aircraft, no UFO.*

Startup's book quotes Powell as saying: "The back of my hair felt peculiar when we couldn't identify the light, and again when it was tracking [pacing] us." Powell might have been relieved if he had known that a very bright planet Venus had started to rise above the horizon to the east about twenty minutes before he, Pirie, Randle, and Heine had first noted a brilliant light to the east. At the planet's great distance, it would seem to an aircraft observer as if it were pacing the Argosy. If the UFO was not Venus, it is curious that not one of the four pilots reported that the UFO was in the vicinity of a very bright planet or star, for certainly Venus was there at the time.

But considering Powell's long-standing interest in UFOs and the "36 years he had searched the skies" in the hope of seeing one, perhaps he would have been sorely disappointed, not relieved, to know that the bright object pacing his aircraft was only Venus—the largest single source of nocturnal-light UFO reports.

Had Quentin Fogarty known that this most-impressive UFO sighted on the night of December 21 was only Venus and that the Wellington radar often shows spurious (non-aircraft) targets, he might have told producer Leonard Lee to find some other means to liven up a dull news period without interrupting Fogarty's vacation. But all that Fogarty and his crew knew as they boarded a Safe Air Argosy at Wellington shortly before midnight on December 30, 1978, was that UFOs had been reported over New Zealand by seemingly reliable observers, including four experienced pilots, and their observations seemingly had been confirmed by Wellington radar. What would transpire on the night of December 30–31 would demonstrate the validity of that old adage: "Seek [UFOs], and ye shall find."

26

UFOs over New Zealand: Southbound

Shortly before midnight on December 30, 1978, the Safe Air Argosy under the command of Captain Startup, with First Officer Robert Guard actually flying the aircraft, lifted off from Wellington with the television crew aboard and headed south for Christchurch. In the large lower cargo cabin, Fogarty was being filmed using a script he had written in advance. "We're now approaching the Clarence River area where the heaviest concentration of UFOs was sighted on December 21," Fogarty narrated. "We're at an altitude of 14,000 feet and we're on exactly the same route taken by Captain Powell when he encountered those mysterious objects. It's a beautiful clear night outside and naturally we'll be looking out for anything unusual." In Fogarty's *Fate* magazine article he noted: "I smiled as we finished that bit. I felt it was good, dramatic television."

Meanwhile, the flight crew had observed some flickering lights to the south in the vicinity of the town of Kaikoura, situated on a small peninsula, and had called the Wellington traffic-control center. From the transcript of a tape recording made of all such communications we know precisely what was said and the approximate time. After identifying himself, Startup asked: "Do you have any targets on the Kaikoura Peninsula range?" Wellington controller Geoffrey Causer replied: "There are targets in your one o'clock position [roughly 30 degrees to the right of dead-ahead of the aircraft] at, uh, thirteen miles . . . appearing and then disappearing. At the present moment they're not showing . . . but were showing about one minute ago."

Although radar blips had disappeared from the radarscope some thirteen miles from the Argosy's position, and the flickering lights were still visible in the vicinity of Kaikoura, more than forty miles away, the flight crew seemingly decided that the Wellington radar report confirmed that the flickering lights were something extraordinary. Startup left his seat to call the television crew to come up to the flight deck, which they did.

235

It is important to note that the controller did not call Startup to alert him to the presence of unknown radar blips ahead of the Argosy until the pilot chanced to inquire. One of a traffic controller's primary functions is to alert a flight crew to potential conflicts with traffic along, or near, its flight path—especially when the identity of the traffic is unknown. Startup admits in his book that the controller "had been watching the curious radar images down the coast for almost half an hour. They were erratic, though, appearing and disappearing in random fashion, and *he did not consider them to be solid objects.*" [Emphasis added.]

Maccabee interviewed the controller by phone on January 14, 1979, barely two weeks after the incident. When Maccabee asked if Causer had ever seen such erratic radar blips previously, the controller replied: "Yes I have. I think if you'd check with most of the radar controllers at Wellington, we've all seen anomalous propagation, or unidentified returns from time to time. We haven't taken too much notice of them. It was only because of the interest shown by this particular flight and by previous [UFO] sightings on the 21st of December, you know. There was a lot of interest shown." Causer told Maccabee that he had been informed by the controller he replaced that Startup had a television crew aboard.

At 12:16 A.M., Wellington reported: "Target briefly appeared at twelve o'clock [dead-ahead] to you at ten miles [range] . . . disappeared again." A short time later, the controller reported: "Strong target showing at, uh, eleven o'clock at three miles." Startup calmly replied: "Thank you. No contact yet"—that is, no light was visible in the direction of the reported blip. If Startup believed that an unknown craft was almost directly ahead, less than one minute's flying time away—a craft he could not see and thus could not hope to avoid on his own—one might expect that Startup would have requested controller assistance to guide him away from a possible midair collision. *Yet Startup made no such request at that time, nor at any time during the flight despite the reported proximity of radar blips.* Nor did Causer volunteer such assistance at any time.

About a minute later, Wellington reported: "Target now at just left of nine o'clock [that is, east] at about two miles." Startup calmly acknowledged and still did not request controller assistance. A short time later the pilot did ask for permission to depart from his original flight plan, not to get out of the area but to make a 360-degree turn so the TV crew could film the pulsating lights near Kaikoura and the aircraft then turned *towards the position* of the unknown radar blip.

Fogarty tape-recorded his impressions at about the same time: "It's fairly hard to describe my feelings at the moment, but we've probably seen six or seven, or even more, bright lights over Kaikoura and a number of these have been picked up by the Wellington radar. We're turning around to see if we can get a clearer sight. It really is just a little strange and a little eerie." Ten days earlier Captain Randle also had spotted lights in the same area, but admitted it was difficult to distinguish them from prosaic light sources in the town.

At around 12:27 A.M., the Wellington controller called the Christchurch center to say the aircraft would be a bit late in entering the latter's airspace because the flight crew "is UFO hunting with me and doing some orbits north of Kaikoura." At about 12:30 A.M., Wellington reported that the radar blip from Startup's aircraft was behaving strangely and had doubled in size, but a short time later it returned to normal. This indicated either that anomalous propagation conditions existed or that if there was a UFO in the area, it now was flying so close to the aircraft that the two appeared to be one to the Wellington radar. Yet nobody aboard the Argosy reported seeing a light close to the aircraft.

Two minutes later, however, the flight crew reported seeing a light to the west (toward land), and Wellington acknowledged that it now had an unknown radar blip in the same general direction at a distance of about four miles. By this time the Argosy had moved into the control area of Christchurch, whose radar showed the aircraft quite clearly. But a transcript of the taped communications between the Wellington and Christchurch controllers reveals that *at the very moment that the Wellington radar showed a "UFO" blip flying alongside the Argosy, the Christchurch radar showed only the aircraft—no UFO.* The same thing had occurred ten days earlier on the flight of Captain Powell when the Wellington radar also showed an unknown blip in the vicinity of Powell's aircraft while the functionally similar Christchurch radar showed only the aircraft.

Convincing evidence which showed that atmospheric conditions were conducive to generating spurious radar blips and that something was awry with the Wellington radar's moving target indicator (MTI) filter would be obtained a few days later, but obviously this was not known to Fogarty at the time when he commented to his tape recorder: "They [UFOs] are airborne. If they weren't, Wellington radar wouldn't be picking them up . . . . Let's hope they're friendly."

Shortly after the incident drew international attention (when the film was shown in the United States on the CBS-TV network and by the BBC in the United Kingdom), the New Zealand government launched an investigation, using a Royal New Zealand Air Force (RNZAF) long-range patrol aircraft and scientists from the government's Physics and Engineering Laboratory (PEL). On the night of January 2-3, 1979, the RNZAF aircraft was directed to the location of each unknown radar blip that appeared on the Wellington and Christchurch radars. When the plane arrived at the area where the radar showed an unknown blip, the crew found a ship at sea, encountered turbulence (which can occasionally generate radar targets), or found nothing at all. In one instance, where the Wellington radar showed an unknown target moving at 30 mph., the RNZAF crew observed *a ship at anchor.* At no time did the RNZAF crew report seeing any unusual lights. It is significant that six times as many of these spurious blips appeared on the Wellington radar as on the Christchurch radar.

One night, PEL scientists were stationed on the Kaikoura coast with radios so they could talk directly with the Wellington center. According to PEL physicist William Ireland, a specialist in radiowave propagation who headed the investigation, "on 18 different occasions he [Wellington controller] reported the position of anomalous echoes or groups of echoes to the visual observers [at Kaikoura]. In only two cases did they see anything near the specified bearings; *in each case [it was] a ship."* [Emphasis added.]

Ireland himself visited the Wellington center on the night of January 7-8; he observed a number of anomalous radar blips, some of which he photographed. (See Plate 22.) Ireland also observed a peculiar of the Wellington radar, later noted by Dr. Bruce Maccabee when he visited the center the following month during a trip sponsored by Australian TV Station "O." Both observed that the *unknown radar blips appeared only when the MTI filter was being used and they disappeared when it was switched off.* During Maccabee's January 14, 1979, telephone interview with controller Causer, he recalled that on the night the now-famous incident occurred, "I did *not* observe the targets with the MTI off." Causer recalled that only once during the incident had he thought to disconnect the MTI filter and that when he did so the mysterious blips disappeared.

Maccabee assumed that the use of the MTI filter *increased* radar sensitivity. But in reality an MTI filter *reduces* the ability of a radar to "see" weak radio-frequency energy reflectors. (This is indicated by radar textbooks and by performance specifications prepared by many different radar manufacturers; it was confirmed to me by several radar-design specialists.) Thus, if there really were UFO objects present that were poorer radar-energy reflectors than the Argosy, they might show up when the MTI filter was disconnected, even if they did not appear when the MTI was in use. But on the night of the filmed encounter, as well as a week later during Ireland's visit and a month later during Maccabee's visit, *the Wellington radar was performing completely contrary to all known radar principles.* Beyond any doubt something was awry with its MTI filter.

But this was not known to the television crew on the night of December 30-31. Fogarty concluded that the radar blips had to be airborne objects. "If they weren't, Wellington radar wouldn't be picking them up," he commented on tape at the time. Thus, in the excitement of the moment, if lights were spotted in the general direction of reported radar blips, it seemed logical to conclude that they too must be airborne. During the Argosy's approach to the Christchurch airport, a controller there reported seeing briefly an unknown radar blip to the right of the aircraft, which he later attributed to prosaic causes. But the flight crew spotted a flashing light to the right near a road, which could have been a car's headlights interrupted by trees along the road. The cockpit observers preferred to believe that the lights belonged to a UFO following them to Christchurch.

Thus it is not surprising that when the party disembarked from the Argosy after landing and spotted a bright light to the southeast of the airport, they quickly decided that this too must be a UFO, and the TV crew decided to set up the camera to film it. In his book, Startup describes the UFO seen near the airport as "brighter than Venus.... It was not pulsating and it did not seem to move." As the crew was setting up to film this UFO, an airport security guard came up and the crew pointed out the UFO to him. The guard dismissed it as a light atop an antenna tower on nearby Sugarloaf Hill, so the crew abandoned plans to film it.

Later, according to Startup, he and co-pilot Guard decided that the light was not atop the Sugarloaf antenna tower and apparently "was something unusual." In October 1979, many months later when PEL's Ireland visited the Christchurch airport at night, he found the same "UFO" was still visible, in the same location, and photographed it. It was two very bright lights atop a 1450-foot hill southeast of the airport, about six degrees to the right of the Sugarloaf Hill antenna. Ireland did not bother to visit the site to determine the function of the lights.

If this prosaic light source was not the "UFO" reported by the flight and TV crews, it is strange that the Christchurch controller, with a superb view of the surrounding area, did not note any unusual lights in the area. Surely he would have been aware of the radio reports from the Argosy which told of numerous "UFO-lights" they had spotted along the coast and which should have alerted him to any unusual lights in the vicinity. But he, like other airport employees, would be familiar with the numerous prosaic light sources in the airport area. Inasmuch as only the Argosy flight and TV crews were impressed by the bright light to the southeast of the airport, it is clear that by this time both crews were inclined to mistake prosaic light sources for UFOs.

If Startup had not asked Fogarty whether he would like to fly back to Blenheim instead of getting off at Christchurch as originally planned, the incident and the resulting film would have attracted scant attention outside of Australia and New Zealand. During the seventy-five-minute trip south, Crockett had managed to obtain less than twenty seconds of film of UFOs—half of which showed faint, flickering lights in the vicinity of Kaikoura. There is nothing in the brief film sequences made on the trip south, nor in Fogarty's taped commentary, to indicate high-speed movements of visible UFOs—that is, nothing that could not be explained as prosaic ground light sources. The flickering seen on the film and the very slight apparent movement could have resulted from atmospheric scintillation effects and severe vibration on the Argosy flight deck. As Fogarty himself admitted in his *Fate* article, the faint lights on the film taken during the southbound trip "could have been anything."

It was not easy to film from the cramped Argosy flight deck. There was a "jump-seat" behind the console that separated the pilot's and co-pilot's seats. It was occupied by Crockett, who typically rested his large, heavy Bolex 16 mm. movie camera on his shoulder. As there were no other seats, Fogarty had to stand, typically behind the co-pilot's seat, while Ngaire Crockett crouched over her tape recorder behind the pilot's seat. The noise level in the cockpit was so high that communication between members of the TV crew was difficult.

On the trip south the visible UFOs had not been very cooperative, as Fogarty himself noted on tape: "We're not having very much luck filming these objects because they just appear and then disappear. A few moments earlier Fogarty had described one UFO as looking "like a faint star, but then it emits a very bright white and green light." This description would be apt for an airport rotating beacon, of which there were several along the coast. On the return flight, the TV crew would be much luckier—obtaining, as we shall see, about seven minutes of a very bright, very photogenic UFO, which would make the incident world famous.

27

UFOs over New Zealand: Northbound

At approximately 2:17 A.M., the Safe Air Argosy lifted off from the Christchurch airport. After reaching a safe altitude, the Argosy made a small turn to the right to acquire the 33-degree (magnetic) radial of an Omnirange radio-navigation aid located at Christchurch to fly an air route called Moto track. It planned to fly Moto track (north-northeast) for about ninety nautical miles to the vicinity of Kaikoura, where it would turn slightly left and head about fifty miles north to Cape Campbell. Then the Argosy would turn left and fly about twenty-five miles to Blenheim, its final destination. (See map, Plate 19.)

There were few prosaic light sources on the surface on the right side of the aircraft, where a bright light was spotted as the Argosy flew over Pegasus Bay. To the east was open ocean. To the south was Banks Peninsula, a mountainous area with scant habitation. There was a lighthouse at Lyttleton Head, just southeast of Christchurch. Roughly twenty miles beyond, on the eastern tip of Banks Peninsula, was another bright lighthouse beacon at Steep Head. The cloud cover over Christchurch might have obscured the Lyttleton beacon, but the Steep Head lighthouse would certainly have become visible when the Argosy reached an altitude of several thousand feet. In his taped commentary, Fogarty does not mention seeing either of these lighthouses, which could have provided a valuable indication of the relative bearing of the UFO.

Later, when the Argosy reached its 13,000-foot cruising altitude, about forty miles northeast of Christchurch, cockpit observers should have been able to see an extremely bright glow on the southeast horizon, coming from a fleet of nearly fifty Japanese vessels that had just arrived in the area to fish for squid. To attract the squid to the surface, each of the small boats had strings of very bright lights around its periphery. At the time of this UFO incident, the bulk of these Japanese squidboats were fishing near

241

Mernoo Bank, roughly 150 miles east-southeast of Christchurch. The illumination from these squidboats was so bright that the fleet showed up on photographs obtained by a U.S. Defense Department meteorological satellite passing overhead *at a height of nearly 500 miles.*

Months after the UFO incident, Startup decided to check with the harbormaster at Wellington to determine if a Japanese squidboat might have been fishing on the night of December 30–31, in Pegasus Bay, the area east of Christchurch where a very bright UFO was sighted and filmed by Crockett. Startup learned that *one Japanese boat had indeed departed Wellington on December 16, listing as its destination the Pegasus Bay area.*

Ngaire Crockett decided not to make the return trip to Blenheim. In her place was Dennis Grant, a journalist friend of Fogarty who lived in Christchurch and who had accepted his invitation to join in the UFO hunt. At takeoff, Fogarty and Grant were seated in the large, lower cargo cabin. Crockett was in the jumpseat on the flight deck, behind the flight crew, where he filmed the takeoff. As the Argosy climbed through the cloud layer over Christchurch, at an altitude later estimated to be about 3000 feet, the crew sighted a very bright light to the right and *below* the aircraft. Startup later recalled that the bright light appeared to be *close to the ocean surface.* And for the duration of the incident, the UFO always appeared to be *below* the Argosy's own altitude.

As best as can be estimated, this visual UFO* was first spotted at about 2:19 A.M., when the Argosy was roughly seven nautical miles northeast of the airport. Crockett promptly began to film the V-UFO. After shooting fifty-three seconds of film, he stopped for an indeterminate period, which is evident from a single red-color frame of film, which shows that the Bolex camera stopped with its shutter open, exposing the film for some time to the red light used to illuminate the cockpit instruments at night. (However, the shutter does not always remain open when the camera is stopped. There are other places in the film where Maccabee deduces that the camera was stopped because of a sudden change in position or appearance of the V-UFO image from one frame to the next. This seems a rational explanation.)

Because of the considerable vibration in the cockpit, which made it difficult for Crockett to hold his camera steady, the initial fifty-three-second segment shows a variety of V-UFO shapes and sizes. But after painstaking analysis intended to try to select frames that indicate minimum camera motion due to vibration, Maccabee concludes that the V-UFO at this point in the flight has the shape of a thin ellipse. By a curious coincidence, a squidboat with strings of lights around its periphery when viewed from the

---

*The term "V-UFO" will be used henceforth to refer to the visual UFO in order to distinguish it from an unidentified blip that appeared briefly on the Argosy's airborne radar, which will be referred to as an "R-UFO."

Argosy's then low altitude, would be expected to appear elliptical. The elliptical image is tilted upward at its left end at an angle of about 45 degrees. During the initial segment, some of the images are surrounded by a faint red fuzz, and periodically the image shrinks, sometimes becoming very faint, then expands and becomes brighter. This prompts Maccabee to conclude that these early frames were filmed as the Argosy was climbing through the upper portion of the cloud layer. I agree.

Fogarty's initial taped commentary, given as he watched the V-UFO, was:

> We are about three minutes out of Christchurch airport and on our starboard [right] side we can see two very bright lights, one much brighter than the other. The only way really to describe it . . . it's like a very, very bright star, and just below it is another light, not quite so bright. [The Crockett film shows only one V-UFO and none of the others recall seeing a second V-UFO.] This is quite incredible, really. We've, as I've said, only been flying for about three minutes and already we've picked up two unidentified flying objects.

Since Fogarty's tape recorder was not synchronized with Crockett's camera, it is impossible to correlate precisely the time of his comments with specific segments of the film. Because of the cramped quarters and Crockett's large movie camera, it is unlikely that Crockett was able to film at the same time that Fogarty was in a position to view the V-UFO except later in the flight when the V-UFO was almost directly ahead of the aircraft. Another indication that Fogarty could not view the V-UFO continuously is the fact that he periodically went to the trouble of shutting off the recorder. Maccabee and I have devoted much effort to trying to correlate Fogarty's comments with both Crockett's film and the Argosy's location and altitude to determine whether it is possible to rule out the prospect that the bright light seen and filmed might have been a squidboat. The effort to reconstruct these key parameters has been difficult, and some uncertainties remain.

The tape recording made by the Wellington center, which includes the content of each radio communication with the Argosy and the time each occurred is helpful. Unfortunately, most of this encounter occurred while the Argosy was still near Christchurch and thus beyond direct radio range of Wellington. The Christchurch center also recorded its communications with the Argosy, but the tape subsequently was reused (thus erasing communication with the Argosy), despite Startup's claim that he requested the tape be saved. (One possible explanation for reusing the tape quickly is that it may have contained derogatory comments expressed by Christchurch controllers about the actions of the flight crew.)

Following the first segment and the red-frame, there are approximately three more minutes of V-UFO film before the next red frame. However, there is circumstantial evidence, such as a sudden change in V-UFO position or shape, that indicates that Crockett stopped filming several times. Approximately forty-eight seconds into this second segment, Crockett fortuitously decided to "zoom" back with the lens to film the interior of the cockpit while simultaneously filming the V-UFO. These frames make it possible to come up with a rough estimate of the V-UFO's bearing relative to the Argosy's flight path because of a cockpit instrument on the right that appears below and to the right of the V-UFO. Maccabee's necessarily rough estimate is that the V-UFO's bearing was about 45 degrees to the right and that it was at a depression angle of roughly 5 degrees below the Argosy's fore-aft axis. Because the Argosy was in a climbing (pitch-up) attitude, the true depression angle to the V-UFO relative to the horizon would have been less than 5 degrees. At the time the V-UFO/meter frames were taken, at around 2:22 A.M., the Argosy would have been about fourteen nautical miles (n.m.) northeast of Christchurch at an altitude of around 6500 feet.

During the second segment, which lasts about three minutes, the V-UFO image changes briefly from a thin elliptical form to a "distorted triangular" shape; then it becomes elliptical, growing in thickness until it appears as a roughly circular blob, frequently distorted. The most likely explanation for these shape changes is optical distortion in the right side windows of the aircraft through which Crockett then was filming. Some days after the incident, a scientist named Dr. N. J. Rumsey, from New Zealand's Physics and Engineering Laboratory, took measurements of the Argosy's windows and reported finding considerable distortion. *At no time during Fogarty's taped comments did he report seeing any significant change in V-UFO shape or size, nor did other observers later recall any.*

Based on circumstantial evidence, Maccabee concludes that Crockett may have stopped filming several times during this three-minute segment. At one of these times Fogarty would have been able to gain access to a window to look at the V-UFO and to have taped the following commentary:

> We're now five or six minutes out of Christchurch and those two lights appear to be travelling with us. They're still off the starboard wing. The bright light is still above the other and it's moved a little further ahead of the other. It's extremely bright, much brighter than any of the other stars in the sky. Now it's just dimmed . . . . It's . . . it's gone. It's back again. It appears to be going behind a cloud. I can't quite make out whether it is in fact going behind cloud or whether the light is just dimming. No, it's . . . it's such a bright light. It's lighting up the clouds around it. *This is by far the best of the unidentified flying objects we've seen so far.* [Emphasis added.]

After a brief pause, with the tape recorder running, Fogarty added: "And we've just heard that Wellington radar have more targets at Clarence, so it looks like this is going to be an eventful trip back to Blenheim." Fogarty then shut off the recorder. Maccabee and I agree that this last comment probably was recorded around 2:24 A.M., when the Argosy would have been about twenty-one nautical miles northeast of Christchurch at an altitude of nearly 9000 feet. This estimate is partially based on notes hastily scribbled by Grant, which mention the R-UFOs near Clarence and indicate that the Argosy was about twenty-one miles from Christchurch—information which Grant had obtained from co-pilot Guard in response to his handwritten question.

The report on R-UFOs near Clarence had come from the Wellington center, relayed through the Christchurch center. When the Argosy crew first spotted the bright V-UFO, co-pilot Guard called Christchurch to ask if its radar showed any unidentified craft in the area. The Christchurch center controller had replied that *its radar showed only the Argosy—no UFO.** Christchurch had relayed the Argosy crew report to Wellington, prompting its reply on R-UFOs.

At some point after takeoff, Startup decided to turn on the Argosy's airborne radar, which can be operated in either of two modes. The primary mode is to detect heavy precipitation along the aircraft's flight path that can cause severe turbulence. When operated in this "weather-mode," the radar emits a conical-shaped beam, roughly four-degrees in diameter, which sweeps back and forth 60 degrees either side of forward searching for storm clouds. If Startup intended to use the airborne radar to search for an airborne object (UFO), as he would later claim, this would seem the best mode to use.

Instead, Startup selected the "ground-mapping-mode," in which the radar energy is diffused into a fan-shaped beam that illuminates the earth's surface. This mode typically is used as a navigation aid to assure that the aircraft's primary radio nav-aids are functioning properly and are showing the aircraft's correct position. Because cloud cover over Christchurch at the time of takeoff obscured familiar landmarks, this mode might logically have been selected, since it enhances radar performance against *surface objects* rather than against airborne objects.

Shortly after Startup turned on the radar, he observed a very large blip at a range of nearly 20 n.m., at a bearing he later recalled was roughly 40 degrees to the right of the aircraft—similar to the bearing of the V-UFO. On February 6, 1979, about a month after the incident, during Maccabee's visit to New Zealand, Startup drew a sketch based on his recollections. The blip he sketched was about 3/8 inch wide—the size of a radar blip that would be expected *from a moderately large ship* in Pegasus Bay.

---

*The Christchurch radar antenna is located near sea level, which limits its ability to see objects at very low altitude. For example, the radar could not see a craft below 2000 feet altitude at a distance of 20 n.m., or below 4,000 feet at a range of 40 n.m. Thus, if there was an *airborne* object in proximity to the Argosy during this encounter, its altitude would have had to remain very low throughout the entire incident to avoid radar detection.

A cryptic note scribbled by Grant suggests that this R-UFO was first seen *before* the Argosy had climbed through the clouds and *before* the crew spotted the V-UFO. Grant's note refers to a "Big Sig" (large signal) at 2:18 A.M. and notes "close as 10 miles" which is Startup's recollection of the closest range observed for the R-UFO on the Argosy's radar. This seems to confirm my view that Startup probably turned on the radar to use it as a nav-aid before the V-UFO was spotted, and this would explain why he selected the gound-mapping mode. When the V-UFO was spotted at roughly the same bearing, it is not surprising that those aboard the Argosy assumed that the V-UFO and the object producing the R-UFO were the same.

However, some weeks afterward when Maccabee had the opportunity to analyze the Crockett film, he found that the V-UFO image dimensions (excluding effects caused by cockpit vibration) indicated that the bright-light source subtended an angle of approximately 0.1 degree whereas the radar blip subtended an angle roughly seventy-five times larger, or approximately 7.5 degrees, *indicating that two different objects were involved.* Additional evidence to confirm my "different objects" hypothesis would come later when Startup decided to turn toward the V-UFO for a closer inspection and did not see any R-UFO blip on his radar even when the bright light was directly ahead of the aircraft. This prompts me to believe that the R-UFO blip on the Argosy radar was generated by a large merchant vessel in Pegasus Bay, located about 20 n.m. east of the airport—somewhat closer to the Argosy than the V-UFO. (See Plate 19.)

Maccabee rejects this hypothesis on the grounds that, more than a month after the incident, Startup claimed that the R-UFO had maintained a relatively constant bearing as it closed from about 18 n.m. to nearly 10 n.m. before the blip began to swing around to the right and disappeared at a bearing of 60 degrees, the limit of the airborne radar's scanning ability. Maccabee assumes that this month-old recollection is accurate, even though Maccabee admits that other Startup recollections, tape-recorded only a few days after the incident, are obviously in error. If the R-UFO was caused by a merchant ship about 20 n.m. east of the airport, its blip would appear to close on the aircraft as it flew along Moto track, as Startup later recalled, and its blip would at first appear to maintain a roughly constant bearing—as best Startup could estimate from the small radar display. If, at the time of the encounter, Startup really believed the R-UFO was holding a precisely constant bearing as it closed from 18 n.m. to 10 n.m., this would indicate that the object posed a potential collision threat. Because an airborne radar shows nothing about a target's relative altitude, Startup would have instinctively alerted co-pilot Guard to the potential danger and asked him to focus his attention on the V-UFO because he had the best view of the object. Yet Startup did not do so, offering additional evidence that the R-UFO did not maintain precisely constant bearing and that the blip could have been generated by a large merchant ship in Pegasus Bay.

At approximately 2:26 A.M., Fogarty taped the following commentary:

> We must now be about thirty miles north of Christchurch and that bright light is still with us. According to Captain Bill Startup it came as close as ten miles to us [based on Startup's assumption that the R-UFO blip came from the V-UFO] and it's remained just as bright, so if any object is that bright ten miles away it must be rather large. [Pause] The bright object is still just off our starboard side. According to our cameraman, David Crockett, who's been filming it for the past few moments, it appears to have a brightly lit bottom and a transparent sort of sphere on top, so it appears to be. . . well, like a . . . a flying saucer. I'm watching it right at the moment. It's extremely bright. It's very hard with the naked eye to pick up any details because [unintelligible] the light is so bright. It must have been following us for close to ten to twelve minutes. [Actually the V-UFO had first been spotted about seven minutes earlier.]

Note that Fogarty does not mention the dimmer V-UFO. If this dim "UFO" was deck/stern lighting from a merchant ship that had generated the R-UFO blip, the ship by this time would have disappeared from view behind the Argosy's wing.

The best V-UFO imagery obtained that night was filmed by Crockett shortly before the foregoing Fogarty commentary, probably beginning around 2:24 A.M. It lasts ninety-one seconds. At the time the V-UFO was nearly broadside, and the image appears to be drifting slowly to the right, as would be expected if the bright object was a squidboat at anchor and the Argosy was flying past it. If only once during this (or other segments) the bright object suddenly had climbed above the Argosy, or had quickly shifted to the other side of the aircraft, the squidboat explanation would be demolished. But neither occurred.

During this third segment, Crockett held his camera relatively fixed and allowed the V-UFO image to drift slowly to the right, then periodically he shifted his camera to the right to re-center the bright object. *Maccabee admits that this suggests that the bright object was maintaining a fixed position* — but of course an extraterrestrial craft could hover in one spot if it so desired. During the first part of this segment, the V-UFO drift rate is about three milliradians per second (roughly 1/6th deg./sec.), which indicates a fixed-location object at a distance of about 20 n.m. Later in the segment, the apparent drift rate decreases, eventually to about one milliradian per second. This apparent change could be the result of Crockett's decision to pan his camera very slowly, to avoid periodic re-centering, or it could result from small changes in aircraft heading introduced by the autopilot to compensate for changing winds aloft as the aircraft climbed.

During this most photogenic film segment, the V-UFO images generally resemble color photos of a Japanese squidboat later taken by Startup using a 35 mm. still camera. (See Plate 21.)

At approximately 2:27 A.M., co-pilot Guard made the first radio contact with Wellington, whose tape recording shows he reported:

> We are just 32 [n.m.] out of Christchurch at the moment on Moto track, and, uh, we've got a great big target sitting at, uh three o'clock [at 90 degrees] to us at the moment with us here at 11,500 feet [altitude]. He's sitting at about twelve miles out. [Because of the difficulty of estimating distance at night of an unknown object, which Guard later acknowledged, his distance estimate of the V-UFO almost certainly was based on his assumption that the bright light was the same object that had produced the R-UFO blip.] We had him on our radar when we were tracking [moving] toward him. Do you have anything as far ranging as that?

Wellington replied that its radar could not see that far. But the controller added: "I've got plenty of targets waiting for you off Clarence and north of Kaikoura." About a minute and a half later, Wellington called the Christchurch to say it now could see the Argosy's blip on its radar. The Wellington controller added: "But I've got nothing showing for the next fifty miles anyway." *In other words, although the Wellington radar could "see" the Argosy, it showed no UFO nearby.*

Although Crockett had obtained what would prove to be the best V-UFO film during the period between 2:24 A.M. and 2:26 A.M., at a time when the Argosy was nearing its cruise altitude and the pilot had throttled back (which reduced cockpit vibration), Crockett did not try to film the V-UFO for the next several minutes. One possible explanation for this is that the V-UFO had drifted too far to the right for Crockett to film with his very large camera. This also would explain why Startup decided to make a right turn after the Argosy reached cruise altitude, to fly toward the bright light source.

At approximately 2:29 A.M., Startup banked the Argosy to the right and turned toward the bright light. Fogarty, who had been alerted by the pilot in advance of his intended maneuver, had turned on his recorder and taped the following: "Well, we're moving towards it and it's now just above us." Because the aircraft was banking to the right and Fogarty had no way of distinguishing aircraft motions from those of the V-UFO in the darkness, he could only describe perceived (relative) motions. At that point Crockett's voice can be heard yelling: "I can't see it." Fogarty continued: "Can't really tell if it's moving . . . it's moving extremely quickly, extremely quickly, it's going down." (This would have been Fogarty's perception as the aircraft levelled off from its right bank turn.)

Fogarty: "It's now moving toward the front of the aircraft . . . or maybe we're moving towards it, I can't really tell. It's quite incredible. It's moving away from us now. It appears to be . . . picking up speed . . . it's now basically level with us . . . almost in front." In the darkness, Grant scribbled: "2:30 [A.M.] directly in front. No radar reading." Startup had glanced at his scope after the turn, but there wasn't any large R-UFO blip like the one he had seen earlier even though the V-UFO was almost directly ahead. (Some weeks afterward, Startup tested his airborne radar against known squid-boats and reported that the small vessels, ranging up to 200 feet in length, typically produced only *very small blips.* If the V-UFO ahead was a squid-boat, Startup could easily have overlooked such a small blip because he would be expecting a very large one such as he had seen earlier.)

The next segment of Crockett's film, which lasts for about thirty-six seconds, indicates that he tried to film the V-UFO as Startup was banking into and out of the right turn toward the object. Because of these aircraft maneuvers and the bulky movie camera, Crockett managed to obtain only smeared, streaked images.

Shortly after the right turn, Crockett decided to go below to the cargo cabin to get his 240 mm. telephoto lens. He returned to the flight deck with the large lens and tried to install it in the dimly lit, cramped quarters. As a result, it was not installed properly so that when he set the lens focus for infinity to film the still distant V-UFO, the lens was significantly out-of-focus for the object. As a result, most of the final seventy-three seconds of film show a very large, diffuse image that resembles a "beach ball." Approximately four seconds after Crockett began filming, apparently he recognized that something might be amiss because the V-UFO image begins to shrink in size, returning briefly to a more solid bright blob of light seen in the earlier segment, as if Crockett changed lens focus. Then the V-UFO image begins to expand in size until, after about eighteen seconds, it again resembles a faint beach ball. Crockett retained this "focus" for the rest of this segment. If Crockett's telephoto lens had been properly focused during this period as the Argosy approached the V-UFO, the question of whether it was a squidboat probably could have been resolved beyond any doubt.

Horizontal streaks that appear on the beach-ball images indicate that they were caused by imperfections in the Argosy windows coupled with a rather large depression angle to the V-UFO. If the bright object was a squid-boat that was roughly 20 n.m. abeam of the Argosy at around 2:27 A.M., then by the time Crockett began to film with the telephoto lens, the object would have been less than 10 n.m. away and at a depression angle of at least 15 degrees.

If Startup had not suddenly decided to turn away from the V-UFO and head back to Blenheim just about the time that Crockett began to film with his telephoto lens, the squidboat issue might have been resolved by members of the TV crew using their eyeballs. *Without a word of explanation or advance warning to any member of the TV crew,* Startup suddenly decided to head for home. He banked the Argosy to the left. This is evident in Fogarty's taped commentary: "It's now dropping away right below us." Shortly after Startup initated the left bank, he spotted a bright light directly ahead or a bit to the left which startled him, so he halted the left turn.

This is confirmed by Fogarty's taped commentary: "It appears in fact to be . . . it's moving at speed and it's rising [Argosy right wing dropping]. It's coming straight for us. It's getting a bit brighter. It's just a bit difficult to say in fact, well, to gauge the movement of the object because the aircraft itself is moving over the sky." In all probability, the bright light that startled Startup briefly was the intense glow from the large fleet of Japanese squid-boats just over a hundred miles to the southeast, which Startup would not have noticed earlier as he tried to focus his attention on the nearby V-UFO to the right.

A short time later Startup again banked to the left and resumed his turn in that direction, as evidenced by Fogarty's commentary: "It's now dropping right away *behind us*. The light that is coming out from it *through the reflection of the window* here is probably about twice the *apparent length* of the object." [Emphasis added.] Fogarty's comment that the V-UFO was falling "behind" the aircraft, and his reference to the "reflection of [in?] the window," suggests the object by now was too far to the right and below the aircraft for Fogarty to see it directly.

Especially interesting is Fogarty's reference to the "apparent *length*" of the V-UFO, at a time when the film images show a roughly circular shape and when he might be expected to refer instead to the object's "diameter." One of the 35 mm. still photos that Startup subsequently took of a squid-boat at a distance of about 15 n.m. shows that a great deal of the illumina-tion from its strings of intense lights is reflected off the ocean surface. A camera and color film cannot match the ability of the human eye to discern subtle details, but with careful study it is barely possible, Maccabee found, to make out the main illumination running the length of the squidboat and distinguish it from the less intense light reflected from the surrounding water.

Thus Fogarty's eyes might have observed an object whose *length* was readily apparent, prompting him to use that term (rather than "diameter") in his commentary. Maccabee informed me that "several of the witnesses referred to the edge of the light [V-UFO] as being 'fuzzy,' or as if some material was moving away or flowing outwards from the edges . . . . I got the impression from the descriptions that the 'flow' was confined to a region close to the V-UFO." This would be an apt description of light reflected from ocean waves bouncing off a squidboat.

In Startup's book, he claims that he decided to turn left and head home after the V-UFO had "disappeared beneath the starboard wing." But this is contradicted by Fogarty's taped commentary and by the beach-ball imagery obtained by Crockett, just before or during the initial left turn.

Another possible explanation, if the V-UFO was a squidboat, is that by the time the Argosy had closed to within perhaps 10 n.m. of the object, Startup or Guard suddenly recognized its true identity and realized how foolish they would appear if the TV crew made the same discovery. Startup and Guard knew that Crockett was in the process of installing his telephoto lens, which would have given him a closeup of the V-UFO, and almost certainly would soon enable him to identify it. They could not know that the telephoto lens would not be properly installed, resulting in a badly out-of-focus image, both on the film and in the view-finder through which Crockett was looking.

Maccabee has suggested that Startup's sudden, unannounced decision to abandon the V-UFO investigation may have been the result of concern that he had wasted enough fuel on an unauthorized diversion. Yet Startup himself did not offer this excuse in his book. And on the trip south, Startup had not hesitated to use a little extra fuel to make several complete orbits to give the TV crew more opportunity to see and photograph the V-UFOs. It strikes me as strange that having decided to "waste" several minutes of fuel to get a close look at the V-UFO, and with Crockett's camera now outfitted with a telephoto lens, that Startup should decide suddenly that "enough is enough." Although Startup had informed Fogarty in advance that he planned to turn toward the V-UFO, he gave no advance warning that he planned to abandon the "close inspection" effort.

At approximately 2:40 A.M., less than eight minutes after Startup suddenly "lost interest" in the brightly illuminated V-UFO and decided to head back toward Kaikoura, something prompted the Argosy to contact Wellington to ask if its radar showed any unidentified blips nearby. (Startup later said he had spotted more R-UFOs on his airborne radar.) Wellington replied that the closest R-UFO was "at ten o'clock at twenty miles, just off the coast—about six miles North of Kaikoura." The Argosy simply acknowledged, suggesting the crew saw no bright light in that direction. About two minutes later Wellington reported "two targets at eleven o'clock at fifteen miles." Again the Argosy acknowledged and added: "We don't appear to be picking it up quite so easily on this leg." No bright lights were visible in that direction.

This is confirmed by Fogarty's taped comments: "We've now just passed Kaikoura and, uh, there's been no further activity. There are pinpoints of light in the sky, but nothing's been confirmed on radar" At approximately 2:51, when the Argosy was headed toward Cape Campbell and about 25 n.m. south of it, Fogarty recorded: "We've got another one right in front of us . . . very bright . . . it seems to be quite a long way away and another one just flashed to the left of it. That one flashed extremely brightly." (Cape Campbell has a lighthouse that emits an extremely bright beam of 1½ million candlepower; beyond are Wellington harbor and Cook Strait, with many flashing beacons that serve as navigation aids for ships.)

Fogarty continued:

> They've both now faded. The other one's flashing again. It's giving off an orange flashing light. It looks like an aircraft beacon and it's moving off. It's

extremely bright . . . It fades . . . and its dropped. It seems to have just dropped at an incredible speed and it seems to be rolling and turning. In fact,
there's one light and another light beside it . . . . It appears to be over the hills
. . . There appears to be a whole cluster of them. [In the background Crockett
is heard to yell: "I can't see anything."] You can see orange and red among the
lights. There's one particular one that keeps flashing to the right side
of . . . you can see three distinct lights. In fact, it looks very much like the
same sort of pattern we saw when we came down over the Kaikoura coast on
the way down, but there wasn't quite as much flashing. It really is quite
strange.

The Wellington center's tape recording shows that at 2:51 A.M., while
Fogarty was recording his observations, the Argosy had called the center to
ask if it had an unidentified blip slightly *west* of Cape Campbell, in the
direction of Blenheim, which had a partial cloud cover at the time. Wellington replied that it had a "strong target" directly ahead of the Argosy,
located about ten miles *south* of Cape Campbell, not west of it. The Argosy
responded: "We have that one also," which indicates that this was not the
direction of the V-UFO about which it had inquired. The Argosy added: "It
looks like a collection of lights," that is, numerous V-UFOs, not one as
Wellington reported. Then the Argosy asked the Wellington center to call
the Blenheim airport controller to ask him to shut off the airport's rotary
beacon "just in case we're mixing it up with that [V-UFO]." Wellington
promptly did so.

A short time later Fogarty recorded:

> Well, you can't be right all the time. It appears the last flashing light we saw in
> fact was the beacon at Blenheim and they, the pilots, asked for the beacon to
> be turned off and we're no longer seeing that light. But at the same time as they
> turned the beacon off, Wellington radar told us that he had targets coming over
> to the left of us. In fact, as I speak now we have another one right over
> Blenheim. Extremely bright . . . and that's not a beacon because it's not in the
> same position as the lights were before. And these sightings at the moment are
> right in the position where Wellington radar says they should be [that is, the
> reported direction to the R-UFO was approximately the same as the bearing to
> the V-UFO].

Fogarty was wrong, as the Wellington tape reveals. At 2:52 A.M., Wellington had informed the Argosy crew that the large R-UFO just south of
Cape Campbell had disappeared and that it now showed *four* R-UFO blips
to the left of the aircraft. The crew acknowledged but did not report seeing
any V-UFOs in that direction. At 2:54 A.M., Wellington informed the crew
that it now had an unidentified blip dead-ahead of the aircraft and only
four miles away. However, Wellington did not suggest that the aircraft
detour for safety, nor did the crew propose such action. Instead the crew
replied: "No sighting of that one."

A short time later the crew reported seeing "a pretty bright light . . . it appears to be behind Woodbourne [in vicinity of Blenheim airport] . . . Do you have anything there?" Wellington replied: "Nothing showing over there"—contrary to what Fogarty reported in his taped commentary. Shortly again the Argosy asked whether Wellington had any R-UFOs to the east of the aircraft. Wellington replied: "Nothing showing up on my radar." But the center added: "I have a target just off the coast at 9:30, or coming up at nine o'clock at about five miles."

The Argosy responded: "Appears to be a large number of small boats [don't know] whether there is a fleet going through or not, but there appears to be upwards of twenty lights on our starboard side, but they all appear to be on the surface." This indicates that propagation conditions were such that the Wellington radar was detecting ships on the ocean's surface.

Shortly after 2:57 A.M., the Argosy was cleared to descend to 7000 feet while flying a circular path, providing cockpit observers a panoramic view of Cook Strait with its numerous flashing marine beacons. When the Wellington center cleared the Argosy to descend, it casually mentioned that it had a radar blip directly ahead of the aircraft and only two miles away. Yet the controller did not suggest an evasive maneuver, nor did the flight crew propose such action. Instead the Argosy replied: "We have a light on the surface . . . appears to be on the surface at about that position." Still another confirmation that the Wellington radar was detecting and displaying surface targets that night.

A short time later, Wellington advised: "As you turn, now, twelve o'clock to you at ten miles, a strong target." The Argosy responded: "We have lights on the surface once again. Does it [R-UFO blip] appear to be moving?" Wellington replied: "It's very difficult to tell whether *any* of these targets I've advised . . . you see them for one sweep [radar antenna scan] and then they miss [disappear for] a couple sweeps and appear somewhere else. Now, whether it's the same target or some other [anomalous?] propagation, I've got no idea." This demonstrates that Wellington controller Causer suspected that the R-UFO blips were due to propagation conditions and explains why he did not offer to detour the Argosy around them. The Argosy inquired whether Wellington had any unknown blips in "the Picton area," suggesting that the crew saw lights in that direction. But Wellington responded: "No. No targets at all." Approximately ten minutes later, the Argosy landed at Blenheim and the flight that soon "would be heard around the world" via television was ended.

With the exception of what Fogarty described as "an orange flashing light" that he said "looks like an aircraft beacon," *none of the V-UFO lights appeared to move or to do anything more mysterious than flash on and off in the manner of marine and airport beacons.*

During the nearly forty minutes flying time after Startup suddenly lost interest in the Pegasus Bay V-UFO until the Argosy landed, Crockett managed to obtain only twenty eight-seconds of additional V-UFO film. This final segment shows a light that fluctuates rapidly from a dim red-orange to a bright white, then back to red-orange, then back to bright white, at approximately the flash-rate of the red-orange anti-collision beacons installed atop and beneath the Argosy's fuselage. Prior to departing for Christchurch, Crockett had filmed the Argosy from outside, showing its rotating orange-red beacon mounted topside just behind the flight deck. Maccabee's analysis shows the topside beacon was flashing seventy-eight times per minute, compared to seventy times per minute for the V-UFO later filmed. But film shot for the southbound leg was photographed at a camera speed of twenty-four frames per second, which is very accurately controlled. On the return trip, Crockett filmed at ten frames per second, to obtain increased exposure time. At this frame-rate, camera speed can vary by approximately 10 percent. This means that the V-UFO's actual flash-rate could really be seventy-seven times per minute, almost identical to the Argosy's topside anti-collision beacon.

Crockett would not have been able to film the topside beacon directly. But its intense illumination could have been reflected off one of the aircraft's rotating propeller blades when beacon rotation rate and propeller speed were roughly "synchronized." Such synchronization could have occurred when Startup began to throttle back for his descent, possibly increasing the propeller's pitch-angle. A short time later, when he throttled back further, the requisite synchronism between propeller speed and beacon rotation rate would be lost and the V-UFO would mysteriously disappear.

The only other time when such fortuitous synchronization might have occurred would have been when the Argosy was approaching the Christchurch airport. But at that time, as Crockett's film shows, the attention of the observers on the flight deck was focused in the forward direction rather than far to the side, where a briefly visible reflection of the topside beacon off the propeller blades might have been seen.

If this final-segment V-UFO was a reflection of the beacon from the curved surface of the propeller blades, whose rotation rate was not perfectly synchronized with the rotating topside beacon, it readily explains the remarkable changes in shape, size, and appearance of the V-UFO images that occur in a fraction of a second. For example, the film shows a UFO that changes from a roughly circular "blob" in one frame to a banana-shaped object standing on end in the next, only 0.1 second later. And in the next frame, 0.1 second later, the single banana-shaped UFO splits into two "string bean" shaped objects in a horizontal position. Two frames later (0.2 seconds), the two string-bean-shaped objects merge into a single, distorted eliptically shaped object. These remarkable "gymnastics" prompted Maccabee originally to characterize this twenty-eight-second segment as the "best" of all the film shot on the night of December 31, 1978.

Maccabee rejects my hypothesis that the V-UFO could be a reflection of the Argosy's topside beacon, and that the bright white color is the result of overexposure of the film because of the intensity of the beacon light when it is aimed directly at the propeller. (Crockett was using extremely sensitive film with an ASA-400 rating.) Maccabee finds it easier to believe that a UFO can change shape, size, orientation, and color, and even divide itself into two separate objects in a fraction of a second, then recombine into one object just as quickly. Yet Crockett's film of the Pegasus Bay V-UFO offers no indication that it could do any of those remarkable things.

Even more significant, not one of the five observers in the Argosy later recalled seeing a V-UFO near Cape Campbell/Blenheim that changed shape from a circular blob to a banana-shape, then split into two objects then merged back into one—behavior so extraordinary that it should have been remembered by all of the flight-deck observers. Nor did Fogarty tape-record any description of such V-UFO gymnastics—only something he described as an "orange flashing light [that] looks like an aircraft beacon."

Maccabee also rejects the hypothesis that the very bright object filmed in Pegasus Bay could have been a squidboat, possibly the ship that left Wellington two weeks earlier after logging its destination as Pegasus Bay. The principal basis for rejecting the squidboat hypothesis, according to Maccabee, is that the illumination from a single squidboat would not be sufficient to produce the overexposed images, even on the extremely sensitive (ASA-400) film at ten frames per second that Crockett used. A typical squidboat, measuring up to 200 feet in length, carries a string of fifty lights, each rated 4000 watts—forty times the brightness of "large" 100-watt bulbs sometimes used for home illumination. Thus the light from a typical squidboat should be equivalent to stringing a total of 2000 bulbs, each 100-watts, side-by-side completely around the ship. (See Plate 20.)

Maccabee's convictions are based on measurements he made on the original Crockett film in early 1979 when it was brought to the United States by a representative of Australian TV station "O." At the time Maccabee analyzed the film he, seemingly, did not fully apreciate that the extent of image overexposure that later would become such a key factor in his argument against a squidboat explanation. As a result, he made densitometer measurements only on six frames out of nearly 4400 frames in the Pegasus Bay sequence—an extremely small sample of the total. And most of these measurements were taken with a "projection-densitometer" that Maccabee built himself, rather than on precision commercial instruments available in the Navy facility where Maccabee is employed. Later Maccabee ran tests to correlate measurements from his "home-made" instrument with Navy densitometers, and found that despite some discrepancies there was moderately good agreement.

But Maccabee's conclusion that the bright illumination from a single squidboat is insufficient to account for the overexposed V-UFO images he measured is based on his assumption that the film manufacturer's data, intended to help photographers obtain properly exposed images can be used to accurately estimate the intensity of a light source that produced much overexposed imagery. On several occasions I have urged Maccabee to check this critical issue with qualified scientists at Eastman Kodak. But, as of this writing, he had not yet done so.

If the bright object photographed in Pegasus Bay was not a squidboat, the only plausible alternative is that it was an extraterrestrial craft from a distant world. But in considering this alternative one ought to ask why it would radiate such intense illumination—the equivalent of several squidboats if Maccabee's basic assumptions are correct. One possible explanation is that the surface of the craft must operate at "white-hot" temperatures of several thousand degrees because of heat given off by its propulsion system. But this would rule out any possibility that such a craft could carry a crew unless the "UFOnauts" were constructed entirely from high-temperature metals or ceramics.

An alternative explanation is that the intense illumination is purely decorative—perhaps intended to attract the attention of earthlings and make them aware of strange craft in our skies. But this could be done without equipping the craft with millions of watts of an extraterrestrial equivalent of lightbulbs and wasting large amounts of energy simply to attract attention, as advertising aircraft do.

A third possible explanation is that squid are as great a culinary delicacy for some distant civilization as they are for some on earth and that an extraterrestrial craft had traversed interstellar distances to fish for squid in the waters off New Zealand. If so, the craft would come equipped with intense illumination to attract the squid from the ocean depths. And if the V-UFO were an extraterrestrial craft fishing for squid in Pegasus Bay, this would explain why the brightly illuminated object did not perform any bizarre maneuvers during the many minutes it was under observation and being photographed lest it interrupt fishing operations. The only characteristic that could distinguish a Japanese squidboat from an extraterrestrial craft also fishing for squid would be the intensity of illumination—*if* Maccabee's assumptions, measurements, and calculations are correct.

Maccabee admits that *some* of the flashing and flickering lights observed from the Argosy and *some* of the blips that suddenly appeared on the Wellington radar and then quickly disappeared *may* have prosaic explanations. In other words, that some of the V-UFOs and R-UFOs may have been what Allan Hendry has called "UFO imposters." But Maccabee repeatedly has refused to indicate which he believes to be "genuine-UFOs" and which he suspects may be UFO-imposters.

My investigation indicates that *all* of the V-UFOs and R-UFOs reported can have prosaic explanations. But if Maccabee's assumptions, measurements, and interpretations of the data are correct, it would indicate that the bright object in Pegasus Bay was an extraterrestrial craft, probably fishing for squid. This raises the question of why Safe Air flight crews, who fly over Pegasus Bay every night, had not previously reported seeing such brightly illuminated objects. One possible explanation is that the night of December 31, 1978, was the first extraterrestrial squid-fishing expedition off New Zealand and just happened to coincide with the flight of a TV crew out on a "UFO hunt." Another possible explanation, of course, is that Safe Air crews may often have seen UFOs engaged in squid fishing, but previously mistook them for a Japanese squidboat, which they so closely resemble.

28

The Public Brainwashed

In 1976, Mensa International, whose members have an IQ of more than 130, which puts them in the upper 2 percent of the population in IQ scores, polled its members on UFOs. One question was: "Do you think UFOs are spaceships from other planets?" Of those responding, 64 percent answered in the affirmative.

Industrial Research/Development magazine polled its readers on the UFO issue in 1979 and received 1200 replies. In response to the question, "Do you believe UFOs exist?" a total of 61 percent of the respondents checked "definitely" or "probably." And 44 percent of the respondents indicated they believe that UFOs originate from "outer space." Analysis of respondents who held Ph.D.s showed that 46 percent believe UFOs definitely or probably exist. The figure for respondents without a college degree was 87 percent.

On this basis it is not surprising that a survey of American adults conducted in 1978 by the American Institute of Public Opinion (Gallup Poll) showed that 57 percent of those surveyed believe that UFOs are "real," as contrasted with "imaginary." Although the phrasing of the Gallup Poll question is ambiguous and misleading,* the most recent survey results, when compared with earlier ones that used the same question, show that an increasing number of American adults "believe in UFOs." And a 1978 Gallup Poll of teenagers shows an even higher figure of 61 percent.

---

*The Gallup Poll question is poorly phrased, because most UFO reports are generated by "real" objects, such as a bright celestial body, a fireball, an advertising airplane or a hot-air balloon. On June 3, 1978, I wrote to Dr. George Gallup to point out this ambiguity and to suggest that future surveys might better phrase the question: "Do you believe UFO reports can be explained in prosaic terms or that they are generated by extraterrestrial spacecraft?" I never received a reply.

Dr. J. Allen Hynek offered the following commentary on this growing public acceptance of UFOs in an editorial published in August of 1979 in *International UFO Reporter,* portions of which are quoted below:

> Suppose you were given the job of selling an idea— not a product—but an idea, an idea quite foreign to popular thinking, and one which runs against common sense, against scientific and military opinion, and against the learned opinions of the intelligentsia . . . Quite a job, you'll agree. You might start by engaging a highly expensive Madison Avenue advertising firm, and obtain prime time TV and radio time in stations all over the country. This would be accompanied by a barrage of newspaper advertising, perhaps full page ads in major newspapers, and you might hire fluent speakers to tour the country, much as in a political campaign.
>
> To attain the actual acceptance of this idea by more than 100 million people, the majority of our population, would be, you'll agree, a major accomplishment, and a very expensive one! Yet this has been accomplished without the spending of one cent, and against a barrage of ridicule, of active opposition from science, the military, *and the press!* Of course it took some thirty years to do it.
>
> The Gallup Poll earlier this year indicated that 57% of the American population feels that UFOs are "for real." Yet thirty years ago, when the "campaign" started, the whole idea was foreign to our thinking, and would have been regarded as preposterous . . . .
>
> Well done, whoever or whatever put on this campaign. Madison Avenue would be proud, and envious of you. To convince 57% of the U.S. population (and probably a high percentage of the world's population) to accept an originally preposterous idea, and against the opposition of many vested interests—well, quite a job!

Obviously Hynek is delighted, as are others eager to promote belief in UFOs. I am very much concerned, because the future of this republic depends upon a well-informed citizenry, which in turn depends on a well-informed and responsible news media.

Consider the one-hour NBC-TV News documentary on UFOs, televised in prime time on December 15, 1974, entitled "UFOs: Do You Believe?" Because of the controversial nature of the subject, one would expect NBC to provide roughly equal time to UFO proponents and to UFO skeptics, but it did not. At the time the program was being taped in mid-1974, Dr. Donald Menzel and I were the two leading experienced UFO skeptics. Menzel was not even invited to participate, and most of the several hours of NBC's taped interview with me ended up on the cutting-room floor. I made three brief appearances totalling less than one minute during the hour-long program.

NBC devoted nearly three minutes to the Coyne/Mansfield helicopter incident (Chapters 16-17), but could find no time to report the results of my investigation, leaving viewers to conclude that there was no possible prosaic explanation for the incident. NBC provided more than ten minutes for Charles Hickson and Calvin Parker to recount their tale of being abducted by a UFO while fishing in Pascagoula, Mississippi. I was given only twenty seconds to characterize the incident as a hoax, but no time to explain the many reasons for my appraisal, which I had detailed at considerable length for NBC.

NBC included many segments showing persons describing their UFO sightings, typically lights in the night sky, but the network did not inform viewers that even UFO-proponents admit that at least 90 percent of such reports have prosaic explanations. Although there were numerous cases that NBC could have included to show that such eyewitness reports are unreliable, it did not do so. Viewers could only conclude that there are many UFO incidents that simply cannot be explained, except as extraterrestrial visitors.

Nearly a year later, on October 20, 1975, NBC-TV offered another prime-time documentary drama "The UFO Incident," a two-hour Hollywood film recounting the story of a New Hampshire woman, Betty Hill, and her late husband, Barney, who say they believe that Betty's dreams of having been taken aboard a flying saucer in 1961 are based on the actual occurrence of such an incident. In the film, the actor playing the late Dr. Ben Simon, a Boston psychiatrist who treated Betty and her husband, expressed uncertainty over whether the alleged UFO abduction had actually occurred. The real Dr. Simon had no such doubts when we first talked in the fall of 1966, shortly after the incident achieved international fame. Dr. Simon told me he was certain the abduction was a dream-fantasy, and he documented the reasons for his conclusion, citing specifics as he played the tape recordings of the Hills recounting their story while under regressive hypnosis.

Dr. Simon was a guest on NBC-TV's popular "Today Show," along with Betty Hill, on the morning of October 20 as the network sought to promote its upcoming UFO spectacular to be telecast that night. When Dr. Simon was asked whether he believed that the Hills "actually went aboard a spacecraft," the experienced psychiatrist who had treated the couple replied: "It was a dream. The abduction did not happen." Several nights later, the Hill incident was the subject of another popular NBC-TV talk show, "The Tomorrow Show," hosted by Tom Snyder. Betty Hill was invited to recount her alleged abduction again, but Dr. Simon had been replaced by Stanton Friedman, who then earned his living as a pro-UFO lecturer and who strongly endorsed the alleged UFO abduction. On September 9, 1976, NBC again televised "The UFO Incident" in prime-time. Undoubtedly it will be repeated again.

In the late spring of 1975, many independent television stations throughout the United States televised a one hour documentary entitled:

"UFOs: Past, Present and Future." When the program was telecast in the Washington, D.C., area, on May 12, 1975, the television critic for the *Washington Post* endorsed the program, saying its producer, Allan F. Sandler, "succeeded in selecting enough scientists and credible-appearing eyewitnesses to give the non-credulous . . . the opportunity for suspended judgement." But in fact the documentary did not include a single UFO skeptic. More than a year earlier, when I heard that Sandler planned to make the film and had hired Hynek as a consultant, I wrote to him on April 18, 1974, offering my own services as a consultant *without charge.* I noted that my soon-to-be-published book, *UFOs Explained,* would offer prosaic explanations for a number of famous cases. Sandler replied promptly, turning down my offer on the grounds that "the film is at such a stage as not to allow any new segments to be added." In reality, Sandler had not even begun to shoot the film at that stage.

The ABC network's popular "Good Morning America" and "Good Night America" talk shows have carried a number of interviews with UFO claimants, including Travis Walton and deputy sheriff Val Johnson. As noted earlier (Chapter 23), ABC-TV allowed Hynek to veto my appearance with Walton despite my many months of investigative effort on the case. And ABC made no effort to obtain a UFO skeptic to counterbalance Allan Hendry for its interview with Johnson. CBS, alone among the major networks, has shown restraint and even-handedness in its treatment of the UFO issue.

NBC-TV News concluded its documentary "UFOs: Do You Believe?" as follows:

> The problem with UFOs is that no one knows *how to collect hard data.* [It would be more accurate to say that despite thirty years of effort, UFO proponents have been unable to come up with hard data.] The people are the evidence—what people say they have seen. When all is said and done, that's all we have to go on. Because that is the case, no one can say for certain whether we do or do not have visitors from beyond earth. All we can say is that we have a very real and persistent phenomenon, sustained by an idea as old as humanity—the belief that we are not alone. And that's an idea so emotionally appealing that UFOs are not likely to go away, regardless of what we or anyone else says about such things as proof, or evidence, or the scientific method. What it comes down to after all is a question of belief, and we must decide that for ourselves.

So long as a major network's "news" department offers its viewers such a one-sided pseudo-documentary on UFOs, we can be certain "that UFOs are not likely to go away." That the idea is "emotionally appealing" is certainly true. Left unsaid is that UFOs are financially appealing, especially to the radio-TV media. For example, the November 24, 1975, issue of *Broad-*

casting magazine carried the following large display advertisement:

DO UFOs REALLY EXIST?

UFO REPORT

DID YOU KNOW . . . there is good reason to believe that Airforce [sic] officials have a captive flying saucer?

. . . thousands of flying saucer sightings are never reported?

. . . many UFO investigations are purposely hidden from the public?

UFO REPORT explores this, and more, in a daily 5-minute radio feature!! All UFO REPORT programs are based on facts from the files of APRO [Aerial Phenomena Research Organization], an international society of scientists devoted to the study of UFOs, with representatives in 47 countries. Strange things are happening in our skies, and UFO REPORT is the first radio feature to raise these questions and deliver the facts from the APRO files.

*After just 2 weeks, 73 radio stations all say the same thing: UFO REPORT is the best audience grabber available!! And, an entire week of UFO REPORT pays for itself in just *one day* of commercial sales!

Creative Radio Shows/ 9121 Sunset Blvd. / Los Angeles, Ca. 90069 CALL COLLECT: (213) 276-5022

Radio and television networks, as well as individual stations, are caught in an intense competition for listeners and viewers. Their success determines the advertising rates they can charge and, in the final analysis, their profits. If a grossly one-sided program on UFOs attracts listeners or viewers, who cares if this serves to brainwash the public into accepting a myth as fact?

I care, very much, and the reader should also. From a purely selfish viewpoint, anything that promotes public interest in UFOs and keeps the myth alive assures continuing sales of my books on this subject. This modestly enhances my financial well-being. One might argue: what harm does it do for the public to have a modern-day, adult substitute for Santa Claus?

The answer is that when a national network documentary is so lopsided in its treatment of this controversial issue, how can the public be sure that documentaries on other controversial issues, such as nuclear energy, or a current Mideast crisis, are not also similarly biased while giving the illusion of being even-handed? The record shows that at least where UFOs are concerned, brainwashing can occur even in a free society.

In recent years, the print media generally have demonstrated a commendable skepticism with respect to UFOs, except for the sensationalist tabloids. Yet periodically even such respected newspapers as the *New York Times* and the *Washington Post* reveal a schizophrenic editorial judgment that is difficult to fathom.

For example, the decision of the *New York Times* to publish a long article on January 14, 1979, claiming that the CIA "is secretly involved in the surveillance of unidentified flying objects" and that "the U.S. Government has been totally untruthful [about UFOs] and the cover-up is massive," would seem to indicate that top officials of the newspaper placed sufficient credence in the charges made by William Spaulding, of Ground Saucer Watch to warrant publication in the *Times*. On this basis one might expect that these officials would assign some of their best investigative reporters to look into the charges, or at least to study the CIA's readily available UFO papers, which formed the basis of Spaulding's charges. Yet so far as is known, the *Times* never did so.

Recalling that the initiative displayed by officials of the *Washington Post* following the breakin at the Watergate served to expose a major scandal and resulted in the resignation of President Richard M. Nixon, one is curious at the apparent lack of interest in pursuing the question of mysterious craft alleged to be overflying vital USAF airbases and missile sites featured on the front page on January 19, 1979.

If senior officials at the *Post* really believed that unknown craft were penetrating American airspace and overflying strategic military installation, regardless of whether the craft were Russian, Cuban, or extraterrestrial, it would seem to be a major story that demanded an all-out investigative effort. Especially since the *Post* article suggested that the USAF and Defense Department either were guilty of a coverup or were ignoring a potential foreign threat to national security. But, so far as the record shows, the *Post* never bothered to pursue the matter further.

In response to an article in The *Skeptical Inquirer** by the editor, Kendrick Frazier, which criticized some news media for their credulous handling of paranormal claims, Doug Clark, editor of the *Coeur d'Alene* (Idaho) *Press,* wrote to acknowledge the validity of the criticism. "Stories on the weird and supernatural, too often, are dealt with for their readership and sensational values," Clark said. "As long as we attribute the wild claims . . . we feel an expiation for any resulting myths, half-truths and outright lies." But Clark said his own newspaper treats such subjects with "a healthy skepticism" in the best journalistic tradition, and he enclosed several examples.

On January 4, 1979, the *Coeur d'Alene Press* reported UFO sightings by several law-enforcement officers, who saw a bright object hovering to the south in the early morning hours. But it did not stop there. The newspaper showed good journalistic enterprise by consulting with a professor of astronomy and also published his comment that a very bright Venus was

*Published by the Committee for the Scientific Investigation of Claims of the Paranormal, Box 229, Central Park Station, Buffalo, N.Y. 14215

visible to the southeast at the time of the UFO sighting. Another example was a feature story in the October 4, 1979, edition, describing a law-enforcement officer's "close-encounter" with a "weird"-looking UFO. The next day the newspaper reported that the UFO was a re-entering Soviet satellite. More important, the explanation was given as much prominence as the original report instead of "burying" it and leaving many of the original readers to conclude that the incident was still unexplained—a more common practice.

29

Abductions, Hypnosis, and Credulity

A remarkable change occurred in the UFO movement during the 1970s that has gone almost unrecognized by those in the movement and which will influence its future. Its leaders became incredibly credulous, willing to accept bizarre tales that in previous years would have been rejected as fantasy. During the 1950s, both NICAP and APRO, the two leading UFO groups, rejected the stories of persons like George Adamski, who claimed to have flown aboard a flying saucer and to have talked with its occupants. During these years, "serious UFOlogists" (as they like to call themselves) viewed such "contactee" reports as an embarassment that could only bring ridicule from the public and the world of science. By the late 1970s, leaders of the UFO movement were endorsing a latter-day variant of "contactee" stories in the form of tales of alleged "UFO abductions."

During the first two decades, there was a general reluctance even to accept as fact reports by persons who claimed to have seen strange-looking creatures near a UFO, referred to as "occupant cases." For example, in 1964 when NICAP published a lengthy report titled *The UFO Evidence,* citing hundreds of UFO sightings, not one of them was of the "occupant" or "contactee" variety. And NICAP cautiously limited its claim to stating that the cases provided "support of the hypothesis that UFOs are under intelligent control, making plausible the notion that some of them might be of extraterrestrial origin."

NICAP later gave a qualified endorsement to a "UFO landing" incident that occurred in early 1964 near Socorro, New Mexico, where a lone policeman claimed to have seen an egg-shaped craft sitting on the ground and what he described as two figures in coveralls who seemed to be working on the craft. The case seemed impressive at the time because of its so-called "physical effects"—depressions in the sand and a slightly burned bush, effects that could easily have been produced by a hoaxer, as my own investigation later indicated. (See *UFOs Explained,* Chapter 12.)

In late 1966, the British UFO magazine *Flying Saucer Review* startled many in the UFO movement by publishing an issue devoted entirely to "occupant" cases, most of which came from France. The issue was entitled "The Humanoids." One of the articles, authored by Mrs. James L. (Coral) Lorenzen, co-founder of APRO, began:

> When I first considered a research article dealing with UFO "entities" in the United States, I anticipated documenting approximately 15 to 20 cases, because landing and occupant cases *prior* to 1964 seemed to have been confined largely to other countries. I was somewhat surprised, therefore, to find that, excluding contactee cases (George Adamski's Venusians, etc.) there were 29 on record. Unfortunately, some of these and others are cases which stretch the credibility [sic] of even the most seasoned UFO researcher.

Within a decade, the UFO movement would drop its standards of credulity and "occupant" cases would become quite commonplace. Mrs. Lorenzen would be in the vanguard of this change, as suggested by her article:

> A certain segment of UFO researchers (which happen to be in the majority in my country, unfortunately) resisted the idea of humanoid UFO objects until the famous Socorro case of 1964 . . . . Therefore, those of us who are deeply interested in *every phase* of the UFO mystery, have been greatly hampered by our own colleagues.

Within two years the Lorenzens would publish a book titled *The Flying Saucer Occupants*.

There is an element of logic to Mrs. Lorenzen's position. If one believes that extraterrestrial craft are visiting earth for scientific exploration, it would be likely that some would carry living creatures to perform functions that could not be conducted by robotic devices. Thus one ought not reject the possibility that some craft might land and that their crew would go outside to perform such functions, perhaps even to stretch their legs. But there was very good reason for skepticism about such occupant tales on other grounds—for example, variation in the reported appearance of the UFOnauts.

For example, in one case from West Virginia cited by Mrs. Lorenzen, the occupant was said to have been a giant, ten to fifteen feet tall, with a blood-red face and "glowing greenish-orange eyes." Another account from California described the UFOnauts as being "the size of a midget." Still another from Kansas claimed the small creature had "a very long nose and very long ears, and when he moved he seemed to fly." Still another report from Kentucky said the creature was *illuminated internally,* had huge elephantine ears and a slitlike mouth that extended from ear to ear. (During the 1970s, as such "occupant" reports gained credence in the UFO movement and were included in new books on the subject, the subsequent descriptions of the UFOnauts began to take on greater uniformity.)

In the early fall of 1966, *Look* magazine published a blockbuster that would forever change the UFO movement's acceptable level of credulity: a two-part series describing an alleged UFO-abduction of Betty Hill and her husband, Barney. The articles by John G. Fuller, a prelude to his book on the incident, generated the highest newsstand sales in the magazine's history. Publication in so prestigious a magazine gave the incident an aura of authenticity and would make it world famous. But in fact the incident had been investigated by NICAP representatives nearly five years earlier and its officials had serious doubts about the alleged abduction. This explains why the Betty and Barney Hill incident was not even mentioned in NICAP's *The UFO Evidence.* *

Even after the widespread public interest generated by the *Look* articles and by Fuller's book, NICAP and APRO showed considerable reluctance to endorse publicly the idea that UFOs, after nearly two decades of benign visits, suddenly had decided to start abducting earthlings for brief, superficial examinations. On July 29, 1968, Congressman J. Edward Roush held a one-day UFO Symposium, at which he invited six scientists to testify, five of them strongly pro-UFO. Although these scientists cited many dozens of UFO incidents to support their views, the Hill case was not even mentioned.

In 1972, when Dr. J. Allen Hynek published his first book on the subject (*The UFO Experience: A Scientific Inquiry,* Chicago: Henry Regnery Company, 1972), he discussed the Hill case very cautiously. He noted that the recollection of the Hills that they seemed to be followed by a nocturnal light as they drove through the White Mountains of New Hampshire "fits the pattern." But Hynek said that the alleged abduction was "atypical," and added: "The atypical portion is not amenable to study except as an atypical event. When and if other cases of hypnotic revelation of close encounters become available for study . . . we will be able to note whether they also form a pattern." Within the next few years, many, many dozens of persons would claim that they too had been abducted and given a brief physical examination, and leading UFOlogists would throw caution to the wind and accept many of these tales after only superficial investigation.

Even Donald Keyhoe, NICAP's director and the person who had dictated its policy against accepting "contactee" and most "occupant" reports, felt obliged to include a chapter on "The UFO Beings" in his book *Aliens from Space* (New York: Doubleday, 1973). Keyhoe discussed the Hill case at some length, but indicated he agreed with the Hill's psychiatrist, Dr. Ben Simon, that the "supposed abduction was a psychological reaction" to their encounter with a nocturnal light. Yet Keyhoe concluded: "Beings from a more advanced world are here now. It is impossible to hide from them." Events that followed seemed to confirm his prophecy.

---

*It was not until eight years later, in April 1972, that NICAP published the highlights of the Hills' alleged abduction in its monthly publication, *UFO Investigator.*

A few months after Keyhoe's book was published, on the night of October 11, 1973, two shipyard workers reported that while fishing near downtown Pascagoula, Mississippi, they too had been abducted by two strange-looking creatures with clawlike hands—*vastly different* from the creatures Betty Hill had described. The men claimed they had been "levitated" aboard a flying saucer, where they too were given a superficial physical examination. The case was given extensive coverage by the networks, including interviews with the principals.

Hynek promptly flew to Pascagoula to investigate the case, as did Dr. James A. Harder, APRO's director of research. Following their brief investigation, they held a press conference at which Harder announced: "There was definitely something here that was not terrestrial. . . . Where they come from and why they were here is a matter of conjecture, but the fact that they are here is true, beyond a reasonable doubt." Hynek was a bit more cautious, saying: "There is no question in my mind that these two men have had a very terrifying experience." And within several weeks, when Hynek appeared on an NBC program, he said, "I do not think the men were perpetrating a hoax." (My own investigation indicated the incident was a hoax, for reasons explained in Chapter 27 of *UFOs Explained*.)

Hynek's views on UFO abductions were undergoing a metamorphosis, as he later explained in an interview published in the August 1976 *UFO Report* magazine. Hynek said:

> The close encounter of the third kind—type six—involves humanoid occupants. Currently we have an estimated 800 sightings of this sort on file [recall that a decade earlier Mrs. Lorenzen reported only twenty-nine such incidents in the U.S., and many of these even she found of questionable veracity] . . . . When I first heard of such episodes, my own natural prejudices told me to throw them out . . . . I've since come to believe that no scientist should discard data simply because he doesn't like it.

Hynek was asked if there was a particular case which had changed his views and he replied:

> I had been building toward a positive attitude for a number of years when John Fuller . . . told me the fascinating story of Betty and Barney Hill. . . . My thinking was altered completely when I was called in, along with Dr. James Harder of the University of California, to interrogate two Mississippi fishermen . . . who insist they were literally "kidnapped" and forced to go aboard a spacecraft, where they were subjected—just as in the case of the Hills—to a physical examination. The tale told by these two rugged shipyard workers held up under grueling cross-examination.

In another interview published the same month, in *People* magazine (August 16, 1976), Hynek was asked, "How seriously do you take reports of

UFO occupants?" Hynek replied, "I take them fairly seriously."* When asked what sort of UFOnauts were being reported, Hynek replied:

> I'd guess you'd say that the average occupant — if you can even think of an average in this area — is three-and-a-half to four feet tall, with a big head, large eyes and a spindly body. But other kinds have also been reported, *everything from huge monsters on the one hand to figures resembling normal humans on the other.* Most reported occupants, however, are small humanoid types; *like slightly overgrown elves and goblins, as a matter of fact.* [Emphasis added.]

In view of Hynek's growing inclination to accept reports of persons who claimed to have been taken aboard craftlike objects, it is curious to find him telling the interviewer in *UFO Report* magazine that "In recent times I have come to support less and less the idea that UFOs are 'nuts-and-bolts' spacecraft from other worlds. There are just too many things going against this theory." Yet in the interview published the same month in *People* Hynek said, "There is so much nuts-and-bolts evidence. How do you explain things you can see on radar? How do you explain imprints on the ground? How do you explain something that comes along and tears off the tops of trees? . . . How do you explain bullets ricocheting off whatever was in the sky?

On October 20, 1975, NBC telecast in prime time a two-hour film recounting the Betty and Barney Hill claim. Barely two weeks later, Travis Walton would "disappear" and return five days later to claim that he too had been abducted by a UFO. Shortly after seeing the NBC show, a North Dakota woman named Sandy Larson contacted a local UFOlogist to claim she, her young daughter, and her boyfriend also had been abducted by a UFO, allegedly two months earlier. Mrs. Larson told her story under hypnosis administered by Dr. R. Leo Sprinkle, a University of Wyoming psychologist and senior APRO consultant; he is the nation's leading advocate of using hypnosis to investigate "abduction" incidents. Under hypnosis, Mrs. Larson claimed that she and her two companions were "stripped naked and all parts of our bodies examined . . . even our heads were opened and all parts of our brains looked at . . . we were dissected like frogs." Yet several hours later, all three of the "victims" returned home, none the worse for their experience and without any physical scars to substantiate her story.

Several months later, two young men from Maine also came forward to claim they too had been abducted several months earlier — just one week after the NBC show. Shortly before the program, a USAF Staff Sergeant named Charles L. Moody had contacted APRO to report he had been

---

*The June 15, 1975, issue of a publication by Hynek's own Center for UFO Studies offered its readers the opportunity to purchase from CUFOS a report entitled: *1973 — Year of the Humanoids,* by David Webb. CUFOS characterized this report as "an excellent publication."

abducted by a UFO on August 13, 1975, but insisted on anonymity. After the show, Moody was willing to have his identity made public. According to Moody's tale, one of the UFOnauts spoke "in perfect English, with an American accent," but without moving his lips. Moody said the UFOnaut informed him "that within three years his people will make themselves known to mankind. It may even happen as early as this summer." (That was seven years ago!)

In early 1976 three Kentucky women reported that they had been abducted several weeks earlier. And the following year a Kentucky teenager reported his abduction, describing UFOnauts that resembled boxlike machines rather than humanoids. If the UFO movement's leaders had doubts about these cases, they did not express them publicly.

One of the most bizarre of the many UFO abductions reported in the months following the NBC telecast came from a Massachusetts woman named Mrs. Betty Andreasson, who claimed the incident had occurred *a decade earlier,* on January 25, 1967. As Mrs. Andreasson recalled the incident under hypnosis, strange-looking creatures, with one black eye and one white eye and insectlike antennae, brazenly entered her home and took her aboard a flying saucer. Mrs. Andreasson recalled seeing ugly creatures that reminded her of monkeys, and a giant eaglelike bird that stood fifteen feet tall. One of the UFOnauts, she said, had inserted thin wires into her nose (reminding her of surgery she had earlier undergone) and withdrew small metal pellets from her nose.

The case was investigated by MUFON's director of investigations, Raymond E. Fowler, who was so impressed that he later wrote a book, entitled: *The Andreasson Affair.* (Prentice-Hall, 1979). The introduction to the book, written by Hynek, read:

> In the past, I frankly would not have touched an invitation to write the foreword for a book treating "contactees," abduction, mental telepathy, mystical contact and examination by "aliens." But across the years I have learned to broaden my view of the entire UFO phenomenon. Those who still hold that the entire subject of UFOs is nonsense will be sorely challenged if they have the courage to take an honest look at the present book.

Could this be the same Dr. Hynek who, in his first book, written only a few years earlier, had sought to disassociate himself from such tales by stressing a distinction between

> . . . cases involving reports of the presence of presumably intelligent beings in the "spacecraft" and the so-called contactee cases . . . . I must emphasize that contactee reports are *not* classed as Close Encounters of the Third Kind. It is unfortunate, to say the least, that reports such as these have brought down upon the entire UFO problem the approbrium and ridicule of scientists and public alike, keeping alive the popular image of "little green men" and the fictional atmosphere surrounding that aspect of the subject.

What a remarkable change had occurred in Hynek's views in less than a decade.

On October 17, 1975, several hundred UFOlogists convened in Fort Smith, Arkansas, for a national conference—the only one to which a lone skeptic (this author) was invited to speak.* APRO's Coral Lorenzen announced that in the future APRO would focus its efforts on "landing and occupant cases," leaving APRO's competitors to investigate the less exotic type of reports. Several weeks later APRO was blessed with the most exciting "abduction" case of all time, involving Travis Walton. Not only would APRO try to keep secret the fact that Walton had flunked his first lie-detector test, but later Mr. Lorenzen would try to pressure me into having another test conducted by a man with whom it had held secret discussions (See Chapters 18-23).

Even Richard Hall, who as NICAP's assistant director in the late 1950s and early 1960s had been reluctant to accept "occupant" and "contactee" cases, also began to show symptoms of hypercredulity in the late 1970s, when he became editor of the *MUFON UFO Journal,* one of the most widely read UFO publications in the United States. In an editorial published in February 1978, Hall wrote:

> Humanoid and abduction reports (or Close Encounters of the Third and Fourth Kind, as they are being called) currently dominate UFO research —whether rightly or wrongly. There is no question but that these reports are central to an understanding of UFO phenomena. Either hundreds of people worldwide are suffering from very similar hallucinations or delusions, in which case the origin of such widespread pathology needs to be studied urgently, or something extraordinary and with sweeping implications for mankind is occuring. A major policy of the *Journal* will be to seek articles that help sort out fact from fiction in these important areas. However, we advise caution in interpreting the bewildering array of sensational reports now coming to light. As a general principle, the more sensational the contents of a UFO report is, the closer critical scrutiny it should receive . . ."

This was very sage advice, but it would be largely ignored by Hall in selecting articles to be published in the *MUFON Journal.*

For example, in November 1981, there was a report by John F. Schuessler, an aerospace-industry engineer and a deputy director of MUFON, on an incident that allegedly occurred on December 29, 1980, in the vicinity of the Houston, Texas, airport. The incident involved two middle-age women, Betty Cash and Vickie Landrum, and the latter's young

---

*This reluctance to invite a single UFO skeptic to speak at such conferences suggests a fear that even one skeptic, although heavily outnumbered by pro-UFOlogists, might somehow raise doubts in the minds of those in the audience.

grandson Colby. It is claimed that the three experienced radiation after-effects, such as loss of hair and a persistent sore, after having viewed a flaming, diamond-shaped UFO. Hall introduced the MUFON article in the following words:

> The update report by John Schuessler on the Cash-Landrum radiation case shows it to be one of the most significant reports in modern UFO history. The possible explanations are only two: either it was some military test device, tested along a highway near a large urban area with reckless disregard for human safety, or it was a strange airborne phenomenon with many of the same features attributed to UFOs over the years. It seems very doubtful that any such highly radioactive device would be tested where this object was seen. Yet that would appear to be the only alternative to a luminous, maneuverable, flame-spewing, noise-making radioactive . . . UFO.

Apparently, the possibility that this case might be a hoax did not occur to Hall, or it seemed too outlandish to even mention. He admits that it is most unlikely that the Defense Department would test some new radiation weapon in a populated area when it has a large desert site in Nevada always used in the past. The only alternative Hall can imagine is that after three decades of benign visits, extraterrestrials suddenly have begun to use radiation weapons against innocent earthlings. Many persons have reported watching a UFO at distances much closer than Cash and Landrum, and many dozens claim to have been aboard a UFO, yet none have reported such symptoms and after-effects.

Earlier Hall had called for "critical scrutiny" of sensational UFO reports. The distinguishing feature of the Cash-Landrum case was the alleged physical after-effects, which should prompt a UFO investigator to begin by talking to the family physicians of the principals to determine *if they had shown any of the symptoms,* like a persistent sore and falling hair *prior to the alleged incident.* (Some of the reported after-effects, such as diarrhea and increased tooth cavities for young Colby also could have prosaic explanations.) Although Schuessler has written several articles on the case over a two-year period, he has never included any details on the health of the two women *prior* to the alleged incident.

The UFO movement experienced a phenomenal growth in "UFO abduction" cases in the late 1970s. For example, according to an article by David Webb, MUFON's eastern regional director, published in the February 1978 issue of the *MUFON UFO Journal,* "Two years ago, in 1976, I presented a paper on abduction cases at the CUFOS Conference in Chicago. At that time I was able to find references to only 50 Type-G [abduction] reports; *the number has grown by a factor of three in only two years!"* [Emphasis added.]

At last count, more than 200 people claim to have been abducted by UFOs. Until recently, a night watchman in Italy held the record with his claim of four "abductions." Now that claim has been tied by a thirty-one-year-old nurse, Barbara Schutte, of Des Moines, Iowa, who is a field investigator for both CUFOS and MUFON. Schutte says she first became aware that she might be an "abductee" in the fall of 1981 while attending a CUFOS conference, during discussions with APRO's Harder. Later under hypnosis by Sprinkle, she "discovered" that she had been "abducted" four times for sure, and perhaps as many as eight times. The first such incident allegedly occurred in 1959, when Schutte was only eight, which would predate the Betty and Barney Hill "abduction." (One can only speculate as to how rigorously Schutte seeks prosaic explanations for UFO cases that she personally investigates.)

One possible explanation for the mushrooming number of "UFO abduction" cases in recent years is that the UFOnauts are growing bolder. Despite having examined dozens of earthlings, the UFOnauts seem to have developed an insatiable curiosity for more. It never has occurred to them to carry a few human specimens back to their native planet for more rigorous study, possibly including dissection. The alternative explanation is that people have discovered how easy it is to fool famous UFOlogists with tall tales and to become instant international celebrities via the pages of sensationalist tabloid newpapers.

One of the most puzzling aspects is that *not a single claimant has reported his or her abduction to the Federal Bureau of Investigation,* which is responsible for investigating kidnappings in the United States. *Nor have any UFOlogists reported an alleged "UFO abduction" to the FBI.* Such a report would, of course, trigger an FBI investigation and *the penalty for reporting a spurious abduction to the FBI is a $10,000 fine, five years imprisonment, or both.*

What rationale can UFOlogists offer for accepting bizarre tales of "abduction" that they, or their predecessors, would have rejected as fantasy during the first two decades of the UFO era? Not one of the roughly two hundred "abductees" has returned with a single physical artifact that could instantly confirm his or her story. Not one "abductee' has returned with new scientific knowledge, say, for example, the existence of a distant, as yet undiscovered planet in our solar system. The only thing that has changed is the credulity level of UFOlogists and the fact that many of the stories are recalled or recounted while the subject is said to be under hypnosis.

For at least some UFOlogists, and for a significant segment of the public, hypnosis is viewed as a "magic road to the truth." If that were true, the nation's polygraph examiners would long ago have taken up new professions, and lengthy criminal trials and litigation could be resolved in less than a day by using hypnosis.

As earlier noted, APRO's Sprinkle is the leading proponent of using hypnosis to investigate claims of UFO abductions, and he is often quoted as an authority by sensationalist tabloids, whose headlines typically read:

"Hypnosis Confirms UFO Abduction." On January 23, 1977, I wrote to Sprinkle to ask:

> To your knowledge, has anyone conducted controlled experiments to evaluate the effectiveness of regressive hypnosis in determining whether a subject is intentionally trying to perpetrate a hoax or a falsehood . . . . [I added that if such experiments had not been conducted it seemed to me that they should] before UFO investigators invest any more time in its use as a means of trying to sort out reality from non-reality.

Sprinkle replied saying that he had first begun to experiment with the use of hypnosis on abduction claimants in the mid-1960s and that he "began to recognize that there was no way for me to 'know' whether the UFO witness did or did not experience an abduction." Then he made a remarkably candid admission: "Now I have persuaded (conned?) [sic] myself that . . . the apparent abduction experiences are 'real' . . . although I'm not in a position to determine the 'level of reality.'" (In response to my subsequent query, Sprinkle tried to explain that there are *many* "levels of reality," a concept that my simple mind was not able to grasp.)

In May 1977, the UFO movement's faith in the use of hypnosis to verify abduction tales were severely shaken by a long-time UFOlogist, Alvin H. Lawson, a professor of English at California State University, Long Beach. Lawson published a paper entitled "What Can We Learn from Hypnosis of Imaginary 'Abductees'?" With the aid of a physician with clinical experience in the use of hypnosis, Dr. William C. McCall, Lawson conducted experiments with persons who never claimed to have experienced a "UFO-abduction." The subjects were placed under hypnosis and told to *imagine* they had been abducted by a UFO, after which they were questioned about their *imaginary* experience. Lawson and McCall found that the subjects were easily able to improvise answers to questions about what had happened aboard the flying saucer. Lawson reported that their stories "showed no substantive differences" from tales recounted under hypnosis by persons who claimed they had been abducted by a UFO.

Lawson's findings were harshly attacked by APRO's Harder, who also uses hypnosis for "abduction" cases, in the September 1977 issue of the *APRO Bulletin*. When Lawson later presented a paper to the American Psychological Association, August 28, 1978, in Toronto, he stuck by his original conclusion that there were "no substantive differences" between the imaginary and "real" abductees, but he then added that "despite the many similarities, there are crucial differences—such as alleged physical effects and multiple witnesses—which argue that UFO abductions are separate and distinct from imaginary and hallucinatory experiences." Lawson warned that "one should be cautious about the results from hypnotic regression in UFO investigations. A witness can lie . . . witnesses [can] subtly confuse their own fantasies with reality — without either the witness or the hypnotist being aware"

Dr. Sprinkle also presented a paper at the same conference in Toronto. Its contents suggest that he preferred to ignore the results of the Lawson-McCall experiments. Sprinkle described his use of hypnosis to investigate the claims of twenty-five "abductees" and said the resulting data "support their claims of 'abduction' experiences." Sprinkle added: "I do not know if these 'abductees' have experienced physical abduction, or whether they have experienced 'out-of-body' events." (This refers to an *alleged* "psychic" phenomenon that enables a person to leave his or her body and view it from a distance.) Sprinkle considers these two exotic alternatives much more plausible than that the subjects are simply telling tall tales. He seems to believe that persons who like to spin tall tales to a credulous listener are too rare to deserve consideration.

Dr. Martin T. Orne, an internationally recognized authority on the clinical use of hypnosis, and past president of the International Society of Hypnosis, published a paper in the *International Journal of Clinical and Experimental Hypnosis,* in October 1979 that demolishes any idea that hypnosis can authenticate stories of alleged UFO abductions. The paper is entitled "The Use and Misuse of Hypnosis in Court." Orne emphasized that "it is possible for an individual to feign hypnosis and deceive even highly experienced hypnotists . . . . Further, it is possible for even deeply hypnotized subjects to willfully lie." Orne added: "We should keep in mind that psychologists and psychiatrists are not particularly adept at recognizing deception . . . the average hotel credit manager is considerably more adept at recognizing deception than we are."

Dr. Orne's paper focused on the potential for misuse of hypnosis in the courts, but some of his warnings are particularly appropriate for persons like Sprinkle and Harder, who are convinced that extraterrestrial craft are kidnapping earthlings. Orne warned: "If the hypnotist has beliefs about what actually occurred, it is exceedingly difficult for him to prevent himself from inadvertently guiding the subject's recall so that he [the subject] will eventually 'remember' what he, the hypnotist, believes actually happened." To minimize the risk of the hypnotist influencing the subject's replies, Orne recommended a number of procedural safeguards.

I sent a copy of Dr. Orne's paper to Sprinkle on March 24, 1980, seeking his reactions. When Sprinkle replied, he acknowledged that Orne was an internationally recognized expert in the field, and he acknowledged the validity of the proposed safeguards "for the forensic uses of hypnosis in court." *But Sprinkle argued that they were not appropriate for use in UFO cases* because there is "no crime, no criminal, no victim." I responded that it seemed to me that a person taken against his or her will onto a flying saucer and subjected to the indignity of a phsyical examination should be considered "a victim." But Sprinkle replied that such persons usually "do not seem to perceive themselves as 'kidnapped.' In fact, they see themselves as citizens of a 'higher civilization.'"

Finally, in reply to my question as to whether Sprinkle still believed that hypnosis was of value in determining whether or not a "UFO abduction" actually had occurred, he replied: "I believe that the use of hypnotic techniques is helpful to UFO abductees and contactees in exploring their memories of their experiences and that it is helpful to them in assisting them to come to terms with the abductions which have occurred—in this very reality!" (Sprinkle is director of student counseling and testing at the University of Wyoming.)

By the very early 1980s, the UFO movement was in the doldrums. There had been no major UFO flap for nearly a decade—the longest hiatus of the UFO era. With the possible exception of the New Zealand incident and the Texas "radiation" case, there was a dearth of cases impressive enough to attract the attention of the respectable news media. A decade earlier, the abduction claims of the two men from Pascagoula had prompted extensive network coverage. By the early 1980s, such claims had become so commonplace that few of them attracted coverage outside the sensationalist tabloids where the story usually was "buried" far back in the newspaper.

Each of the new "abduction" cases faintly resembled those that had been reported in the tabloids so often before. The creatures were said to be small, bald, with large heads and eyes who always performed superficial physical examinations. But each new story was embellished with a few new details to distinguish it and its claimant from many predecessors.

The UFO movement had become a victim of its own credulity—the inability of its leaders to discriminate between fact and bizarre fantasy, and their reluctance to publicly expose hoaxers—with rare exceptions. As a result, the movement was being inundated with "abduction" reports, each more bizarre than the other. Then, in the early 1980s, an even more fantastic story burst on the scene. A similar tale had surfaced thirty years earlier, but at that time it had been rejected by "serious UFOlogists" who then were much less gullible.

30

Crashed Saucers
and Credulous Dementia Syndrome

In the fall of 1950, barely three years after UFOs first burst on the American scene, the public was stunned by a book that claimed that the United States government had managed to recover three flying saucers that had crashed in New Mexico in 1948, and the bodies of thirty-four tiny occupants. The book, titled *Behind the Flying Saucers* (New York: Henry Holt & Co.) quickly became a best-seller and was discussed widely in newspaper and magazine articles. Its author was Frank Scully, then a well-known columnist for *Variety*—sometimes called the "Bible of show business." Scully said the information about the crashed saucers came from a "Dr. Gee"—a pseudonym for a man said to be a top scientist who allegedly had been one of many scientists brought in by the government to analyze the strange craft—and from a Colorado businessman named Silas M. Newton.

Two years later Scully's crashed-saucer tale was exposed as a hoax by an investigative journalist, J. P. Cahn. He revealed that "Dr. Gee" was a Mr. Leo GeBauer who operated a radio-parts supply store in Phoenix, that Newton had a reputation for questionable business practices, and that there was no basis in fact for their crashed-saucer tale. Within weeks after Cahn's exposure, GeBauer and Newton were arrested by FBI agents, charged with selling a device called a "Doodlebug," which they claimed could discover oil deposits. One victim had been swindled out of more than $230,000. Within a year the two men were convicted of operating a "confidence game," that is, fraud.

Ironically, Cahn's expose was published in *True* magazine, which had helped to launch the UFO era by publishing an article authored by Donald Keyhoe in its January 1950 issue, claiming that UFOs were extraterrestrial and that the U.S. government was trying to cover up that fact. In an editorial

279

that accompanied Cahn's expose of the crashed-saucer tale *True* (September 1952) noted that "this magazine first stated the premise that flying saucers were real . . . that they are in all probability extraterrestrial in origin . . . . This was the belief of the Editors of True in 1950 and it remains their belief today . . . True does not argue that proof of the extraterrestrial contention is presently available. We believe it will soon be available . . . . we are bitterly opposed to attempts to convince the public that it already exists."

Three decades later, when a similar crashed-saucer story was ressurected in a new book *The Roswell Incident* (Grossett and Dunlap, 1980), none of the leaders of the UFO movement spoke out to question it, as *True* had done many years earlier. And this despite the fact that at least one of the book's two authors, Charles Berlitz, had earlier demonstrated his proclivity for promoting fantasy as fact. (Berlitz first achieved fame for two books dealing with the so-called Bermuda Triangle where, he claimed, ships and aircraft disappear mysteriously without leaving a trace, perhaps being carried off by UFOs.) The co-author of the crashed-saucer book was William L. Moore, at the time the MUFON state section director in Arizona who later would be named APRO's director of special investigations in recognition of his efforts on the thirty-year-old crashed-saucer case. Moore and Berlitz had collaborated earlier on a book that claimed that during World War II, the U.S. Navy had successfully discovered and demonstrated a technique to make its ships invisible, but had decided against using it because it caused a ship's crew to suffer adverse after-effects.

The origin of the crashed-saucer tale was some debris found by W. W. Brazel on his ranch on June 14, 1947—ten days *before* Kenneth Arnold reported seeing nine saucer-shaped objects while flying near the Cascade Mountains. The debris later was identified as instrumentation from a crashed radar calibration balloon, but following Arnold's reported sighting, rumors spread that it was a UFO that had crashed on the ranch. However, in the July 9 1947, edition of the Carlsbad, New Mexico, newspaper, *Daily Current-Argus,* three weeks after the incident occurred, Brazel was quoted as saying he "was amazed at the fuss made over his discovery."

Were Brazel alive today he would be flabbergasted at the tale that has emerged more than thirty years later, and the credulity of those who accept it as fact. According to Berlitz and Moore, the incident occurred on July 2, 1947, more than two weeks after the correct date. The authors claim that a UFO was struck by lightning about seventy-five miles northwest of Roswell, New Mexico, scattering the debris later found on Brazel's ranch. Yet despite this seemingly severe damage, the authors claim that the UFO managed to fly for another 150 miles before crashing near Socorro, New Mexico, on the Plains of San Agustin.

According to Berlitz and Moore, military personnel were hastily brought in to cordon off the site near Socorro, and government scientists were brought in to examine the crashed saucer. Despite what the authors claim were all-out efforts to impose secrecy, word of the debris found by Brazel quickly reached the news media. News of the crashed saucer itself spread rapidly, according to the authors, even to a group of students on an archaeology expedition nearby. Others who learned of the alleged secret included railroad personnel who helped load the craft onto a car for shipment to Edwards Air Force Base, in California, and military personnel there who unloaded the craft. Within a short time, according to Berlitz and Moore, dozens of persons had first-hand knowledge of the alleged craft and, not surprisingly, at least some of these told close friends and relatives. But, curiously, several years later when Scully's book about crashed saucers was making headlines across the nation, and the "secret" now was "out," not one of these many persons stepped forward to confirm Scully's tale, or to point out that the saucer had not crashed near Aztec, New Mexico, as Scully claimed, but near Socorro.

If the U.S. Army Air Force really captured a flying saucer in mid-1947, as Berlitz and Moore claim, one of the first persons who should have been informed of this extraordinary fact would have been General Dwight D. Eisenhower, then Army chief of staff. Yet according to Berlitz and Moore, Eisenhower was not told of the crashed saucer because "he did not possess the necessary clearances," and was not informed officially even after he became president!

Another high military official who failed to "get the word" was General Hoyt S. Vandenberg, who would become the chief-of-staff of the then newly created U.S. Air Forces in 1948. In the fall of 1948, after a year of investigating UFO reports, the USAF's Air Technical Intelligence Center prepared an Estimate of the Situation, classified "Secret," which suggested that *some* UFOs *might* be extraterrestrial. General Vandenberg rejected this report on the grounds that the extraterrestrial hypothesis was based on speculation and lacked any proof. Yet Berlitz and Moore claim that incontrovertible proof had been in hand for more than a year, but no one had thought to inform the USAF's chief-of-staff or the USAF's Air Technical Intelligence Center.

A once-classified CIA memorandum, dated August 14, 1952, shows that someone had forgotten also to inform that agency. That CIA memo, which discusses several possible explanations for UFO reports, cites the extraterrestrial hypothesis briefly but notes that "there is no shred of evidence to support this theory at present."

Still another once-classified CIA memo shows that the UFO question was discussed on December 4, 1952, at a meeting of the nation's top intelligence officials, including those from the USAF, Navy, Army, Atomic Energy Commission, FBI, CIA, and the Defense Department's Joint Chiefs of Staff. This memo shows that these intelligence officials, with access to the nation's top secrets, endorsed the CIA's plan to convene a panel of distinguished scientists to "appraise the available evidence" to try to explain UFO sighting reports. There would be no need for such an effort if the U.S. government had recovered a flying saucer five years earlier.

The U.S. government has gone to court to try to block publication of books that threaten to reveal important secrets, such as *The CIA and the Cult of Intelligence,* by former CIA employee Victor Marchetti and former State Department employee John D. Marks, and *The Pentagon Papers,* by Daniel Ellsberg. But the government took no such action to try to block publication of *The Roswell Incident,* which claims to reveal the biggest secret of all time.

Based on the contrary evidence available to UFO movement leaders since late 1978, when the CIA papers were declassified, one would expect at least the more responsible leaders to denounce the Berlitz-Moore book. (As Charles Peguy once observed: "He who does not bellow the truth when he knows the truth makes himself the accomplice of liars and forgers.") But that has not happened. The book was recommended by Dr. Bruce Maccabee, head of the Fund for UFO Research* when he reviewed it in *Frontiers of Science* magazine (July-August 1981). Maccabee said of the book:

> [It] is probably the first of several books to come from authors who will try to convey to the general public why the UFO "community" is presently becoming more involved with the Crashed Disc Syndrome (CDS) . . . . More and more people are "suffering" from CDS these days because of recent revelations under the Freedom of Information Act (FOIA), and, more importantly, because many reputable witnesses of such crashed discs are now speaking out about their experiences.

Maccabee implies that documents released under FOIA offer support for the crashed-saucer tale, when in reality they show just the opposite. He concludes that the Berlitz-Moore book is "well worth reading." But he cautions that "if you read it, don't be surprised if you come down with a sudden case of CDS." Maccabee's "CDS" would be more aptly termed "Credulous Dementia Syndrome."

That Maccabee himself is suffering symptoms of CDS became apparent when he spoke at a UFO symposium held in Washington on September 6, 1980, sponsored by the Smithsonian Institution. (Other panelists included

---

*Maccabee's Fund for UFO Research also helped to promote the book by including Moore as a featured speaker at its press conference on October 27, 1981, in Washington. Later FUFOR disclosed it would provide funds to Moore for additional research into the "crashed-saucer" incident.

Hynek and Allan Hendry, while UFO skeptics included Robert Sheaffer, James Oberg, and myself.) During the question-and-answer period, panelists were asked if any of them "believe that the U.S. government or Air Force . . . [has] in storage, extraterrestrials from crashed spacecraft . . . is there any evidence for this?" Only one of the three UFO proponents – Maccabee – was willing to admit support of this hypothesis. He said: "Speaking for myself, I have no direct evidence, but I wouldn't be surprised."

The U.S. government, which Maccabee suspects of trying to withhold significant information on UFOs, is his employer. The Fund for UFO Research, which Maccabee heads, has donated money to attorney Peter Gersten to support legal efforts to force the U.S. government to release a handful of still classified papers held by the CIA and National Security Agency. Maccabee not only has made no effort to hide this but his organization has issued press releases to publicize its efforts to force the U.S. government to take action against its wishes. Maccabee, as earlier noted, even has used government laboratory facilities for his analysis of the New Zealand films. If the U.S. government really knows something of significance about UFOs that it is trying to keep secret, one might expect that Maccabee would have been told either to cease such activities or to look for another job outside the government. Yet in response to my question, Maccabee told me that he has never detected any such pressure from his employer.

In the early years of the UFO movement, before the Watergate scandal and the Pentagon Papers demonstrated how difficult it is for the U.S. government to keep secrets despite determined efforts, a rational person might have speculated that the U.S. government could have captured a UFO but was keeping this fact under cover until it could master the very advanced extraterrestrial technology and exploit it in new-generation military aircraft and missiles. (In the mid-1950s, Canada's A. V. Roe Ltd., did build a small model of a saucer-shaped craft, but the design soon was abandoned because such shapes are poorly suited for flight in the earth's atmosphere.)

But, today, more than three decades after Berlitz and Moore claim that the U.S. government recovered a crashed saucer, our newest military aircraft and their propulsion systems still do not employ any revolutionary new technology that could have been derived from UFOs – only improved versions of traditional technology. We continue to launch satellites – and even the Space Shuttle – using the same type of chemical rocket engines first demonstrated sixty years ago by Dr. Robert H. Goddard.

But more significant, if Berlitz and Moore are correct, and one UFO was critically damaged more than thirty years ago by a lightning stroke which our "primitive" terrestrial aircraft usually are able to survive, *why have there not been any additional UFO crashes during the past three decades?* If one is so credulous as to believe that there *have* been more UFO crashes, and that many different American presidents all have insisted on keeping this fact secret from the public, surely there are other governments around the globe whose leaders would be eager to publicize a history-making event that occurred in their countries. Or is it possible that UFOs only crash in the United States and not elsewhere?

If UFOlogists now are ready to accept the idea that one or more flying saucers have crashed in the States, this negates a basic tenet that UFOlogists earlier were forced to invent to explain why they have not been able to come up with a single, incontestible piece of physical evidence to support the extraterrestrial hypothesis despite tens of thousands of UFO cases during the past third of a century. That tenet* is that the technology of UFOs is so very advanced that nothing ever fails, and that UFOnauts themselves never commit "pilot error." When UFO movement leaders embrace the Berlitz-Moore tale, or fail to denounce it, they provide still another example of the inconsistency that pervades UFOlogy. None have asked publicly: Why are there not more crashed saucers to provide the incontrovertible physical evidence that has been sought for so many decades? Why only one?

Within the UFO movement, consistency must take a back seat to other priorities, such as getting publicity in the news media to generate more public interest and more dues-paying members upon which UFO organizations depend for survival. Although the leaders of the numerous UFO groups profess a willingness to cooperate toward their *stated* common objectives, there is sharp rivalry for members and for the attention of the news media. In the late 1950s and early 1960s, APRO—the oldest UFO group—was upstaged by NICAP's Keyhoe with his charge that the USAF was involved in a UFO coverup.

Persons interested in UFOs, who became bored with mundane accounts of seemingly mysterious nocturnal lights and metallic disks reported in NICAP's *UFO Investigator,* began to turn to *The APRO Bulletin* for more exciting "occupant" tales. By the late 1960s, NICAP was in serious financial trouble because of declining membership. Keyhoe and Hall were replaced with persons who proved to be more "UFOlogically conservative." Stuart Nixon, who assumed Hall's position, aroused the wrath of many NICAP members when it became known that during a radio interview he had publicly admitted that NICAP lacked proof that UFOs were extraterrestrial and even lacked "solid proof that something extraordinary occurred." Nixon soon was replaced.

NICAP's problems in the late 1960s, like those of other UFO groups,

*Another basic tenet of the UFO movement was shattered in 1982 with the release of Steven Spielberg's movie *E.T. — The Extraterrestrial.* UFOlogists, attempting to rationalize their charge of a government coverup, long have claimed that the government feared the public would panic if they learned that strange-looking creatures were visiting earth. But when Spielberg's movie opened, millions of persons flocked to see his "ugly" but charming extraterrestrial creature and there were no reports of panic when it appeared on the screen.

resulted primarily from the UFO investigation conducted by the University of Colorado, directed by world-renowned scientist, Dr. Edward U. Condon, under government sponsorship. In the final report, issued in early 1969, Dr. Condon concluded that the lengthy investigation had found no evidence to support the extraterrestrial hypothesis—a conclusion bitterly attacked by UFOlogists. Soon afterwards the USAF announced it was closing down its UFO investigations effort after more than twenty-two years. As a result, responsible news media lost interest in the subject, and without news coverage, public interest also dropped sharply.

Another blow came in the mid-1970s when the USAF declassified all of its Project Blue Book UFO files, which were made available to the public at the National Archives. UFOlogists poured over the voluminous files but were unable to find a "smoking gun" to support charges of a USAF coverup. Rather than abandon this basic tenet of UFOlogy, some UFOlogists concluded that the USAF effort was only a "cover," and that the CIA must have been the U.S. government's "real" center of UFO investigations. This hypothesis was shown to be false when the CIA released its UFO files in late 1978, as described in earlier chapters, but UFOlogists are reluctant to abandon long-held beliefs.

The UFO movement got a much-needed lift in 1972 when Hynek, who for nearly two decades had served as a paid consultant to the USAF on UFOs, formally shifted sides with the publication of his first book on UFOs. But the real turning point came in the fall of 1973, when the public and news media—weary of many weeks of sordid disclosures of wrongdoing at high levels in the Nixon administration found relief in reports of a few nocturnal-light UFO reports from the southeastern states. Soon the news media, and the public, refocused their attention on UFOs. Then came the report of the two men in Pascagoula who claimed to have been abducted by a UFO.

If officials of the news media really believed that UFOs had begun to kidnap earthlings, this was the biggest news story of all time and deserved their all-out investigative efforts. Such an effort would have shown the incident to be a hoax. But instead the two men were allowed to tell their fantastic tale to tens of millions of viewers on the news and on network talk shows without challenge, leaving many viewers to conclude that the networks believed the tale was true, or at least might be. One could hardly expect the leaders of the UFO movement, or UFOlogists, to be less credulous. This would encourage APRO to decide to focus its efforts on "abduction" and "occupant" cases.

NICAP, whose "UFOlogically conservative" leadership suspected the Travis Walton case was a hoax, and candidly informed its membership of these suspicions, soon became financially insolvent and never recoverd. MUFON, originally created by Walter Andrus in 1969 as a regional group under APRO, would in 1973 split with APRO and become a national organization that would attract many former NICAP members. By the late 1970s, MUFON also was focusing more attention on the more exotic type of reports.

When Hynek created his Center for UFO Studies in late 1973, he stated that it was being "established for those who wish to see positive scientific action taken to end a quarter of a century of misrepresentation and buffoonery." Barely a year later, on January 20, 1975, Hynek described the objectives and projected the modus operandi of CUFOS at a UFO symposium presented at the prestigious Aerospace Sciences Meeting of the American Institute of Aeronautics and Astronautics, in Pasadena, California. Hynek acknowledged that many scientists had ignored the UFO question, which he attributed primarily to "the poor presentation of the subject matter . . . mostly in tabloids, in pulp magazines, and in the sensationalist press."

Hynek said that CUFOS, "guided by a scientific board of established scientists" would remedy this and would provide "authoritative and reliable information about the UFO phenomenon, documents, reports, etc., which are not easily available elsewhere." Hynek told members of the AIAA: "We who have worked in the UFO field are somewhat in the position of Einstein who wrote to Arnold Sommerfeld in response to Sommerfeld's skepticism of the General Theory of Relativity: 'You will accept the General Theory of Relativity when you have studied it. Therefore I will not utter a word in its defense.'" Hynek added: "Emotional defense of the UFO phenomenon is pointless; the facts, properly presented must speak for themselves." That was what Hynek intended to do.

Barely two years later, CUFOS' official monthly publication, *International UFO Reporter,* was offering its readers reports of alleged UFO abductions. One, involving three Kentucky women, reported in the March 1977 issue, quoted Dr. Leo Sprinkle as saying: "I believe that the Stanford, Kentucky, case is a good one for several reasons." The next month's issue reported the tale of a nineteen-year-old truck driver from Kentucky who claimed his abductors were rectangular in shape, resembling machines rather than humanoids. The October issue that year reported the story of a young couple who claimed to have been abducted in western Kansas, although *IUR* noted that the tale might be fantasy. In April 1978 the use of hypnosis in "abduction cases" was discussed, but readers were cautioned that "it cannot be stated definitely whether or not the accounts provided . . . under hypnosis are entirely accurate."

The next month the CUFOS publication carried a review written by Hynek of the book by Travis Walton. In support of Walton's claims that he was abducted, Hynek wrote that "the Walton case does not stand alone. Today we have dozens of 'abduction' cases."* Hynek said, "I believe we must

---

*There also are hundreds of reports over several centuries of persons who claim to have seen ghosts or mermaids. Early in this century people in the United Kingdom reported seeing tiny "fairies," and two young girls even had photographs to back up their claims.

accept most of them [abduction reports] as a real part of the UFO phenomenon, or cast all of them out entirely," which clearly he was reluctant to do. Hynek rejected the possibility that the Walton case might be a hoax, despite extensive documentation which I had sent him, when he wrote: "Walton's story seems more self-consistent than that of his detractors, the latter containing a number of ad hoc assumptions."

When Hynek was invited to write an article for the prestigious *Technology Review,* published by the Massachusetts Institute of Technology, there was no mention of any "abduction" or "contactee" cases. In Hynek's long article, in the July 1981 issue, he drew a parallel between the contradictions of UFOlogy and the seeming contradictions in quantum mechanics when it was first proposed. And the UFO skeptics were compared to those who questioned Galileo's claims of what he reported seeing through his primitive telescope. (Hynek was called the "Galileo of UFOlogy" in a feature article on his activities published in *Qui* magazine, May 1977.)

But when Hynek speaks to those inclined to believe in UFOs and other paranormal claims, he is much more candid, as when he addressed the Spiritual Frontiers Fellowship, on July 11, 1979, at its annual retreat. "In speaking to this very special group," Hynek began, "I can feel freer to discuss the more esoteric aspects of the subject of UFOs . . . . You have an awareness of the possibilities that the solely materialistically oriented person, like scientists in general, do not have. Talking to them about certain subjects would be like trying to explain calculus to a kindergarten student. He has the potential of learning it, but it hasn't developed yet." Hynek predicted that UFOs "foreshadow a coming revolution in scientific thinking which will be more far-reaching than the Copernican revolution."

More than a decade earlier, when Hynek's position on UFOs was more middle-of-the-road, he had published an article in *Playboy* (December 1967) which began with an expression of his grave concern that the Russians might beat the United States in solving the UFO mystery, creating a "UFO gap" more worrisome than the then recent "missile gap." To prevent this from happening, Hynek had recommended that "a central UFO center in the United States should be established. A central telephone exchange . . . could be manned 24 hours a day by competent interrogators." Teams of UFO investigators would then be dispatched quickly to regions of UFO activity.

Hynek wrote: "If UFOs . . . actually exist, we would have photographs, movies, spectograms, plaster casts of indentations (if a landing occurs) and detailed measurements and quantitative estimates of brightnesses, speeds, and so on, within a year of the initiation of such a no-nonsense program." Hynek added that if such a "program is sincerely and intensively carried out *for a full year and yields nothing, this in itself would be of great negative significance.*" [Emphasis added.] Hynek noted: "I will be surprised if an intensive, yearlong study yields nothing."

In the fall of 1973, Hynek created such an operation. CUFOS had a toll-free long-distance telephone line whose number was made available to law-enforcement agencies around the country, and the CUFOS switchboard was manned around the clock, as Hynek earlier had recommended. CUFOS lacked sufficient resources to dispatch a team of headquarters investigators to distant regions of reported UFO activity. But with the cooperation of MUFON, Hynek soon developed a nationwide network of experienced UFOlogists who could rush to the scene for prompt investigations.

Nearly a decade now has passed since CUFOS was created — nearly ten times the period that Hynek estimated would be sufficient to obtain convincing evidence if there really was an extraordinary phenomenon occurring in our atmosphere. Today all that CUFOS has to show for this effort are several thousand additional reports, most of them similar to the many thousands of earlier reports, plus a growing number of bizarre tales of "occupants" and "abductions." *Thus, this decade of CUFOS effort has provided what Hynek in 1967 called evidence of "great negative significance," that is, that there is no mysterious UFO phenomenon.* If Hynek is surprised, as he predicted he would be, he has never admitted it publicly.

When CUFOS was created, Hynek cited "a growing number of scientists, engineers and other professionals generally associated with universities, laboratories and industry" whom he claimed were interested in UFOs. Hynek said that CUFOS would provide "an avenue whereby the interests and talents of these scientists and other professionals can be focused and brought to bear on this challenging problem. A significant number of them have become actively associated with the Center and have volunteered their talents and facilities." One of those scientists was Dr. Peter A. Sturrock, an astrophysicist on the staff of Stanford University.

Nearly a decade later, in the spring of 1982, Sturrock announced the formation of his own Society for Scientific Exploration of anomalous phenomena, in which UFOs would be a major issue. Only persons with a "demonstrated ability in science" would be allowed to join. In one published interview, Sturrock explained the need for his new group: "If anybody wanted to know the facts about the UFO phenomenon, he couldn't go to a physics library and find journals covering the subject, couldn't find textbooks written by responsible, well-known people covering it. *There's nowhere that you can go for reputable information.*" [Emphasis added.]

Sturrock's rationale sounded like one offered nearly a decade earlier by Hynek to explain his formation of CUFOS. Sturrock, as an Associate of CUFOS, periodically receives a long list of reports and books that CUFOS recommends and offers for sale. A recent one lists more than fifty reports, including papers presented at two CUFOS-sponsored conferences, and approximately forty books. One is the Berlitz-Moore book on the "crashed-saucer" and another is *The Andreasson Affair,* one of the wildest abduction tales.

Sturrock stressed that his new group "will be neutral" and that "most of our members are completely uncommitted." It is useful to examine Sturrock's decade-long record in the UFO field for insights into his interpretation of "neutral" and "uncommitted." In the late 1960s, Sturrock, like Hynek and many UFO proponents, harshly criticized the Condon Report on the University of Colorado UFO study. When Sturrock became chairman of the UFO Subcommittee of the American Institute of Aeronautics and Astronautics, whose membership did not include a single experienced UFO skeptic, the only significant change Sturrock made was in the name: Anomalous Phenomena Subcommittee. In 1975, as chairman of the UFO symposium for the AIAA's Aerospace Sciences Meeting, Sturrock's choices of seven panelists were all UFO proponents. Not a single experienced skeptic was invited to speak. Two years later, when Sturrock sought advice for his UFO survey of American Astronomical Society members (see Chapter 7), he consulted several UFO proponents, including Hynek, but not a single experienced UFO skeptic.

Sturrock's new group held its first conference in early June 1982. One of the featured speakers was Dr. Ron Westrum, a professor of sociology at Eastern Michigan University. Westrum, a long-time UFOlogist and member of the CUFOS Scientific Board, has publicly stated his views as follows: "UFOs may or may not be extraterrestrial spaceships. Actually the question is of little importance for it is obvious that the intelligences which direct them are technically far more advanced than we are, and it seems very likely that interstellar travel is well within their competence."* Westrum spoke on a wide range of "anomalous phenomena," including "spontaneous human combustion" where, it is claimed, persons suddenly burst into flame without external cause. Another invited speaker was Dr. Bruce Maccabee, who discussed the New Zealand case.

Although the conference was held near my home in Washington, D.C., Sturrock did not invite me to speak, nor did he invite any other experienced UFO skeptic to counterbalance Westrum and Maccabee. Although Westrum has been named to the position of Councilor in Sturrock's new group, he has not appointed any experienced UFO skeptic to a comparable post. Yet Sturrock claims that his new Society for Scientific Exploration "will be neutral," and that "most of our members are completely uncommitted." Presumably Sturrock includes himself in these categories.

---

*From a prepared position statement by Westrum, published in *The Encyclopedia of UFOs*, by Ronald D. Story (New York: Doubleday/Dolphin, 1980).

31

"The Greatest Derangement of the Mind . . ."

In 1977, a man in his early thirties named Todd Zechel, from Prairie du Sac, Wisconsin, quickly rose from obscurity to become one of the most well-known figures in UFOlogy. Soon Zechel was named director of research for Ground Saucer Watch (GSW), and in the Spring of 1978 he created his own national organization, Citizens Against UFO Secrecy (CAUS), whose publication, ironically, was named *Just Cause*. Zechel became the first UFOlogist to be honored with a feature-story interview by CUFOS in its *International UFO Reporter* (May 1978). Still further accolades came from Jerome Clark, an editor of *Fate* magazine, in an article published in *UFO Report*'s August 1978 issue. Clark wrote: "At this moment in history, it's distinctly possible that Todd Zechel is UFOlogy's major figure." Zechel and CUFOS chief investigator Hendry journeyed to Jackson, Mississippi, to speak on UFOs before a subcommittee of that State's House of Representatives.

Zechel's rapid rise stemmed from his claim that he had been employed for ten years by "two civilian intelligence agencies" where he said he had discovered hard evidence of a government UFO coverup. One of the two agencies he identified as the National Security Agency. The other he implied, but never stated, was the CIA. On several occasions when Zechel telephoned me, my suspicions were aroused by his manner of making sweeping claims and his evasiveness in replying to questions, but this demeanor aroused no suspicions in other UFOlogists, who warmly embraced Zechel and his claims. (Francis Bacon once observed: "What a man would like to be true, that he more readily believes.")

In August of 1977 *UFO Report* carried a feature story by a "Ted Zachary," whose initials matched those of Todd Zechel, and who also claimed that he had been employed by two different civilian intelligence agencies, one of them NSA, where he had seen evidence of a UFO coverup. In the article "Ted Zachary" wrote: "Since leaving intelligence work, I have become a freelance writer and researcher. About a year ago, I joined a civilian UFO research organization, Ground Saucer Watch, and was eventually appointed Director of Research." That statement revealed that the author was Todd Zechel because he was the only person to hold that title at GSW.

If Zechel was revealing government secrets, it would be natural for him to try to hide his identity with a pseudonym. But how could anyone who had spent ten years in intelligence work be so careless in disclosing his real identity? Also I found it surprising that anyone who had been employed by the National Security Agency would refer to it as a civilian agency. NSA is one of nearly a dozen Defense Department agencies, its stationery carries the official Pentagon seal, and the agency is headed by a high-ranking military officer who reports to the secretary of defense. This prompted me to make an inquiry through the Defense Department, which later informed me that NSA could find no record of Zechel having been on its payroll.

Knowing that Zechel had worked as a freelance sports writer for his hometown newspaper, I called its editor, Pat Peckham. His candid comments confirmed my growing suspicions that Zechel was a spinner of tall tales. Peckham suggested others I should call, and these in turn suggested still others, some of whom had been victimized financially by Zechel. Some sent me hard evidence to confirm their stories. After making only a few telephone calls I had discovered what Zechel really had been doing during the ten years he claimed to have been employed by "two civilian intelligence agencies." For the first three years he had served in the U.S. Army. For the next six years he had worked at a small factory in Baraboo, Wisconsin, first as a carpenter and later as a fireman. Then he had gone to Milwaukee, where he worked in a "sex-shop" and pornographic book store. That was how Zechel had discovered the inner secrets of the government "UFO coverup."

On September 1, 1978, I prepared a White Paper detailing my findings on Zechel, including the names of those who supplied my facts so others could verify them if they wished. Copies of my White Paper were sent to all of the leaders of the UFO movement, and to writer Jerome Clark and to Zechel. Although Zechel and I had corresponded extensively prior to my exposé, and I would receive brief notes from him subsequently, Zechel never wrote to deny or challenge any of my findings.

None of the leaders of the UFO movement responded to my White Paper, except for GSW's Spaulding. He wrote to thank me for the information, but gave no indication that as a result he planned to drop Zechel from his high position in GSW. Clark wrote to attack my efforts sharply, saying that he and CUFOS' Hendry had gotten to know Zechel very well and knew him to be a person of "uncompromising integrity." Within a year, Clark and another UFOlogist, Brad Sparks, would join the long list of persons cited in my White Paper who had been victimized by Zechel. But Clark would be much too embarrassed to disclose the circumstances. By the late 1970s, Zechel, after having become a nationally known figure in UFOlogy and having been introduced on network television as a leading expert on the subject, departed for greener pastures. His own organization, CAUS, was left without funds to publish its newsletter, to which many of us had subscribed.

The UFO movement's leaders and its leading writers have never revealed to UFOlogists why the man earlier hailed as a "major figure" suddenly disappeared from the scene. Obviously it would be embarrasing to reveal how very credulous all of them had been, and it was more expedient to accuse others, such as the U.S. government, of resorting to coverup. UFOlogy is the exception that proves the maxim offered by Petronius, the seventh-century Roman satirist, who observed: "He will never do well who easily believes." *To succeed in the UFO movement one must be credulous, if only to maintain the support of those who provide the membership dues for survival.*

While Sturrock says his new group will attempt a "scientific" attack on UFOs and other anomalous phenomena, one of the most experienced UFOlogists, APRO's James Lorenzen is convinced that scientific methodology simply can't cope with UFOs. In an interview published in *Frontiers of Science* magazine (May-June, 1982) on APRO's thirtieth anniversary, Lorenzen was quoted as saying that "physical science as it is currently conducted, doesn't lend itself to a solution to the UFO mystery. *But that's a shortcoming of science. If your techniques won't accomodate the problem, then change your techniques."* [Emphasis added.] Even Hynek, a trained scientist, expressed a similar view in his 1975 AIAA paper, claiming that "our present scientific framework is severely strained to encompass [UFOs] . . . probably necessitating new departures in methodology."

Although scientific methodology has demonstrated it can provide valuable insights into many diverse and complex mysteries of nature and is continually discovering and illuminating new phenomena, Lorenzen is convinced—and Hynek suspects—that it simply cannot handle the UFO mystery. The same complaint could be voiced by those who are eager to believe in ghosts, poltergeist, and monsters, such as Sasquatch ("Big Foot").

A basic principle of scientific methodology, which is repugnant to all "believers," is known as Occam's Razor: Given a choice between a simple, direct explanation and one that is extremely convoluted and depends upon many unlikely assumptions, the simpler explanation is preferred. Mathematical-physicist J. Williard Gibbs stated it more eloquently a century ago in his letter to the American Academy of Arts and Sciences: "One of the principal objects of theoretical research in any department of knowledge is to find the point of view from which the subject appears in its greatest simplicity."

UFOlogists reject this approach and prefer to invent complex explanations, for, as an example, the reason why UFOs never crash to leave behind incontrovertible physical evidence. Or why one "saucer" that they claim crashed was recovered more than thirty years ago by the U.S. government. During this time, many different American presidents with a wide spectrum of political differences have been able to agree on only one thing—to keep the news of the crashed saucer from the public.

UFOlogists cite hundreds of physical-trace cases, such as Delphos, where they believe UFOs left behind physical evidence of their visits—yet all such indentations in the ground, burned spots, or broken tree branches could have prosaic explanations. They ignore the fact that no one has found what would have been the greatest discovery of all times, a physical artifact —such as one of the many scientific instruments placed on the Lunar surface by American Apollo astronauts, or the equivalent of the expensive camera accidentally left behind on the moon by one forgetful astronaut. The UFOnauts are more careful and never, in hundreds or thousands of "visits," leave behind an extraterrestrial artifact that could resolve the issue for all time.

UFOlogists devise convoluted explanations to explain why UFOnauts for so many years showed no interest in earthlings, but in recent years seem to have developed an insatiable appetite for giving superficial examinations. Yet the UFOnauts never carry a few earthlings back to their native planet for a truly rigorous examination. And why do UFOs, presumably operated by creatures of super-intelligence, only abduct and communicate with dull, uninteresting earthlings rather than seek out more intellectually stimulating subjects? (A friend suggests that perhaps the answer is that UFOnauts are making a study of the earth's "kooks.")

In an effort to rationalize why most scientists are not impressed by UFOlogy's favorite cases, Hynek, Sturrock, and Westrum often cite the fact that nearly two centuries ago, the French Academy of Science found it difficult to believe reports from peasants who claimed that "stones fell from the sky," but later reversed its position on what are known as meteorites today. UFOlogists who cite this example gloss over the fact that the French Academy reversed its position *within three decades* when analysis of meteorites recovered from many different areas showed similar compositions. In a comparable period of time, UFOlogists have not been able to come up with any scientifically credible physical evidence, only increasingly bizarre tales of "abductions." The reluctance of eighteenth-century French scientists to accept credulously what seemed to be incredible stories from uneducated observers with a proclivity for superstition, until there was hard physical evidence to support their tales, deserves commendation, not ridicule.

Sturrock, in describing plans for his new Society for Scientific Exploration, said: "We also hope to learn from history by reconsidering, for instance, the meteorite controversy. How could the French Academy of the 18th Century have saved itself from a historic 'boo-boo' when it decided that meteorites are stones struck by lightning since 'stones cannot fall from the sky'? How can scientists of the 20th Century avoid making a similar mistake?" Sturrock and his associates would do better to study a much more grievous mistake made by the French Academy of Science more than a century later—one which has more direct application to UFOs.

The closing years of the nineteenth century had seen the discovery of mysterious "rays" that were invisible to human eyes and other senses. First had been Germany's Wilhelm Roentgen's discovery of X-rays, which would gain him a Nobel Prize. This was followed shortly by France's Henri Becquerel's discovery of the even more mysterious rays emitted by pitchblend—today known as nuclear radiation. Then, in the fall of 1903, Professor R. Blondlot, a respected member of the French Academy reported still another which he named "N-Rays," for the University of Nancy, whose physics department Blondlot headed.

Blondlot reported that N-rays were emitted by a variety of metal objects and that they enhanced human vision. For example, if the gas lights in his laboratory were turned down to where an observer could not quite read a clock on the wall, when a metal object was brought into the room, its N-rays enabled an observer to read the clock. Other French scientists rushed to perform experiments and before the year was over the French Academy had published a dozen papers that seemed to confirm the existence of the mysterious N-rays. Within a year, the Academy had published nearly a hundred papers by many different scientists, which not only confirmed the existence of N-rays but reported even more mysterious effects. For example, that N-rays also were emitted by the human brain and they enhanced the senses of hearing and smell, as well as vision. One scientist reported that N-rays also were emitted by plants and even by a human corpse. *But all experimenters agreed with Blondlot that objects made of wood never emitted N-rays.*

The French Academy announced that it would award its LaLande prize of 20,000 francs and a gold metal to Blondlot for the "discovery of N-rays." But when an American physicist named Dr. Robert W. Wood, working in London, tried to replicate Blondlot's experiments, he was unable to detect any evidence of N-ray effects. This prompted Wood to visit Blondlot's laboratory for a demonstration. When Dr. Wood, in Blondlot's dimly lit laboratory, secretly substituted a wooden ruler for what Blondlot thought was a metal file, Blondlot still reported seeing N-ray effects. And when Dr. Wood secretly removed a vital element from Blondlot's spectroscope, the French scientist still reported observing the expected N-ray effect. Dr. Wood concluded that Blondlot was the unwitting victim of self-delusion, and that dozens of other French scientists had become victims of the same malaise in their understandable desire to participate in exciting scientific discoveries.

Dr. Wood reported the results of his visit to Blondlot's laboratory in the

September 29, 1904, issue of Britain's *Nature* magazine. After Wood's article was published, N-rays disappeared as mysteriously as they had emerged.
UFOlogists often cite the French Academy's initial error in appraising the
source of meteorites but they never mention the N-ray incident, with good
reason.*

The N-ray affair is one of several examples of scientists who became victims of wishful thinking, or what has been called "pathological science" by
the late Dr. Irving Langmuir, Nobel-Prize-winning scientist and former
associate director of General Electric's Research Laboratory. Langmuir
discussed "pathological science"—"the science of things that aren't so"—at
a research laboratory colloquium on December 18, 1953, to alert researchers to the dangers of the malaise. One of the symptoms, Langmuir warned,
are "fantastic theories contrary to experience." Another indication,
Langmuir noted, is that "criticisms are met by ad hoc excuses, thought up
on the spur of the moment." Langmuir said, "There is no dishonesty involved but people are tricked into false results by a lack of understanding of
what human beings can do to themselves in the way of being led astray by
subjective effects, wishful thinking, or threshold interactions."

A century earlier, the famed Louis Pasteur offered a similar warning: "I
should like to see these profound words inscribed on the threshold of all the
temples of science: *'The greatest derangement of the mind is to believe in
something because one wishes it to be so.'*"

My own—admittedly limited—study of scientists who have become victims of "pathological science" suggests that those who are most vulnerable
are persons who are approaching the end of their careers without having
achieved great prominence and younger scientists whose achievements have
fallen short of their ambitions.

In an interview with Hynek published in the May 17, 1973, issue of the
British *New Scientist* magazine, given at a time when Hynek was nearing the
end of his career as a professor of astronomy, he spoke with remarkable
candor: "When I look back on my career, I've done damn little that was
original . . . I've never launched any new theories; I've never made any
outstanding discoveries. I guess I'm not very innovative."

When interviewer Ian Ridpath suggested that Hynek "would be
remembered not as an astronomer but as the man who made UFOs respectable," Hynek replied: "I wouldn't mind it, I wouldn't mind it. It's always
nice to add one stone to the total structure of science. If I can succeed in
making the study of UFOs scientifically respectable and do something con-
structive in it, then I would think that would be a real contribution."

Two years later, in Hynek's talk to the AIAA at its UFO symposium, he

*A more detailed account of the false N-rays can be found in the book *Doctor Wood,* by
William Seabrooke (New York: Harcourt, Brace & Co., 1941.)

said: "It is indeed sobering, yet challenging, to consider that the entire UFO phenomenon may be only the tip of the proverbial iceberg in signalling an entirely new domain of the knowledge of nature, as yet totally unexplored and as unimagined as nuclear processes would have been a century ago." And in 1979, speaking to the Spiritual Frontiers Fellowship, Hynek said he believes that UFOs "foreshadow a coming revolution in scientific thinking which will be more far-reaching that the scientific revolutions of the past, greater even than the Copernican revolution."

It is much more alluring to hope to become the "Galileo of UFOlogy," or its Albert Einstein, than to opt for the simple, Occam's Razor alternative—that roughly 98 percent of all UFO reports are simply misidentifications of prosaic, if sometimes unfamiliar objects by basically honest observers. And that the balance, roughly 2 percent, are self-delusions or hoaxes by persons who like to spin tall tales and become instant celebrities. There is no prospect of a Nobel Prize, or long-lasting scientific fame, for anyone who proposes prosaic explanations entirely within the framework of existing scientific knowledge, only harsh criticism from those eager to promote UFOs.

Hendry's investigations of 1305 CUFOS cases showed that at least 91 percent of the witnesses failed to recognize prosaic objects, sometimes with good reason. Hendry discovered that many witnesses were unwitting victims of their imaginations, fed by exposure to UFO accounts in the news. If Hendry had been able to spend more than an average of only a couple of hours investigating each case, and with a little more luck and a bit more skepticism, the percentage of IFOs would certainly have exceeded 91 percent. Hendry candidly admitted in his book: *"How can I be sure if my remaining 'UFOs' aren't simply IFOs misperceived (sincerely) . . .?"*

There is not a shred of scientific evidence from any of numerous experiments to show that even a tiny percentage of the population is immune and *never errs* in attempted recollections of brief, unexpected, and/or unusual events. Quite the opposite. The UFO data itself demonstrates that pilots, scientists (including astronomers), law-enforcement officers and even a member of Mensa can mistake a prosaic object for a UFO. And that has been true since the birth of the UFO era. Even a scientifically trained naval officer, who later would become president of the United States— Jimmy Carter—has demonstrated that he can mistake a bright Venus for a UFO.

Only the "occupant" and "abduction" cases defy explanation as possible misidentifications. The fact that Hendry and some other UFOlogists have been able to detect a few hoaxes, despite the hypercredulity of many UFOlogists, shows that *at least a few people will concoct a tall tale and attempt to pass it off as fact*. If all UFOlogists readily agreed that the Travis Walton and Pascagoula "abduction" cases were hoaxes, and that Betty Hill and Betty Andreasson were not really abducted by strange-looking creatures, leading UFOlogists might be able to claim that they are able to distinguish fact from fantasy, and are willing to expose hoaxers publicly. The rapid rise of Todd Zechel in the UFO movement, and his disappearance without explanation, demonstrates the credulity of the movement's leaders and their reluctance to be candid with the public. CUFOS rejects the possibility that Deputy Sheriff Johnson might have been involved in a hoax which leaves "malicious UFOnauts" as the only alternative explanation for the car's damage.

In early 1967, two teenage boys in Michigan claimed to have photographed a craftlike UFO in daylight and their photos were endorsed by Hynek, despite important discrepancies between the boys' story and the chronological sequence of the pictures. (I characterized the photos as a hoax in my book *UFOs—Identified,* published in 1968.) A decade later, the two principals wrote to Hynek to confess the photos were a hoax, made using a small model suspended from a white thread. But not all hoaxers are as honest, especially if it might embarrass friends who earlier gave them a character endorsement or if it will cost the principals their celebrity status.

Some UFO incidents are more accurately characterized as practical jokes. For example, a neighbor of mine confided to me that he had generated a few UFO incidents during the 1950s when he was a Navy fighter pilot based on the West Coast. He explained that Navy pilots would practice intercepting an enemy bomber in darkness by using an unsuspecting airliner as a mock target. The authorized procedure called for the Navy aircraft to come no closer than about ten miles before breaking off. However, this former Navy pilot (who requested anonymity) said that if he felt in a "playful mood" he would turn off his aircraft's external lights and approach quite close to the airliner.

Then, he said, he would reach for his emergency cockpit flashlight and flash it on and off until he could see passengers in the cabin reacting to it. Then he would maneuver to the other side of the airliner and give a repeat performance. Finally, he told me, he would drop below the airliner and turn on his jet-engine's afterburner, creating greatly increased thrust and a long rocketlike plume, and would zoom out in front of the relatively slow-moving airliner. Then he would return to base. "The next day I would scan the newspapers and sure enough there would be a story about an airline flight crew who reported seeing a rocketlike UFO, with confirming reports from a number of passengers who described seeing a bright flashing light," my neighbor told me.

During one of my UFO lectures, I recounted the story of how this former Navy pilot had generated UFO reports that would be extremely difficult to explain in prosaic terms had he not chosen to confide in me. After the lecture, a man came up to tell me that he was a former USAF interceptor pilot and that while based on the East Coast he also had generated a few such airliner UFO-encounter reports "for kicks." He added: "Here I was creating UFO incidents that another branch of the Air Force (Project Blue

Book) was trying to solve, but I dared not reveal my role because it was a serious infraction of the rules."

For more than three decades, UFOlogists have been searching for the evidence that could substantiate their hopes—but without success. They recall the turning point in the meteorite controversy that occurred on April 26, 1803, when so many meteorites fell near the French village of L'Aigle that the physical evidence overpowered prior scientific skepticism. UFOlogists continue to hope that UFOs will eventually be equally obliging. But have UFOlogists really considered the consequences for them personally and for the UFO movement if a real extraterrestrial craft were to crash, or, better still, if one landed safely with its crew? When news of this historic event flashed around the world, as surely it would, UFOlogists would be ecstatic—*but only briefly.*

If an extraterrestrial craft crashed and there were no survivors, only the world's leading scientists would be brought in to investigate the craft, its occupants, and their technology. None of the leaders of the UFO movement have the stature or technical expertise to qualify. If the craft and its occupants landed safely, the extraterrestrial visitors would be entertained by the political leaders of the host-nation and their selected invitees. I doubt very much whether any heads of state would even think to invite Hynek, the Lorenzens, Andrus, or other famous UFOlogists. The reporters and writers invited to cover the event would come from the world's leading news media and scientific journals, not from *Fate* or *UFO Report.*

Very quickly it would become obvious that there no longer was any need for UFO organizations to promote public belief in extraterrestrial visitors. No longer would Hynek, Sturrock, and others need to urge top-ranking scientists to take an interest. No longer would once-famous UFOlogists be invited to appear on radio and TV talk shows, and no longer would they be featured in the sensationalist tabloids. No longer would Hynek be able to command a $2000 fee for one of his UFO lectures. And who would pay a large fee to hear Stanton Friedman deliver his colorful lecture: "Flying Saucers Are Real!"? UFOlogists would return to their humdrum lives and jobs.

Clearly UFOlogists have the most to lose if an extraterrestrial craft were to land or to crash. Using the convoluted logic of UFOlogy, one could argue that if UFOlogists ever found hard, incontrovertible evidence, they would have great incentive to keep it secret so as to preserve their celebrity status. And if one were to employ the conspiracy theories so popular in UFOlogy, one might begin to suspect that perhaps UFOlogists already have found such hard physical evidence and that they accuse the U.S. government of a coverup to obscure their own guilt. If this strikes you as an incredible hypothesis, I agree. But it is no more incredible than those that have been used by leaders of the UFO movement during the past three decades.

If the past is any portent of the future, the sensationalist tabloids and avant-garde UFOlogists will eventually become bored with still more reports of UFO "abductions," and there will emerge more exciting tales of "visitations" to distant worlds. The claimants will report that these very advanced societies have eliminated disease, poverty, pollution, and war. But not one of the claimants will be able to show a clearly extraterrestrial physical artifact to substantiate the tale.

I predict that Sturrock will be no more successful than Hynek in his efforts to arouse the interest of truly outstanding scientists in UFOs. Sturrock assumes that they have ignored UFOs because the subject has not been treated in respectable scientific journals. Sturrock, like Hynek, will discover that it is not where, or how, the UFO evidence is presented. *It is the intrinsic lack of scientific credibility of the evidence itself.*

However a significant segment of the public will continue to suspect that perhaps a few UFO reports may involve extraterrestrial visitors, because the idea is so universally appealing. It is what psychologist Joseph Jastrow called a "congenial conclusion," in *Error and Eccentricity in Human Belief* (New York: Dover, 1962). Jastrow defines a congenial conclusion as "beliefs which would make life more interesting if true, and have an engaging air of plausibility."

With billions of stars in our own galaxy, and possibly billions of such galaxies in the universe, these sheer numbers seem to suggest that there should be other stars with planets inhabited by intelligent life. If so, certainly some of these would be much more advanced than our own civilization and their guidance could help us solve some of the problems that plague our planet. The prospect of finding intelligent life elsewhere is universally appealing, and the search for it has attracted the attention, and efforts, of many competent scientists, including Dr. Carl Sagan. One of the few critics of this legitimate scientific search for intelligent extraterrestrial life which uses radio telescopes to try to detect signals from distant worlds, is sociologist Ron Westrum, who was named a Councilor in Sturrock's new society. In a talk given at MUFON's 1981 international conference, Westrum criticized radio-astronomers for their costly programs and asked: "Can't we spend perhaps one billion dollars on UFO research to find out what might be going on right over our heads?"

Those who engage in the legitimate scientific search for extraterrestrial intelligence recognize that if it exists, it very probably will be much too distant to ever visit earth, unless such creatures have lifetimes measured in many thousands of earth-years, or can travel faster than the speed of light, which Einstein's Theory of Relativity indicates is impossible. Yet some clear night when you are gazing at the heavens and wondering what life might be like in a distant world, should you see a light that seems to be unfamiliar and perhaps behaving in an unusual fashion, don't be surprised, or even feel guilty, if you begin to speculate that perhaps it *might* be an extraterrestrial craft, possibly bearing creatures as engaging as Steven Spielberg's "E.T."

But recall the caveat on UFOs expressed by the science and science-fiction writer Arthur C. Clarke in *The Promise of Space* (New York: Harper & Row, 1968): "Much of the trouble arises from the fact that the sky presents an almost endless variety of peculiar sights and objects, only a few of which are likely to be encountered by one person in a lifetime. And when this does happen, he may be misled into thinking that he has seen something extraordinary—instead of merely unfamiliar."

Commenting further on UFOs, Clarke, who is himself a great space enthusiast, wrote: "Seldom has any subject been so invested with fraud, hysteria, credulity, religious mania, incompetence, and most of the other unflattering human characteristics."

Of these, I would single out the credulity of UFOlogists and some segments of the news media, recalling Francis Bacon's sage warning: *"A credulous man is a deceiver."* If UFOlogists and some journalists only deceived themselves, it would be simply their personal problem. But for much too long, they have deceived the public as well.

"The great enemy of the truth," the late President John F. Kennedy observed, "is very often not the lie—deliberate, contrived and dishonest —but the myth, persistent, persuasive, and unrealistic." Belief in myths, Kennedy added, allows "the comfort of opinion without the discomfort of thought."

Appendix: UFOlogical Principles

*UFO*LOGICAL PRINCIPLE *1:* Basically honest and intelligent persons who are suddenly exposed to a brief, unexpected event, especially one that involves an unfamiliar object, may be grossly inaccurate in trying to describe precisely what they have seen.

*UFO*LOGICAL PRINCIPLE *2:* Despite the intrinsic limitations of human perception when exposed to brief, unexpected and unusual events, some details recalled by the observer may be reasonably accurate. The problem facing the UFO investigator is to try to distinguish between those details that are accurate and those that are grossly inaccurate. This may be impossible until the true identity of the UFO can be determined; in some cases this poses an insoluble problem.

*UFO*LOGICAL PRINCIPLE *3:* If a person observing an unusual or unfamiliar object concludes that it is probably a spaceship from another world, he can readily adduce that the object is reacting to his presence or actions, when in reality there is absolutely no cause-effect relationship.

*UFO*LOGICAL PRINCIPLE *4:* News media that give great prominence to a UFO report when it is first received subsequently devote little, if any, space or time to reporting a prosaic explanation for the case after the facts are uncovered.

*UFO*LOGICAL PRINCIPLE *5:* No human observer, including experienced flight crews, can accurately estimate either the distance/altitude or the size of an unfamiliar object in the sky, unless it is in very close proximity to a familiar object whose size or altitude is known.

*UFO*LOGICAL PRINCIPLE *6:* Once news coverage leads the public to believe that UFOs may be in the vicinity, there are numerous natural and man-made objects which, especially when seen at night, can take on unusual characteristics in the minds of hopeful viewers. Their UFO reports in turn add to the mass excitement, which encourages still more observers to watch for UFOs. This situation feeds upon itself until such time as the media lose interest in the subject, and then the "flap" quickly runs out of steam.

*UFO*LOGICAL PRINCIPLE *7:* In attempting to determine whether a UFO report is a hoax, an investigator should rely on physical evidence, or the lack of it where evidence should exist, and should not depend on character endorsements of the principals involved.

*UFO*LOGICAL PRINCIPLE *8:* The inability of even experienced investigators to fully and positively explain a UFO report for lack of sufficient information, even after a rigorous effort, does not really provide evidence to support the hypothesis that spaceships from other worlds are visiting the earth.

*UFO*LOGICAL PRINCIPLE *9:* When a light is sighted in the night skies that is believed to be a UFO and this is reported to a radar operator, who is asked to search his scope for an unknown target, almost invariably an "unknown" target will be found. Conversely, if an unusual target is spotted on a radar-scope at night that is suspected of being a UFO, and an observer is dispatched or asked to search for a light in the night sky, almost invariably a visual sighting will be made.

*UFO*LOGICAL PRINCIPLE *10:* Many UFO cases seem puzzling and unexplainable simply because case investigators have failed to devote a sufficiently rigorous effort to the investigation.

Index

Acuff, John, 52, 125
Adamski, George, 161, 267
Advertising aircraft, 69–74 passim
Aerial Phenomena Research Organization (APRO), 8, 13, 62, 162, 181–88, 195–97, 207, 220, 263, 267, 273, 280, 285. *See also* Lorenzen, Coral and James (L. J.)
AIM-9 (Sidewinder) air-air missile, 112, 119
Air Force. *See* U.S. Air Force
Alvarez, Luis W., 7, 27
American Airlines, 121, 141
American Association for the Advancement of Science (AAAS), 210
American Astronomical Society (AAS), 57–63 passim, 289
American Broadcasting Company (ABC), 136, 219, 227, 262
American Institute of Aeronautics and Astronautics (AIAA), 286, 289, 293, 296
American Institute of Public Opinion. *See* Gallup Poll
American Polygraph Association, 217–18
American Psychological Association, 276
Amory, Robert, 36
Andreasson, Betty, 272, 288, 297
Andrus, Walter, 125, 285, 299
APRO. *See* Aerial Phenomena Research Organization

APRO Bulletin, 173, 181, 183, 196, 276, 284
Arizona Daily Star, 172
Arizona Republic, 195–96
Arnold, Kenneth, 280
Associated Press, 2, 188
Astronomers. *See* American Astronomical Society
Aviation Week and Space Technology, 11, 142
A. V. Roe Ltd., 34, 283
Azerbarzin, Abdullah, 116–17

Backster, Cleve, 207–15, 217
Bacon, Francis, 291, 301
Ball lightning, 20, 60
Balloons, weather and other, 13, 14, 17, 18, 29
Baltimore News American, 90
Baltimore Sun, 44
Bangor (Me.) *Daily News,* 95, 96
Barry, Bill, 193, 221
Battelle Memorial Institute, 9
Bell Helicopter UFO incident, 135–60
Berkner, Lloyd V., 7, 27, 37
Berlitz, Charles, 280–83, 288
Bird-generated UFO reports, 19
Bissonnette, William E., 69–71
Blondlot, R., 295
Blue Book Project, USAF, 6, 41, 78, 84, 285
Brazell, W. W., 280–81
Brekke, Dennis, 225

305